THE NEW ENGLAND MAFIA

New England's Mob Bosses

Raymond L.S. Patriarca

(1950-1984)

Raymond Patriarca, Jr.

(1984-1991)

Nicholas "Nicky" Bianco

(1991)

Francis "Cadillac Frank" Salemme

(1992-1996)

Luigi "Baby Shacks" Manocchio

(1996-2009)

A

Acorn Social Club: Operated by Frank "Bobo" Marrapese it was off Atwells Avenue in the heart of Federal Hill. The club was basically a barroom, was a key meeting spot for Marrapese and other mobsters from across New England. On March 15, 1975, mobster Dickie Callei was probably killed there.

Alogna Ignazio AKA Iggy Born 1931. Operative in the Gambino Crime Family Alleged Gambino operative and one time body guard to John Gotti. In 2003, Alonga, a Capo, and a slew of other Colombo associates were indicted on large-scale racketeering charges, with the primary charge resting on the extortion of a Fairfield county Connecticut nightclub owner for $2,000 a month. Alogna, who claims to have retired to Pocono Lake, Pa., faced up to 20 years in prison in the case but was given six months home confinement and three years' probation after Alogna said he was a down-on-his-luck retiree and his family's only caregiver. Stamford Connecticut businessman Harry Farrington ran two successful strip clubs in Stamford, Beamers on Richmond Hill Avenue and Harry O's Café. According to the Stamford Police Department, his businesses were legitimate. No history of prostitution or
Fights. In 2002, Alogna, 72, came into one of Farrington's clubs with enforcers

Joseph "Joey Mash" Mascia and his brother John "Johnny Mash" Mascia Jr., and two associates of the Patriarca family, Alfred "Chip" Scivola Jr. and Henry "Hank" Fellela Jr.

"We're taking over the whole East Coast now," Alogna said and demanded $4,000 a month in protection payments from Farrington.

"You've had a free ride for years," Farrington says Alogna told him, boasting about extorting 50 other New England strip clubs for similar payments. "Come on, you know the routine, you gotta start paying." The money was to be left in an envelope marked

"grocery money" and picked up at the start of each month. If not, he promised, someone would come in and wreck the place, and he could get hurt.

Farrington went straight to the FBI. The FBI wired him and rigged his club for sound and film. On direction of the FBI, Farrington called Megale for help after Alogna demanded his extortion payments.

Anthony Megale, the so-called Tony Soprano of Connecticut, was born in Italy and moved to the US as a young man, settling in Connecticut. He became a US citizen and

attended Post University in Waterbury for two years, majoring in recreation. At some point, he moved into the Mob and became the Gambino family illegal gambling guru in Southern New England. Known for his taste for expensive cashmere and high life style that included a mini-mansion in an upscale house in the picturesque suburbs of North Stamford, Megale met regularly with top-ranking Gambino members from New York.

Megale was a new generation who hood who held his meetings in Starbuck's, Home Depot, and McDonald's or anywhere else he felt free from FBI bugs. Megale did a stretch in prison in the 1990s for racketeering, but was soon back in charge of Fairfield County, running a crew of his own men in Bridgeport, Stamford, Norwalk and Waterbury.

Anthony Megale (FBI)

Megale went to Beamers to meet one-on-one with Farrington. On the wiretaps, Megale bragged "They made me the acting underboss of this family. So I'm over everybody."

The two men exchanged updates about their wives and children. Farrington flattered his old acquaintance by asking if he too could join the Gambino family.

"What about me bein' a soldier?" Farrington asked.

"Your father Italian?" replied Megale.

"No, Indian," Farrington said.

"You're probably better than 90 percent of the guys. But if you were Italian..."

Regarding the extortion payments, Megale was outraged that Alogna, who lived in eastern Pennsylvania, was trying to extort a business in Stamford, Megale's territory.

"I just don't want to be embarrassed," said Megale. "You gonna let a guy from out of town take a guy you know all your life?" He explained to Farrington how he got clearance from New York, then sent one of his crew, Angelo Ricco, to deliver a message to Alogna and the others at a roadside diner: "Stay out of Stamford. I've got a message, it's coming from the boss--stay out of Connecticut."

"I'm going to make this fucking asshole bleed, though," said Megale about Alogna.

And he did, although not literally. According to court documents, Megale used his power as underboss to demote the older man from a captain to soldier. On July 26, 2005 Alogna pleaded guilty to attempted extortion.

Almonte, Robert AKA Bobby A. A Rhode Islander, Almonte was arrested as the get-away drive in the Marfeo-Melei murders. He was arrested and convicted in 1976 on counterfeiting charges.

Arsenal According to the FBI, in 2001, Michael Flemmi, the brother of alleged Boston gangster Stephen "The Rifleman" Flemmi, allegedly tried to hide 80 weapons, including 10 machine guns, 13 rifles, nine shotguns and dozens of handguns, U.S. Attorney Donald Stern said. The guns were found during searches over the past 10 months, Michael Flemmi, 63, who retired this year after 32 years on the Boston police force, was arrested and charged with obstruction of justice and perjury, possession of unregistered weapons and transfer and possession of machine guns.
Prosecutors said the weapons were stashed at a Boston-area home of a gang member who has since died and then were moved to the back yard of a home owned by Flemmi's parents. In January, apparently anticipating a search warrant to uncover the weapons, Stephen Flemmi enlisted his brother's help to move the cache to other places, authorities said.
U.S. Attorney Stern stated "The recovery of this mind-boggling arsenal, including ten machine guns and numerous other high-powered firearms, together with return of these serious charges result from the continued determination of

investigators and prosecutors to uncover the full scope of the Bulger Group's criminal activities and to eliminate any remaining threat this organization might pose to the public safety. The calculated efforts to thwart the recovery of these weapons, through lies and evidence tampering, were unsuccessful. The Bulger Group's storehouse of weapons has been safely dismantled."

The following weapons were found

- Two .45-caliber fully automatic pistols without markings - .45-caliber United States Military submachine gun with attachable 13 1/4" silencer and no visible markings relating to serial number. - .45-caliber Auto Ordinance Thompson submachine gun
- Three 9mm-caliber German MP40 submachine gun serial no. obliterated
- 56mm-caliber Colt fully automatic rifle
- .45-caliber M3 submachine gun
- .30-caliber U.S. carbine fully automatic rifle
- .30 carbine-caliber Plainfield Machine rifle with pistol grip, telescoping stock, and ability to accept detachable magazine.
- 9mm-caliber Uzi rifle, model A
- Two .30 carbine-caliber Universal rifle, model M1
- 30-06-caliber Remington rifle, model 742, serial no. 140619
- 30-06-caliber Springfield Armory rifle, model M1 garand
- .30-carbine caliber Universal rifle, Model M1
- .44 magnum-caliber Sturm, Ruger rifle
- 308 win-caliber Browning rifle, serial no. 69373M70
- 30-06-caliber Remington Wingmaster rifle, model 742
- .30 carbine-caliber Universal rifle, model M1
- .30 carbine-caliber Universal rifle, model M1
- 20-gauge Browning shotgun with cut-down barrel
- 12-gauge JC Higgins shotgun with cut-down barrel, model 120, and with no markings relating to serial no.
- 12-gauge Ithaca shotgun with cut-down barrel
- 12-gauge Winchester shotgun, serial no. 825678(E)
- 12-gauge Browning shotgun, serial no. 382736
- 12-gauge Mossberg shotgun, model 500A
- 12-gauge Winchester shotgun, model 12, serial no. 1670091
- 12-gauge Remington shotgun, serial no. 468099
- 16-gauge LC Smith shotgun

- .380-caliber Beretta pistol with attached silencer/suppressor
- .32-caliber Spanish-made pistol with attached silencer/suppressor
- .32-caliber Walther pistol with attached silencer/suppressor device
- .380-caliber Beretta pistol with attached silencer/suppressor
- .380-caliber FN Browning pistol with attached silencer/suppressor
- .22-caliber Colt Woodsman pistol with attached silencer/suppressor
- .22-caliber High Standard derringer pistol
- .38 special-caliber F.I.E. derringer pistol, serial no. 006539
- .22-caliber Sterling Arms pistol
- .357 magnum-caliber Astra revolver
- .38 special-caliber Smith & Wesson Airweight revolver
- .44 magnum-caliber Smith & Wesson revolver
- .357 magnum-caliber Smith & Wesson revolver
- Two .380-caliber Walther pistol, model PP, serial no. 38030A
- .22-caliber High Standard pistol
- 9mm-caliber Walther pistol
- .38 special-caliber Smith & Wesson revolver
- 9mm-caliber Walther pistol
- .38 special-caliber Smith & Wesson revolver
- Frame of .45-caliber Government pistol, model 1911A1, with no markings relating to serial no.
- .25-caliber Beretta Jetfire pistol
- Two .45-caliber Colt pistol, model NM
- .45-caliber Ithaca pistol, model 1911A1
- .25-caliber Astra pistol
- .22-caliber Sturm, Ruger pistol
- .30 mauser-caliber Mauser Broomhandle pistol
- .38 special-caliber Smith & Wesson revolver
- .22-caliber Smith & Wesson revolver
- .22-caliber H&R revolver
- .22-caliber Ruger Mach-II pistol
- .45-caliber R.P.B. Industries pistol, model M10, serial no. obliterated
- 9mm-caliber Walther pistol, model P-38
- .38 special-caliber Smith & Wesson revolver
- .38 special-caliber Smith & Wesson revolver
- .38 special-caliber Smith & Wesson revolver

- 9mm Walther pistol, model P38, serial no. 746h
- Eight silencers
- Approximately 80 boxes and other containers of ammunition
- Assorted magazines of various types and calibers
- Assorted holsters and gun cases
- Assorted firearm tools and lubricants
- One blue light
- Assorted handcuffs
- Assorted brass knuckles
- Assorted knives
- Assorted badges
- Assorted face masks and gas masks

Amico Joseph W. AKA "Chico", Born January 15, 1942. He was a member of the Barboza East Boston crew. When Barboza broke with the mob, the mob began killing off his gang. On December 8, 1966, Amico left Alphonse's Broken Hearts Club with another member of the gang. As they drove away, gunmen in another car opened fire, wounding the driver and killing Chico instantly.

Angiulo Gennaro AKA Jerry. March 20, 1919 – August 29, 2009. Angiulo was a New England mob boss who rose through the Mafia under Raymond L. S. Patriarca. He was convicted of racketeering in 1986 and was in jail until being released in 2007. One of the Angiulo Brothers, Angiulo was "probably the last very significant Mafia boss in Boston's history

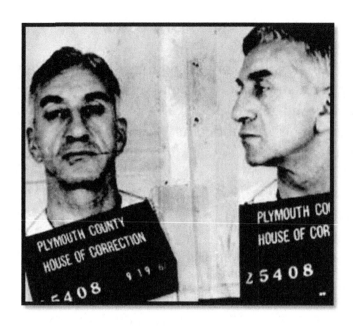

Jerry Angiulo

Angiulo was born in 1919 to Italian immigrants Caesar and Giovannina (Jeannie) Angiulo, who owned a mom-and-pop grocery store. Angiulo enlisted in the U.S. Navy at the beginning of World War II and served 4 years in the Pacific theater The Angiulo brothers, who owned nightclubs, were publicly named as members of Cosa Nostra, more commonly known as the American Mafia. In 1963. Gennaro's reputation for being a shrewd businessman, along with his successful racketeering, led to Patriarca appointing him underboss of the Providence, Rhode Island-based Patriarca crime family. Angiulo later headed up Boston's underworld from the 1960s to the 1980s. He and his brothers ran the criminal organization out of Francesco's Restaurant at 98 Prince Street in the North End, the neighborhood in which he grew up.

In 1981, the Federal Bureau of Investigation placed wiretaps in the restaurant and at a nearby social club, located at 51 North Margin Street, for three months. It was later revealed in a federal court that rival gangsters Whitey Bulger[6] and Stephen Flemmi drew a diagram for FBI agents telling them where to plant the bugs. As Angiulo was being taken in handcuffs from the restaurant on September 19, 1983, he yelled, "I'll be back before my pork chops get cold." As Angiulo sat in jail without bail awaiting trial on federal racketeering charges, he was demoted from the mob.

At the highly-publicized trial, jurors heard hours of taped conversations of Angiulo and his associates planning numerous illegal activities, including murder, gambling, loan sharking and extortion. In one conversation, Angiulo ordered the killing of a bartender after concluding that was set to testify before a federal grand jury investigating gambling and loan-sharking. The FBI thwarted the plot by warning the witness.

At the eight-month-long trial, the mobster often sarcastically commented on the evidence presented and cracked jokes, prompting District Court Judge Davis Nelson to repeatedly reprimand him. In February 1986, Angiulo and his co-defendants were convicted of "an avalanche of charges". He was sentenced to 45 years in prison on 12 counts of racketeering, gambling, loan sharking, and obstruction of justice. As his own lawyer, Angiullo argued numerous times, unsuccessfully, to have his conviction overturned. One argument claimed that he was framed by the FBI, Bulger, and Flemmi.

In an affidavit filed in federal court in 2004, he wrote that he was in poor health and his term was "tantamount to an illegal death sentence". Angiulo, who had been incarcerated at the federal prison hospital in Devens, was paroled on September 10, 2007. He died on August 29, 2009 at the Massachusetts General Hospital of renal failure from kidney disease.

Brothers Donato "Danny" and Nicky Angiulo

Boston's Little Italy where the Angiulo's ran their operations

Anzalone Ralph. A Quincy based hood who was found shot to death in his car on Second Street in South Boston, January 1973. It is suspected that Whitey Bulger gave the order.

Ashe George E Born 1923 Died 1964 FBI Informant. Ashe was a local Boston knock around hood that was released from prison in 1964 just as the Boston Irish Wars were escalating. The FBI recruited him as a snitch but before he could do them any good Jimmy Flemmi, the younger brother of Stevie Flemmi, stabbed Ashe 57 times and then shot.

B

Baiona Philip AKA "Sonny", Boston hood related to Larry Baione, a South End Boston hood who died in prison

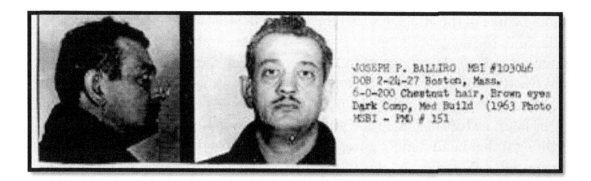

JOSEPH P. BALLIRO MBI #103046
DOB 2-24-27 Boston, Mass.
6-0-200 Chestnut hair, Brown eyes
Dark Comp, Med Build (1963) Photo
MSBI - PMD # 151

Bauco, Phillip J.: Of Bridgeport, Ct. In 2010, Bauco was accused of being a collector for a gambling ring. He pled guilty to a charge of racketeering conspiracy that same year. Bauco claimed that he had Gambino family backing.

Barboza Joseph AKA The Animal Born September 20, 1932 – February 11, 1976) Barboza was a Portuguese-American mafioso and one of the most feared mob hitmen during the 1960s. He is reputed to have murdered at least 26 men in his lifetime—yet never proven.
Barboza, also known as "The Animal", "The Wild Thing", "The Nigger", "Joseph Donati", "Joseph Bentley" and "The Joe Valachi of New England", was born to Portuguese-American emigrants from Lisbon, Portugal who settled in the old whaling city of New Bedford, Massachusetts
He earned the nickname "The Animal" after an altercation at a Revere, Massachusetts club that was patronized by figures of organized crime and Patriarca crime family underboss Henry Tameleo. Barboza was at the nightclub drinking and carrying on when an older Italian patron who did not enjoy Barboza's crude behavior told him so. Barboza approached the man and slapped him hard across the face. Tameleo, who was seated not far away, shouted angrily, "I don't want you to ever slap that man. I don't want you to touch anybody with your hands again." Barboza, now brooding at the bar, suddenly leaned over and bit the man's ear. "I didn't touch him with my hands", he snarled at Tameleo.
Barboza was first sent to prison in 1950 to the Massachusetts Correctional Institution - Concord for five years. Barboza would later lead a wild prison break in the summer of 1953, which would become the largest in the prison's seventy-five year history. Joe and six other fellow inmates had guzzled contraband whiskey and pilfered amphetamine tablets, overpowered four prison guards and

raced away in two separate cars. During their furlough of freedom they beat random people in the street, cruised the bars in Boston's Scollay Square, wandered to the neighborhoods of Lynn and Revere, and were finally apprehended at a subway station in East Boston. The escape party had barely lasted twenty-four hours. That November, while awaiting trial for his prison break, Barboza slugged a prison guard in the cafeteria for no reason. Three months later, he tossed a table at a guard's chest when he entered his cell.

It is thought that he first met figures of Boston organized crime while incarcerated at Walpole, and it is thought that they arranged to have him paroled in 1958. He became a recognized figure in East Boston's organized crime circles and was a regular habituate of a bar on the corner of Bennington Street and Brook Street which became known among local criminals as "Barboza's Corner". His crew of small-time burglars and thieves consisted of Joseph W. Amico, Patrick Fabiano, James Kearns, Arthur Bratsos, Thomas DePrisco, father and son team Joseph Dermody and Ronald Dermody, Carlton Eaton, Edward Goss and Nicholas Femia. All of his crew would all later be murdered by rival mobsters including himself. The crew was officially supervised for the Patriarca crime family by Stephen Flemmi.

It was widely believed in law official circles that Barboza had performed contract killings for Raymond L.S. Patriarca. By January 1966, Barboza was considered a powerful crime figure in the Boston underworld and was often represented by F. Lee Bailey which proved to be a huge mistake-But he was also facing major problems.

Raymond Patriarca with his attorney Joseph Balliro leaving a Boston court around 1967.

The authorities were constantly on his heels. For disturbing the peace one night at the same Revere nightclub where he chewed the ear off, he slugged a Boston Police Department Detective and received a six-month sentence. After his release from prison and his graduation from an expensive cooking school he was shipped out on the S.S. President Wilson to the Orient.

By 1966, Barboza he had a very turbulent position in the Boston underworld. Before he had chewed off the mobster's ear, he had been shot at while standing outside his home in Chelsea. The local authorities believed there had been other unreported attempts. Brimming with reckless power, he was not abiding to the traditional rules of the La Cosa Nostra. One night he went into a nightclub that was paying Gennaro Anguilo for protection and demanded that the owner make payments to him as well. By mid-1966, the unrelenting attention from the law Barboza received from the authorities only made his standing in organized crime more tenuous.

In October 1966, he came to terms with his falling-out with the organized crime element after he and three local hoodlums were arrested on weapons charges while cruising the Combat Zone in Boston. His accomplices were released on bail, but Barboza had his bail set at $100,000 which he could not afford. Nobody from the Patriarca crime family came down to post his bail and he heard that it was the Mafia family who tipped off the cops.

Two of his fellow compatriots and members of his crew, Arthur C. Bratsos and Thomas J. DePrisco, went to raise Barboza's bail. Five weeks later, after raising $59,000 the pair were murdered in the Nite Lite Cafe by soldiers serving under Ralph "Ralphie Chong" Lamattina, who served in the crew of Ilario Zannino. After relieving them of their bail money, they stuffed their bodies in the back seat of Bratsos's car and dumped it in South Boston, hoping to throw blame onto the Irish gangs. However, a mob associate named Joseph Lanzi tipped the cops about the murder. He was later murdered by Mafia associates Carmen Gagliardi, Frank Otero and Ben DeChristoforo.

The FBI began diligent efforts to turn Barboza into an informant. In December, Joe Amico, another friend of Barboza's, was murdered. The following month, after a ten-day trial, Barboza was sentenced to a five-year term at Walpole on the weapons charges. In the summer of 1967, Steven Flemmi met with Joseph and informed him that Gennaro Anguilo and his brothers had plans to murder him. In June 1967, Barboza turned FBI informant while imprisoned for murder, and eventually testified against Raymond Patriarca, Sr. before becoming one of the first informants to enter the Witness Protection Program. The government would not protect his wife and two young children if he refused to testify and even after the ordeal ended never kept any of their promises—he traded one evil for another.

Barboza went on to testify against Raymond Patriarca and many high-ranking members and associates of the New England family. On June 20, Patriarca and Tameleo were indicted for conspiracy to murder in the 1966 killing of Providence bookmaker Willie Marfeo. On August 9, Gennaro Angiulo was accused of participating in the murder of Rocco DiSeglio. Finally in October, six men were charged with the March 1965 murder of Edward "Teddy" Deegan. Shortly after the indictment of Raymond Patriarca, which drew front page stories about Barboza as a turncoat, Barboza wrote to the Boston Herald: "All I want to be is left alone." The La Cosa Nostra was willing to pay Barboza $25,000 to quit talking. He showed some interest in the deal raising the price to $50,000 which was agreed upon but later turned down after consulting his lawyer.

Gennaro Anguilo was later found not guilty. Despite efforts by reporters to coax jurors to explain their deliberations, none did. Twenty years later, however, jury foreman Kenneth Matthews said none of the sixteen jurors had found Barboza believable stating: "He didn't help the state at all. He wasn't reliable. He was nothing as a witness."

While the trials were going on, the mob tried to get at Barboza by planting a bomb in the car of his attorney, John Fitzgerald. Resulting in Fitzgerald losing his right leg below the knee. After that Barboza was moved around frequently from Thacher Island to Fort Devens and even to the Junior Officers' quarters located in Fort Knox, Kentucky. Barboza owned a German Shepherd Dog and while at Fort Knox he would walk his dog with future FBI agent John Morris. John Morris was a member of the military police at the time. In May 1968, the Deegan trial began. After 50 days of testimony and deliberations, the jury returned a guilty verdict. Found guilty and sentenced to death were Peter J. Limone, Louis Greco, Henry Tameleo and Ronald Cassesso. Sentenced to life in prison were Joseph Salvati and Wilfred Roy French.

Barboza was given a one-year prison term, including time served. He was paroled in March 1969 and relocated to Santa Rosa, California where he enrolled in a culinary arts school and is rumored to have killed ten more men. In 1971, he pleaded guilty to a second-degree murder charge in California and was sentenced to five years at Folsom Prison. At prison Barboza became an amateur poet and wrote poems portraying the evils of the La Cosa Nostra and his own fearlessness, "Boston Gang War", "The Mafia Double Crosses", "A Cat's Lives" and "The Gang War Ends". Additionally, he was a talented artist.

Barboza was paroled in October 1975 and moved into a $250-a-month apartment under the name "Joseph Donati". He took the last name from small-time underworld figures, identical twin brothers Richard and Robert Donati. After he was befriended by small-time South Boston hoodlum James Chalmas, Gennaro Anguilo was at last informed of his whereabouts. On February 11, 1976, Barboza left Chalmas' San Francisco apartment and walked towards his Oldsmobile. He was armed with a Colt 38 but never had a chance to draw it. He was hit by four shotgun blasts from close range, killing him instantly. F. Lee Bailey was quoted as having said his client's death (referring to Joseph Barboza) was "no great loss to society," but his young daughter never recovered from his death and was consumed by grief. Ilario Zannino, chief enforcer of Gennaro Anguilo, was later overheard saying to an associate on a hidden bug that it was J. R. Russo who had assassinated Barboza. In the conversation, Zannino described Russo as "a genius with a carbine".

While working with the corrupt FBI agent H. Paul Rico, he helped to frame Mafia associates Joseph Salvati, Peter Limone, Louis Greco as well as his former mob superior, Henry Tameleo for the murder of a small time criminal named Edward "Teddy" Deegan in Chelsea, Massachusetts, protecting the real culprit. Deegan was the maternal uncle of Gerry Indelicato, future aide to Governor Michael Dukakis.

Peter Limone

Deegan had been marked for death by the New England family in 1965 for several burglaries which he had committed with future Winter Hill Gang heavyweight, Stephen "The Rifleman" Flemmi.

Out of the six people convicted for the murder, only Ronald "Ronnie the Pig" Casseso and Wilfred Roy French were actually involved and present in the alley where the murder took place. FBI agent Paul Rico had offered French and Casseso leniency if they would corroborate Barboza's false testimony. Both French and Casseso refused the offer and when French was threatened with the death penalty he responded by telling Rico to "warm up the electric chair." Cassesso died in prison 30 years later. French was finally freed 34 years later.

Winter Hill enforcer John Martorano became a government witness in 1999 after learning that both Steven Flemmi and James "Whitey' Bulger were FBI informants and have been delivering information about the Mafia and the Winter Hill Gang to them. In his plea agreement, he told the Drug Enforcement Administration agent that Barboza had admitted to lying about the men convicted of killing Teddy Deegan. Barboza allegedly said that the Patriarca crime family had "screwed me and now I'm going to screw as many of them as possible."

Martorano also revealed that Vincent "Jimmie the Bear" Flemmi, the brother of Stephen Flemmi, had admitted to murdering Deegan. Vincent Flemmi and his brother were both acting as informants to the FBI. Instead of arresting Vincent Flemmi, the FBI knowingly let four men go to prison for a crime they didn't commit. Barboza used this opportunity to settle some old grudges with some local North Enders and Mafia associates who he felt had not shown him the proper respect.

Greco

Tameleo and Greco died in prison after serving almost 30 years, and Salvati and Limone were finally released in 1997 and 2001, respectively. Lawyers representing the families of Greco, Tameleo, Salvati and Limone currently have lawsuits totaling in excess of one billion dollars filed against the Federal government.

Dermody

Barnoski Billy: A member of the Winter Hill gang in the 1960s and 1970s, who worked as a strong arm man for Tony Ciulla. Ciulla is most remembered implicating dozens of jockeys, trainers and others in an effort to lower a long prison sentence he was facing. He admitted to fixing several hundred races at 39 tracks all over the country during the 1970s. The end came in 1971 when a low level hood named Bobby Byrne was arrested, of all things for climbing a fence at Suffolk Downs race track. Police found hypodermic needles and syringes on him provided information on the Ciulla's crew of veterinarians, exercise riders and jockeys who were on the take. The information provided by Byrne resulted in Ciulla being convicted of drugging horse in Massachusetts and the bribery of racing officials in Rhode Island.

Benjamin Frankie: A native of Roxbury Mass. and a lifelong criminal. Released from a prison sentence in 1964, he dropped by a neighborhood bar where something happened between him and Vincent "Jimmy the Bear" Flemmi, it is clear exactly what happened. Flemmi had served time with Benjamin in the 1950's. Flemmi left the bar and came back with a gun, owned by a cop, and shot Benjamin through the head, killing him. To avoid an identification of weapon used, Flemmi cut its head off and left the headless torso in a stolen car. The head was never found.

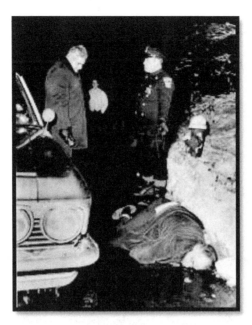

Wimpy Bennett

Nicholas Bianco

Bianco Nicholas: Providence underboss to Mr. Patriarca. Former Colombo crime captain. AKA Nicky March 21 1932 – November 14 1994. Bianco was originally a Brooklyn-based mobster and a member of the Colombo crime family. He was also associated with Mafia renegade Joey Gallo before moving to Rhode Island to become one of Patriarca's leading tough guys.

Bulger, William Michael AKA Billy . Born February 2, 1934 Bulger was forced to resign from the office of president of the University of Massachusetts after it was revealed that he had communicated with his fugitive brother, James J. Bulger. Bulger became interested in politics in 1959 and was first elected to the Massachusetts House of Representatives in 1961. After serving four terms, Bulger was elected to the Massachusetts State Senate in 1970 representing the First Suffolk District. He was elected President of the Massachusetts State Senate in 1978 and re-elected every two years to 1996, making his time as State Senate President the longest tenure in Massachusetts history.

Heroically, Bulger joined other Irish American neighborhood leaders in opposition to court-ordered desegregated busing. Like other Massachusetts politicians who were elected leaders of their legislative chambers, Bulger was frequently pilloried in the media, but remained very popular in his district. He won his district election every two years from 1961 to 1994 without ever facing a challenge more serious than he faced in the Democratic primary in 1988, when

Stephen Holt, a neophyte liberal activist and bookstore owner from Dorchester won 31 out of 60 precincts, only to lose the district by a landslide due to the huge turnout of Bulger supporters in South Boston.

During the 1960s, he led efforts to write the first child abuse reporting laws in the state. He was supportive of environmental protection legislation.

Bulger was among the first advocates of charter schools and public school choice. During the 1980s, he advocated funding of public libraries, the expansion of childhood nutrition services and fuel assistance programs. As Senate president, Bulger led the debate on welfare reform in the early 1990s, with the resulting legislation becoming the model for a national law.

For many years, Bulger hosted the annual St. Patrick's Day Breakfast in South Boston. This is a "roast" of politicians.

Although a Democrat, Bulger was appointed President of the University of Massachusetts by Republican Governor William Weld in 1996.

On August 6, 2003, Bulger announced that he would resign as President of the system effective September 1, 2003. His resignation came due to pressure from Governor Mitt Romney after Bulger had refused to cooperate with authorities who were searching for Bulger's brother, the notorious mobster James "Whitey" Bulger. In addition to Bulger the entire Senior Staff of the Office of the President of the University of Massachusetts resigned. Jack Wilson, a hand-picked Bulger staffer, who was overseeing the creation of the University Online Web Learning Portal was tapped to be the interim President. He would later take the post in whole.

Bulger's older brother James J. "Whitey" Bulger, is an alleged former Boston crime boss accused of murder and several other crimes. Whitey was a fugitive from justice from 1995 until his arrest in June 2011. William Bulger's role in his brother's escape from authorities is a matter of some dispute. On June 19, 2003, he testified to a House of Representatives committee about an incident in which, while still President of the Massachusetts State Senate, he "went to an arranged location in 1995 to take a call from his fugitive brother, apparently to avoid electronic eavesdropping. He said that accepting the call from the gangster without bothering to inform the FBI was 'in no way inconsistent with my devotion to my own responsibilities, my public responsibilities.'"

During the hearing, when asked what he thought James (Whitey) did for a living, William Bulger said: "I had the feeling that he was in the business of gaming and... whatever. It was vague to me but I didn't think, for a long while he had some jobs but ultimately it was clear that he was not being, you know, he wasn't doing what I'd like him to do".

He added that he loves his brother and hopes that the most brutal rumors concerning him will be proven false. In addition, he grudgingly admitted to visiting an isolated pay phone in order to speak to his older brother, who was by then a fugitive. As fallout from these remarks, he was forced out by then-Governor of Massachusetts Mitt Romney from his position as president of the University of Massachusetts in 2003.

Bulger also testified that the FBI never asked if he knew of Whitey's location. Those remarks were disputed by a former FBI agent who claimed Bulger declined to submit to an interview with the bureau. Months later, the committee report found Bulger's testimony "inconsistent" about whether the FBI had contacted him in its search for his fugitive brother.

Upon Whitey's arrest in California in June 2011, William Bulger issued a statement expressing his "sympathies to the families hurt" in the case, and asking for privacy for his family.

Boston Irish Gang Wars: The Boston Irish Gang War started in 1961 and ended in 1966. The war was a series of skirmishes fought between the McLaughlin Gang of Charlestown, headed by Bernie McLaughlin and the Winter Hill Gang of Somerville, headed by James "Buddy" McLean. On Labor Day weekend 1961, while at a party (locally called a "Time") Georgie McLaughlin made several crude remarks to the girlfriend of a Winter Hill Gang member. Gang members beat McLaughlin unconscious and then dumped him outside of a local hospital. Bernie McLaughlin demanded that Jimmy McLean turn over the men who had beaten his brother. McLean refused. The McLaughlin's then attempted to wire a bomb to McLean's wife's car. In retaliation McLean shot McLaughlin twice in the back of the head. Then, in 1965, Mclean was shot and killed. The killing ended five years later.

Bratsos Tash. Born April 11, 1930. Bratsos worked for Joe Barboza as a Loanshark before he was murdered by persons unknown in the Nite Lite Café on Commercial Street in the North End of Boston.

Bratsos, a Greek, was in the midst of raising bail money for Barboza.

In October, Barboza was arrested in Boston's notorious "Combat Zone" on a concealed weapons charge and bond was set at $100,000 and Patriarca and

Angiulo made no efforts to furnish his bail. Five weeks later Barboza was still languishing in jail. The Mob didn't want Barboza out of prison since he was deemed a loose cannon beyond control. Another Barboza associate was loan shark, James Chalamas, who was also a hired thug for the mob. He was offered $25 thousand to murder Barboza but Chalamas declined. Bratsos and Thomas J. DePrisco Jr. had collected $59,000 in bail money when they went to the Nite Lite Café that was managed by Ralphie Chang Lamattina. Both men were shot to death and dumped in South Boston to make it look like a rival Irish gang murdered them.

Buccola

Bruno Adolfo M: An alleged mobster from Agawam, Mass, in November of 2004, on the night before his 59th birthday Bruno was shot six times in the face and chest with a .45-caliber handgun while walking to his car with a friend outside a Springfield social club and died instantly. Bruno was thought to be a member of the New York Genovese crime family that runs gambling rackets in Springfield. Why he was killed is unknown.

Buccola, Philip. Born 1886. Died 1987. Buccola is widely believed to have ascended to the leadership of the Boston-based Mafia Family in the Prohibition Era. Some sources indicate he became boss upon the death of Gaspare Messina in 1924. However, it is not at all certain that Messina died in that year - Nick Gentile indicates that Messina briefly served as American Mafia boss of bosses about 1930. Gentile's account fits better with the traditionally accepted 1932 timing of Buccola's recognition as Boston boss from the national Mafia commission. Born in Palermo, Sicily, Buccola arrived in the United States in 1920 and worked for a time as a fight promoter.

He appears to have led a Sicilian gang in Boston's East Side for a while. His education, relative affluence and links to the Palermo underworld served him as he rose to the top of Boston's Sicilian underworld. Buccola might have cooperated with non-Mafia bootlegging czar Charles "King" Solomon and the rest of the Seven Group ("Big Seven") in rum-running operations in the late 1920s and early 1930s. However, his name is conspicuously absent from lists of Seven Group members. It is possible that Solomon's leadership in the New England bootlegging rackets was a cause of some friction between him and Buccola. At least one source indicates that Solomon's 1933 murder was ordered by Buccola.

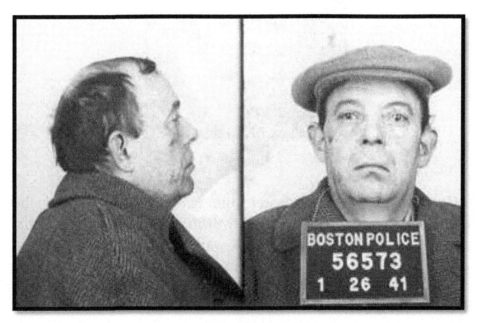

Joe Lombardo

The relationship between Buccola and Mafioso Joe Lombardo is something of a mystery. It appears that Lombardo, deemed responsible for the December 1931 assassination of Irish Gustin Gang boss Frankie Wallace, was at least part of a New England-wide Mafia leadership in the 1940s. There are several theories regarding Lombardo's poorly documented role: He might have been an overall boss, using others as front men or division leaders; He might have served as Buccola's underboss; or he might have led an ethnic faction within the North Side Mafia. Based upon information provided by turncoat Vincent Teresa, Lombardo was overall boss. It remains possible, however, that Lombardo was less a regional crime czar than an influential member of a panel of Mafia leaders, which might have included Boston's Gaspare Messina (if alive) and Providence's Frank Morelli. Targeted by law enforcement as a result of assuming control over Morelli's Rhode Island operations around 1947, Buccola retired to his Sicilian estates in 1954. Day-to-day Mafia affairs in Providence and Boston were turned over to Raymond Patriarca. Buccola kept a hand in Boston affairs while chicken farming outside Palermo. He died at the age of 101 in 1987.

Buccelli, John F. AKA Fats Born 1914. Died (Murdered) June 19, 1958. Buccelli was arrested for his role in the Brinks robbery but released due to lack of evidence. Buccelli was later shot to death and left in car.

Buffoli Leo AKA Chipper. Patriarca Family Informant

New England Mafia boss Harry Anguilo talking to Boston murderer Whitey Bulger

Bulger, James J. Sr: Whitey Bulger's father. An honest and hard- working Irish immigrant he worked most of his life in the United States as a longshoreman. Bulger's mother was a housekeeper.

Bulger, Whitey: Born September 3, 1929 The FBI's Ten Most Wanted Fugitives list turned fifty years old this year, and sitting at the very top of the list Tis Himself, Whitey Bulger, Boston own home-grown gangster and brother to the former president of the Massachusetts Senate.

FBI surveillance

FBI agent John Connolly, and bad guy James "Whitey" Bulger, both the sons of Irish immigrants, grew up in drab housing projects of South Boston, or Southie, as the natives call it, a close knit, depressing and dreary, mostly Irish, mostly working poor, neighborhood.

FBI surveillance

Jimmy Bulger, he detests the name Whitey, knew Connolly from the neighborhood, not well, but he knew him. Connolly was closer to Billy Bulger, the brother who went straight, and as a result, went places. A brilliant student with an earthy sense of humor, Billy entered politics and eventually became President of the state Senate, and is currently the head of the University of Massachusetts, Billy Bulger took a liking to the young Connolly, and mentored him, guiding the sharp young man out of South Boston and into Boston College for a Bachelor's degree and to Harvard for a Masters.

FBI surveillance

Connolly reciprocated by becoming a loyal Bulger man, working in his various campaigns, and parading each new Bureau chief to Bulger's office when he sat in the State Senate Presidents chair.

FBI surveillance

Jimmy Bulger took a different route to fame. He robbed a bank and ended up in Alcatraz. He got off The Rock early by volunteering for government sponsored LSD experiments.

Whitey Bulger

Released back to the streets of Boston, Jimmy Bulger returned to Southie and to the mostly Irish, Winter Hill gang that ruled over the area.
At the same time, John Connolly was working in the FBI's Organized Crime Unit in Boston, charged with busting up the growing power of the New England mob. It was Connolly who flipped an informant named Sonny Mercurio, and in turn, the hood tipped him off about Mafia induction ceremony. Connolly bugged the place, and got the most valuable evidence the FBI has ever obtained, a live recording of a Mafia swearing in ritual

FBI surveillance

When Connolly started hauling in that sort information, the Bureau pressured him for even more miracles, and Connolly delivered.

As part of his mission to smash the Outfit, in October of 1975, Connolly and Jimmy Bulger met in a darkened parking lot that overlooked the Atlantic Ocean, and Connolly made his pitch to flip Bulger.

"Jimmy" Connolly said "Your buddies in the Mafia want to give you up to the cops. Why not give up your buddies in the Mafia to us?" working under the code name "Charlie," Whitey Bulger fed Connolly a steady stream of reliable information on the New England Mafia.

FBI Agent Connelly

But did it go further than that?

The stories of the Connolly's protection of Bulger, and his Winter Hill gang, are now the stuff of legend around Boston. Like the time that the gang fixed races at Suffolk Downs in East Boston, and several other racetracks, by paying jockeys to hold back their horses. A score of Winter Hill hoods went to jail on that one, but not Bulger. In fact, when the smoke cleared, Bulger was the gang's leader. Connolly admits that after working closely with Bulger, that he and other agents exchanged holiday gifts with the gangster and accepted dinner party's invitations as well.

That would have been marginally acceptable, but, if the testimony of John Morris, a Bureau field supervisor, is to be believed, even though Bulger was released as an informant in 1990, Morris says that Connolly stayed close to the gangster, and even warned him about the pending indictments, allowing the gangster ample time to escape justice.

Morris also claims that he accepted $7,000 in cash bribes from Bulger, and that Connolly delivered at least two of those pay off's, of $1,000 each, which were placed under the bottom of a case of expensive wine that Connolly delivered to Morris in the garage below the FBI's Boston offices.

Connolly also allegedly received free household appliances from Broadway Appliance, a South Boston store controlled by Bulger. The reports said that the hoods gave Connolly a refrigerator, dishwasher and stove, among other things. Adding to Connolly's woes is federal grand jury probe into a series of highly suspicious real estate deals by him that appear to have Jimmy Bulger's markings all over them.

Earlier this year, Connolly, who has long since retired from the Bureau, was indicted, charged with racketeering and obstruction of justice. That case hinges on the government's assertion that Connolly's relationship became so close with Bulger and the gang, that he became a partner in crime with them.

The Fed's charged Connolly with warning Bulger and others of up and coming investigations, falsifying reports to hide their crimes, passing bribes, and allege that Connolly derailed an investigation into the extortion of a South Boston family forced to turn over its liquor store to Bulger. If that's true, its pathetic and unforgivable.

In 1984, Stephen Rakes was allegedly approached by Bulger with a bag containing $64,000, and told by Bulger that he wanted to buy the store. Rakes said it wasn't for sale.

According to Rakes, Bulger drew a pistol, complimented Rakes young daughter and said "It'll be a shame not to be able to see her grow up"

Rakes went to the Boston police, who took the case to Connolly, who, according to the indictment, falsely told the cops that unless Rakes agreed to wear a wire to record Bulger, that the FBI was unlikely to take action on the complaint.

Prosecutors say that not only did Connolly fail to pursue the case, he allegedly warned Bulger about Rakes complaint to the Boston P. D.

On an even more sinister scale, Bulger allegedly had one of his enforcers pump a bullet into the back of the head of Roger Wheeler, the chairman of Telex Corporation, as he finished a round of golf in Tulsa, Oklahoma.

Wheeler

According to Brian Halloran, a former member of the Snow Hill gang, who was supposed to do the killing, Bulger wanted Wheeler dead so he could take over his Jai Alai frontons in Florida and Connecticut.

Halloran identified professional hitman John Martorano as the killer, and said that Bulger was at the scene of the crime, in a getaway car. But, despite the wealth of evidence he provided, the Boston FBI Bureau refused a deal with Halloran, and concluded he wasn't credible.

Shortly afterwards, person's unknown gunned Halloran as he walked down a Boston Street. Through it all, Connolly denies any wrong doing "He was a hell of guy" Connolly told an always indignant Washington Post about Bulger "I know damn well the guy is no Boy Scout. But, I'd be lying if I said I didn't like him" When asked to explain the G man's behavior, one of the lawyers in the case said "This indictment is a whitewash, designed to cover up the institutional practices and philosophy of the FBI in the 1970s and 1980s, which encouraged the kind of relationship Bulger had with the FBI to achieve a perceived greater goal - the destruction of La Cosa Nostra"

Maybe so, but more than one Law Enforcement official was overjoyed to hear that Connolly had been arrested and hauled out of his comfortable suburban home in handcuffs.

" I feel for his family" one former DEA agent said "But John was a (X@C&*#@) of the highest order. He hurt a lot of people. A lot of blood, sweat and tears went down the crapper, thanks to John. I can still see the wardrobe. The cuff links. We gave John a nickname "Giovanni Connollino". He was the only agent I knew who took style tips from John Gotti"

If Connolly's name in the halls of power in Washington, down in the narrow streets of Southie, Bulger still enjoys a sort of Robin Hood reputation as the guy who kept drugs and violence out of South Boston's neighborhoods, which is not true. At all.

Bulger's status as a local hero was confirmed when Boston City Council President James Kelly called him "A gentleman" and has openly defended him in the past. The endorsement is questionable.

Mr. Kelly's name popped up during a hearing into the Bulger gangs extortion of a Raymond Slinger, a South Boston Realtor.

According to Slinger, in 1987, Bulger and his boys threatened to kill the Broker if he didn't fork over $50,000 in protection money.

Slinger said he went to Kelly for help. A day later, Kelly called Slinger and told him that the issue was resolved and that he would have no other troubles out of the Winter Hill mob.

Shortly afterwards, Slinger was called to a meeting at one of Bulger's bar rooms where he was severely beaten.

However, Jimmy's reputation as a likable rouge took a turn for the worst at the start of this year when one of his gang members led investigators to a spot in Dorchester where the skeletal remains of three mob victims were buried.

The bones belonged to John McIntyre, Arthur Barrett, and Deborah Hussey, the daughter of Flemmi's longtime girlfriend, all of whom disappeared between 1983 and 1984.

They may have killed Barrett, a bank robber, for his share of the $1.5 million take from a robbery he pulled with the Winter Hill gang. The women, Hussey, may have been killed because she simply knew too much about everything.

 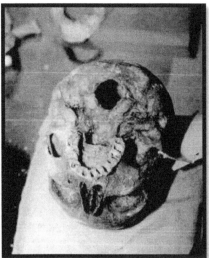

Deborah Hussy

McIntyre was an otherwise honest man, deeply committed to the cause of freedom in Northern Ireland, who got involved with Bulger's convoluted gun running schemes to the IRA.

And where is Jimmy Bulger today?

Well, the FBI certainly doesn't know, even though they've tried to squeeze Bulger's family for information. But that's not going to happen, since Bulger's sister, Jena Holland, has been battling the state for five years to have herself declared her brothers "absentee receiver"

And understandably so. It seems that before he disappeared, Jimmy Bulger's Irish luck came into play one more time, when he won the state lottery, some 1.9 million dollars, or $119,000 for twenty years. Back in the 1980's, the son of Chicago's mob boss, Tony Accardo, also won the lottery.
After sixteen years at large and twelve years on the FBI Ten Most Wanted Fugitives list, Bulger was arrested in Santa Monica, California, on June 22, 2011.

Bulger had $822,000 in cash and a dozen weapons when captured.

Bulger kept a cache of cash and weapons behind a mirror in his Santa Monica, Calif., apartment.

C

Dickie Callei

Candos, Bobby: In 1967, word leaked that Candos, a bank robber, planned to testify against the Rhode Island mob. In 1970, his skeleton was found in North Attleborough, he had been shot in the head three times. Raymond Patriarca was arrested for the murder in 1980

Carr, James: AKA Jimmy. Carr worked closely with mobster Dick Callei. In 1974, while stopped at a light Providence, someone walked up to his car and fired a shot into his head. Remarkably, the ling in his hat stopped the bullet and Carr survived. He disappeared a short time later.

Carrozza Robert AKA "Bobby Russo", (born January 9, 1940 East Boston, Massachusetts) led a bloody internal rebellion against the leadership of the Providence-based Patriarca crime family.

"Gigi" Portalla, enforcer for the renegade faction of the Boston mob led by Mafia Capo Robert Carrozza

Carrozza became the stepbrother of Patriarca crime family capo Joseph (JR) Russo born May 5, 1931 in East Boston, Massachusetts after his mother remarried Russo's father. After his stepmother married his father, he used his adopted named "Robert (Bobby) Russo" as a criminal alias among associates. His stepbrother became notorious for murdering mob contractor killer Joseph Barboza in San Francisco, California in 1976. Russo was later convicted of RICO and sent to prison where he died of natural causes in 1997. Robert would later the last name of his stepbrother's Christian name 'Russo' as an alias when involved in organized crime. Journalist Howie Carr would write that unlike the respect his stepbrother Russo earned from mob capos such as Ilario Zannino and Angelo Mercurio, Carrozza was "considered such a complete moron by Patriarca crime family underboss Gennaro Anguilo that he was told that if he set foot in the city proper, excluding East Boston, Massachusetts, that he would be shot on sight." In 1989, a violent internal conflict fractured the Patriarca family. A "renegade faction" led by Carrozza, his stepbrother and family Consiglieri Joseph Russo, and mobster Vincent Ferara challenged the leadership of boss Raymond Patriarca and family associate Frank Salemme.

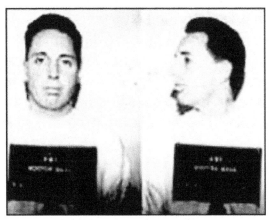
Vincent Ferara

By seizing family leadership, Carrozza and the other renegades sought to control illegal gambling and the extortion of bookmakers, drug dealers and restaurant owners in Massachusetts. This takeover attempt provoked a gang civil war that lasted until 1996 and claimed over a dozen lives. On June 16, 1989, Patriarca underboss William P. Grasso's body was found with a bullet wound to the head along the banks of the Connecticut River in Massachusetts.

Five hours after the discovery of Grasso's body, gunmen shot and seriously wounded Salemme at a restaurant in Saugus, Massachusetts. On June 27, 1989, informant and former Patriarca family member, Angelo Mercurio told Federal Bureau of Investigation (FBI) agent John Connolly that Russo, Ferrara and Carrozza had planned and executed both shootings. Much of the Patriarca family's legal troubles resulted from this relationship between Whitey Bulger, leader of Boston's Winter Hill Gang, and Connolly. In exchange for Bulger providing Connolly with incriminating information on the Patriarca family, Connolly protected Bulger and his criminal operations from law enforcement.

On March 26, 1990, Carrozza and twenty other family members were indicted on racketeering, extortion, narcotics, illegal gambling, and murder charges. The Patriarca arrests were described as "the most sweeping attack ever launched on a single organized crime family." One of the most damaging pieces of evidence was a tape recording of a Cosa Nostra induction ceremony attended by 13 Patriarca family members. On January 6, 1992, Carrozza's attorney, Henry D. Katz, offered Carrozza a plea bargain in which the government promised not to prosecute him for the Grasso murder, an offense that could carry a life sentence, and for the attempted murder of Salemme. Carrozza accepted the plea bargain and was sentenced to 19 years in prison. In 1993, 26 others were indicted and convicted for running a bookmaking operation. In 1991, Salemme became boss of the Patriarca Family and the family conflict escalated. Both factions wanted to collect the family's extortion payments and control its other business. Anthony Ciampi, a key Carrozza faction member, owned a club on Bennington Street in East Boston, the site of gambling and illegal card games, that was frequented by Carrozza faction members.

Following Carrozza's sentencing in April 1992, it took nearly two years for the "renegade faction" to plan its revenge. Ciampi and Michael P. Romano, Sr. visited Carrozza several times in prison in Pennsylvania. The FBI contended that the two men sought Carrozza's permission to continue the war against Salemme. Assistant United States Attorney Jeffrey Auerhahn claimed, "Robert Carrozza supplied legitimacy. You can't take on a Mafia member unless you have one with you." Using Ciampi's social club as the group's headquarters, the "renegade faction" in 1994 retaliated against Salemme by killing several of his supporters. On April 8, 1997 federal authorities indicted 15 members of the "renegade faction" for three murders, seven murder attempts, and seven planned murders. Carrozza was named as the sole made man, or full member, of the Patriarca family of those indicted. Sean Thomas Cote, the first of four indicted members to turn government witness, dominated the grand jury testimony that produced the indictments. Carrozza was accused of orchestrating the "renegade faction's" activities from prison, largely through Ciampi and Michael Romano, Sr. At a July 1999 court hearing, Carrozza announced that he would represent himself at the new trial. Despite efforts by District Judge Nathaniel Gorton to dissuade him, Carrozza remained adamant. On November 1, 1999, Carrozza began his opening statement at the trial with the comment "I'm a little nervous." He then told the jury that he previously confessed to being part of an "enterprise" during his 1992 trial and then stated, "Unlike some witnesses in this case, I accept the fact that I'm guilty of crimes and accept punishment for them." Carrozza informed jurors that despite prison authorities monitoring his mail and phone calls since 1989, prosecutors lacked any evidence that he had conspired with the other indicted men.

One month into the trial, Carrozza's former attorney offered prosecutors a plea bargain agreement from Carrozza. In exchange for pleading guilty to a felony charge of gambling across state lines, two more years would be added to

Carrozza's existing prison sentence and he would be exempted from testifying in any federal grand jury investigation of the Patriarca Family or from cooperating with the government. A deal was worked out and Carrozza served his expanded sentence at the Federal Correctional Institution - Medium Allenwood in White Deer, Pennsylvania. On March 23, 2008, Carrozza was released from prison.

Cassesso

Cassesso Ron, Born December 12, 1931. AKA Ronnie the Pig. Of Revere Beach, Mass. Long suspected as one of Teddy Deegan's killers in March 1965. He died in prison

Castagna, John F AKA Sonny: During the RICO trials of the Providence Mob in March of 1990 Castagna, a former associate of the Patriarca family turned government witness, revealed that Raymond Patriarca Jr. would be killed by the Boston mob if he didn't step down. Castagna, testifying in May 1991, said the story was relayed to him by J. R. Russo. "Raymond Junior had tears in his eyes and he was begging for his life," Castagna quoted Russo as saying. Castagna, now in the Federal Witness Protection Program with his son Jack Johns, also claimed that Gaetano Milano murdered William Grasso.

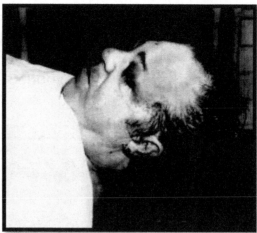

Richie Castucci, alive and dead

Richie Castucci, who owned the Ebb Tide lounge on Revere Beach, where Teddy Deegan's murder was plotted was an FBI informant and told the government men where they could find Joe McDonald and James Simms. The FBI told members of the Winter Hill Gang who lured Castucci to Somerville, Mass. and had Johnny Martorano shoot him through the head. Stevie Flemmi and Whitey Bulger cleaned tossed Castucci's body was in the trunk of his Cadillac and left it in Revere, Mass.

Cesario, Aurelio H: Cesario was gunned down on Federal Hill in Providence. Dickie Callei was charged in the murder in 1972. In turn, on March 17, 1975, Callei was murdered by Bobo Marrapese. Callei's body was found (he had been shot, knifed, and beaten with a blunt instrument) in Rehoboth, Massachusetts.

Charlestown Mob was an Irish Mob organized crime group in Charlestown, Massachusetts, which figured prominently in the history of Boston for much of the 20th century. The gang was headed by the McLaughlin Brothers (Bernie, Georgie, and Edward "Punchy" McLaughlin) and their associates, brothers Stevie and Connie Hughes from Charlestown. Some of its notorious members included Arthur Doe, William Bennett, Edward Bennett and John Shackelford. They were involved in the Boston Irish Mob Wars of the early to mid- 1960s against Somerville's Winter Hill Gang led by James "Buddy" McLean. The decade long gang war left both Bernie and Punchy dead and Georgie in prison. The Hughes

Brothers later suffered almost identical fates, as they were both shot to death in their cars on two separate occasions

Chodor John J. Born January 1, 1939. A knock around hood active in the late 1960s

Cincotti, John: A soldier in the New England mob in the 1970-1980s. In 1986, he was jailed for twenty years on a massive loansharking indictment.

Coakley, Daniel H: A Massachusetts Governor's Councilor, impeached and removed from office for his involvement in the early parole of Raymond Patriarca in the late 1930.

Coia Arthur Sr., vice president of Laborers International Union of North America. In 1981, Coia and his son, Arthur Jr. along with Raymond Patriarca, former Rhode Island state Rep. Albert LePore, a law partner of the elder Coia were named in a sealed indictment that accused them of violating the Racketeer-Influenced and Corrupt Organizations (RICO) Act. The indictment charged that the Coias, Lepore and Patriarca conspired to skim money intended for union members' insurance benefits through the use of kickbacks, payoffs and improper personal expenses and that in 1976, Patriarca stated that the insurance business of the Laborers Union would be controlled by "The Family." Patriarca would control business in the Northeast, Trafficante in the South and Anthony "Big Tuna" Accardo in the Midwest. The charges would eventually be dropped.

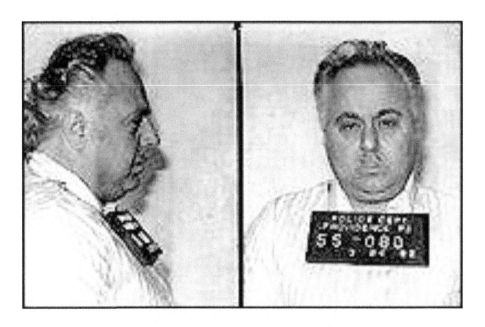

Coppola Ronald AKA Ronnie. A loan shark and bookmaker with longtime ties to the Patriarca family. In the early 1970s Coppola and Bobby DeLuca were arrested for pistol-whipping a man outside a social cub. In 1973 Coppola received a 10-year prison term in Oklahoma after trying to scam horses from a local rancher. Returning to Providence, Coppola worked for Edward "Mulligan" Romano, a capo in Boston's North End. Romano and Coppola soon had a falling out. Coppola went to work for the so-called
"Boston faction" of the Patriarca Family and became one of the most powerful figures in the loan sharking and bookmaking rackets during the early part of the 1990s. Coppola was murdered on April 1, 1994. He was killed in an argument with Antonia Cucinotta, AKA Nino, who also killed Peter Scarpellino in the same argument. A made member of the New England crime family. Cucinotta became Junior Patriarca's driver and gofer for a salary of $100 a week. After Patriarca was forced out, Cucinotta worked as a flagman on a roadwork construction site. Cucinotta eventually pleaded guilty to two counts of second-degree murder in

May 1995, and agreed to become a government witness and testify against the Patriarca family.

Coin-O-Matic Distributors, a vending machine and pinball business owned by Raymond Patriarca and housed in the Mobs "office" on Atwell Avenue in Providence.

Connecticut River: The Connecticut River was considered the dividing line between the New York and New England Families. However, the Genovese Family controlled Hartford, Springfield, and Albany, while New England controlled the cities of Worcester and Boston, and Maine. Raymond Patriarca had a strong relationship with the Genovese and Profaci/Colombo crime families and they considered Patriarca a reliable friend.. Patriarca's underboss, Henry Tameleo, was a member of the Bonanno crime family

Condon Dennis. Born in Charlestown Mass. In 1971, J. Edgar Hoover ordered Condon to recruit Whitey Bulger as an FBI informant. Condon attended the 1985

Lexington dinner in 1985 with Bulger, and Stevie Flemmi, at which crooked FBI agent John Morris was given a $5,000 bribe.

Connolly, John J. Jr. Born August 1, 1940 is a former FBI agent, who was convicted of racketeering and obstruction of justice convictions stemming from his relationship with James J. "Whitey" Bulger, Steve Flemmi, and the Winter Hill Gang. Connolly was released from federal prison June 28, 2011, and was transferred to Massachusetts state prison to serve the remainder of his sentence for his 2008 second degree murder conviction.

As the FBI handler for Bulger and Flemmi, Connolly (who had grown up in the Old Harbor Housing Project with Bulger) had been protecting them from prosecution by feeding Bulger information about possible attempts to catch them.

Connolly was indicted on December 22, 1999 on charges of alerting Bulger and Flemmi to investigations, falsifying FBI reports to cover their crimes, and accepting bribes. In 2000, he was charged with additional racketeering related offenses. He was convicted on the racketeering charges in 2002 and sentenced to 10 years in federal prison.

Connolly Jr. is the son of an Irish immigrant John Connolly Sr. known as "Galway John" who worked for Gillette Company for 50 years; his mother Bridget T. Kelly was a housewife. As a boy, Connolly would later tell reporters his first memory of James J. Bulger, using his illicit earnings to buy ice cream cones for all the boys that swarmed around him in adoration.

Before he became an FBI agent Connolly worked as a teacher at South Boston High School and Dorchester High School In 1968 he met with H. Paul Rico's FBI partner Special Agent Dennis Condon, and Boston Police Department Detective Edward Walsh, an old friend of the Connolly family. Both Condon and Walsh would later brag that they had 'recruited' Connolly. Then he stopped by his old neighbor and state representative Billy Bulger to discuss career opportunities in law enforcement. On August 1, 1968 U.S. House Speaker John William McCormack wrote a personal note to J. Edgar Hoover on behalf of a constituent. The letter began, "Dear Edgar, It has come to my attention that the son of a lifelong personal friend has applied to become a special agent of the Federal Bureau of Investigation..." He was appointed to the FBI in October 1968. FBI Supervisor John M. Morris, who would also face charges of corruption, was Connolly's supervisor during much of his time working for the FBI

As an agent he was also one of the primary agents involved in developing the Top Echelon Criminal Informants Program in New England.

He is the brother-in-law of Arthur Gianelli who was later indicted with Joe (Joey Y) Yerardi who oversaw John Martorano's criminal operations when he was a federal fugitive in Florida between 1978 and 1995. In 1989 the DEA was probing the Winter Hill Gang for suspected drug trafficking.

The DEA was well aware that John's brother James, and a former roommate of his both worked for the DEA. An FBI supervisor later noted in a memo, the head of the DEA's Boston office, "quietly changed the duties of both these DEA special agents so they would not become aware of this matter." Boston FBI Special Agent Robert Fitzpatrick said, "Connolly just became a force unto himself, a vortex in a constantly changing system. He stayed put as new agents in charge came and went. And he could take care of other agents. He became the guy who could get you sports tickets. He could help you get a day off through the secretaries. He made no secret that he could help you get a job after retirement through Billy Bulger. But he wasn't that much of an agent. He couldn't write a report. He was no administrator. He was just this brassy bullshit artist. We enabled him to some extent. No one had the stomach for examining what he was up to. We just never came to grip with that guy."

In 1990 after he retired from the FBI, Billy Bulger lobbied with Boston Mayor Ray Flynn to have Connolly appointed Commissioner of the Boston Police Department.

In 2005, Connolly was indicted on murder and conspiracy to commit murder charges in the 1982 slaying of Arthur Andersen certified public accountant John B. Callahan and the 1981 murder of Roger Wheeler, owner of the World Jai Alai sporting corporation. Connolly stood trial in 2008 in Miami.

Callahan

Callahan was murdered by John Martorano who shot Callahan and left his body in the trunk of his Cadillac in a parking lot at Miami International Airport. Prosecutors alleged that Callahan was killed on the orders of Whitey Bulger and Stephen Flemmi after Connolly told them that the FBI was investigating his ties to the Winter Hill Gang in their ongoing investigation into Wheeler's death. Wheeler had been killed by Martorano in Tulsa, Oklahoma in May 1981. During the trial, Bulger associates Stephen Flemmi, Kevin Weeks and John Martorano testified for the prosecution detailing Connolly's ties to Bulger and Flemmi. Long time Bulger girlfriend Teresa Stanley testified for the defense about her travels with Bulger. Flemmi testified that Connolly warned them that the FBI wanted to question Callahan in the death of Wheeler, telling them that Callahan "wouldn't hold up" and would probably implicate them.

Callahan

Also testifying against Connolly was his former FBI boss, John Morris, who admitted that he accepted $7,000 in bribes from Bulger and Flemmi. He stated he began leaking information to them after Connolly delivered a case of wine and an envelope stuffed with $1000 cash from the pair. On November 6, 2008, a jury convicted Connolly of second-degree murder.

Cuccharia Frank AKA The Cheeseman. Died January 23, 1976. Cuccharia was appointed to run the Boston mob by Raymond Patriarca after the departure of boss Phillip Bruccola and his Consigliere Joe Lombardo. A cheese importer by trade, it was thought by the FBI that the business clocked his money made through gambling. Cucchiaria had European contacts through Lucky Luciano and Vito Genovese. In 1976, Cuccharia shot gunned his wife to death in a fit of anger and then killed himself.

Curcio, Raymond AKA baby, a 31-year-old drug addict shot six times in the back of the head and neck in 1965. Curcio had burglarizing the home of Patriarca's brother Joseph.

Cufari Salvatore AKA Big Nose Sam. Cufari was a capo in the Springfield LCN crews and managed to live to age 82 and die of natural causes.

O'Toole

Connors Eddie, Born 1933 Connors owned barrooms in South Boston and Dorchester, Mass. One of the places he owned was the Bulldog, was a bookie hang where Spike O'Toole, the last survivors of the McLaughlin gang, was usually found. Connors set O'Toole up for a hit in December of 1973. Howie Winter learned that that Connors was bragging about his role in the O'Toole hit.
 In 1975, Connors stopped to use a pay phone at gas station and was gunned down by Whitey Bulger and Stevie Flemmi.

D

Davis Debra: Davis was 17 and working in a suburban Boston jewelry store when Steve Flemmi, who was then in his late thirties. He set Debra up in a luxurious apartment and gave her cars, clothes and very expensive gifts. Only Debra's father disapproved of his daughter's choice, because of the age difference. Davis stayed with Flemmi for nine years. In 1980, he finally divorced his wife and asked her to marry him but she had also met a Mexican businessman, and fallen in love. In 2009, Flemmi testified in open court about killing 26-year-old Debra Davis and said that the murder was "a very traumatic moment in my life" as he watched her being strangled by Whitey Bulger. Flemmi said he brought Davis to a vacant South Boston home he had purchased for his parents. Then Bulger, who was hiding in a bedroom, snuck up behind Davis and grabbed her by the throat. "There was a struggle going on there," Flemmi said matter-of-factly.
"What did you do?" asked the Judge
"I didn't do anything," Flemmi said.
"You watched it?"
"Yes," said Flemmi.

Debbie Davis

Flemmi said Bulger brought Davis down to the basement with his hands still wrapped around her throat. He said he didn't know if Davis was still alive at that point, but he recalled telling Bulger, "Let her pray." And later they extracted Davis's teeth to make it more difficult to identify her remains, wrapped her body in plastic, and dumped it in the trunk of a car. They buried her body in an unmarked grave alongside the Neponset River in Quincy

Deegan

Deegan Teddy. Deegan, an ex-boxer from Malden Mass. was marked for death by the mob for several burglaries that he committed with Stevie Flemmi. The mob dropped what Deegan thought was a hint about a big score bank burglary in Chelsea. But when Deegan arrived at the designated spot, an alleyway near the bank, on March 11, 1965, he was met by the Flemmi brothers, Joe Barboza, Wilfred Roy French and Romeo Martin, who killed him. In 1967, Barboza named four innocent men in the killing, which the FBI knew about but did nothing to stop. Two of the men died in prison.

Delaney Wilfred. A South Boston, a rapist and armed robber associated with the McLaughlins. In August of 1964 he was strangled to death and tossed into Boston Harbor by members of the Winter Hill Gang.

Deleo Crew: Allegedly under the direction of Ralph Deleo of Somerville, Mass. who was reputed to be, 2010, a ranking member of Colombo crime family. The crew accused of loansharking and extortion and violation of the RICO act.

DeLuca, Vito: A longtime member of the Rhode Island mob, DeLuca has a record for extortion and mail fraud.

DePalma, Angelo: One of the largest shylocks in the State of Rhode Island Patriarca crime family was murdered in 1966 in his own back yard at 516 West Exchange Street, Providence on Raymond Patriarca orders.

Depergola Frank: Depergola was Springfield Mass. and a friend of Mob boss Al Bruno. Depergola was playing cards with Bruno on November 23 2003 when two men ran into the private club where the regular Saturday night card game was held and fired six shots into Bruno hitting him in the head, torso and groin. Depergola, who has never been officially recognized as a member of organized crime, was later convicted of loan sharking and sent to federal prison.

DePrisco Thomas. DePrisco was a member of Joe Barboza's crew and in November 1966 he and Tash Bratsos were raising money for Barboza's bail on a gun charge. Their last stop that night was the Nite Lite, a Mafia hangout on Commercial Street. DePrisco and Bratsos were killed there and the bail money, about $11,000, was stolen. Their bodies were left in a car in South Boston.

Georgie McLaughlin

Dermody Ronald: Dermody was a second generation Irish-American gangster from Cambridge, Mass. he was part of Whitey Bulger's bank robbing team. In the early 1960s, Dermody fell in love with James "Spike" O'Toole's girlfriend and cut a deal with George McLaughlin, of Charlestown mobster and an enemy of Winter Hill Gang leader Buddy McLean, to kill O'Toole, and in turn Dermody would kill

Buddy McLean. Dermody did take a pop shot at the boss but missed and then went into hiding. Unfortunately he made the mistake of calling corrupt FBI agent H. Paul Rico, for help. Rico scheduled a meeting with Dermody at the Watertown-Belmont line. When Dermody arrived he was met by Buddy McLean who murdered him.

DeScicio Vincent Crime partner of Joseph A. "J.R." Russo, future Mafia capo and murderer of Joe Barboza, now deceased. DeScicio came down with cancer, committed suicide.

DiNunzio Salvatore Carmen. Alleged Underboss in the New England Mafia in the beginning of the 21st century.

DiSiglio, Rocco AKA Rocky DiSiglio (born April 11, 1939 Newton, Massachusetts - April 3, 1966 East Boston, Massachusetts) was an American professional welterweight boxer and associate of the Patriarca crime family who was involved in armed robbery and illegal gambling.
 Little is known about his personal life except that he was born in Newton. DiSiglio fought his first professional fight on June 10, 1960. His last professional

boxing match was against Jesse Ammons on February 17, 1964 which he lost. His overall professional boxing record was three wins, four losses and one withdrawn match in a total of twenty-seven matches fought.

It was rumored that DiSiglio supplemented his petty boxer's income by being a prizefighter for members of the Patriarca crime family who had interests in illegal betting and professional sports. In 1964 he gave up his dreams of being a professional boxer entirely and became active in the Patriarca crime family. He was married to an Italian-American housewife and drove a burgundy 1962 Ford Thunderbird on a desolate street at night in his home city of Newton. He left behind a wife and no children.

In 1966 Stephen Flemmi, acting as an informant told FBI agent H. Paul Rico that DiSiglio was robbing illegal card and dice games. There had been two dice games and three high-stakes card games that were held up by DiSiglio within three weeks. The most recent brazen robbery was on April 9, 1966 when five men burst in on a dice game that was happening at an address on the corner of Morton and Blue Hill Avenue in Mattapan, Boston with Bernard Zinna and Richard DiVincent, armed with sawed-off shotguns. They were robbing lucrative card games that he controlled in his territory of Newton and Lowell, Massachusetts overseen by Gennaro Anguilo, gambling czar for the Patriarca crime family which at the time was headed by Raymond Patriarca. They robbed the players of an estimated $4,500. None of the individuals bothered to wear ski masks during and all appeared to be of Italian ethnic extraction. DiSiglio was the "inside man" who saw to it that the door was unlocked for Zinna and DeVincent to come in unannounced and surprise the card players. One of them made a comment to the card players, "Larry told you not to run." Flemmi advised the Federal Bureau of Investigation (FBI) that this was a reference to Ilario Zannino who oversaw a lucrative illegal barboot game that ran on Sundays in the neighborhood. One of the card players at this game had been relieved of $10,000 and he had just borrowed the money from a Jewish loan shark named "Richfield" in the North End, Boston so he could act as a loan shark at the high stakes card game for unfortunate players.

Patriarca crime family underboss and acting boss Gennaro Anguilo of the Angiulo Brothers quickly became infuriated with DiSiglio's maverick actions and robbing the patrons of his gambling operations.

In 1968, Patriarca crime family capo Gennaro Anguilo and two others were arrested and charged with first degree homicide but later acquitted. In August

1967, after H. Paul Rico testified before a Suffolk county grand jury about his conversations with Joseph Barboza concerning the murder of DiSiglio, the Boston SAC sent an urgent teletype to J. Edgar Hoover at 1:03 a.m. The Special Agent in charge noted that Suffolk County District Attorney Garret Bryne was commented that this "tremendous penetration into the La Cosa Nostra and the hoodlum element was effected through the outstanding investigative efforts of the FBI and his office." Joseph Barboza stated that Gennaro Anguilo summoned Bernard Zinna and Richard DeVincent and gave them a choice, to either carry out the murder of their former gang mastermind or be murdered themselves.

The following week, Zinna and DeVincent set up DiSiglio at a bar in East Boston, luring DiSiglio to ride with them. They drove over to a dark street and Mario exited the Thunderbird under the guise of picking up a stolen car for a robbery they had planned. As he sat in the driver's seat of his Ford Thunderbird Landau on a desolate street he was shot three times at close range in the head by DeVincent. They drove the car out to Danvers, Massachusetts and left it in the woods. Shortly after his murder Joseph Barboza became a stool pigeon and he identified DiSiglio's triggermen as police officers in the Boston Police Department, including the murderers of Edward Deegan.

One bullet tore off part of DiSiglio's face; another went through his head and out an eye socket. The murderers drove to Topsfield, Massachusetts and dumped the body in the Ipswich River Wildlife Sanctuary. Barboza told the jury that he knew this because the accused triggermen Zinna and Richard "Vinnie the Pig" DeVincent told him so after the slaying. DeVincent bragged about it. Barboza even went to see Gennaro Anguilo at his office: "I told him that Benny Zinna and Vinnie DeVincent told me that he gave the order to whack out Rocky DiSiglio or he would whack them out. The reason I wanted to know this was that DiSiglio was a friend of mine and to find out if he had done anything wrong on his part to be killed. I told Anguilo they were running at the mouth. That they came down and told me everything. Anguilo said that he would talk to Zinna and that he didn't trust 'the Pig.'" Joseph Barboza later revealed the location of where they had dumped DiSiglio's corpse to the police. They found him in the backseat of his Thunderbird in the woods abandoned outside of Danvers, Massachusetts. Soon after the charges against Bernard Zinna for his involvement in the murder of DiSiglio were dropped, he was executed gangland style by being shot twice in the back of his head as he sat in his own car by unknown gunmen. Homicide investigators were never able to charge anyone with the homicide, except

Gennaro Anguilo most likely ordered his death for his mother who he allowed to give an interview to television reporter John Henning during the trial. DeVincent was murdered by unknown members of the Patriarca crime family in Medford, Massachusetts on April 3, 1996.

DiStasio Raymond Bartender at the Mickey Mouse Lounge in Revere, alleged member of the McLaughlin gang. Joe Barboza caught him in the bar in November 1965, a couple of weeks after the murder of Buddy McLean. After killing DiStasio he shot down John O'Neil, the father of four young children happened to be in the bar, buying cigarettes.

Doe Arthur: AKA Butchy Born 1960. An alleged Charlestown Mass. Hoodlum. His father Arthur Sr. was killed in the Boston Irish wars

Dog House' 98 Prince Street, the Boston mob's headquarters also known as The Doghouse.

Donati, Robert. Born October 4, 1940. September 24 1991. Of Revere Mass. Donati was strictly a small timer who occasionally worked as a money collector for Vinny "the Animal" Ferrara while Ferrara was serving time. In September of 1991, Donati disappeared. He was found a week later, a block from his home, dead stuffed into a car trunk. Why he was murdered remains unknown.

E

Eaton Carlton Born 1937. Eaton was from Revere Mass. He was murdered with two shots in the head in September 1964 by Joe Barboza who was acting on orders from Providence since the bosses were certain that Eaton was robbing their poker games.

Elliott Buick on Elmwood Avenue, Providence: On October 8, 1964 Joseph "Jo Zita" Schiavone, drives his car to the station to have the engine checked. A mechanic opens the hood and finds the engine wired with a stick of dynamite.

Enrico Henry AKA The Referee AKA Tameleo: Died August 1985. Underboss for Raymond Patriarca in Providence, RI. Enrico had ties to the New York families. During the late 1960s he was hit with a string of murder indictments. In 1968 he was convicted for the murder of Teddy Deegan, a Boston hood. He was sentenced to death in the murder, but in 1972 the sentence was commuted to life. Died in prison.

F

Fabiano Patsy of East Boston, Barboza crew member.

Feragnani William. A businessman from suburban Boston . He was kidnapped in October 1964 and killed on May 20, 1965 after he cooperated with the police Vinnie Teresa later wrote "I found out later that two car thieves, one named Chuck and another called Mike, were hired to hit Fergnani. They got close to Fergnani because one of them, Chuck, dressed up like a woman."

Ferrara

Ferrara Vincent J. AKA Vinny the Animal. Born 1949. A mobster from Boston, Massachusetts and former Capo of the New England based Patriarca crime family of La Cosa Nostra. On March 22, 1990, Ferrara was indicted on racketeering and related charges with six other alleged members and an associate of the Patriarca Family. Three years later, under a plea agreement with the government just as his case was about to go to trial, he pleaded guilty to racketeering, extortion, gambling, and ordering the 1985 slaying of Boston mobster Vincent "Jimmy" Limoli. The murder was apparently the result of a narcotics transaction gone bad. Ferrara received a 22 year sentence. He served 16 years and was released on April 12, 2005 when U.S. District Judge Mark L. Wolf decided to cut several years off his sentence after finding that a prosecutor, Assistant United States Attorney Jeffrey Auerhahn, had withheld evidence during plea negotiations that a key witness had tried to recant his claim that Ferrara had directed his codefendant Pasquale Barone to murder Vincent Limoli. Wolf concluded that Ferrara was denied due process and was probably innocent of Limoli's slaying but pleaded guilty rather than risk a wrongful conviction.

Robert Fairbrothers, Rhode Island Mob

Flynn

Flynn, Charles AKA Chucky. Born May 16, 1940. Flynn, of Somerville Mass. was reported to be one of the toughest criminals in all of New England. He was sentenced to life for his role in a $3 million dollar heist on the Bonded Vault Company in Providence in 1975.

Flynn James P. Born February 5, 1934. From Boston, Massachusetts. Flynn was reputed to be a member of the Winter Hill Gang and was framed for the murder of Brian Halloran in 1983 by Whitey Bulger. In 1986 he was tried and acquitted for that murder. He was used as an F.B.I. informant by agent John Connolly in the 1980s.

Brian Halloran

Femia Nick, a former member of Joe Barboza's crew. Femia was born in Somerville, Massachusetts to first generation Italian immigrants from Cittanova in the region of Calabria, Italy. He was a hulking, overweight man with a cocaine addict who wore flashy flamboyant clothing and had a troubled relationship with James J. Bulger when he became of an associate of the Winter Hill Gang in 1976. Nicholas lived with a girlfriend of Stephen Flemmi's mistress, Marilyn DeSilva in an apartment across the street from Chandler's Restaurant located at 25 Deerfield Road in South Deerfield, Massachusetts. He first began a career criminal under the tutelage of Joseph Barboza. Nicholas was introduced into the gang to assist with extra muscle for their extortion and protection rackets..

As Whitey Bulger aged, he became more obsessed with physical fitness. Bulger would often wear tight jeans and t-shirts, and grow increasingly disgusted with Nicholas's protruding gut. He lived off a diet of fat food and was a habituate of McDonald's, of which one was close to the gang's headquarters on Causeway Street. On one occasion, when Nicholas returned from the McDonald's with a bag of Big Mac hamburgers and French fries and began spreading out his fast food feast on the hood of Bulger's black Chevrolet, Bulger erupted in a fit of anger, screaming at Nicholas and pelting him with French fries.

On June 28, 1978 Nicholas became one of the prime suspects of the 1978 Blackfriars Pub Massacre, when gunmen had burst into Blackfriars, a downtown

Boston bar located at 105 Summer Street and murdered the pub manager John A. Kelly, a former local television reporter for Channel 7, Vincent E. Solmonte of Quincy, Massachusetts, Peter F. Meroth of Jamaica Plain, Massachusetts, Charles G. Margarian of North Andover, Massachusetts and Frederick R. Delavega of Somerville, Massachusetts. The armed robbery was allegedly over several kilos of cocaine. Vincent E. Solomonte was a close friend of Stephen Flemmi. Two of the suspected gunmen who allegedly partook in the gangland style shootings, Robert Italiano and William N. Ierardi were later tried for the murders and acquitted in 1979.

When Femia began hanging around Lancaster Foreign Motors garage, Bulger wanted it established that Nicholas had nothing whatsoever to do with the Blackfriars massacre, although his involvement in considered highly suspect by law enforcement circles. Bulger did this to reduce any pending surveillance and subpoenas or investigations by ambitious policemen who would try to prosecute Bulger just because of his association with a suspected killer with a higher profile like Nicholas.

Soon after Nicholas joined the Winter Hill Gang, a brief notice appeared in one of FBI Special Agent John Connolly's reports clearing Nicholas of any involvement in the Blackfriar's Massacre. Later, after Bulger and Nicholas parted ways, Connolly put another report in Bulger's file, suggesting that Nicholas had in fact been one of the triggermen in the Blackfriars killings. His involvement in the Blackfriars' Massacre was never successfully proven and remains unsolved. Nicholas would be recognized as one of the few associates in the Winter Hill Gang that were able to part from the group and not be murdered in retribution for something foul for their actions, like Richard Castucci and Louis Litif. Femia would later be shot to death by police during a botched bank robbery in East Boston in 1983.

French Wilfred Roy Born March 13, 1929. From Swampscott MA. French set up Teddy Deegan for murder by hitmen Joe Barboza and Jimmy the Bear Flemmi. Spent 35 years in prison and was released in 2002.

Castucci with Sammy Davis Jr.

Fusaro, Joseph AKA Davey Crocket. A member of the Genovese Crime Family. In the 1990s, Fusaro swore out a statement that he collected tribute, paid to John Gotti Jr., by a Connecticut gambling ring

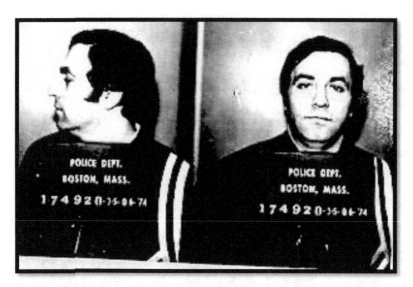

Stephen J. "The Rifleman" Flemmi, Whitey Bulger's right hand man (Boston PD photo)

Vincent "Jimmie Da Bear" Flemmi

Fox Louis: Fox ran the rackets in Revere, Mass. for a while in the 1940s and retired rich. Died in 1963 of natural causes.

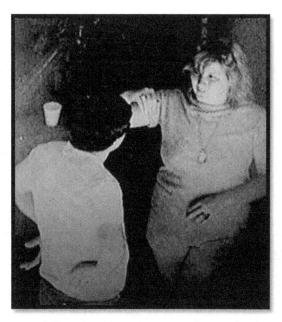

Flemmi, left and Nick Giso's girlfriend

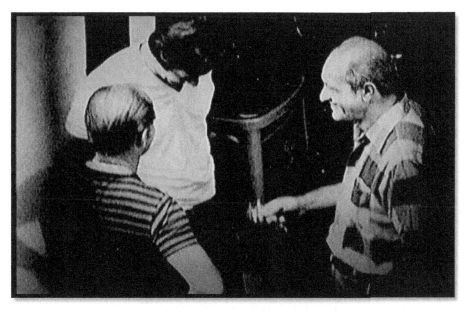

Whitey Bulger, Stephen Flemmi and Nick Giso

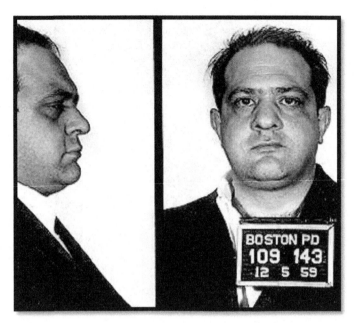

Nick Giso as a young man

Johnny Martorano

Frizzi Guy D. Born July 7, 1927. Associate of Mafia hitman Joe Barboza and Chico Amico and part of the Revere, Mass. fraction.

G

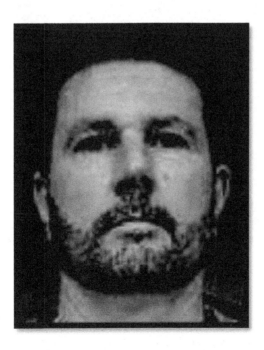

Galante James Born. 1936 and reputed to be a member of the Genovese Crime Family. He is a a convicted felon owner of the Danbury Trashers minor league hockey franchise and CEO of Automated Waste Disposal, a company which holds waste disposal contracts for most of Western Connecticut and Westchester and Putnam Counties in New York. Galante was sentenced in 1999 to 12 months and a day in federal prison after pleading guilty to tax evasion. Galante was charged along with 29 others for paying a 'mob tax' to Matthew "Matty the Horse," Ianniello, the alleged boss of the Genovese crime family. Galante's business, which handles 80% of garbage hauling in Western Connecticut was accused of muscling out local competition through no-bid contracts and payments of up to $120,000 per year to Genovese crime family boss Matthew "Matty the Horse," Ianniello. In September of 2006, Ianniello pled guilty to racketeering, and interfering with a federal grand jury probe and was sentenced to between one and a half to two years in prison.

Arthur Gianelli, left

Gianelli, Mary Ann: Wife of reputed Patriarca associate Arthur Gianelli and sister-in-law of former FBI agent John J. Connolly Jr., She pleaded guilty to 19 counts of racketeering, money laundering, filing false tax returns, and illegal structuring of cash transactions in connection with an illegal gambling ring.

Under a plea agreement the government dropped an additional 141 money laundering counts against her.

Gianelli

Gianelli Arthur: Gianelli, who is said to have a vicious temper, is an alleged Mafia associate who has been accused by the federal government of dabbling in gambling, money laundering, loan sharking, arson, and extortion. In 2009 he was convicted of arson, racketeering, extortion, gambling, and money laundering and sentenced to 22 years in prison. Gianelli is also the brother-in-law of convicted FBI agent John J. Connolly Jr. He and Connolly purchased property in Lynnfield, Mass. that was sold to them by alleged mobster Rocco Botta.

Gilbert, Peter: In 1983 Peter Gilbert, a career criminal escaped from a Florida prison and phoned Gelardo Mastracchio an alleged member of Rhode Island organized crime. Mastracchio told Gilbert to return to Rhode Island and join up with him. And he did. A year later, Gilbert was arrested by the Providence Police on drug and gun charges. Believing that Mastracchio had set him up, Gilbert agreed to become an informant. He was a better than average informant whose information solved many unsolved murders in the Providence area. He even fingered Mastracchio's son in a murder of a man named Richie Valente, who was kidnapped, beaten and tossed off of the Jamestown Bridge. In 1988, Gilbert died of a heart attack after a case road rage.

Gomes, Richard AKA Red Bird" a violent, powerful Rhode Island mobster. In 1972 he tabbed Robert Cullen, 46, of Providence, to death in the basement of a Johnston RI bar. Gomes pled guilty to second-degree murder and was sentenced to 25 years in prison. John Gotti Jr. once asked his lawyer to send $500 to a Rhode Island mobster long rumored to be behind the murder of a Howard Beach neighbor who accidentally ran down Gotti's younger brother in 1980. "He was very dear to my father," Gotti told his lawyer on March 11, 2004, while Gotti was on trial for racketeering. "I want to send $500 to him. I know he's in jail. I know that he's broke, people that come through here told me this. This is a great guy. This is a real man." Gomes admitted that he participated in the revenge killing of John Favara, a Queens New York man who killed John Gotti's 12-year-old son in a tragic car accident. Gomes personally notified Gotti that the murder had been done. In his final years outside of prison, Gomes began using cocaine and drinking heavily. Gomes, whose first arrest was at age 12 for breaking into a freight train in Providence, spent 50 years in reform school and prisons for crimes ranging from desertion to murder. Gomes died alone in his apartment in North Providence at age 73 of natural causes in 2006.

Guglielmetti, Matt, Jr.: Matthew L. Guglielmetti, Jr., also known as "Matty" (born 1949), an alleged high-ranking mobster from Cranston, Rhode Island who is alleged to be a Caporegime in the New England-based Patriarca crime family. Guglielmetti is said to be closely aligned with former family boss Luigi Mannochio.

In 1984, Guglielmetti and his father, Matthew L. Guglielmetti Sr. were arrested for hijacking a truckload of Canadian whisky. However, the case was later dropped. In 1989, while the Patriarca family was in the midst of an internal factional war, Guglielmetti came to the attention of law enforcement authorities when it was discovered that he had attempted to act as a peace broker. In return for his efforts, he inherited the rackets previously overseen by the murdered underboss William Grasso. On October 20, 1989, Guglielmetti was recorded by the FBI while the Patriarca family conducted a Mafia induction ceremony in Medford, Massachusetts. Guglielmetti served nearly five years at the federal prison in Sandstone, Minnesota during the 1990s after pleading guilty to federal racketeering charges in Hartford, Connecticut.

In April 2002, the FBI launched a probe into the Rhode Island construction industry. As part of the investigation, they created a fake company called Hemphill Construction in Johnston, Rhode Island. At the time, Guglielmetti served as steward for Laborers' International Union of North America (LIUNA) Local 271. After Hemphill opened, an undercover FBI agent met with

Guglielmetti and offered him the chance to buy into the company. According to an FBI affidavit, Guglielmetti became a silent partner in Hemphill and started taking company funds, "including a share of the profits from laundering what Guglielmetti believed were drug proceeds through the undercover business."

In 2003, Guglielmetti served as union steward for Capital City Concrete, which was chosen as a minority contractor for a $5.8 million parking ramp at the Kent County Court House in Warwick, Rhode Island. The company was also selected for $7 million in contract work on a sewage overflow tunnel at Narragansett Bay in Rhode Island. As work on the Warwick ramp progressed, state court officials pressed local contractors for payroll records in order to conduct criminal background checks on their employees. Capital City was among the last contractors to comply with this request. About a week before Guglielmetti stopped working on the ramp, Capital City finally turned over the records. Nothing emerged in the state files - apparently, Guglielmetti had unspecified charges expunged.

In October 2003, Rhode Island and Massachusetts police visited the Warwick construction site to tell Guglielmetti that he and Manocchio had been recorded on undercover wiretaps discussing the collection of gambling debts and the mediation of a mob dispute. On January 20, 2005, FBI agents and Rhode Island State Police detectives raided the headquarters of Local 271 and Capital City Concrete in Cranston. Earlier that day, Guglielmetti and a pair of associates were arrested in Johnston.

On March 31, 2005, Matthew Guglielmetti signed a plea agreement admitting that he conspired to distribute more than five kilograms of cocaine. Later in 2005, Guglielmetti was sentenced to 11 years in prison.

Nick Giso, right, a lieutenant in the Angiulo crime family, with his girlfriend, Eva McDonough.

Gustin Gang: A Boston-Irish gang during the prohibition. It was founded in 1910 as the "Tailboard Thieves" in South Boston, then a large Irish ghetto, by the Wallace Brothers (Steve, a one-time prize fighter, Frank and Jimmy) The gang started as a receiving agent for bootleg shipments for other bootleggers and soon decided it was more profitable to simply hijack the product, disguised as Prohibition agents, and sell it themselves. In 1931, a shipment the gang had intended to rob was ambushed and the bulk of the gang was wiped out. The stayed in power until the 1960s and then disbanded.

H

Hanrahan

Hanrahan Kevin T. Born June 25, 1953 Died September 18 1992. A freelance hood based in Providence, Rhode Island, Harahan was an occasional enforcer for the Patriarca Crime Family. Police suspected Hanrahan in the murder of Raymond "Slick" Vecchio as well as many other murders in the 1980s and 1990s. Hanrahan did a series of prison sentences for jury tampering, intimidating witnesses, drug trafficking and counterfeiting. In 1975 he was shot in the chest in a nightclub but refused to finger the gunman to police. In 1990, Hanrahan and Cadillac Frank Salemme and several others tried to kidnap Patriarca bookmaker Blaise Marfeo in Providence but the plan backfired and Hanrahan barely escaped arrest. He was arrested the following day in relation to the foiled plot. He was sentenced to two years in the Walpole state prison. Upon release he took to robbing drug dealers in ambush situations. On September 18, 1992, Hanrahan was shot and killed by persons unknown while walking through the federal Hill District of Providence.

Connie Hughes

Hughes Cornelius AKA Connie Died. May 26, 1966. A mobster from Charlestown, Massachusetts and one of the most feared assassins of the 1960s. he worked for the McLaughlin Brothers gang with his brother Stevie. It was Hughes that killed Somerville, Mass. gang leader James "Buddy" McLean during the Boston Irish Gang Wars which left over forty men dead from both Somerville and Charlestown. Hughes was later shot to death in his car by Winter Hill Gang member Cadillac Frank Salemme and Joseph "The Animal" Barboza, while driving in Revere, Mass.

Former prizefighter Rico Sacramone of Everett Mass. Was acting as a body guard Winter Hill Gang boss Buddy McLean. He was with McLean in 1965 when Steve Hughes caught Buddy McLean as he was leaving the Peppermint Lounge. Hughes fired with an automatic carbine from the other side of the street. Rico was murdered by parties unknown in 1976.

Hughes Stevie was a Charlestown Mob assassin along with his brother Cornelius Hughes. He is reputed to have worked for Sammy Lindenbaum. Both Lindenbaum and Hughes were shot dead on September 23, 1966 while driving through Middleton, Mass.

I

The Irish Mob Wars The Boston Irish mob wars was a conflict in the 1960s between the two dominant New England Irish-American organized crime gangs in Massachusetts: the Charlestown Mob in Boston, led by brothers Bernard, George and Edward "Punchy" McLaughlin, and the Winter Hill Gang of Somerville (just north of Boston) headed by James "Buddy" McLean. It was widely believed to be started when Charlestown's George McLaughlin tried to pick up the girlfriend of Winter Hill associate Alex "Bobo" Petricone, also known as actor Alex Rocco. McLaughlin was then beaten and hospitalized by two other Winter Hill members. After this Bernie McLaughlin went to Buddy McLean for an explanation. When McLean refused to give up his associates Bernie swore revenge but was soon killed by Mclean in Charlestown City Square. The war resulted in the eradication of the Charlestown Mob with all its leaders having been either killed or put in prison. The remnants of the Charlestown Mob were then absorbed into the Winter Hill Gang, who were then able to become the dominant Mob in the New England area.

J

Journal-Bulletin. A Rhode Island newspaper sued for libel by Raymond Patriarca in 1961. Patriarca also paid for a large advertisement in the paper criticizing them for what he saw as its campaign against him.

K

Kazonis, William: AKA Skinny. The Anguilo brothers kept Kazonis on the payroll as their driver. Kazonis was caught on an FBI bug shaking down a loan shark victim who was delaying payments. His partner in the shakedown was

Joseph "Joe Porter" Patrizzi. Both Kazonis and Patrizzi served 8 years for the shakedown and didn't talk, which garnered them great respect from the hierarchy In 1987, Kazonis served another 6 years for conspiring to derail a grand jury investigation.

Killeen Donald. Born 1924 Died May 13, 1972. A Boston mobster who controlled criminal activity in South Boston during the 1960s and 70s. Killeen's organization included Whitey Bulger and Billy O'Sullivan. He was involved in a turf war with South Boston's Mullen gang before he was murdered outside his home in suburban Framingham, Massachusetts on May 13, 1972. Whitey Bulger has been accused of the murder. However, former Mullen gang member Patrick Nee said that the murder was actually committed by Mullen enforcer Paul McGonagle, who was angered over the murder of his brother Donald.

The weapon used to kill Killeen

Killeen Gang After his release from prison, Bulger worked as a janitor prior to becoming an enforcer for Donald Killeen, the boss of the dominant crime family in South Boston. In 1971, the Killeen gang became involved in a turf war with the

Mullen gang, headed by Paulie McGonagle and Patrick Nee. The Killeens soon found themselves outgunned and outmanned by the younger Mullens.

The end of the war has usually been related as follows. Bulger, realizing that he was on the losing side, secretly approached Howie Winter, the leader of the Winter Hill Gang. He allegedly told Winter that he could end the fighting in South Boston by murdering the leaders of the Killeen gang. Shortly thereafter, Donald Killeen was gunned down outside his home in suburban Framingham, Massachusetts.

L

LaMorte Michael. AKA Big Mike Morello, reputed Boston Mafia hoodlum of 1940's and 50's worked as a bookie and gambler. He was acquitted in 1949 of the

Hotel Bostonian murder of a Charlestown Mass. thug who had held up one of his dice games.

La-Z-Boy lounge chairs. In October 1981, Bobo Marrapese was arrested for receiving and possessing a truckload of La-Z-Boy lounge chairs. A trailer carrying 109 loungers worth $21,000 was stolen from a truck terminal in Alexandria, Va. The chairs were en route from Tennessee to three stores in Connecticut. The thieves brought the hot chairs to Providence, where they sold them for $5,000 to Marrapese. The government seized two of the recliners from the homes of the mobsters.

Lazzarini, Barry: Killed in Manmet Mass. in 1991

Frankie Lepere, alleged narcotics dealer

Lombardo

Lombardo, Joey: Died 1969. AKA "Joe the Gentleman" One of the Mafia members who shot their way to dominance in New England. He served as Consigliere to Boss Philip Buccola. He lived long enough to retire from the rackets and died from natural causes. The five-foot-six with thick glasses Lombardo, despite his efforts to appear to the public as a soft spoken and reasonable man, was feared in the underworld.

LoStocco Joe. LoStocco is an alleged member of the Genovese Crime Family. LoStocco owns and operates LoStocco Services, a carting company located in Danbury Ct. He was one of nearly 30 people arrested in a federal crackdown on organized crime's influence in the trash hauling industry. He pled guilty for his role in a federal racketeering case with alleged ties to organized crime. Federal prosecutors said LoStocco admitted that he knew others were involved in a so-called 'property rights' scheme, in which trash haulers carve out routes for each other and agree not to poach customers. Authorities said LoStocco failed to report the activity to law enforcement, which is a crime

M

Marfeo, Willie: A Rhode Island hood shot gunned to death in the telephone booth of a Federal Hill restaurant the Korner Kitchen in 1966 probably on orders of Raymond Patriarca. Marfeo and Joe "Jo Zita" Schiavone were running a dice game without Patriarca's permission.

Mannocchio Louis "Baby Shanks" AKA Luigi Giovanni, a long time member of the Providence Mafia. In 1999 he was convicted of receiving stolen goods. (A refrigerator which he claimed was for his mother) The name Baby Shanks comes from a restaurant he ran in Rhode Island. He served as Boss of the local mob in the late 1980s. His criminal record dates back to at least the 1940s

Manocchio, Nick: Of Providence, a former director of the Laborer's New England Region Organizing Fund, was sentenced to three years' probation in 2000 and banned Manocchio from seeking or holding any positions in labor organizations and fined $2,500 in fines and sentenced to perform 200 hours of community service for each year of probation. Manocchio pled guilty to accepting gifts from an undercover FBI agent posing as a contractor looking for business in Rhode Island.

Marfeo, Willie: A Providence, RI, Bookmaker who killed in 1966 for holding back from the Patriarca family. In 1968, based on testimony given by John "Red" Kelly, a Boston associate, Raymond Patriarca, Rudolph Sciarra, Maurice "Pro" Lerner, Robert Fairbrothers, Louis Manocchio, John Rossi and Frank Vendituoli were indicted by a Grand Jury on a variety of charges related to the Mafeo murder. Sciarra, Manocchio and Vendituoli fled the state.

Vendituoli   Sciarra   Fairbrothers   Rossi   Mannocchio

McElroy, Ronald: McElroy, of East Providence, was beaten to death with a baseball bat shortly after midnight on August 23, 1982, in what was probably a case of road rage involving Bobo Marrapese. McElroy, only 20, was driving a Volkswagen and inadvertently cut in front of Marrapese's Ford Mustang. Marrapese was drag racing down Broadway against a mobster named William "Billy" Ferle in his red pickup truck. The two mobsters chased McElroy, and catching him, beat him with baseball bats in the parking lot of a gas station. The prosecution contended that Marrapese leveled the swing that killed McElroy. The defense argued that it was Ferle, not Marrapese.
While facing the murder charges, Marrapese was accused of threatening to kill a government informant, telling the informant's brother that if he got his hands on the turncoat, he would "chop him up and cook him and eat him and whatever … " Marrapese beat the charge.

McLaughlin Bernard "Bernie" Bernard "Bernie" McLaughlin was an Irish-American gangster from Charlestown, Massachusetts and leader of "The McLaughlin Brothers" gang. Before Bernie formed his own gang he was a loan shark and enforcer for the Angiulo Brothers of Boston's North End. After the Irish gangs decided to break away from the Italians and Whitey Bulger became an informant for the FBI, giving information that would ruin his Italian mob enemies, Bernie and his brothers (Edward "Punchy" McLaughlin and George McLaughlin) started the McLaughlin Brothers. Soon after, while drunk at a Labor Day party on Salisbury Beach, Georgie was badly beaten by two members of The Winter Hill Gang for groping the girlfriend of mobster Alex Rocco (then known as Alex 'Bobo' Petricone).

When Bernie found out about this he demanded that his then friend Winter Hill leader James "Buddy" McLean turn over his two men (Bernie and his brothers had been known to perform hits for gangs all over New England, including The Winter Hill Gang). McLean said Georgie had it coming and refused to turn them over, so the next night Bernie wired a bomb under Buddy's family car. When Buddy found out about this he immediately went looking for Bernie. Buddy, Alex Rocco, and driver Russell Nicholson found Bernie in Charlestown's town square and shot him dead. Despite the large crowd, not one witness agreed to testify and the three went free. Soon after, Russ Nicholson was taken from the street and murdered by Bernie's brothers Punchy and Georgie.

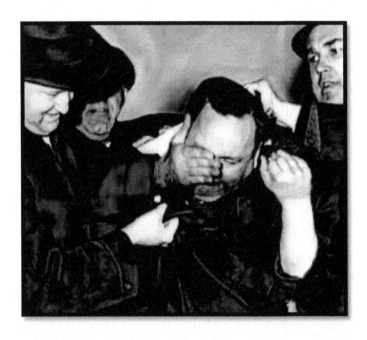

The FBI and Boston Police struggle with George McLaughlin after his capture in a third floor apartment in Dorchester. McLaughlin had been on the FBI's 10 most wanted list for 11 months.

Edward "Punchy" McLaughlin (died October 20, 1965) was a former boxer and a member of the "The McLaughlin Brothers" gang of Charlestown, Massachusetts. After his brother Bernard McLaughlin was murdered in October 1961 by their former friend, "Winter Hill Gang" leader James "Buddy" McLean (Punchy and his brothers had been known to perform hits for gangs all over New England, including the Winter Hill Gang), Punchy and brother George McLaughlin murdered Russell Nicholson who was rumored to be McLean's driver in the shooting. After surviving many assassination attempts, one where he lost a hand and another where he lost half his jaw, Punchy was on his way to the Court House for his brother Georgie's murder trial, and was shot dead at a bus station in West Roxbury, Massachusetts.

McLean James AKA Buddy. Born 1929-October 31, 1965. McLean was an Irish-American mobster and the original leader of the Somerville, Massachusetts-based "Winter Hill Gang" during the 1960s. Buddy was well known throughout Boston as a tough street fighter and eventually accumulated injuries including several scars on his neck and face as well a damaged left eye. A friend of Buddy's once said, "He looks like a choir boy, but fights like the devil".

Born to longshoreman William McLean, in Somerville, Massachusetts, McLean had been orphaned at a young age and adopted by an immigrant Portuguese-American family. Working as a longshoreman during his teenage years on the docks of Charlestown and East Boston, he would become close friends with future president of the International Brotherhood of Teamsters William J. McCarthy as well as a later member of the ILA. After marrying a local Portuguese nurse in 1955, McLean began to slowly amass a formidable criminal organization which would dominate the local underworld in northern Boston which included running numbers, loansharking and truck hijackings.

In early-September 1961, two of his Winter Hill associates and their friend, 22-year-old Charlestown mobster George McLaughlin rented a cottage on Salisbury Beach for a Labor Day party. Drinking with his friends throughout the day and into the late evening, McLaughlin attempted to grope one of the gangster girlfriends. Confronted by the two men, McLaughlin received a savage beating until losing consciousness. Not sure if he was still alive, they dumped him at a nearby hospital and went to tell McLean what had happened. Buddy told them he would take care of it and absolved them of responsibility while he would have a talk with his friend, and Georgie's brother, Bernie.

When Buddy found that Bernie wanted revenge, and Buddy's help in doing it, Buddy told him his brother had been out of line and had the beating coming. McLaughlin stormed out of Buddy's house in a rage. Later that night, Buddy awoke to the sound of his dogs barking, and saw two men under his car. He went outside firing a .38 revolver, and found plastique wired to the ignition of his car. Immediately suspecting the McLaughlins, he began stalking Bernie McLaughlin throughout Charlestown until he took his shot and killed McLaughlin in front of the Bunker Hill Monument in Charlestown's town square, during broad daylight and in front of almost one hundred witnesses, on October 31, 1961.

Although he was acquitted of the murder charges, he went to prison for two years for illegal possession of a firearm. Leading the Winter Hill Gang against their Charlestown rivals for more than two years, McLean was finally shot dead by the McLaughlin Brothers, Stevie and Cornelius Hughes as he left the Tap Royal. He was succeeded by his right hand man Howie Winter and later James "Whitey" Bulger.

Melei, Rudolph, and Anthony. Brothers. Both were shot gunned to death on April 20, 1968, in a Providence grocery store. Patriarca was accused of the crime.

Mercurio Angelo AKA Sonny. Born 1936 – December 11, 2006. Mercurio was a member of the Patriarca crime family who became a government informant and recorded a Cosa Nostra induction ceremony.

Sonny Mercurio

Born in the West End section of Boston, Massachusetts, Mercurio grew up working in the family bakery in Malden, Massachusetts. He had a fleeting resemblance to actor Dayton Callie. After serving time in prison for stealing securities, Mercurio opened an Italian food shop in the Prudential Tower in Boston. Mercurio was soon working for the Patriarca family, serving as a liaison between the family and the Irish Winter Hill Gang in Boston. During the 1980s, the Federal Bureau of Investigation (FBI) obtained incriminating evidence on Mercurio by electronic surveillance at his food shop. The FBI had gathered enough evidence to indict him and others for extorting a couple of elderly bookmakers. In order to avoid a prison term, Mercurio became an FBI informant in 1987.

Mercurio lured mobster Francis "Cadillac Frank" Salemme to a meeting in June, 1989, outside a Saugus, Massachusetts International House of Pancakes restaurant, where gunmen ambushed the unarmed Salemme as restaurant patrons dining inside ducked for cover. Wounded in the chest, Salemme took cover in the restaurant's vestibule, but ran back outside to prevent bystanders from being hurt, suffering a wound to his leg.

In 1989 Mercurio informed the FBI about an upcoming family induction ceremony at a home in Medford, Massachusetts. Mercurio surreptitiously recorded the ceremony, the first time in U.S. history that a mob induction was taped. Attendees at the ceremony included Raymond Patriarca Jr., underboss Nicholas Bianco; consigliere Joe Russo; and caporegimes Biaggio Digiacoma, Vincent Ferrara, Matthew Gugleilmetti, Dennis Lepore, and Robert Carozza. (Below)

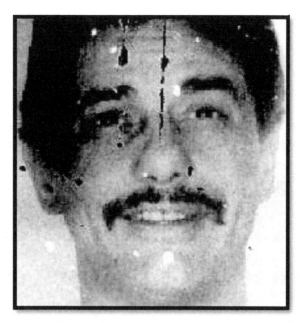

While the ceremony was taking place, Mercurio even turned down the television volume in the home to improve the recording. Mercurio's recordings led to the prosecution and conviction of dozens of criminals. In 1991, Patriarca pleaded guilty to racketeering and conspiracy charges and was sent to prison for seven years. After Patriarca's indictment, Mercurio disappeared from New England to avoid indictment himself.

Angelo said he innocently met FBI Special Agent John Connolly in the Prudential Center in the fall of 1987, after Vanessa's had been searched. He was still disgruntled from the humiliation of being successfully bugged, accused the FBI of trying to "plant" evidence during their secret forays into the store and bragged that the Mafia had outsmarted them. He was trying to best John Connolly in a battle of insider information. It was a mistake. Connolly calmly rattled off the name of the Patriarca crime family's inside source for law enforcement information. Angelo had stupidly confirmed that the Patriarca crime family had a law enforcement source, and he knew what it meant if the FBI exposed his Top Echelon Informant status. Angelo's conversation earned Stephen Flemmi restored Top Echelon Informant status in November 1987. In less than a year, Angelo had joined Stephen as a Top Echelon Informant, and was constantly feeding the FBI inside information on his associates in the Patriarca crime family.

John Connolly with FBI agent Joe Pistone (Donnie Brasco)

In some ways he even supplanted Whitey Bulger and Stephen Flemmi in importance- the FBI and the Organized Crime Strike Force were targeting the Patriarca crime family, Robert Carrozza, J.R. Russo and Vincent Ferrara, and as a member of their inner circle, Mercurio was privy to information that even Stephen Flemmi could not obtain. He threw himself into his informant role enthusiastically- even though he had been the best man at Vincent Ferrara's first wedding did not stop him from thoroughly informing on the illicit activities of his old friend. Angelo's value as an informant made protecting him a priority.

In 1994, Mercurio was convicted in Georgia of possessing 150 pounds of marijuana and was sent to prison there. He was also arrested because he tried to shoplift a $500 Shimano fishing reel in a Sandy Springs sporting goods store. He put the fishing reel in his pocket and just walked out of the store, giving the manager at the front a "Stop me, I dare you" look. The manager, a marathon runner, gave chase, and Mercurio made it about two blocks before collapsing in a breathless heap on the sidewalk. Mercurio was booked on shoplifting but released since the fake name he was using that day wasn't in the FBI national crime database.

Bulger

A short time later, though, he was pulled over for suspected drunk driving, and this time his fraudulent driver's license was a match. When word got back to the Boston FBI that Angelo had been arrested, FBI Special Agent Michael Buckley visited him in jail. Soon afterward, he pled guilty in the Vincent Ferrara case. The government just asked for nine years. Despite his obvious role in the attempted murder of Frank Salemme, it was significantly less time than J.R. Russo, Vincent Ferrara and Robert Carrozza received. Not only that, but federal prosecutors recommended that it be served concurrently with Mercurio's ten-year sentence in Georgia. In effect, Angelo received no jail time at all. In June 1997, Mercurio was brought back to Boston from prison in Georgia to testify in the trial of Patriarca boss Frank Salemme. His revelation in court as a government informant was a tremendous surprise to the Patriarca family. After this testimony, Mercurio was sent back to prison. In 2000, Mercurio's sentence was reduced. On his release from prison, Mercurio entered the federal Witness Protection Program and was secretly relocated to Arkansas. According to Mercurio's lawyer, Mercurio in later years felt guilty about becoming an informant and betraying the Patriarca family. On December 11, 2006, Mercurio died of a pulmonary embolism in Little Rock, Arkansas.

Mirabella, Anthony AKA The Moron. In 1982 Mirabella, a mobster known for following his own rules, was shot and killed at Fidas' Restaurant, Valley Street, Providence. Frank "Bobo" Marrapese, considered one of the most cold-blooded killers in the Patriarca crime family, (Marrapese once promised to kill a state witness, and then chop him up and eat him). was convicted of the crime. He was also convicted of killing Dickie Callie. Marrapese beat the charge.

Morelli Frank: AKA Butsy. Morelli was an immigrant who probably settled in Brooklyn, New York before moving to Providence where he and his brothers began pulling day-light, big dollar robberies. During prohibition, by 1917, he may have built a tiny Mafia fraction in the state based in Providence. In 1947, Morelli was summoned to testify before a jury to answer questions about harboring Genovese Family capo Michael "Trigger Mike" Coppola and his family. Coppola was a suspected in the beating death of republican political district captain Joseph Scottoriggio. By the mid-1940s Morelli began to drink heavily and Phillip Buccola, boss of the Boston fraction, forced Morelli to retire. Morelli died in the 1950s. The Morelli gang was absorbed into the New England Mafia while Filippo Buccola's was boss.

Mullen Gang: The Mullen Gang were an Irish-American gang operating in Boston. Paulie McGonagle (died November 1974) was a Boston mobster and onetime leader of the Mullen Gang, a South Boston street gang involved in burglary, auto theft, and armed robbery. During the war against Donald Killeen and his brothers, McGonagle successfully led the Mullens in a string of shootings which finally ended with Killeen's murder in 1972. After a truce was arranged with Whitey Bulger and the remnants of the Killeen organization, McGonagle remained angry about Bulger's accidental murder of his younger brother, Donald McGonagle. It is believed that this was one of the reasons for his disappearance in November 1974. His body was later excavated from a shallow grave on Boston's Tenean Beach.

King Tommy (died 1975) was a Boston mobster and member of the Mullens during their gang war against Donald Killeen and his lieutenants Billy O'Sullivan and James J. Bulger during the early 1970s. Following Killeen's murder in 1972, he became an associate of Bulger and the Winter Hill Gang after his alleged involvement in the death of Paul McGonagle. In 1975, he disappeared following an altercation with Bulger in a Southie watering hole. He was suspected of having been killed by hitman John Martorano.

Patrick Nee was born to an Irish speaking family in Rosmuc, County Galway, Ireland in 1943. He was brought to America by his parents in 1952 and became a member of the Mullens at the age of 14. He fought in several turf battles before joining the U.S. Marine Corps. He arrived in Vietnam in 1965 and saw combat at Phu Bai. After his return to South Boston in October 1966, he rejoined the Mullens and became one of their leaders in the war against the Killeen brothers. It was Nee who arranged the truce that ended the war by arranging a sit-down in Boston's South End. After being supplanted by Bulger, he moved to Charlestown, Massachusetts and switched increasingly to smuggling arms to the Provisional IRA. He currently resides in South Boston and is the author of the memoir, "A Criminal and an Irishman."

The Killeen brothers - Donald, Kenneth, George and Edward - were an Irish-American crime family which ran the bookmaking and loansharking in South Boston, Massachusetts. The Killeens controlled every illegal activity that emerged in South Boston for nearly two decades. They used muscle to make collections, and to make examples of those who didn't pay in a timely fashion.

The Mullens, by contrast, were a loosely organized crew of thieves. But being in Southie, it was just a matter of time before they butted heads with the Killeens. The Mullens Gang were mostly thieves who stole from the ships that brought goods into Boston Harbor and from the warehouses where they were stored. The crew was particularly talented and opportunistic, as likely to steal a truckload of Easter hams as one of televisions. They also had strength in numbers, the Boston Police Department at one time estimated there were as many as sixty members.

In 1971, Donald Killeen's younger brother, Kenneth, bit off the nose of Mickie Dwyer, a member of the rival Mullen Gang, at The Transit, a local watering hole. Paulie McGonagle, Francis (Buddy) Leonard, Thomas King, and Dennis (Buddy) Roche went to The Transit (the Killeen Gang's main base of operations) looking to confront the Killeens who had already left the bar. The presence of the Mullens at the Killeens headquarters was viewed as a direct challenge by Donald Killeen. A gangland war soon resulted, leading to a string of slayings throughout Boston and the surrounding suburbs.

Several weeks following the Transit incident, Killeen enforcers Billy O'Sullivan (mobster) and "Whitey" Bulger encountered Mullen member "Buddy" Roache, brother of future Police Commissioner Francis "Mickey" Roache, in a bar on Broadway in South Boston. After a heated argument, Roache was shot and left paralyzed for life.

A short time later, Bulger and O'Sullivan killed Donald McGonagle. Donald was not a member on the Mullens and was killed by mistake. His brother, Paulie McGonagle vowed revenge and according to Patrick Nee personally murdered O'Sullivan near his house at Savin Hill.

The killing of O'Sullivan revitalized the Mullins and the Killeens quickly found themselves outgunned and outmaneuvered.

On May 13, 1972, South Boston mob boss Donald Killeen was shot to death by Mullen gang enforcer Jimmy Mantville outside his home in suburban Framingham, Massachusetts. The leadership of the Killeen faction then devolved on Bulger, who was then in hiding on Cape Cod. Rather than murdering Bulger as some Mullens, including Paulie McGonagle desired, Patrick Nee arranged for their dispute to be mediated by Howie Winter, the godfather of the Irish-American Winter Hill Gang of Somerville and Joe Russo of the Patriarca crime family.

Howie Winter

After a sit-down at Chandler's restaurant in the South End, Boston, the two gangs joined forces with Winter as overall boss.

By 1973 Bulger was in control of the rackets in South Boston. He began to use his influence to remove opposition, by persuading Winter to sanction the murders of those rivals whom he viewed as having stepped out of line. These included former Mullens Spike O'Toole and Paulie McGonagle, who was murdered by Bulger and buried in a shallow grave in Boston's Tenean Beach. It is also alleged that Bulger had direct involvement in the murders of Eddie Connors, in January 1975 and Mullens, Tommy King and Buddy Leonard in November 1975.

N

Nazarian, John F AKA Jackie, AKA Mad Dog, an enforcer for the Patriarca crime family is shot by two men in an ally way next to 13 Vinton Street in Providence where Joseph "Jo Zita" Schiavone and Willie Marfeo, ran an unsanctioned crap game. Nazarian lingers for a few days before dying. The story in town was that Nazarian, a crude and simple man, had made a remark about Henry Tameleo's girlfriend. Patriarca Family member Rudolph Sciarra was arrested and charged with the murder.

Sciarra

National Cigarette Service Company: A company owned by Raymond Patriarca and housed in the Mobs "office" on Atwell Avenue in Providence.

Nee Patrick Born Born 1943. Nee is an Irish immigrant, former mobster. Raised to speak in the Irish language, Nee and family moved to Boston in 1952. He later served in US Marines in Viet Nam and upon returning home, joined the South Boston Mullen gang and became embroiled in the gang's war against the equally Irish Killeen brothers. On May 13 1972, Mullen gang enforcer Paulie McGonagle killed Donnie Killeen which allowed Whitey Bulger to take over the Killeen gang. Nee arranged for a truce to be held by Howie Winter at a sit down held at Chandler's restaurant in South Boston. There, it was agreed that the two gangs would join as one under the leadership of Howie Winter. In 1979, after Winter was convicted of fixing horse races, (In a set up by Whitey Bulger) Bulger took over the gang and Nee slowly drifted out of the gang. However that same year he attempted to smuggle seven tons of assault rifles to the IRA but was found out by US Customs, probably through information provided by John McIntyre, a low level associate whom was later tortured and killed by Whitey Bulger. Nee fled Boston but was arrested by the FBI in 1987 and served an eighteen month sentence in Federal prison. He was released in 1989 but became involved in a plot to rob banks to support the IRA. On January 13, 1990, he was sentenced to 37 years in prison for an armored car robbery in Abington Mass.

Nicholson Russell was a member of Somerville, Massachusetts' "Winter Hill Gang" and a former MDC (Metropolitan District Commission) police officer, he was rumored to be the driver for James "Buddy" McLean during the assassination of Charlestown gangster Bernard McLaughlin. Nicholson, one of the only Protestant members of the gang, was later murdered by the surviving McLaughlin Brothers, Edward "Punchy" McLaughlin and George McLaughlin for his involvement in their brother's murder.

Oaths: On October 29, 1989, in Medford, Massachusetts, the FBI successfully taped an initiation ceremony of New England's Patriarca crime family. There has been some controversy surrounding this bugging, given that the warrant for the 'roaming bug' used to tape the ceremony was given on false information.
One source details that the members involved in this ceremony were the consiglieri Joseph Russo, who conducted parts of the ceremony; mobster capos Biagio DiGiacomo, who administered the oaths; Robert F. Carrozza; Vincent M. Ferrara; Charles Quintina—all from Boston—and Matthew Guglielmetti, from the Providence, Rhode Island area; and inductees Robert DeLuca, Vincent Federico, Carmen Tortora, and Richard Floramo. Another newspaper article states that there were 17 Mafiosi present, including the current boss, Raymond Patriarca Jr., and other high ranking officials in the family.

The FBI surveillance of this ceremony was the tail end of a five year investigation about the crime families in the area, which resulted in a host of indictments and arrests. Among those indicted were Patriarca, DiGiacomo, Russo, Tortora, Ferrara, Carrozza, and Guglielmetti, all of whom were present at the ceremony. Additional big names of those that were indicted are Antonio L. Spagnola, Nicholas Bianco, Louis Failla, and John E. Farrell. Information from the ceremony was used in the case against the Mafiosi.

FBI Boston Mafia specialist Thomas A. Hughes speculated that the Patriarca crime family lost honor and favor as a result of the sacred ceremony being taped under their watch.

O'Brien Carleton Born 1903- Died May 1952. A Rhode Island mobster and one of the last independent gamblers in the state before the Patriarca family took over, completely. O'Brien was also involved in the 1950s Brinks Robbery through his friend Joe "Specs" O'Keefe. O'Brien was murdered, probably by the mob in May of 1952.

Boston's Spec's O'Keefe

O'Brien Gordon Born 1947. An associate of the Patriarca family, he acted as a go between for the mob and independent hoods, largely working in narcotics and gambling. In 1992, O'Brien was convicted and sentenced for dealing in heroin.

Ouimette, Gerard T. Ouimette was a feared mobster known for his ruthlessness whose arrest record went back to the 1950s. In 1972 Ouimette was found guilty of conspiring to murder a former associate and sentenced to 10 years. Prison didn't harm him much. He held so much sway inside the Rhode Island Correctional Institution that he had a phone installed in his maximum-security cell and had his five year old son in for a sleepover. After he was released he returned to the streets and was arrested again on March 18, 1995, and sentenced to life in prison after he was found guilty of trying to extort $125,000 from two other hoods.

P

Patriarca Raymond Loreda Salvatore, Sr. (March 18, 1908 – July 11, 1984) was a mobster from Providence, Rhode Island who became the longtime boss of the Patriarca crime family, whose control extended throughout New England for over three decades.

One of the most powerful crime bosses in the United States, Patriarca often mediated disputes between Cosa Nostra families outside the region. He was the father of Raymond Patriarca, Jr.

Raymond Patriarca Jr, son of Boss Patriarca

Born to Italian immigrants in Worcester, Massachusetts, Patriarca was charged during his teenage years for hijacking, armed robbery, assault, safecracking, and auto theft. He was indicted as being an accessory to murder before Prohibition's end, in 1934.

During the 1930s, the Providence Board of Public Safety named Patriarca as "Public enemy No. 1". However, when Patriarca was sentenced to five years in prison for robbery, he was paroled in 1938 after serving just a few months in prison. An inquiry revealed that Executive Councilor Daniel Coakley, a close associate of Governor Charles F. Hurley, had drawn up a parole petition based on the appeals of a "Father Fagin", whom Coakley had fabricated. Coakley was impeached and dismissed from the Governor's office. This scandal enhanced Patriarca's reputation in the underworld, as it demonstrated the power of his political connections. During the 1940s, Patriarca continued to rise in power. In 1950, family mobster Philip Bruccola fled the country to avoid prosecution for tax evasion. Patriarca took control of Bruccola's criminal operations. Patriarca's reign as leader of the New England syndicate was reportedly a brutal and ruthless one. In one incident Patriarca allegedly ordered an elderly mafioso to murder his own son, after Patriarca lost a substantial amount of money on a bad deal. When the father pleaded for his son's life, Patriarca exiled him from the family. (Underboss Henry Tameleo later persuaded Patriarca to relent). In another incident,

Patriarca demanded that several members of the crime family pay him $22,000, after federal authorities seized a hijacked shipment of cigarettes he had financed. Patriarca allegedly ordered the murder of his brother for failing to notice an electronic surveillance device placed by federal agents in Patriarca's office. During the Irish Mob Wars between the Charlestown Mob and the Winter Hill Gang, Patriacra allegedly ordered the murder of several members of the McLaughlin Gang. This occurred when Bernard McLaughlin started interfering with Patriarca's loansharking operations in Boston. On July 11, 1984, around 11:30 AM, the North Providence, Rhode Island Fire Department Rescue Squad received an emergency call from a Douglas Avenue address. It was later revealed that this was the home of Patriarca's girlfriend. His first wife died in 1965. He then married a former nightclub hostess and was living with her in Johnston, Rhode Island at the time of his death. When emergency workers arrived, they found Patriarca to be in full cardiac arrest. Rushed to Rhode Island Hospital, doctors tried to revive Patriarca with electrical defibrillation and the implanting of a cardiac pacemaker. At 1:00 PM, Patriarca was pronounced dead of a massive heart attack at the age of 76. Patriarca is buried in Gate of Heaven Cemetery, East Providence, Rhode Island. " At the time of his death, Patriarca was under indictment for two murders. Patriarca was succeeded by his son Raymond Patriarca, Jr.

Vincent "Gigi" Portalla, alleged enforcer for the renegade faction of the East Boston mob said to be led by Mafia Capo Robert Carrozza

Q

Quintino, Charles. Of Revere, Massachusetts, believed to have been elevated to Underboss at age 70 in the 1980s because Raymond Patriacra Jr. needed someone closer to the Boston operations.

R

Rico Harold Paul (April 29, 1925 – January 14, 2004) was an FBI agent. Indicted for murder in 2003, he played a significant role in the 1968 framing of four men for murder, unjustly imprisoning them for decades. Rico was born in 1925 in Boston. He joined the FBI in 1951 at the age of 26. He used members of the Winter Hill Gang as informants and in 1956 he recognized a disguised James "Whitey" Bulger in a Revere bar and arrested him. In 1965 Rico received word that gangster Edward Deegan was going to be killed by members of the The Winter Hill Gang but did nothing. He then watched as Joe Barboza testified in court against four men they both knew to be innocent of the crime: Peter Limone, Henry Tameleo, Joe Salvati and Louis Greco. Tameleo died in 1985 in prison. Salvati was released in 1997, and Limone in 2001. During U.S. House Judiciary Committee hearings in October 2003 looking into the Deegan killing, Rico responded to questions about the innocent men imprisoned with "What do you want, tears?" Greco died in prison. The two survivors and the estates of the deceased were awarded $101.7 million.

Reputed mob associated and loan shark Vincent "Fat Vinnie" Roberto

Rocco Alex (born Alexander Federico Petricone, Jr. on February 29, 1936) Rocco was born in Somerville, Massachusetts to Mary and Alexander Petricone. Known by the nickname "Bobo" as a young man, Rocco had connections to the Winter Hill Gang in the early 1960s (a mostly Irish gang, despite his Italian-American background). George McLaughlin, of a rival gang, tried to pick up on Rocco's girlfriend may have helped to start the the Irish Mob Wars.

Rocco was a suspect in the October 1961 murder of Bernie McLaughlin, but was never charged. He moved to California, began using the name Alex Rocco, lost a considerable amount of weight, and got into Hollywood. Rocco played the part of Moe Greene, a Las Vegas casino owner, in the film *The Godfather*.

Roche Frankie A: Born 1973. Alleged gunman accused of killing Genovese New England based gangster Adolfo Bruno in November of 2003. Roche was later arrested by the FBI and is suspected of cooperating with the police in the Bruno murder investigation because he was believed to have gotten into a petty beef with Bruno over money shortly before the shooting.

Rossi Alfredo AKA The Blind Pig. An alleged fence for stolen goods in the Providence area for Patriarca's mob

Rossi John: Patriarca enforcer

Rossi Tommy: Bank robber and enforcer for Patriarca's mob

Russo Joseph AKA J.R Died June 1 1998. A Capo in the New England Mob. By the mid-1980s Russo controlled most of the rackets in the east Boston area. However, Raymond Patriarca, nervous over Russo's growing power base, officially place Russo under the control of Boston capo Charles Quinito. In 1987 Russo replaced the imprisoned Illario Zannino as Consigliere of the New England LCN Family. On January 6, 1992 Russo was indicted on a RICO case involving drug trafficking, extortion and murder. He was found guilty, fined $758,000 and sentenced to 16 years. Russo died at the Springfield Federal Prison Hospital, at Springfield, MO.

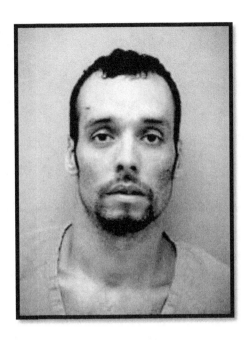

S

Sacramone Americo AKA Rico. One time boxer and bodyguard for James Buddy McLean and was with him on the night he was killed. Sacramone was wounded, but survived and was sent back to prison for a parole violation.

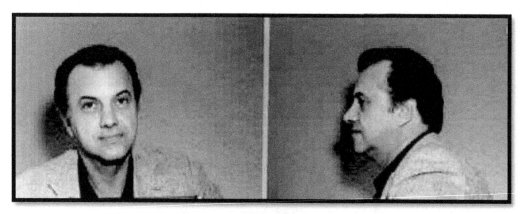

St. Laurent Michael Anthony St. Laurent's arrest record dates back to 1959 and includes many offenses associated with illegal gambling and bookmaking. St. Laurent has also been identified as a member of the New England organized crime family. In 1999 he was convicted in Rhode Island for extortion, loansharking and conducting an illegal sports book. While incarcerated he was again charged with overseeing a gambling ring from his prison cell. St. Laurent remains in federal custody.

Scanlon, Joseph AKA Joey Onions. On April 3, 1978, Joe Onions Scanlon disappeared from the streets of Providence. For first time in Rhode Island's history, prosecutors tried the related case without a body, in this case Joe Onions' body. Mob associate Nicholas Pari and Andrew Merola were tried and convicted of the murder and served ten years in prison as a result. Testimony at trial indicates the pair thought Scanlon was an informant for police. At the time, police believe Joey Onions body was dumped in Narragansett Bay. But in 2008, the police dug up Onions body behind the Lisboa Apartments at 378 Bullocks Point Ave. in East Providence. Nick Pari, 71 and dying of cancer, told police where he had buried the body. Pari had been picked up in the state police sting dubbed "Operation Mobbed Up" the week before. According to accounts at the time of their trial, Pari was accused of punching Scanlon in the face to distract him, Merola then shot Joe Onions in the back of the head.

Louis Mannochio

Schiavone, Joseph AKA Jo Zita. In 1966, Schiavone was arrested for firing several shots at Louis Mannochio, a Patriarca family, inside the mobs hang out at Atwells Avenue and Ridge Street in Providence. A .38 cal. Colt Cobra, a black silk mask and black leather gloves were found in Schiavones pocket.

Sciarra, Rudolph: Sciarra, a mob regular, was convicted in 1983 of providing the guns for the 1965 murder of Raymond "Baby" Curcio. He was sentenced to life but only served ten years. Curcio was marked for death because he burglarized Raymond Patriarca's brothers home.

Shamrocks: A juvenile South Boston street gang active in the 1940s that once included Whitey Bulger as a member.

Solomon Charles AKA King (Seated) Charles "King" Solomon was a Boston racketeer who controlled New England's bootlegging, narcotics and illegal gambling during Prohibition. One of the earliest crime figures in New England's history, Solomon emigrated from his native Russia as a boy settling with his family in Boston's West End. The son of a local theater owner, Solomon and his three brothers came from a middle class background and, during his teenage years, worked as a counterman in his uncle's restaurant. However, by his early 20s, he had had become involved in prostitution, fencing and bail bonding prior to Prohibition. By the early 1920s, he controlled the majority of illegal gambling and narcotics such as cocaine and morphine before expanding into bootlegging with Dan Carroll during Prohibition owning many of the city's most prominent speakeasies including the Coconut Grove nightclub night club. He enjoyed extensive contacts throughout the underworld including the Bronfman's in Canada as well as associates in New York and Chicago. Although never indicted on bootlegging charges (due to his political connections), he was tried on narcotics charges in 1922. He was later acquitted of charges. He would however serve thirteen months of a five year prison sentence for intimidating a witness into perjury for his narcotics trial. During his imprisonment, a request for his transfer to a prison closer to Boston was made by two Boston Congressmen. Attending the Atlantic City Crime Conference in 1927, Solomon was one of the several leaders in the Big Seven who helped negotiate territorial disputes and establish policies which would influence the later National Syndicate in 1932. Solomon continued to control illegal gambling in New England until his death on January 24, 1933 when he was killed in Boston's Cotton Club by rival gunmen.

South End Mutual Benefit Association: AKA The Oxy, Was a credit union in Hartford, CT which the FBI suspected of providing "instant credit" during the 1980s to gamblers who played in games run by the Patriarca crime family. Banking regulators shut down the company because the New England Mafia was said to be using it as a private bank to underwrite a multimillion-dollar, illegal gambling business. Mobsters who ran illegal casino games at social clubs in Meriden, New Britain and Hartford had access to stacks of pre-approved credit union loan applications and used them to extend instant money to tapped out players. When FBI agents raided a mob game at the Meriden Independent Club in June 1988, they seized $42,000 in cash, gambling records, gambling paraphernalia and, according to an FBI affidavit, "numerous loan applications for the South End Mutual Benefit Association (a state chartered and federally insured credit union)."

Spinale Anthony Dominic: Spinale has two convictions for bookmaking and has alleged ties to the New England organized crime family. In 2000, Spinale was convicted on federal racketeering charges, along with members of the Los Angeles organized crime family.

T

Taglianetti Louis, AKA The Fox. a Patriarca family member.. In 1970, Taglianetti and his girlfriend Elizabeth McKenna, were shot to death 2045 Broad Street Cranston RI. At the time of his death Taglianetti was under indictment for the 1962 murder of John F "Jackie" Nazarian.

The Taglianetti Logs: The names given to recorded conversations and logs for telephone wiretapped conversations recorded by a bug placed inside the Patriarca family. The logs were released on May 19, 1967.

Henry Tameleo

Tameleo Enrico AKA Henry, AKA The Referee,. Died 1985, was an underboss in the New England-based Patriarca crime family of La Cosa Nostra from 1952 to 1968. Tameleo was a long time participant in organized crime and is considered one of the founding fathers of the Patriarca family. in 1967, Tameleo, Raymond L.S. Patriarca, and Jerry Anguilo were charged with the murder of bookmaker Willie Marfeo . Before the trial's conclusion, on March 12, 1965, Tameleo, Peter Limone, Louis Greco, Wilfred Roy French, Ronald Cassesso and Joseph Salvati were indicted for the murder of hoodlum Edward "Teddy" Deegan . In 1968, all six men were found guilty of the Deegan murder in the Superior Court of Suffolk County, Massachusetts. Tameleo, Limone, Greco and Cassesso were sentenced to death by the state, with Salvati and French receiving life sentences. The death sentences were later reduced to life in prison, where Tameleo died in 1985. By 2000, all charges had been dismissed against Tameleo and the other accused men amid accusations of a government frame-up and cover-up extending over thirty years.

FBI agents H. Paul Rico, Dennis Condon, John Morris, and John Connolly withheld evidence of the defendants' innocence in order to protect FBI informants Vincent "Jimmy the Bear" Flemmi and Joseph Barboza. Out of this settlement, $13 million went to the estate of Enrico Tameleo, specifically his son, Saverio, as administrator of the Tameleo estate, and Tameleo's wife Jeanette.

Teresa, Vincent. AKA Fat Vinnie (1930 – 1990) was a mobster in the Boston branch of the Patriarca crime family who was a lieutenant of boss Raymond Patriarca.

After he entered witness protection, Teresa wrote three books including the 1973 My Life In The Mafia which chronicles Teresa's path to a life in organized crime, his time as a lieutenant for Raymond Patriarca, his fall in the Patriarca crime family, and the circumstances that led to him to seek the protection of the Federal government and the Federal Witness Protection Program. Intelligent and personable, Teresa was as good a federal witness as he was a criminal. His testimony put a large number of the Patriarca crime family in jail. Teresa was bitter against the Federal government for his treatment in the Federal Witness Protection Program, feeling they used him with no regard to his safety, or an appreciation of his value. Teresa claimed that while he reached the position of lieutenant in the Patriarca crime family, this was mainly due to his prowess as a money maker for Raymond Patriarca, and that he never murdered anyone. In February 1990, Vincent Teresa died of kidney failure in Seattle, Washington.

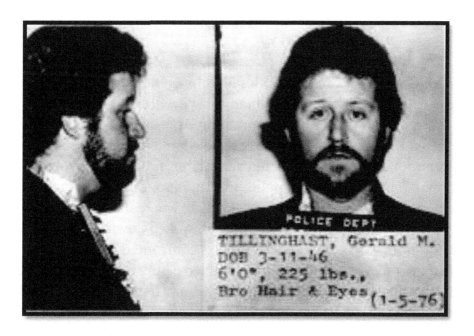

Tillinghast Gerald M. AKA Gerry, Alleged mob hit man who was convicted of shooting loan shark, George Basmajian nine times, in a stolen car near T.F. Green Airport in Warwick RI. He was also accused of participating in the Bonded Vault heist of 1975, when mobsters cleaned out safe-deposit boxes of an estimated $3 million in cash, gold and jewelry reputed to have been stashed by other members of organized crime. When a state police detective bumped into him in prison and asked how he was doing, Tillinghast responded, "Not guilty." In a more candid moment, Tillinghast attributed his criminal conduct to poor judgment, stupidity and putting himself in risky situations. Tillinghast was accused of running a gambling ring from his prison cell in New Hampshire. Tillinghast, 62, was accused of resuming his storied criminal career upon his release from prison in 2008 after serving 30 years for the 1977 George Basmajian murder. Tillinghast allegedly ran a narcotics and gambling ring in Cranston, Rhode Island in a second-hand furniture and appliance store that went out of business, forcing him to move to a Flea Market.

V

Vecchio Raymond AKA Slick. In 1982, Vecchio, a noted as an underworld loose cannon with a smart mouth and many suspected he was also a police informant, was shot at Vincent's restaurant on Atwells by two masked men. Police suspected Kevin Hanrahan, who, as fate should have it, was shot outside of the Arch restaurant, also on Atwells, ten years later in 1992. On September 18, 1992, Hanrahan had dinner with a police informant and two other mob associates. He then went to a bar called The Arch, where he told others he was expecting a big score. After leaving the Arch he walked down Atwells Avenue to go to a restaurant in North Providence. He was confronted by two men at the corner of Pequot and Atwells. One of them pulled a gun and fired three bullets into Hanrahan's head. Hanrahan died not far from where Raymond Vecchio had perished ten years earlier. Hanrahan's killers have never been found.

W

Wady, David. A Boston drug dealer, he was shot to death in an alley by Wimpy Bennett 1964 on orders of Raymond Patriarca who had a no Heroin rule for his territory.

Alleged Boston mob associate Phil Waggenheim

Wagenheim Philip AKA Phil (February 2, 1915-April 1989) was a Boston mobster and a close associate of Larry Baiona and Whitey Bulger. Based in the neighborhood of Jamaica Plain, he was a key contact between the New York and Boston underworld between the 1960s until his death from natural causes in April 1989. In November 1966, he was present at Ralph Lamattina's Nite Lite Café with Joseph Lamattina and Larry Biona when two members of Joe "the Animal" Barboza's "crew", Tash Bratsos and Tommy DePrisco, were murdered (the two had previously been extorting money from local residents to raise bail for Barboza).

Walsh Daniel L. AKA Danny: Born 1893   Died February 2, 1933, Providence Rhode Island based bootlegger during the prohibition. Springing out of what was then the village of Pawtucket, he built an impressive bootlegging operation. He earned a fortune and although Rhode Island did not ratify the 18th Amendment, it did indict Walsh for tax evasion. He was said to have been occasional partners in bootlegging and in residential real estate (apartment buildings) with Joe Kennedy. He claimed his partner in New York was Owney "The Killer" Madden. There is some dispute over his attendance at the Atlantic City Conference but it's doubtful that he was there. On the night of February 2, 1933, Walsh disappeared off the streets of Pawtucket. Several days later his brother Joey received a ransom note that demanded he drive to Boston and pay $40,000. Joey drove to Boston with the money, and he too, disappeared. Walsh's bodies have never been found.

Weeks. Kevin Born March 21, 1956, South Boston, Massachusetts. Weeks is a former Irish-American mobster of and a longtime friend and confidant to James J. Bulger.

Whitey Bulger in the 1980s

After his arrest and imprisonment in 1999, Weeks became a cooperating witness. His testimony is viewed as responsible for the convictions of FBI agent John Connolly and mobster Stephen Flemmi.

Weeks graduated from South Boston High in 1974, ending his formal education. His two brothers would later go on to graduate from Harvard University. His brother John (Jack) Jr. became an advance man for Massachusetts Governor Michael Dukakis, and William became a selectman in Acton, Massachusetts.
In 1976, after Weeks gave up on college, he became a bouncer at a popular neighborhood bar, "Triple O's". a frequent hangout of the Winter Hill Gang, which was then headed by James J. Bulger. It was here that Weeks first met Bulger, as well as Bulger's partner Stephen Flemmi. Beginning in 1978, Weeks began working for Bulger part-time as muscle and a personal driver. Impressed by Weeks' knack for making money and genuinely liking him, Bulger decided to bring him in closer than any other associate. Meanwhile, Weeks turned to running a loansharking business on the side.
On the night of May 11, 1982, Bulger was told the whereabouts of a former associate turned Federal informant, Edward Brian Halloran, known on the streets as "Balloon head".

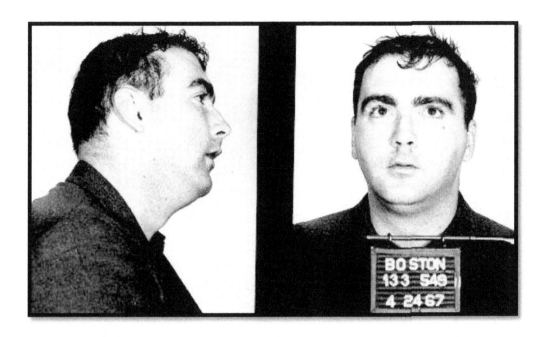

After arriving at the scene, Weeks staked out Anthony's Pier 4 Restaurant, where Halloran and construction worker Michael Donahue were dining together. As Donahue and Halloran drove out of the parking lot Weeks signaled Bulger by stating, "The balloon is in the air", over a hand held radio. Bulger drove up with a masked man armed with a silenced Mac 10; Bulger himself carried a .30 caliber carbine. Bulger and the other shooter opened fire and sprayed Halloran and Donahue's car with bullets. Donahue was shot in the head and killed instantly. Halloran lived long enough to identify his attacker as James Flynn, a Winter Hill associate, who was later tried and acquitted. Flynn remained the prime suspect until 1999, when Weeks agreed to cooperate with investigators.

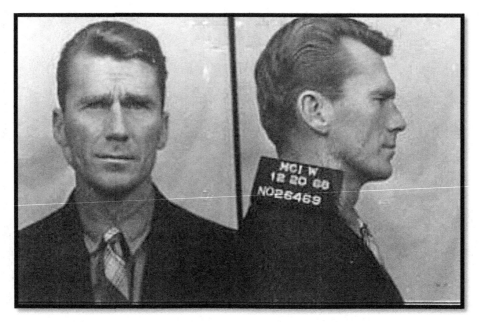

James P. Flynn, once a reputed member of the Winter Hill Gang.

Bulger, Weeks, and Flemmi became heavily involved in narcotics trafficking in the early 1980s. Bulger began to summon drug dealers from in and around Boston to his headquarters. Flanked by Kevin Weeks and Flemmi, he would inform each dealer that he had been offered a substantial sum to assassinate them. He would then demand a large cash payment not to do so. Eventually, however, the massive profits of drugs proved irresistible.

According to Kevin Weeks "Jimmy, Stevie and I weren't in the import business and weren't bringing in the marijuana or the cocaine. We were in the shakedown business. We didn't bring drugs in; we took money off the people who did. We never dealt with the street dealers, but rather with a dozen large-scale drug distributors all over the State who were bringing in the coke and marijuana and paying hundreds of thousands to Jimmy. The dealers on the street corner sold eight-balls,…grams, and half grams to customers for their personal use. They were supplied by the mid-level drug dealer who was selling them multiple ounces. In other words, the big importers gave it to the major distributors, who sold it to the middlemen, who then sold it to the street dealers. In order to get to Jimmy, Stevie, and me, someone would have had to go through those four layers of insulation."

In South Boston, most of the neighborhood's drug trade was managed by a handpicked crew of prize fighters led by John Shea. Edward MacKenzie Jr., a former member of Shea's crew, has stated that this was done because Shea viewed athletes as less likely to abuse the drugs they were selling.

According to Weeks, Bulger enforced strict rules over the dealers who were paying him protection. "The only people we ever put out of business were heroin dealers. Jimmy didn't allow heroin in South Boston. It was a dirty drug that users stuck in their arms, making problems with needles, and later on, AIDS. While people can do cocaine socially and still function, once they do heroin, they're zombies."

Weeks also insists that Bulger strictly forbade PCP and selling to children and that those dealers who refused to play by his rules were violently driven out of the neighborhood.

In 1990, "Red" Shea and his associates were arrested as part of a joint investigation involving the Drug Enforcement Administration (DEA), the Boston Police Department and the Massachusetts State Police. All refused to testify against Bulger, Flemmi, and Weeks.

According to Weeks "Of course, Jimmy lost money once the drug dealers were removed from the streets in the summer raid, but he always had other business going on. Knowing I had to build something on the side, I had concentrated on my shylocking and gambling businesses. The drug business had been good while it lasted. But our major involvement in it was over."

In 1997, shortly after the Boston Globe disclosed that Bulger and Flemmi had been informants, Weeks met with retired Agent John Connolly (later sentenced to 40 years in prison), who showed him a photocopy of Bulger's FBI informant file. In order to explain Bulger and Flemmi's status as informants, Connolly said, "The Mafia was going against Jimmy and Stevie, so Jimmy and Stevie went against them."

Weeks and Whitey Bulger

On November 17, 1999, Weeks, Kevin O'Neill, and other Winter Hill associates were arrested in South Boston by agents of the Drug Enforcement Administration and the Massachusetts State Police. The next afternoon, he was presented with a 29-count indictment under the Racketeer Influenced and Corrupt Organizations Act (RICO). At first refusing to cooperate, Weeks was transferred to a Federal penitentiary in Rhode Island.

Imprisoned in Rhode Island, it took about two weeks for Weeks to decide to cooperate with authorities, leading some in South Boston to dub him "Kevin Squeaks" or "Two Weeks". He has stated that he was approached by one of his fellow prisoners, a Made man in the Patriarca crime family, who asked him, "Kid what are you doing? Are you going to take it up the ass for these guys? Remember you can't rat on a rat. Those guys have been giving up everyone for thirty years." In addition, Weeks was also deeply impressed by the cooperation of John Martorano, a legendary enforcer for the Winter Hill Gang.

He led authorities to six different bodies buried by the Winter Hill Gang, including the triple grave of Hussey, McIntyre and Barrett. He implicated Bulger in the murder of Brian Halloran (nicknamed "Ballonhead" by Bulger) as well as agreeing to testify against Stephen Flemmi, Special Agent Connolly, and Whitey Bulger. He was then sentenced to five years in federal prison.

Weeks married his longtime girlfriend, Pamela Cavaleri, on April 26, 1980 at the Gate of Heaven Roman Catholic Church in their native South Boston. They have two sons, Kevin Barry Weeks, to whom Whitey Bulger stood as godfather, and Brian Weeks. The couple later separated.

He was released from Federal prison in early 2005. After a major bidding war over his memoirs he chose to collaborate with journalist Phyllis Karas (of People magazine). Weeks' account of his life with Bulger and Flemmi was published in March 2006.

Werner, Maurice: A Brookline, Massachusetts, convict, whom Vincent Teresa testified was chosen to kill Fidel Castro for the CIA in 1960 but the plot was never carried out.

Westerman, Gary: Westerman was the brother-in-law of Anthony Arillotta, a reputed Genovese capo, or at least he was until he disappeared in 1980. His remains were found in 2010 on a residential parcel of vacant land at 160 Springfield Street in Agawam, MA. He had been shot twice in the head at the site, and then buried a short distance away in a hand-dug grave approximately 8 feet deep" Arillotta was charged in 210, for his alleged role in the 2003 murder of his predecessor, Adolfo "Big Al" Bruno in Springfield, Mass. Arillotta became a cooperating witness and told investigators where to look for Westerman.

Winter, Howie Born March 17, 1929: Leader of the Winter Hill Gang after the gang's originator, Buddy McLean was killed during the Irish Gang Wars of the 1960s. Whitey Bulger replaced Winter as leader of the gang after Whitey provided the FBI with enough information on Winter to have him jailed for ten years. Winter was released from prison in 1987. In 1993, he was caught dealing cocaine. When the FBI informed him that Whitey had been a snitch all those years and offered Winter a deal if he would inform on Bulger, Winter refused the deal telling the FBI he was no rat, despite facing another decade behind bars, which he would serve, being released from prison in July 2002

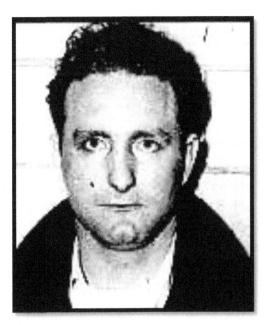

Howie Winter, the gang leader who helped to ignite Boston's Irish Wars of the 1960s

Winter Hill Gang took its name from the Winter Hill neighborhood of Somerville, Massachusetts north of Boston. Its members have included notorious Boston gangsters Howie Winter ("Howie"), James McLean ("Buddy"), James J. Bulger ("Whitey"), and hitman Stephen Flemmi ("The Rifleman"). They were most influential from 1965 under the rule of McLean and Winter until the takeover led by Bulger in 1979.

The Winter Hill Gang was given its name in the 1970s by journalists at The Boston Herald, although the name was hardly ever openly used as a reference to them While Winter Hill Gang members are alleged to have been involved with most typical organized-crime-related activities, they are perhaps most known for fixing horse races in the northeastern United States. Twenty-one members and associates, including Winter, were indicted by federal prosecutors in 1979. Winter Hill no longer exists in its original state.

The Boston Irish Gang War started in 1961 and lasted until 1967. It was fought between the McLaughlin Gang of Charlestown, led by Bernie McLaughlin and the Winter Hill Gang of Somerville, led by James "Buddy" McLean.

The two gangs had co-existed in relative peace for a number of years until an incident on Labor Day weekend 1961. While at a party, Georgie McLaughlin made an advance on the girlfriend of Winter Hill Gang member Alex Rocco.
 He was subsequently beaten unconscious by members of the Winter Hill Gang and was dumped outside of the local hospital. Bernie McLaughlin went to see James McLean and demanded that he hand over the members of the gang who beat his brother. McLean refused. The McLaughlins took this refusal as an insult and attempted to wire a bomb to McLean's wife's car. In retaliation, McLean shot and killed McLaughlin coming out of the "Morning Glory" bar in Charlestown, Massachusetts in October 1961. This was the start of Boston's Irish Gang War.
In 1965, McLean was shot and killed by one of the last survivors of the McLaughlin Gang, Steve Hughes. Howie Winter then assumed control of the Winter Hill Gang. A year later, in 1966, the last two associates of the McLaughlin Gang, brothers Connie and Steve Hughes, were killed.
After the Irish Gang war, the Winter Hill Gang was reputed to be not only the top Irish Mob syndicate in the New England area, but along the east coast as well. In the book Black Mass, by Dick Lehr and Gerard O'Neill, the authors claimed that the Winter Hill Gang were far more feared and powerful than their rivals in the New England Mafia, run by the Angiulo Brothers. The Angiulo Family of the North End was responsible for most of the Italian mafia operations in Boston and points north. They answered to the Patriarca crime family of Rhode Island.
The Winter Hill Gang was quite proficient at murdering rival mobsters in order to take over their rackets. But once they gained control, they had no idea how to run them. They learned the lesson of their gang's disastrous foray into gambling after wiping out Joseph (Indian Joe) Notranagelli's crew. In what should have been a fabulously profitable illicit gambling enterprise, the gang lost it. As the years went by, James Bulger and Steven Flemmi lost interest in running any kind of gambling operation. They would eventually only provide protection for bookmakers, drug dealers and truck hijackers. By 1975, Howie Winter and John Martorano were going broke. Eventually they had to go to Gennaro Anguilo to borrow money. To make the weekly payments, they began going into businesses with people they didn't know and couldn't trust. These activities included rigging horse races and drug trafficking.
It was the decision to involve outsiders with their business that led to their downfall. By 1979, Howie Winter and the rest of the Somerville crew were all sent to prison for fixing horse races, leaving Whitey Bulger and Stephen Flemmi as the

new leaders of the Winter Hill Gang. By 1991, even as James J. Bulger's criminal career was winding down, he remained the undisputed mob boss. His criminal associate Kevin Weeks was not considered a threat, and neither were John Shea, Eddie Mac, "Polecat" Moore or John Cherry. Howie Carr comments, "they hadn't really been gangsters so much as they'd been ex-boxers and bar-room brawlers who had become cocaine dealers". One problem that arose with the gang was that they enjoyed partaking in their own vices. Like their customers, they spent afternoons in the fall drinking beer and watching professional football on television, often doubling up wagers on late West Coast games as they desperately tried to break even and chased their losses.

Leaders of the Winter Hill Gang

1960s-1965 - James "Buddy" McLean - Boss, killed 1965.

1965-1978 - Howard "Howie" Winter - Boss, Jailed in 1978, released in 2002.

1978-1995 - James "Whitey" Bulger - Boss, one of the most infamous Irish Mob bosses. Fled Boston in 1994 due a pending federal indictment. He was on the FBI's Ten Most Wanted list until his arrest in Santa Monica, California on June 22, 2011. He had a $2 million bounty on his head.

1995-2000 - Kevin Weeks - Boss, was Bulger's lieutenant, he was arrested on November 15, 1999 and becoming a cooperating witness in January 2000. Released from federal prison on February 4, 2005, he wrote a book in 2006 entitled Brutal, The Untold Story Of My Life Inside Whitey Bulger's Irish Mob.

2000–2009 - George "Georgie Boy" Hogan –Alleged Boss of the Winter Hill Mob, (Headquarters in South Boston)

Members of the Winter Hill Gang

Salvatore Sperlinga ("Sal") - Howie Winter's lieutenant and bookkeeper, killed in 1980.

Johnny Martorano - Top hitman for James Bulger & Flemmi, indicted and arrested 1995, became an informant in 1999, sentenced to 14 years in 2004, with time served released 2007. He is half Italian-American and half Irish-American.

Edward "Teddy" Deegan - Bank robber and associate of Stevie Flemmi.

Patrick Nee - Associate of Bulger's with close ties to the Provisional Irish Republican Army, arrested in 1990 by the FBI, but was released after April 2000. Now works in South Boston.

Anthony D'Agostino ("Tony Blue") - Buddy McLean's bodyguard, with McLean at Peppermint Lounge in Somerville when he was killed 1965.

Thomas Ballou, Jr. ("Tommy") - Buddy McLean's driver and bodyguard. He was killed in 1970.

Joseph McDonald ("Joe Mac") - An original member of the gang. McDonald was a hitman, World War II veteran and street fighter. FBI's Top Ten Most Wanted List until he was arrested by the FBI before he could turn himself in. The FBI received information on his whereabouts from Whitey Bulger. He died in 1997 after being released from prison.

Joey McDonald

Jeffrey Dorr – Alleged known associate. Deceased 2006.

Alexander Federico Petricone Jr. ("Bobo") - It was Petricone's girlfriend on Labor Day weekend of 1961 that McLaughlin hit winter Hill and the Charlestown gangs. The following year Petricone moved to California and changed his name to Alex Rocco, acting in the film The Godfather as well as nearly 200 other movie and television roles from 1965 to present.

Russell Nicholson - was an original member of the gang as well as a police officer. He reportedly was the driver during the 1961 gangland slaying of Bernie McLaughlin and subsequently fired by the police force shortly thereafter. He was later kidnapped and killed in retaliation by the Charlestown Gang (McLaughlin Bro's) in 1964.

James Simms ("Jimmy") - Released from prison in 1986, his Whereabouts are unknown.

Mike Iavello - (narcotics, alleged) left Boston area for Florida.

John Shea AKA Red – Alleged known associate and narcotics dealer for the gang.

Vincent Teresa - became an FBI informant against the Patriarca crime family after he was arrested in 1967. He wrote the book My Life in the Mafia, although he was never inducted into La Cosa Nostra.

John "Mick" Murray - Irish-American gangster and professional Bank Robber from the Boston neighborhood of Charlestown. Reputed to have ties with organized crime in Montreal, and the Irish Republican Army. Murray was also implicated along with South Boston gangster Pat Nee with planning a series of gun shipments to the Irish Republican Army. Plead guilty and was sentenced to nine years in federal prison on July 1,2002 to embezzlement, extortion, racketeering and theft for shaking down a Southie bookmaker, stealing computer equipment from UPS trucks and attempting to defraud the union pension and welfare fund.

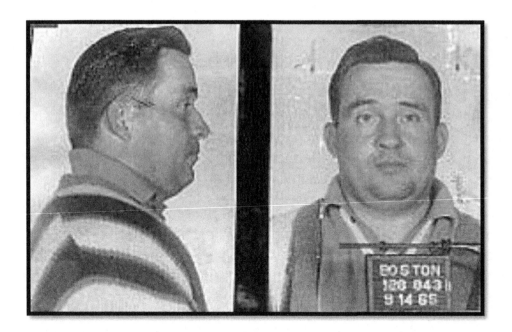

Ballou Tommy, Jr. A former longshoreman and member of the Winter Hill Gang, and former bodyguard and driver to Buddy McLean. Ballou was murdered in Charlestown, Mass. 1970.

Louis Litif - was recruited by Bulger for extra muscle in the 1970s and a suspect in the 1978 Blackfriars Massacre.

Anthony Veranis - local boxer who was murdered by John Martorano in 1966.

George W. Holden - professional welterweight boxer and small time criminal.

Timothy A. Connolly 3rd - was a soldier for Bulger until becoming an informant in 1989, owned the Corner Cafe

James M. Murphy - was on Boston Police Department's "Most Wanted List".

Dennis Horkenbach ("Blumpkin") – Alleged known associate.

Ronnie Fronduto - former associate.

Jimmy Flynn –Alleged, was a soldier who later became an actor.

Tommy McKinnon – Alleged known associate.

Edward "Eddie Mac" MacKenzie, Jr- Alleged enforcer and narcotics dealer for the gang, co-author and subject of the book: "Street Soldier: My Life as an Enforcer for Whitey Bulger and the Irish Mob."

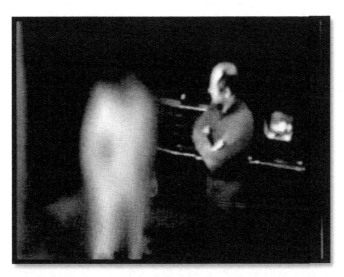

Whitey Bulger speaking to an undercover FBI agent in a parking garage (FBI photo)

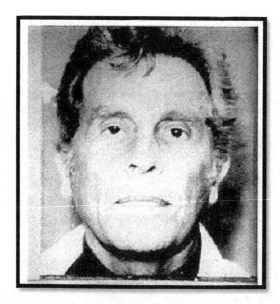

Larry Baione

Ilario "Larry" Zannino, also known as Larry Baione, a top figure in the Angiulo crime family

Zannino Ilario Maria Antonio "Larry Baione" (June 15, 1920 Swampscott, Massachusetts– February 27, 1996 Springfield, Missouri) was the muscle and chief gambling honcho for Raymond J. Patriarca and the Patriarca crime family.

Zannino was said to be the second-highest-ranking figure in the Boston faction of the Patriarca family. He is a paternal nephew or a paternal first cousin of Boston Patriarca crime family mobster Phillip Zannino. Zannino was born to Joseph Zannino and Isabella LaGrada.

He stood at 5'7 and weighed 160 pounds with brown eyes and dark brown hair. He is the husband of Isabella Tawa. He was one of the richest mobsters in the New England mob. The Boston stated that that Zannino had a wallet that looks like the inside of the New England Merchants Bank vault and a bookmaking and loansharking operation more successful than most American car companies. He was often found bouncing with Stephen Flemmi. He attended Boston's Franklin High School, even though he was from South Boston, Massachusetts, graduating in 1938. In his high school yearbook at graduation he stated intentions to attend medical school. His fellow classmates called him "Zip" which later become ironically the same nickname of FBI Special Agent John Connolly who would later successfully prosecute him for his criminal activities.

He was classmates with a future elementary school principal named Larry who were in the "Let's Go" youth gang together. In 1954, Illario attended his old friend Larry's wedding, pressed a $100 bill in his hand and said, "Buy yourself a necktie kid." In 1985, FBI agents acquired details on the interiors of two Mafia controlled apartments in the Boston's North End. With court approval, agents picked the locks early in the morning and planted bugs that produced 800 hours of recordings. Ilario Zannino was heard explaining how dangerous it is to kill just one member of the Winter Hill Gang. "If you're clipping people," he said, "I always say, make sure you clip the people around him first. Get them together, 'cause everybody's got a friend. He could be the dirtiest motherfucker in the world, but someone that likes this guy, that's the guy that sneaks you." Zannino and Patriarca family soldier, John Cincotti were complaining to each other about the problems that they were having with the Irish American gang. Cincotti said: "They don't have the scruples that we have." Zannino agreed. "You know how I knew they weren't Italiano? When they bombed the fucking house. We don't do that." Sent to prison for loansharking and illegal gambling, Zannino died on February 27, 1996, of natural causes at the Medical Center for Federal Prisoners in Springfield, Missouri.

Zinna Benny an Angiulo enforcer; murdered by the mob.

Zoglio, Louis R: Zoglio was a small time clothes boaster and Patriarca associate. He was murdered in 1967 and dumped in Attleboro Massachusetts. His crime may have been murdering another crook named Angelo DePalma.

IN THEIR OWN WORDS

".....in this thing of ours, your love for your mother and father is one thing, your love for The Family is a different kind of love." **Raymond Patriarca from an FBI bugs placed in Patriarca's office from 1962 to 1965. The bug helped to indicate legislators and judges in both Rhode Island and Massachusetts.**

"(He) doesn't have enough the brains or the power to lead the family. He couldn't lead a Brownie troop." **Rhode Island State Police investigator Junior Patriarca taking over the family.**

"If that job had gone to Angiulo, we would have bodies all over the place." Providence Police Detective on top lieutenant Ilario **"Larry" Zannino throwing his support behind the late mob boss's son, Raymond J. "Junior" Patriarca over Angiulo in 1984 after Raymond Patriarca died.**

"The toughest guy you ever saw." **Massachusetts State cop on Raymond Patriarca**

"No one in the New England mob ever starved, whether they were made guys or working for the organization. Patriarca wasn't like Genovese or old Joe Profaci. He made sure his men got paid well" **Vincent Teresa**

"....in this thing of ours, your love for your mother and father is one thing, your love for The Family is a different kind of love." **Raymond Patriarca overheard on a government tape talking to Nicholas Bianco**

"You two don't have the brains of your retarded sister." **Raymond Patriarca to John and Robert Kennedy during the McClellan committee hearings**

'We're going after that pig on the hill,' **Bobby Kennedy referring to Raymond Patriarca's Federal Hill stronghold in Providence.**

"I met him as a soldier when I met him," **Joe Valachi on Raymond Patriarca. They met in 1938.**

"How do you think I feel? I got three houses, five businesses, five kids, two girlfriends and a wife, and now I'm right there. I'm almost at the top, where I'm set for life." **Bobo Marrapese**

"Bang, bang, bang, bang. There were five or six shots and Callei fell to the floor shaking," I picked up the stool. I was going to hit him [Callei] with it. Bobo said, 'No, I'll have enough of a mess to clean up around here." **William "Billy" Ferle**

"Don't even fuck'n bother"
"Thanks, Bobo,"
"It's Frank"
Conversation between Bobo Marrapese and the state police who wanted answers about past mob murders.

"I learned my lesson. Shame on me if I didn't know after what happened to me in the last 35 years with my best friend (Flemmi). Shame on me if it happens again." **Salemme to U. S. District Court Judge Mark L. Wolf after finding out that his two co-defendants in the case, Flemmi and Bulger, were long-time FBI informants and had used him.**

TESTIMONEY OF FRANK SALEMME OF THE NEW ENGLAND MAFIA

About Frank P. Salemme

Francis P. Salemme [Salemone], also known as "Cadillac Frank" and "Julian Daniel Selig" (born August 18, 1933), is a Boston, Massachusetts mobster who became a hitman and eventually the boss of the Patriarca crime family of New England before turning government witness.

In 1957, while in prison, Salemme became acquainted with Patriarca family mobster Anthony Morelli. After Salemme's release from prison, he started working with Morelli in criminal activities.

Although Salemme quickly gained stature in the Patriarca family as an associate, he could not become a made man, or full member. Patriarca boss Raymond Patriarca respected Salemme for his obedience to the family and his skill as a money maker. However, Patriarca only allowed full-blooded Italians to become made men, and Salemme was part Irish from his mother Anne Salemme (née Haverty).

During the early 1960s, Salemme participated in the Irish Gang Wars in Boston. Testifying before Congress in 2003, Salemme admitted to murdering numerous rival gang members in Charlestown, Massachusetts: "The Hugheses, the McLaughlins, they were all eliminated, and I was a participant in just about all of them, planned them and did them."

In 1968, Salemme arranged a car bombing of John Fitzgerald, a lawyer representing Patriarca mob informant Joseph Barboza. The point of the attack was to scare Barboza into not testifying against Raymond Patriarca and other mob leaders. Fitzgerald survived the attack, but lost his left leg. It was later established in testimony by several witnesses and confirmed by the U.S. House of Representatives Organized Crime unit investigation that Salemme was involved in the bombing, but did not carry it out.

After the unsuccessful attack, Salemme went into hiding. He remained a fugitive until 1972, when he was captured by FBI agent John Connolly on a Manhattan street in New York City. Salemme was convicted and sentenced to prison for 16 years.

In 1986, family boss Jerry Angiulo had been sent to prison on racketeering charges, leaving a power vacuum in the Patriarca family. In previous years, Salemme had forged strong ties to Whitey Bulger and the mostly Irish Winter Hill Gang. Salemme was especially close to Bulger's lieutenant Steve Flemmi (who by this time had been a federal informant for ten years).

In early 1989, soon after his release from prison, Salemme attempted to gain control of the Patriarca family. Patriarca caporegime Joseph Russo opposed Salemme's move, fearing the loss of his lucrative rackets.

In June 1989, Angelo "Sonny" Mercurio, a Russo loyalist, lured Salemme to a meeting outside a Saugus, Massachusetts IHOP. Gunmen then ambushed Salemme, wounding him in the chest and leg.

Mercurio (right), with Raymond Patriarca Jr. (left)

The feud between Salemme and Russo continued until John Gotti, the boss of the New York Gambino crime family, brokered a peace agreement. Under the agreement, Salemme loyalist Nicholas Bianco became boss and Russo became consigliere. By 1991 Salemme, with the support of Bulger and Flemmi, had become the defacto boss of the Patriarca family.

During the 1990s, at the urging of Frank Salemme Jr., Frank Sr. started extorting money from a film crew that wanted to avoid paying high salaries to union workers while filming in Boston and Providence, Rhode Island. As it turned out, the film crew was actually a Federal Bureau of Investigation (FBI) front. These events were highly fictionalized in the 2004 film The Last Shot. At the end of the operation, Frank Sr. was arrested in Fort Lauderdale, Florida and charged with racketeering, crossing state lines for criminal activity, extortion, conspiracy, and loansharking.

In January 1995, Salemme was indicted on racketeering charges along with Bulger and Flemmi. Salemme was convicted and sentenced to 11 years imprisonment. In 1999, while serving his racketeering sentence, Salemme learned that both Bulger and Flemmi were government informants, and that both men had provided information on Salemme to their FBI handlers. Salemme now agreed to provide the government with information on the FBI handling of Bulger and Flemmi. Salemme's testimony would help convict FBI agent Connolly, the same man who had arrested him 20 years earlier in New York.

In 2003, in return for assisting the government, Salemme was released early from prison and brought into the Federal Witness Protection Program. Shortly after his release, Salemme appeared before a Congressional committee to testify on the Connolly case.

In November 2004, Salemme was arrested for perjury during a federal investigation of the 1993 murder of nightclub owner Steve DiSarro. Prosecutors alleged that Frank Salamme Jr., had strangled DiSarro in a Sharon, Massachusetts home and Frank Salemme had helped dispose of the body. However, Frank Jr. had died in 1995 and Frank Sr. denied any involvement in the murder. On July 16, 2008, Salemme pleaded guilty to perjury and obstruction of justice and was sentenced to five years in prison. Since the plea deal gave Salemme credit for four years already served in prison, he was expected to be released in January 2009. As of February 2009, it is assumed that Salemme is out of prison and re-enrolled in the Witness Protection Program.

TESTIMONEY OF FRANK SALEMME
UNITED STATES OF AMERICA HOUSE OF REPRESENTATIVES COMMITTEE ON GOVERNMENT REFORM

Washington, D.C.

Statement of FRANK SALEMME, pursuant to agreement, in the offices of the United States Department of Justice, Pennsylvania Avenue, N.W., Washington, D.C, before Keith Wilkerson, a notary public in and for the District of Columbia, when were present on behalf of the parties:

Francis P. Salemme [Salemone], also known as "Cadillac Frank" and "Julian Daniel Selig" (born August 18, 1933), is a Boston, Massachusetts mobster who became a hitman and eventually the boss of the Patriarca crime family of New England before turning government witness.

Raymond L.S. Patriarca

In 1957, while in prison, Salemme became acquainted with Patriarca family mobster Anthony Morelli. After Salemme's release from prison, he started working with Morelli in criminal activities. Although Salemme quickly gained stature in the Patriarca family as an associate, he could not become a made man, or full member. Patriarca boss Raymond Patriarca respected Salemme for his obedience to the family and his skill as a money maker. However, Patriarca only allowed full-blooded Italians to become made men, and Salemme was part Irish from his mother Anne Salemme (née Haverty).

During the early 1960s, Salemme participated in the Irish Gang Wars in Boston. Testifying before Congress in 2003, Salemme admitted to murdering numerous rival gang members in Charlestown, Massachusetts: "The Hugheses, the McLaughlins, they were all eliminated, and I was a participant in just about all of them, planned them and did them."

Joey Barboza

In 1968, Salemme arranged a car bombing of John Fitzgerald, a lawyer representing Patriarca mob informant Joseph Barboza. The point of the attack was to scare Barboza into not testifying against Raymond Patriarca and other mob leaders. Fitzgerald survived the attack, but lost his left leg. It was later established in testimony by several witnesses and confirmed by the U.S. House of

Representatives Organized Crime unit investigation that Salemme was involved in the bombing, but did not carry it out.

After the unsuccessful attack, Salemme went into hiding. He remained a fugitive until 1972, when he was captured by FBI agent John Connolly on a Manhattan street in New York City. Salemme was convicted and sentenced to prison for 16 years.

In 1986, family boss Jerry Angiulo had been sent to prison on racketeering charges, leaving a power vacuum in the Patriarca family. In previous years, Salemme had forged strong ties to Whitey Bulger and the mostly Irish Winter Hill Gang. Salemme was especially close to Bulger's lieutenant Steve Flemmi (who by this time had been a federal informant for ten years). In early 1989, soon after his release from prison, Salemme attempted to gain control of the Patriarca family. Patriarca caporegime Joseph Russo opposed Salemme's move, fearing the loss of his lucrative rackets. In June 1989, Angelo "Sonny" Mercurio, a Russo loyalist, lured Salemme to a meeting outside a Saugus, Massachusetts IHOP. Gunmen then ambushed Salemme, wounding him in the chest and leg. The feud between Salemme and Russo continued until John Gotti, the boss of the New York Gambino crime family, brokered a peace agreement. Under the agreement, Salemme loyalist Nicholas Bianco became boss and Russo became consigliere. By 1991 Salemme, with the support of Bulger and Flemmi, had become the defacto boss of the Patriarca family.

Nicholas Bianco

During the 1990s, at the urging of Frank Salemme Jr., Frank Sr. started extorting money from a film crew that wanted to avoid paying high salaries to union workers while filming in Boston and Providence, Rhode Island. As it turned out, the film crew was actually a Federal Bureau of Investigation (FBI) front. These events were highly fictionalized in the 2004 film The Last Shot. At the end of the operation, Frank Sr. was arrested in Fort Lauderdale, Florida and charged with racketeering, crossing state lines for criminal activity, extortion, conspiracy, and loansharking.

Bulger

In January 1995, Salemme was indicted on racketeering charges along with Bulger and Flemmi. Salemme was convicted and sentenced to 11 years imprisonment. In 1999, while serving his racketeering sentence, Salemme learned that both Bulger and Flemmi were government informants, and that both men had provided information on Salemme to their FBI handlers. Salemme now agreed to provide the government with information on the FBI handling of Bulger and Flemmi. Salemme's testimony would help convict FBI agent Connolly, the same man who had arrested him 20 years earlier in New York. In 2003, in return for assisting the government, Salemme was released early from prison and brought into the Federal Witness Protection Program. Shortly after his release, Salemme appeared before a Congressional committee to testify on the Connolly case.

In November 2004, Salemme was arrested for perjury during a federal investigation of the 1993 murder of nightclub owner Steve DiSarro. Prosecutors alleged that Frank Salamme Jr., had strangled DiSarro in a Sharon, Massachusetts home and Frank Salemme had helped dispose of the body. However, Frank Jr. had died in 1995 and Frank Sr. denied any involvement in the murder. On July 16, 2008, Salemme pleaded guilty to perjury and obstruction of justice and was sentenced to five years in prison. Since the plea deal gave Salemme credit for four years already served in prison, he was expected to be released in January 2009. As of February 2009, it is assumed that Salemme is out of prison and re-enrolled in the Witness Protection Program.

Salemme

PROCEEDINGS

MR. WILSON: Mr. Salemme, thank you very much for being here. I would like to point out before we start that we have provided Mr. Salemme with a copy of an immunity order that has been immunity signed by Judge Hogan and which is a direct result of a vote of the Committee on Government Reform yesterday to confer immunity on Mr. Salemme. Prior to taking this step, the committee consulted with a number of local jurisdictions, the Suffolk County district attorney, the Middlesex County district attorney, and the Tulsa district attorney, and they informed us that they had no objections to our taking that step. With that said, first, thank you very much, Mr. Salemme. You voluntarily appeared before us a couple of weeks ago to be interviewed, and we really appreciate your taking that step, and we also appreciate the fact that you answered the questions that we asked you. There were some concerns at the time that caused us to move forward and go through the process that conferred immunity on you. I understand there are some concerns that you have with process that brought you here, and I think perhaps at the end of this proceeding it might be entirely appropriate for us to discuss that. Now, as you're aware, the last time we spoke, the first questions I asked you about were concerning John Fitzgerald. And to the extent possible, if you can do what you did before, which was to just provide a narrative account of what happened, that will save me asking a lot of questions and will get the story down on the record as clearly as possible. With that, if you would, just tell us as much as you can about what happened with John Fitzgerald and the bomb that ultimately caused him injury.

John Fitzgerald

MR. SALEMME: Where do I start? In the middle? In the beginning? At the end? John Fitzgerald was representing Joseph Barboza, as we all know. John Fitzgerald was laying both ends against the middle. He was a lawyer, and he was also, as I like to say in the vernacular, a crook. He was running Joe Barboza's loan shark operation for him. They were meeting in Al Farese's office, which was also John Fitzgerald's office in Everett, and they would cut up his money.

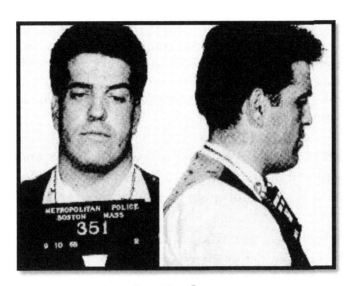

Joe Barboza

John Fitzgerald was, from my understanding, going to be a witness --he was going to write a book with Barboza, but he was going to be a witness against Raymond L.S. Patriarca. So word came from Providence; I was called to eliminate John Fitzgerald. That was agreeable to me, why he had to be eliminated, because he was going to be a witness against Raymond L.S., and I would take care of it my way. I did some preliminary work on Fitzgerald and saw that it would not be that difficult a job. He was kind of a romancer. He had a girlfriend and would spend a lot of time there. And he was a drinker, and he spent a lot of time in certain bars. One in particular was the Irish Ale House out in Dedham, Massachusetts, which was like a very rural type area. Then the second word came from Larry Baione.
Larry came to my club one day, our club, Peter Poulos and myself, and said that Raymond now is going to handle this, they're going to blow him up. Blow him up for what? He wants to make an example. That's when I withdrew. I abandoned it. Flemmi stayed on board with Zannino and Baione and put the thing together.

Within a week, five to seven days or so, Steve got a call at the club, left, and went to Sherman Avenue, to Baione's joint, the Sharma Tavern. He met him, and they went off, and Frankie Balliro and Joe Russo, they went to Everett and put the bomb in the car. They came back to the club, I was still there, and we waited for the news to come on that the bomb had gone off. Basically, simply put, that's what happened. _

NOTE ON THE TEXT: Peter Poulos (Born July 31, 1930) Boston Mass. Poulos was indicted with Stevie Flemmi and Frank Salemme in the Wimpy Bennett murder case because he had witnessed the actual murder in January of 1967. Flemmi and Salemme insisted that Poulos leave the city and head out to Las Vegas to avoid the trial. He did. Several weeks later his body was found in the desert, dead, two bullets in the back of the head.

MR. WILSON: Let's move back and take a few various bits and talk about them. The statement you made about Mr. Fitzgerald being involved in Joe Barboza's loan shark business, how do you know about that?

MR. SALEMME: Well, we knew who he was working with and would get information back from people that they were his crew. I watched them on Saturdays when they went and cut up for Mrs. Baron, and Frank Imbruglia and Al Farese was there, and John Fitzgerald was there. We knew some of the customers, so it was pretty easy to put the thing together, the puzzle together, what they were doing, and Mrs. Baron would be there to pick up her money on Saturday mornings. That's when it was, Saturday mornings. the cut-up of his loan shark business. Plus the automobile that he was driving was Barboza's automobile. It was like a payment type thing to him that he was part of the Barboza's gang, so to speak.

NOTE TO THE TEXT: Frank A. Imbruglia, (East Boston Mass, August 28, 1942- November 14, 2009) was a partner with Robert "Bobby Russo" Carrozza. In June of 1989, someone shot Frank Salemme, wounding him as he left an IHOP in Saugus, Mass. Imbruglia was stopped by police who found the license number of a rental car used in the assassination attempt. Remarkably Imbruglia was not arrested in connection with the shooting.

MR. WILSON: So Barboza had given Fitzgerald the automobile?

MR. SALEMME: Right.

MR. WILSON: You mentioned that Flemmi was involved with Larry Baione. Were you referring to Stevie Flemmi?

MR. SALEMME: Yes.

MR. WILSON: Was Jimmie Flemmi involved at all in this whole endeavor.

MR. SALEMME: No. Jimmie Flemmi had very little to do with us on a personal basis, except he was the instigator in us getting involved in the gang war. He was a loose cannon, Jimmie Flemmi, very similar to Joe Barboza, and I wouldn't have him in my business. We went through that gang war without him knowing (indicating) about what was happening before or even what happened afterwards. As far as I was concerned, he never knew. I don't know if his brother told him, but he never told him before the fact. Obviously I never got caught for it.

MR. WILSON: I just want to point out when Mr. Salemme was saying Jimmie Flemmi didn't know anything, he made a hand signal, and it was a signal for zero, so he was indicating Jimmie Flemmi didn't know anything about the business that Mr. Salemme was involved in at the time. Going back to the purpose or the motive for the bombing, you indicated that it was because Raymond Patriarca wanted to set an example. Can you tell us a little bit more about that, and can you tell us about how you came to that understanding?

MR. SALEMME: Well, like I said, I had been called to Providence and told that this man had to be eliminated because he was going to be a witness in the Barboza case, .

Mr. WILSON: You're referring to the Marfeo murder conspiracy case?

Blaise Marfeo

MR. SALEMME: Right.

MR. WILSON: Did it have any relationship to what was --

MR. SALEMME: Well, I'm not sure now if it was that case, if he was going to be indicted for the case in Boston.

MR. WILSON: That being the Deegan case or the DiSeglio case?

MR. SALEMME: Either/or. He was afraid he was going to get indicted, that John Fitzgerald was going to cooperate with Joe Barboza and suck him into it. He had to be eliminated for that reason, to prevent that from happening.

MR. WILSON: So Joe Barboza appeared to be cooperating with government officials, but obviously in the beginning nobody knew what he was going to say. Tell us what you can about your interactions with Patriarca and other people about what they thought was happening at the time.

MR. SALEMME: Well, right. I don't think they a hundred percent knew who he was going to go after. I don't think the government knew. They were positioning different people to get indicted, but Raymond Patriarca wanted to eliminate the possibility of him getting indicted. That was the key to it for his mind. What happened in Boston happened in Boston as as DiSeglio goes or Deegan. I don't think he had any notions about it. I don't know, but I know he anticipated him to be a witness, a potential witness against him.

MR. WILSON: There's one story I've been told that indicates that you and Stevie Flemmi went into a garage in Somerville -- and I'm not talking about the testimony at Flemmi went into a garage in Somerville, asked if you could get into a garage because you had some work to do on a car, that you got into this garage, and that you and Stevie ing with blasting caps, trying to figure out essentially how to wire explosives to a car. Is there any truth to that story?

MR. SALEMME: Absolutely not. I think I know where it came from. What year was that? Does it say?

MR. WILSON: Well, this was just before the time that Fitzgerald ultimately was injured in the bombing.

MR. SALEMME: Well, I had body shops, so I don't know why I would go to Somerville, Massachusetts and go into a body shop to practice, number one. Number two, there's nothing to practice on. It's a very simple thing, a blasting cap. I mean, I'm a licensed electrician, journeyman and master's, so I don't think I'd have to practice on any blasting caps, and I certainly wouldn't have to go to a garage in Somerville. To me that was like the suburbs even though they're right next to each other, Boston and Somerville.

MR. DURHAM: You say you had garages. Explain what kind of garages you had and what kind of access you had to vehicles.

MR. SALEMME: I owned them. Central Auto Body and Intercity Motors. One was on Dudley Street and one was on Massachusetts Avenue, both in Boston, the Roxbury section of Boston.

MR. WILSON: Since we're on the subject of blasting caps, and this is a little bit out of order right now, but there's one indication that a state prosecutor from Massachusetts spent time with a witness who testified against you and who took him and showed him blasting caps and explained what they were so as to better permit him to testify in court. Do you know anything about that subject?

MR. SALEMME: No. Obviously I wouldn't know about it until I heard it from the witness, but it doesn't surprise me. My question on that would be why would he have to shoot him blasting caps if this witness starts testing blasting caps in some garage. Wouldn't he have seen them already? That's a common sense point. I mean, there would be no need to taking him and saying this is what you saw.

MR. WILSON: You gave us the names of people who were involved in this Fitzgerald matter. Robert Daddeico, what was his role, if any, in what happened with the Fitzgerald bombing?

MR. SALEMME: Absolutely none. Robert Daddeico had absolutely nothing to do with it. He had nothing to do with that whatsoever. I think he gave testimony that he witnessed or overheard a conversation in Somerville at a bar, a lounge, between a number of people. Winters and McDonald, myself, Flemmi, a bunch of people, that this was going to take place. That was his grand jury testimony, which he rescinded and said it didn't happen afterwards, as you know. But we were the only two to get indicted. The other ones at this so-called meeting never got indicted. That's strange, isn't it? Now, the garage that you're referring to, I believe, is the garage on Marshall Street. That's the garage that he hung around at, and my partner was over there periodically trying to get them started. That was the initial garage that Winters and that Somerville crew started on, and my partner had been in the business years by then, and he was putting it together for them. That was the relationship. George was supposed to be at that meeting, too. They never got indicted, and I'm glad they never did, but it seems strange that nobody else did. And just to back up a little bit, I had practiced or looked at different starters and neutrals and all the rest of it as potential weapons against the Irish gang, and if anybody's Irish here I apologize, but the Irish gang that we were fighting, which was the McLaughlin group. So in my garages in Roxbury I had done that, you know, and I had done remotes. I would tend to be partial toward a remote with a backup and check, but that wasn't a good policy. I had numerous opportunities to eliminate the McLaughlins and the Hugheses, especially Stevie Hughes, he was the most dangerous one of the Hugheses, but I wouldn't do it. Most of the time it was in downtown Boston or it was in an urban area. Boston's a very compact city. It wasn't a necessary tool of elimination. It could be done other ways with a little bit of work. That's the point I'm making.

MR. DURHAM: In fact, you had indicated to Mr. Wilson and others prior to the meeting that with respect to some of these meetings that they were eliminated using other means.

MR. SALEMME: Absolutely. I mean, the Hugheses, the McLaughlins, they were all eliminated, and I was a participant in just about all of them, planned them and did them.

MR. WILSON: When you talked to Patriarca, my assumption, but I'll ask you directly, when the decision was made to make an example of Fitzgerald, that came directly from Raymond Patriarca?

MR. SALEMME: From Raymond, yes.

MR. WILSON: Were there any other steps that he was prepared to take to attempt to ensure that he ultimately didn't get prosecuted for anything that Joe Barboza was prepared to say?

MR. SALEMME: Off the top of my head, no. Off the top of my head, not directly from him, no. Off the top of my head, I can't think of anything.

MR. WILSON: It was just a question that arose from what you were saying. I'm not trying to trick you. I don't know of anything myself.

MR. SALEMME: We had numerous conversations, especially about the gang war, who was going to get eliminated and who wasn't. I was trying to keep him abreast of what happened. Stevie Hughes got killed, and he was a dangerous guy, Stevie Hughes, but he ran with a guy named Samuel Linden. Samuel Linden did tickets all over New England, treasury tickets, which was a big source of income, and my initial feeling was not to make a move on Stevie Hughes while he was with Sammy Linden, because Sammy Linden was with Raymond, and I'd just get Raymond to tell this guy to back off. He used to use Stevie Hughes, Linden did, for his muscle, picking up this money. It would be a large amount of money that he'd be picking up. He warned him once, warned him twice, and I went back and said he's still with him, and he said well, that's it, take him out, and that's what happened. He was taken out.

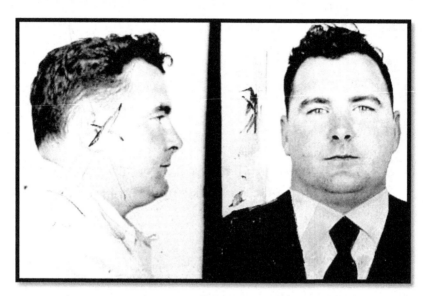

Stevie Hughes (Above and below)

Connie Hughes, another Winter Hill hood who was also murdered

MR. DURHAM: Stevie Hughes and Linden were killed in the same event? ...

MR. SALEMME: Right.

MR. WILSON: Let's move forward a little bit, fast forward a while. At some point there's an indictment that's going to come down, and you're going to be involved in this indictment. Did you get advance warning about the indictment, and if so, how did you get the warning?

MR. DURHAM: You've asked about the Fitzgerald bombing, but there's also a murder that was involved there involving Edward Wimpy Bennett that had also occurred prior to the time you're talking about.

Edward Wimpy Bennett

George and Edward McLaughlin guessed that Wimpy Bennett had helped in setting up the failed murder attempt of Edward McLaughlin. James O'Toole and (allegedly) Francis X. Murray, who worked for the McLaughlin's, tried to shoot Edward Bennett, the criminal mentor of Stephen Flemmi and Vincent Flemmi. Bennett had stepped out the front door of his home and O'Toole shot at him from where he hid in the bushes nearby. Bennett quickly drew his revolver and returned fire and fled from the home. O'Toole's accomplice had been waiting nearby with the car idling but panicked and deserted O'Toole after he realized that Bennett had not been murdered. Francis X. Murray, (1929)essentially disappeared, by his own design, shortly afterwards

MR. WILSON: I was going to inquire about that, but he may as well bring it up right now. If you can give us some information about the Edward Bennett murder, that would be helpful.

MR. SALEMME : Well, Stevie had a business going with Wimpy Bennett and Peter Poulos, and there was a confrontation in my garage one day in the office between Stevie Flemmi and Peter Poulos about his money. He wasn't getting any money from the numbers business. He pulled a pistol out and put it to Peter Poulos ' s head, and Peter Poulos was a real nonviolent guy. He handled the books on Stevie ' s numbers, and he did the books on my football card business, a pretty smart guy with numbers, and he'd take the time and the patience to do it. He claimed that he gave the money to Wimpy to give to him. I could tell he was telling the truth, and I stepped in between Steve and Peter Poulos and told him you can't eliminate this guy, he's telling you the truth, get Wimpy up here with him and we'll decide who's telling the truth, then you can decide. It's your business, really, not mine, except that he was my friend and my partner, but I wasn't in that business. He was my friend and partner in other things, but not that numbers business. So we got Wimpy up there either that; night or the next night at six o'clock. There was a meeting with everyone there. And the next thing you know, Peter put it right on him, I gave the money to you, you did it before. Bennett couldn't even out and shot him in the head. _ ,

REDACTED

But there's two things with Flemmi paramount to everything, his money and his women. He was a womanizer, and you know what happened with this case, what took place with this stepdaughter and the other little girl, Debbie Davis. But that was his MO all along. That's what it was to him, his money and his women, not necessarily in that order.

MR. WILSON: If we could just step back for a minute to the indictment and what happened as far as the indictment for -- well, I guess I shouldn't step out of order cause here's the William Bennett situation first. If you could give us a sense of what happened with the William Bennett murder.

MR. SALEMME: Well, that's number three now. You've got Walter in the middle.

MR. WILSON: Then we may as well move to Walter. I was probably going to skip over Walter.

MR. SALEMME: Walter was naturally upset because his brother's missing. The word got out that Stevie Flemmi did it for the Italians, for lack of a better -- the guineas is what he said. And he kept - -

MR. WILSON: I didn't fully understand that. The word got out that Stevie Flemmi did it on behalf of Italian interests?

Flemmi

MR. SALEMME: Walter Bennett was partners with Petey Baione, who was Larry's brother. When Larry went to jail, Walter ended up screwing Petey for a large amount of money. So Walter always had that in the back of his mind, that the Italians eventually make a move on his brother. And so when that happened he naturally blamed, not owing the circumstances of what happened, he r blamed the Italian element, But Stevie, because of his relationship with Larry, and even though I had a friendly relationship with Larry, I had more of a friendly relationship with Raymond L.S., but Stevie was more with Larry and them at that time. But anyway, we lured Walter to the garage to a meeting with me at six o'clock one night. Peter Poulos drove him to the garage, and I had a big door that you press a button to open, it was a huge garage, and he drove in and walked up the stairs to the office. Stevie was waiting at the end of the stairs, shot him, and he took him out to the car and carried him. He was seeing me to elicit myself and to see if I could be the one that would help him take Stevie out.

MR. WILSON: That takes us to William Bennett. What happened there?

MR. SALEMME: The same thing. He's now concerned that both his brothers are missing, but he's not blaming Stevie, he's blaming Stevie and Frank.

MR. WILSON: Stevie, and Frank being you?

MR. SALEMME: Me, right. So he elicits help from Sonny Shields and Richard Grasso, and they're going to make a move on Steve, on me and Steve, both of us or one moves. So Grasso met with Steve Flemmi. Shields and Grasso met with Steve Flemmi and put this plan together to take him out one night, bang him, and then we would pick him up, take him and put him with his brothers. So that's what happened, except that he fell out of the car. When they shot him, he hit the door, the car door opened, and he fell out in the middle of the street, and a taxi driver came out and there wasn't a chance to pick him up.

NOTE ON THE TEXT: Flemmi was later accused of murdering Grasso in 1967 and stuffing his dead body in the trunk of a car.

MR. WILSON: Who was in the car at the times you shot him?

MR. SALEMME: Grasso and Shields.

MR. WILSON: So it was Grasso, Shields and William Bennett in the car at the same time?

MR. SALEMME: Right.

MR. WILSON: And he was shot how, by somebody outside the car?

MR. SALEMME: No, inside. Sonny Shields shot him.

NOTE ON THE TEXT: Hugh Sidney Shields AKA Sonny Shields (Feburary 21, 1937) Was charged with murdering Billy Bennett but was never convicted. In 1973, Whitey Bulger shot him with a machine gun, but Shields, remarkably, survived and fled the city. He returned in 1975 and claimed that the FBI over a contract to murder the Angiulo Brothers.

MR. DURHAM: His body was recovered. Right?

MR. SALEMME: His body was recovered.

MR. DURHAM: But the bodies of Walter and Edward Wimpy Bennett weren't recovered

MR. SALEMME: No

MR. DURHAM: That sort of all occurred before Mr. Salemme became a fugitive. ?

MR. WILSON: So the indictment is going to come down. Tell us what you can about what you knew in advance of the indictment, if anything.

MR. YEAGER: Which indictment are you talking about?

MR. WILSON: There's an indictment from the Fitzgerald bombing and the William Bennett murder

MR. SALEMME: I think the William Bennett murder is first, and the Fitzgerald bombing comes second, I think.

MR. WILSON: I don't know what you knew at the time, and to be honest, I don't remember which occurred chronologically first, but what was the first indication that you had that there might be some legal consequence to either of those
events?

MR. SALEMME: I get a call from Steve Flemmi one morning, I don't know, five, six o'clock in the morning. He didn't live too far from me. I was in Sharon, Massachusetts, and he was in Milton. He said come by and pick him up, it's something very important. I knew it had to be something important, and I got in the car and drove fast and
picked him up in Milton. He said we have to go see Paul Rico in Revere Beach. I said what's up, and he said Paul said there's going to be indictments and he'd

explain it to us when he seen us. We didn't get into it too much. They had a signal which I never knew until it came out in the hearings, Jack from south Boston or whatever it was, so it didn't make any difference what was said on the phone anyway. But we went to Revere and met Paul Rico.

Paul Rico

Now, he was with an agent, not Dennis Condon, and he pulled up not too far from us, and the other agent got out of car. Now, I backed up and drove out because I didn't want this other agent to be around. I said well, what's up with this.

MR. WILSON: Why didn't you want the other agent....

MR. SALEMME : Because I didn't know him. I figured if Dennis was there -- Dennis always knew enough to keep a little distance anyway so they ' weren't like elbow to elbow. That's the way you wanted it, you know. But he came up and explained
to us what was happening. "

Rico

MR. WILSON: He, being Paul Rico?

MR. SALEMME: Paul Rico, that there was going to be an indictment, that we should get out of town for a while, and that this guy is – how serious is it, that was what my question was. I'm pretty sure that he said it was about the Bennett murder and that they're looking at Fitzgerald, but I think the Bennett murder came down first. He
knows Joe Barboza, that was his statement, but that was enough to get us out of town for a while.

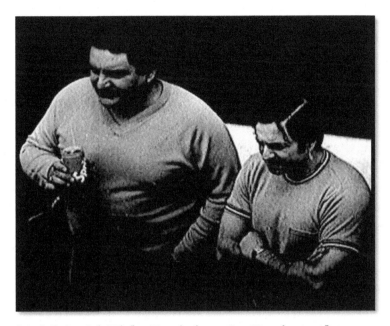

Flemmi (Right) with Nicky Femia in 1980. Femia was later murdered

MR. WILSON: You said something that surprises me a little bit, and that's that you went with Stevie Flemmi to talk to Paul Rico. Why did Paul Rico want you there? '

MR. SALEMME: Well, I was a concerned party

MR. WILSON: Well, I understand why he wanted to communicate, but why were you enough in his confidence that he would tell you this? I understand the historical record is such that Rico had a relationship with Stephen Flemmi, but you're there and he's telling you and Stephen Flemmi about the indictment . Why would he have been comfortable enough to tell you this?

MR. SALEMME: Well, we had a history up to that point. He used to come to the garage and the real estate office, mostly the garage, probably three times a week, mostly him and Dennis during the gang war.

MR. WILSON: Dennis being Dennis Condon?

MR. SALEMME: Dennis Condon. Paul Rico was very concerned about the McLaughlins and that crew. He had an ongoing feud with the Hugheses and the McLaughlins.

MR. WILSON: Why did Paul Rico by your characterization have animosity to the McLaughlin side of the gang war?

MR. SALEMME: Well, they were always on the phone, according to him, and they would – and the feds would pick up the McLaughlins and the Hugheses casting aspersions on Paul's manhood and his relationship with J. Edgar Hoover, and J. Edgar
Hoover was, excuse me again, a fag, and that Paul used to go down there and have a relationship with Colson. They had a ménage a trios with a guy by the name of Colson, I think.

MR. WILSON: I believe the name was Tolson.

MR. SALEMME: So Paul didn't naturally like that, but he was always on their case, Paul was. Paul had a relationship with Buddy McLean. I say to this day, knowing what I think now but not then, that Buddy McLean was actually an informant for them. That's what I saw, that you can only have a relationship with Paul if you give any information. The quid pro quo was I was performing a deed that nobody else had performed, to get rid of his arch enemies. He knew that I could do it. That's why he sent me information about them. He gave me addresses.

Buddy McLean

MR. WILSON: So this is Paul Rico giving you addresses and information about people who are tied in with McLaughlin and the McLaughlin gang?

MR. SALEMME: One address in particular led to McLaughlin's demise, which was Helen Kronis. That was Edward Punchy McLaughlin's girlfriend, his common law girlfriend or wife. They lived in Canton, but I could never find out where, off of E
Street, as it turned out, but he gave me the address and I was able to find him. We killed him at eight o'clock in the morning at a bus stop there, but that was a very, very important piece of information.

MR. DURHAM: Who killed Punchy McLaughlin?

MR. SALEMME: Stevie Flemmi and myself.

MR. DURHAM: Are you familiar with the background of McLaughlin actually being killed, that there had been two prior attempts?

MR. WILSON: While we're there, if you would, just sort of go through that situation.
Where I want to ultimately get to is why Paul Rico would give you this information, what more you know about this information you're saying Rico gave you. If you could just maybe back up about the other attempts.

MR. SALEMME: I had met Paul in Somerville with Buddy McLean. Stevie was also there, and Howie Winters wasn't there. Buddy McLean never had a real --he liked Howie as being somebody around, but he didn't have confidence in Howie. Howie was basically a bookmaker until they tried to put the bomb in his car and it went off, the McLaughlins did. Buddy's a good kid, you'd like him, and I had known Buddy just as kids at sporting events and all that stuff. But looking at it in retrospect, I would have to say that Buddy was probably giving him information, but maybe not. Maybe he was doing the same thing. I mean, Paul hit on me. He tried to make an informant out of me, and I think there's a or a or something to that effect when he asked me to lunch -- and if I'm getting too far ahead, stop me - - and I went to lunch with him. Before I did, I went to Raymond L.S. and told him I'd been invited. Raymond L.S. knew I had a relationship with this guy, because I was bringing him information about various things that were happening, for instance the prosecution with Limone, whether they were going to present ' evidence, that is, Limone ' s defense team, that Limone never met Patriarca. Well, they had a picture this big that Paul Rico gave them. You have a photograph of Limone and a few other guys meeting with Raymond L.S. on Ash Street by the New England health clinic where his first wife Helen was dying. They would have got shot out of the water with that bit of defense, that type of thing.
Anyway, I went to see Raymond and told him I was going to lunch with Paul Rico, and so he said go, by all means, be a good listener, but remember, he's a -- and he used a part of male anatomy, he's a P, be careful of him, just be careful. Unbeknownst to me, it's on tape. I got it in one of the papers, a or a . But anyway, I gave -- you wanted to know what his relationship, why he would ....

MR. WILSON: Just develop as much as you can why Rico would give this information to you. He gave the information to Stevie Flemmi because Stevie Flemmi was an informant, but it's a little surprising that he included you in this conversation.

MR. SALEMME: Well, he knew that I was Stevie's friend. He knew that I was a capable person as far as getting a job done, and this was a job he wanted done, there's no question about that. Plus, I had done little things for Paul, like I got his FBI car fixed, which was certainly not enough to warrant him giving me that kind of information.
That wasn't the quid pro quo, fixing his car and giving him the information. The information was to eliminate these people.

MR. WILSON: We'll talk about the cars in a little bit. As far as you're able to come to a
conclusion, the reason that Rico gave you the address for Punchy McLaughlin was for you to go after Punchy McLaughlin and kill him?

MR. SALEMME: There were two attempts earlier that were unsuccessful, two attempts that I did not want to sanction, but I went ahead and participated in them anyway. After the second one, when he was ambushed and he lost his hand, the first one, he lost his jaw, and that was in the Beth Israel parking lot. Not a good spot at all. The bus stop was much better, boom, boom, and out. But Beth Israel, you had to drive in, they had security, not a good spot, so you couldn't really finish off what you started. We had dressed as rabbis.

MR. DURHAM: That was the first one. The first time you tried to kill him, you and Stevie Flemmi tried to kill him at Beth Israel hospital dressed as rabbis, shot him, took out his jaw.

MR. SALEMME: He was set up by a fellow named Earl Smith.

MR. DURHAM: And there was a second attempt to kill him at a Rotary.

MR. SALEMME: Right.

MR. DURHAM: In that one he lost his hand, but there was some other collateral damage to houses and stuff.

MR. SALEMME: There were ricochets. It was a rural area, but there was still houses around, and those high powered weapons, they hit and they ricochet and they travel. There was some collateral damage, as John said, to houses around. So I had a conversation with Paul about it afterwards. He said boy, that was a sloppy piece of work.

MR. WILSON: So you had a conversation with Paul Rico about that second attempt to kill McLaughlin?

MR. SALEMME: Right.

MR. WILSON: To the extent you can remember, and I know it's a long time ago, what did you tell him and what did he say to you?

MR. SALEMME: See, Paul had a way. Paul was a very shrewd individual. He'd make it like, he'd have the papers and say boy, what a sloppy piece of work that was, other people could have got hurt . There were a lot of other words and a lot of other conversation in with that, but the bottom line is Paul, I don't have his address, he's a tough guy to pin down, but I don't know where his starting point is.

MR. WILSON: So you told Rico you didn't know where he was?

MR. SALEMME: Right. Within a day or two days he came back, and he'd just be patting your shoulder like he usually does, and he hit my hand, I went like this, he kept walking, and there was a piece of paper with an address, and I didn't have to ask anymore. I knew who it was. It was Helen Kronis, Punchy 's girlfriend or common law wife or whatever. So I went out and started to work on that, and I put the finishing touches on that within three or four days.

MR. WILSON: So when you saw the address. you knew what the address went to? You knew what that address was basically?

MR. SALEMME: Well, it took me like that to figure it out. I saw the name Helen, and I
didn't know the last name, but I knew his girlfriend's name was Helen.

MR. WILSON: Was the name on the address?

MR. SALEMME: Yes.

MR. DURHAM: You might want to also explain for the record, you and Stevie Flemmi made all three attempts, the last one of which was successful. Describe, generally speaking, what your role was in these matters and what Stevie's role was, like who planned these things and how were they executed.

MR. SALEMME: I planned them. Stevie wasn't a planner. He would go if you took him by the hand, but he wasn't a planner at all. He had his own agenda, and he wasn't deviating from that. Money and women, I told you, he wasn't going to deviate from that. He had somebody to do the grunt work, and that was me, so I planned them and executed them, him and I.

MR. DURHAM: And similar to the Fitzgerald car bombing, generally speaking, when
you were doing these sorts of things, how many people knew what you were doing?

MR. SALEMME: What I was doing?

MR. DURHAM: What you were doing.

MR. SALEMME: Nobody except Stevie and Raymond L.S. as far as the initial way I wanted to take them out. As far as the other thing went, when it got into the bombing stuff, I wouldn't do it to save my life. During the gang war I certainly wasn't going to do it to eliminate a witness, not when you could do it a simple way.

MR. DURHAM: With respect to the Fitzgerald situation, you didn't have any qualms
about taking Fitzgerald out, you just didn't want to do the bombing.

MR. SALEMME: I didn't want to do the bombing. I don't know what the legal term would be. I was going to do it that way, you know, just take them out. I could take them out very easily with a silencer, pick them up and bury them and they'd never be found. That was the way to do it from my looking at it. A bomb, no matter where it was going to be, whether in Everett, in Al Farese's office or wherever, that was not my MO at all, not that violence wasn't. I mean, I was involved in violence, but I'm not that type. That's the point I'm making. You could do it another way. '

MR. WILSON: I think you said this before, but when the bomb ultimately went off, you didn't know it was going off at that time and you didn't know where it was going to go off. Is that correct?

MR. SALEMME: That's correct. That's correct. When Stevie got the call at the club to
go meet Larry, he didn't stop and tell me that the car's over here or the car's there, we're going to get it.

MR. WILSON: There are a couple of ways to go right now. I think what we might do is just talk a little bit about Deegan, but I do want to go with the chronology. I don't know which makes more sense. You might tell me. Chronologically should we talk about what happened when you left Boston, to my understanding, with Stephen Flemmi and Peter
Poulos, or is it better to go to Deegan? Which makes more sense chronologically at this point?

MR. SALEMME: Well, you could clean up Poulos kind of quick. We're ahead of Deegan now anyway.

MR. WILSON: So let's just go with that. You're at Revere Beach with Stephen Flemmi and Paul Rico.

MR. SALEMME: Right, and this other FBI agent.

MR. WILSON: What did he look like?

MR. SALEMME: He was young.

MR. WILSON: Tall guy? Short guy?

MR. SALEMME: Medium height, slender, athletically built, younger guy. He finally
decided to stay, and he did get out of the car and just stood there by his door. He didn't even walk around to the driver's side. Paul understood. You know, when I pulled out and then he pulled back in, he understood to have the kid stay there and not
try to walk out with him.

MR. WILSON: So Rico told you what he told you, and I think you told us everything you know about that. Was it a long meeting, a short meeting?

MR. SALEMME: minutes, just to get out of town and play it by ear, he's no Joe Barboza. I'm trying to remember his words. How serious was it was one of my questions, you know, and he explained what it was. I'm almost positive he said something about the Bennett murder.

MR. WILSON: I didn't understand what you said before, and you said it a second time and I still don't understand it fully. When you said that Paul Rico said he's no Joe Barboza, explain what you mean by that .

MR. SALEMME: That he doesn't have the potential that Joe Barboza had to involve all these other people into it, that he won't make the type of witness that Joe Barboza made. In retrospect, I know that he was after getting all these documents that he nurtured Barboza, him and Condon, that this is what was in his own Machiavellian mind, so to
speak, that he couldn't be any Joe Barboza. That's the type of fellow he was. In my opinion now, he had that kind of a mind, devious and Machiavellian and very smooth, very suave, just to go along with it. That's what I felt he meant.

MR. WILSON: So Rico, from what you said, it sounds like he clearly communicated to you that there was a witness out there that was going to testify against you.

MR. SALEMME: Against us.

MR. WILSON: Well, you and Stephen Flemmi.

MR. SALEMME: Right.

MR. WILSON: Did he say who that witness was?

MR. SALEMME: Daddeico. We knew Daddeico got arrested and went back on a parole violation to Walpole. He was taken out of Walpole, and we knew that, because people in Walpole sent word out to Howie and Howie got word to us that they took Daddeico out of there, we don't know what's up with him.

NOTE ON THE TEXT: Daddeico later entered the federal witness protection program

MR. DURHAM: Howie being Howie Winters?

MR. SALEMME: Yes.

MR. WILSON: Did you have a suspicion that something was going on? .

MR. SALEMME: That's why people were sending word out, and they didn't indicate against who it was happening, but that he was doing something. He had been arrested for a bank robbery in Somerville with a bunch of Canadian kids that came down from Canada robbing banks all over the northeast. They moved out to Michigan, out that area too, but they had been very successful, Mcintosh. One of them was Eddie Johnson's, the goal tender for the Bruins, the old goal tender for the Bruins, Eddie Johnson, it was his brother, Billy Johnson. Daddeico was supposed to be a backup for them so they could get out of the bank. But what happened was during the robbery this bank security guard with a gun disarmed Daddeico and had him on the floor and these guys all got arrested. So now when he goes back up to Walpole and they're up there pinched too, now they've got that much against him, and he knows he's got to be looking at them and they're looking at him to see what kind of a backup were you, and now people are looking at him up there. And he decides well, there's only one thing for me to do and this is the way I'll go with it, and they took him out, as it turned out. We didn't know that at the time. But that's why he was back on a parole violation, for this bank robbery.

MR. DURHAM: Did Daddeico have anything to do with the Bennett murder? You might just want to explain that for the record also.

MR. SALEMME: We had two cars. Daddeico shows up with Steve Flemmi in one car, and I come up in my car. I had already made the plans with Flemmi that I'll pick the body up out of the car and take them out and bury them. I wouldn't leave that to anybody else. I don't want anybody else knowing where these spots are and who goes. But I pull up, and there's Flemmi sitting with Daddeico. That didn't surprise me. I said I'm taking the body, so it won't matter. The next thing I know these two clowns come down and they're all in a panic, he fell out. What do you mean, he fell out. We're at some kind of a charcoal meat stand down there in Boston, and they said he fell out, he's lying on the side of the road, so I shoot up the street. And I swung around to pick him up and put him in the car, and there's a cab driver that pulls up, he's put the high beams on, and now I can't - even stop, so I made a U-turn and drove by it and kept stepping. Bud I could see that he was gone, that they were going to find him.

MR. WILSON: So you're at Revere Beach and Paul Rico has told you Daddeico 's going to testify. Is that correct?

MR. SALEMME: Right.

MR. WILSON: And he tells you to get out of town?

MR. SALEMME: Right.

MR. WILSON: Does he tell you anything else at this time? '

MR. SALEMME: I'm sure there was conversation, but I can't remember just what --
again, in retrospect, he didn't have to say too much to make me go. But also, as far as communications go, we know what happened with him and Steve from

south Boston. They had their way of communicating, and I had no way of knowing that at that time .

MR. WILSON: If you can walk us through what happened next with your departure from the Boston area.

MR. SALEMME: Well, we drove to Illinois, to Chicago.

MR. WILSON: Let me back you up here. It's my understanding you left with Stephen Flemmi and Peter Poulos and got a car from Peter Poulos . Is that correct?

MR. SALEMME: I don't know if we got the car from him or my garage. I'm not sure. I think it was a Cadillac we left in, so it might have been from the garage. We had access to plates. At that time we had direct access to the registry of motor vehicles. We could go anywhere in the city and get identification, get plates, talk to jurors after hours at night in the court, anything. We had that kind of access in the city of Boston. But we drove to Chicago, and then we flew to Los Angeles from Chicago. Now, they were going to stay out there, but I didn't think it was a good idea for us to stay together. I don't know how long I stayed there. I don't even think I left the airport. But I flew back to New York, and I hooked up with a fellow by the name of William Candelmo, who was a king man with Raymond Patriarca, with our New England group, and I stayed there. Steve stayed in LA and eventually drove back with Poulos, and he eliminated Poulos in Las Vegas, in Clark County. Now, we got some kind of papers or information from Los Angeles while we were down in Plymouth that prints of Poulos and Flemmi were , found in some rooming house or some house in Los Angeles. And when they found the body in Las Vegas they put out an arrest warrant for him and I. And he ends up in New York, Steve Flemmi. He goes to Billy Candelmo 's store. There were different places that we had around so in case of emergencies you can go to these people. I knew Billy. Stevie knew him, but I knew him better than he did. We stayed in Billy's apartment on th Avenue and th Street. The Man from La Mancha was playing right across the street. I used to look out and watch the lines. That's the year it was. But I got into a conversation, why did you do that to Pete Poulos, there was no plan to eliminate Poulos. He would have been a threat, you know, he witnessed the murder. Wimpy 's murder, he drove Walter there, he would have been a threat. And I said -- I don't even think Peter Poulos got indicted. To the best of my knowledge, he never got indicted for either one, the car bombing or the Billy Bennett murder. We didn't know he wasn't getting indicted, and that's why he came. But to eliminate him like that, Steve, you know, come on, oh, it had to be done, he would have been a weak link, they would have made a witness out of him. That's what happened to him.

MR. WILSON: Just to back up for a second, you've come back to New York, Poulos and Stephen Flemmi are still out in Los Angeles, and then at some point after that Stephen Flemmi comes to New York. Is that correct?

MR. SALEMME: Right, by way of Las Vegas.

MR. WILSON: Let's leave that out, because you don't know that's happening at that point. But you see Stephen Flemmi, you come to this place in New York, and what does he tell you? When did you first learn that Poulos had been killed?

MR. SALEMME: It was on the news. It came on the news.

MR. WILSON: So you learned about it from the news before talking to Stephen Flemmi?

MR. SALEMME: Right. Billy Candelmo found out because he used to go back and forth to Providence just to talk to Raymond, to talk to JP, Raymond's brother, when Raymond was back in ACI in Rhode Island. Joe Patriarca would go see him and talk to Billy and see what was happening, keeping abreast of things, so he learned that Peter Poulos got killed. He used to get the Boston newspaper. Billy would go down to Times Square and get the paper at some out-of-town newspaper stand.

MR. WILSON: At that point did you know where Stephen Flemmi was? You said you knew that Poulos was dead from the newspapers.

MR. SALEMME: When I found out about Poulos, no, but I knew he was there. I mean, I knew Poulos was with him, so it was just a simple deduction to figure out what happened. When I saw it --

MR. WILSON: So when is the next time you saw Flemmi?

MR. SALEMME: When he came to New York.

MR. WILSON: And did he tell you what happened?

MR. SALEMME: Yes, that he would have been a weak link, that he had to do it.

REDACTED

I said what are you going to Las Vegas for, and he said, I had an apartment set up and I wanted to stop over somewhere before I continued the drive in.

REDACTED

That would be his way of operating. He wouldn't do that in front of her, but he'd want to solidify his safety, to travel with a woman and not be traveling alone. He got stopped, too, he said, by a Las Vegas state trooper and he had all kinds of material in the trunk. I said, what do you mean. He said he had a shovel and a rope and all that shit in there. He had a gun under the seat. They didn't hold him, but they did stop him. I don't know if there's any record of that, but they stopped him, him and Poulos, but he couldn't put him under. He said the desert's not soft. I said, what were you thinking, it's the Sahara? I said this is Nevada, this isn't north Africa.

MR. DURHAM: Well, you said he wasn't a planner.

MR. SALEMME: Definitely not a planner, no. The word to describe Steve Flemmi was a spontaneous reactor. If you messed with either one and two or two and one, forget it.

MR- WILSON: Now I'd like to step back to Deegan.

(Discussion off the record.)

MR. WILSON: Let's Start a new subject. We're going to get back to the chronology we were just discussing in a minute, but let's discuss the murder of Teddy Deegan. I'm going to try and not cover things that we covered completely in our last interview, but I'll ask a few preliminary questions. Did you know anything about the proposal
to murder Deegan before the actual event happened?

MR. SALEMME: Before the fact?

MR. WILSON: Correct.

MR. SALEMME: No

MR. WILSON: It would probably just be best if you give us a chronology of what you knew about the Deegan murder, when you knew it, and move to sort of when you first heard about the Deegan murder and move chronologically forward in time.

MR. SALEMME: I first heard about the murder from James Vincent Flemmi. Steve and I knew about it from the newspaper, but down at the garage we didn't know what happened with Teddy Deegan. Teddy Deegan was kind of friendly with Steve and had done a few scores before with Steve. I think we went over that before, you know, about rappelling to get in houses. Stephen got a call at the garage from his brother, he was down at the real estate office, and he said take a ride down to the real estate office. The market and the real estate office were right next to each other. So if I say the market or the real estate office, it's the same thing. It's one building with upstairs rooms to it.

MR. WILSON: It's my understanding that Stephen Flemmi owned that premises.

MR. SALEMME : Right, that whole premises, with the rooms he rented out at the top. We took a ride down, it was a short drive, not more than a hundred yards, and his brother told him what had happened, that they had killed Teddy Deegan. And the whole conversation, there's a lot to it, but just to get to the pertinent parts about what did you kill him for, why did Teddy have to go, well, he was helping the McLaughlins, bullshit, Steve said, that wasn't true.

MR. YEAGER : You were present during this conversation?

MR. SALEMME: Yes. He made out that he had to go because he was helping the McLaughlins. We knew he wasn't helping the McLaughlins. Vincent Flemmi had to make up an excuse. I told you we never had anything to do with him or never let him know what was happening. He never knew his brother was burglarizing bookmakers' homes with this guy. So he made up an excuse that he was killed because he was helping the McLaughlins, but we knew it wasn't true. So Steve kept pushing him and pushing him, who was there, who was there, and he told him who was there, who was in the car. And Stathopoulos, they were supposed to kill him, too, but he got away. Vincent Flemmi was more concerned about Stathopoulos getting away, that eventually he would be a problem if he opened up. That's my interpretation, because he said it, you know, but also it would make sense.

MR. WILSON: Let's just stop for a second. He said that he killed Deegan, and he said
that he did it because of what appears to be a gang war motive.

MR. SALEMME: Right. At that time it was hot and heavy in the gang war, so he was helping that side, which wasn't true.

MR. WILSON: Who did he say was involved?

MR. SALEMME: He never made himself as the shooter, but there was him, Joe Barboza, Ronnie Cassesso, Roy French, Romeo Martin. Is that five?

MR. WILSON: I think you mentioned before another name, Imbruglia, the last time.

MR. SALEMME: He wasn't there. Imbruglia was part of the pickup crew. Imbruglia wasn't a shooter or that type of a guy, but he knew the area, where they would pick up Joe Barboza 's shylock money, Revere, Chelsea, east Boston.

Imbruglia knew those areas and he knew the persons they owed money to. That's why he would be picking up money with Nicky Femia for Joe Barboza and Fitzgerald and Mrs. Baron.

MR. WILSON: When he mentioned this in the real estate office, did he talk about planning the Deegan murder? Did any type of conversation take place about when did you think you'd do that, did you make any plans to do the Deegan murder?

MR. SALEMME: Not really. We were more interested in why he got killed and who was there. We always wanted to know who was capable of doing that, because you had to know who was out in the street that would do that. Now, when we heard that Barboza was involved with him and Cassesso – there were six guys there, I think, five or six guys, that killed this guy in an alley. One or both of them was supposed to - - Barboza and Flemmi was supposed to kill Stathopoulos , but he got away. That's typical of them. He lets the guy get away, and now he's concerned about the guy.

MR. WILSON: So what did he say? Did they say they were going to do something to
Stathopoulos?

MR. SALEMME: That if he could find him he'd kill him. But the odds are if this kid stayed out of Chelsea and went next door to his boss, he'd be safe as a bug in a rug with them. I mean, they couldn't find their way off of Hanover Street, believe me, so they would have no chance of finding this guy, little or none.

MR. WILSON: Were you aware at the time of any police reports about the Deegan murder?

MR. SALEMME: At the time, no. Excuse me. There was a police report of - - I don't know if it was Chelsea police or Revere police. I think it was the Chelsea police. A police captain, a police officer or somebody with authority, had gone by the car and witnessed the back plate was turned up .

MR. WILSON: I'm asking here about that time, at the contemporaneous time period. Did you know about any police report or police information? Let me cut to the chase here. You had some sources in various police departments and you talked to a lot of people. At the time of the Deegan murder, not two years later or three years later

MR. SALEMME: This was right then.

MR. WILSON: Right at that time did you or Stevie Flemmi check around and learn anything more?

MR. SALEMME: The Boston police and the FBI would come in the garage. The state police -- there was two state police, the state police and the Metropolitan District Commission in Massachusetts. Until they merged, the Metropolitan District Commission would be around the city somewhat in beach areas, but the state police, they had jurisdiction to arrest, naturally, but to come off the turnpike and chase somebody around Boston, they couldn't do it. There was no jurisdiction unless there was a murder that took place in their jurisdiction. Then they could come in and investigate it, look around for an intelligence, report or go to Boston, but they were very seldom in Boston at that time, the state police, except for a marked car occasionally that turned in to Boston.

MR. WILSON: Until Joe Barboza was picked up and it looked like something might be happening, is there something more you can tell us that you knew about the Deegan murder? '

MR. SALEMME: No, not really...............

MR. WILSON: You had this one conversation in the real estate office, and you talked to Jimmie Flemmi, and he told you what he told you. Did you go back in the next few days or did Stevie ask him any more questions?

MR. SALEMME: It's very possible that he did. Something came up when Barboza had decided to flip after they killed DePrisco and Tash Bratsos, after they killed them and he decided -- and they robbed him of $,, his bail money, and he needed $, cash to get out of jail. But they killed those two guys and they took the money. And somewhere in there it came out that Stathopoulos, Steve told me that, had identified the people that were involved in the case and that Jimmie Flemmi was a participant, was a participant in it, but they never used Stathopoulos. That's when Rico and Condon come into the picture. It's not a hundred percent clear to me, but that's when he went up to Walpole, Steve Flemmi, to visit his brother after conferring with Rico, not so much Condon, but Rico, and that's when they concocted the story and put -- I don't remember who they put in the back seat with a bald headed wig on. That was Jimmie Flemmi in the back of the car with the bald headed wig.

MR. WILSON: So chronologically, you're at the real estate office, and then you go forward a couple of years and nothing happens. The Deegan murder is more or less forgotten.

MR. SALEMME: There were so many murders at the time. It was an incidental murder. It didn't pertain to anything that was reflecting back on Steve or myself. That's what our concern was. And I was mostly concerned for Steve, because Steve was more Deegan's friend than I was, and Roy French. I mean, they had done a few things together as far as robberies went.

MR. WILSON: It sounds like the next time that Teddy Deegan comes back into your life in any way is this time when Stephen Flemmi came to Walpole prison. Is that correct??

MR. SALEMME: No. He doesn't come --

MR. WILSON: Well, just the name comes up.

MR. SALEMME: That's when Stevie went to visit Jimmie. Unbeknownst to me he visits Jimmie and Joe Barboza.

MR. WILSON: And how do you know about this visit of Stevie Flemmi to Walpole?

MR. SALEMME: Well, we knew he was going to see his brother. I didn't know what the context of the visit was going to be, but he used to periodically go visit his brother in jail. And one of the concerns was that -- and there had been like street talk that Jimmie was going to get named in this indictment because of Stathopoulos, his identification of who was there.

MR. WILSON: Where were you at the time that Stevie Flemmi told you he was going to Walpole?

MR. SALEMME: Either the garage or --percent of the time during the day I was in the garages. That was my business, so I would be in there unless I went out for lunch or went over to buy cars or one of those things.

MR. WILSON: So Stevie Flemmi came in and told you he was going to go talk to - -

MR. SALEMME: He said he was going to see Jimmie.

MR. WILSON: Did he also mention he was going to talk to Joe Barboza?

MR. SALEMME: Absolutely not, because that -- well, what are you talking to him for. We supposedly didn't like this guy, both of us. Barboza, I would not let him around my area, my garages, my Roxbury south end area. He wasn't a welcomed guy, and he knew it because I told him.

MR. WILSON: So Stevie said he was going to go talk to Jimmie. Tell us with as much specificity as you can what Stevie said he was going to go and talk to Jimmie about.

MR. SALEMME: He never elaborated and I never would ask. You just don't do those things. If he volunteered something, fine, but nine times out of ten he wouldn't volunteer it. Most of the time it was always looking for money, I got to go see Jimmie, he's looking for money. He was a junkie, and that's what he wanted most of the time from Steve, and he'd have to leave him a couple of hundred dollars. They'd have those type of arguments, and he'd end up buying drugs or paying off drug bills in Walpole, which he eventually OD'd in state prison, as you know, which was inevitable.

MR. DURHAM: I don't know that Mr. Salemme's ever seen this. You know this document that you all received previously, right? There's reference to some of this at the bottom. That's a June ' memo.

MR. WILSON: Just to get back to this particular time when Stephen Flemmi said to you he was going up to Walpole, you said Stephen had already gone up to visit Jimmie a number of times. What was it that particularly singles out this particular visit? What did Stephen Flemmi tell you? Why are you telling us now that this particular encounter between you and Stephen Flemmi might have had something to do with the Deegan
situation.

MR. SALEMME: There was nothing unusual about it at the time. He was going to see his brother, and that was the end of it, he probably wants money or something, one of those remarks. It was unusual when he came back and said Jimmie was concerned about the Stathopoulos guy, Stathopoulos ,whatever his name was, but he didn't really know specifics about it. He was just more or less making conversation as we went out, I believe, to dinner, which we did quite frequently, three or four times a week. We'd hit some little restaurant or whatever. But there was nothing at that time that really made any antennas come up.

MR. WILSON: So his going out wasn't remarkable, but then Stephen Flemmi came back and had a conversation with you.

MR. SALEMME: That was part of the conversation, you know, is he still doing the drugs, he's concerned about Stathopoulos and all that, but he never told me he met with Barboza, too.

MR. WILSON: But it's fairly clear from that conversation in your mind that Stephen Flemmi was told by his brother that he was worried about this fellow Stathopoulos in connection with the Deegan murder?

MR. SALEMME: That was part of the conversation. And in retrospect, it was also clear that that was the meeting that he was sent to by Mr. Rico. That became clear from Plymouth, when I picked up documents that could put two and two together, and I accused him of it.

MR. WILSON: So you confronted Stephen Flemmi with this information that you're putting together in your own mind. Is that correct?

MR. SALEMME: I'm not putting it together in my mind; I'm putting it together from the documentation. And I believe -- I know historically what transpired back then. I knew in my own mind this is what happened. I wasn't, you know, putting together something that may have happened. I knew this happened now, and I accused him of it in Plymouth. I put it right on him.

MR. WILSON: And when you talked to Stephen Flemmi about this, what did he say to you?

MR. SALEMME: He didn't deny it. He said, what could I do, you know, he's my brother. I accused him with words that I wouldn't want to repeat here, but he said, I had to protect my brother. I accused him right out, you went up there for this guy, Rico, and he just put his head down and was nodding his head yes. When I left the conversation, DeLuca was there. Now, he thought he had DeLuca's confidence, and he made a disparaging comment about the fact that he wanted to F with Dennis Condon. He said
Dennis straightened him out. The general, he said. He said he wanted to F with Dennis Condon.

MR. DURHAM: Would you explain to Mr. Wilson the reference to Dennis Condon, wanting to mess around with Dennis Condon? Did an event occur at the garage after the convictions had been obtained in the Deegan murder that you associated that comment with?

MR. SALEMME: Yes.

MR. DURHAM: Why don't you explain that?

MR. SALEMME: Well, shortly after the conviction of the fellows that got convicted, I knew it was a wrong conviction, but what are you going to do? You live and die by the sword. That's the way it is. But Dennis came in with Paul Rico. He was elated this day about getting these guys convicted, and he made the statement, I wonder how Louie Greco likes it on death row, and he wasn't even there. I was thinking, why was he saying that. There were four or five of us in the room. Steve, Rico, myself, and Dennis Condon. I don't know if George was there that day or not. They were ecstatic that they had pulled this off. And I got into a heated conversation with them and said how can you say that, Dennis. Now, mind you, I don't know Louie Greco, but he was specifically zeroing in on Louie Greco, for whatever he did to him, except he was an LCN member. I said you're a Knights of Columbus, you're a holy name society, and I know this because we had conversations about this. We used to get into it. I don't know anything about the Knights of Columbus. If I even suggested to my father to take me into the Knights of Columbus, he might have hit me in the head with a hammer.

MR. DURHAM: He didn't think you were ready yet for that?

MR. SALEMME: I wasn't ready yet for that, but come to find out they have quite an
initiation. The Mafia induction ceremony has nothing compared to theirs.

MR. DURHAM: Yours was short and sweet in comparison?

MR. SALEMME: In comparison. But anyway, he said well, if you're so smart and you think you know so much, why don't you get on the stand and testify. I said Dennis, who's going to listen to me, who's going to believe me. I'll go on the stand if you do. I said you won't get by St. Peter in the gate, you can't, you broke one of the ten commandments, thou shalt not bear false witness, you can't get by him, Dennis. The more I kept hitting him with that, he got mad, and there were words back and forth. It was much more extensive. Once I hit the sore spot of the religious aspect with him, then he really blew his top. Rico was on the other side looking at Flemmi. In retrospect I knew what it was. I could catch the look, but I didn't know at the time. The look in my estimation now was him, Rico, saying to Flemmi, does he know, meaning what they had done with Barboza and the rest of it. I know what that look is now. I wasn't told that. It's just my own visual conception of what happened then. Do you follow me?

MR. WILSON: It's fair to say, then, from what you knew at the time, that Stephen Flemmi did not confide in you specifically.

MR. SALEMME: No. I never could have tolerated that. George McLaughlin was one of the participants in the McLaughlin and McLean feud, our feud, and they wanted to keep -- Rico hated him, too, and he made a suggestion --he got indicted for murder, George McLaughlin. That's when Punchy McLaughlin, Eddie McLaughlin got killed. He was on the way to the trial of Georgie McLaughlin. He had to show up at a certain time in the courthouse, but this was the Suffolk Superior Court house in downtown Boston. It's tough to walk up to a guy and snuff him right there. I mean. that's too much. But he had to get to there, so that's what made me - - that's how important that address was...That address was a starting point, and then picking him up in different spots until he finally got to the VA hospital at West Roxbury, when the bus made a turn around, at the bus stop, make the hit, back out again on the road, and there was no jeopardy to people around. You could back out again, and you were blinded from trees and everything, and nobody could really see what happened unless they witnessed the murder, and they couldn't get back outside on the road. Paul Rico had made a suggestion to Stevie that there was a kid -- Georgie killed a kid at a project at a christening right down the street from my garage, and there were some girls that were going to go in and testify that Georgie wasn't the one that did it. Paul Rico had got this information, and he said to Stevie while I was there in the garage, you know, it would be nice if these girls didn't show up, if somebody could talk to these girls and not have them show up for Georgie. So after Paul left, I said Steve, no way. we hope this little clown comes out, you don't want to get involved in something like that. Unbeknownst to me, that was the first thing he wanted to do. But anyway, it wasn't done. He got convicted anyway.

MR. YEAGER: You had talked earlier about putting two and two together and looking at documentation and concluding that Stevie Flemmi had gone to Walpole to talk to Barboza instead of his brother. Maybe this came up in the interview, but I'm not understanding what you're talking about.

MR. SALEMME: We got arrested in , or the indictments came out in '. We filed a motion about , I think, to disclose informants. Anthony Cardinale put the motion in on my behalf. I sat down and told him something doesn't smell right, Tony. He said he was going to put in a motion to disclose. I said disclose everybody. That's when we got the coconspirators and all that stuff. But this documentation came out, and Steve Flemmi was disclosed as an informant during these hearings.

MR. DURHAM: Well, he had disclosed himself. He identified himself eventually in his affidavits that he was an informant.

MR. SALEMME: Not beforehand. He didn't disclose himself; we disclosed him. And when the Bureau went in with the documentation to say Steve Flemmi was an informant, Judge Wolf excused us from the room. We were in an in camera session, much as we are now, and we left the room and sat outside saying what's this all about, and Tony said what do you think, and I said I think you're right. So then Judge Wolf said, I have to make this disclosure to you people, which he knew all along, but it's not within his legal right to say it until he put in this documentation, that Mr. Flemmi is an informant for the Federal Bureau of Investigation for so many years, I forget how many years, years or whatever it was, but he said he has chosen not to put himself in protective custody, he wants to stay down and fight the case. That's when he said to see, Mr. Salemme, I don't want any problems to happen to Mr. Flemmi because there's documentation coming out that you might not be happy with. So I said well, your Honor, you have my word nothing will happen to him, but I can't give you everybody else's word, I'm not God here. That's why I brought it up in court to Judge Wolf, but he knew what I meant. I said all right, I'll give you my word that nothing happens. And he said well, I'm quite sure if you give me your word you'll see that nothing happens. I said I'll do my best, your Honor. But there came out documentation, this

much (indicating), every single day. So one day he said, when stuff was coming out, he said that f'ing Paul Rico, he told me this wasn't going in writing. And I said well, so much for Paul Rico's word. He would tell me things before it would even come out because he knew it was coming out when it pertained to me. They put a Title in in December of I wasn't even out of prison yet, and they said Steve Flemmi was going to be the informant for me and they were going to set a Title on me. It was Operation Jungle Mist, I think, an extension of that. But to answer your question, it was kind of a long way to get there.

MR. YEAGER: Much later in time, though.

MR. SALEMME: Exactly. And I confronted Stephen Flemmi after that time, when that documentation came out in Plymouth. Now it's like the proverbial light bulb or hammer, bong, everything goes off at once, and I knew then. I could see that scene in the garage just like it was yesterday, and I could see the visit to Walpole just like that. It just put it together. It was just the last piece of the puzzle. That was it. We had a ton of documentation probably this high (indicating) . You could probably fill this room with all the stuff that was out there. '

MR. WILSON: There may be something sort of in the middle of this chronology, sort of walking through your interaction with Stephen and Jimmie Flemmi . There's the real estate office, and that's right after the Deegan murder, and then a couple of years go by, and then there's the situation where Stephen Flemmi goes into Walpole. It's my recollection that you described to us another meeting where you had a conversation with
Jimmie Flemmi in Walpole.

MR. SALEMME: That was afterwards. That was. Chronologically it wouldn't fit in right where you are right now. It was afterwards.

MR. WILSON: We may as well talk about that now. There was this meeting between yourself and Jimmie Flemmi in Walpole in approximately.

MR. SALEMME: It wasn't a meeting. We were incarcerated in Walpole. I got arrested in and incarcerated and convicted in June. When I got to Walpole, Limone and Tameleo and Greco and all those guys were out in population. They were off death row at that time. Joe Barboza had been arrested for a gun violation and went back into Walpole. He was in Block, in isolation. That's when he decided he was going to recant, when
he recanted the recantation and all that. You know all about that. When I got there, Henry, who I was friendly with --

MR. WILSON: Henry Tameleo?

MR. SALEMME: Yes. He was the elder statesman of the New England crime family. He was around before Raymond was even thought of. They were having conversations, and naturally they would call me into the conversation. I lived in Al, and Jimmie Flemmi would come in and be all paranoid because he would see us talking. He didn't know Joe Barboza was recanting, and he didn't know what Joe Barboza was putting in their heads and telling them he was part of this thing. So when I would finish with a meeting with those -- not a meeting, but a conversation in Henry's rooms. Henry lived in the Flats, we called, it, so there would be three or four of us talking, and he would come by and look in but never interrupt. So when I'd leave and go back up to the block, he was also curious. One day he was stoned out of his mind and decides to come into my cell on
the third tier. He said, what are you going doing, what were you talking about down there, were you talking about me, in other words. I said, what do you mean, what were we talking about. You don't ask those questions. I don't ask you what you're talking about when you're with Dick or somebody. I said, why, what's the matter. You know, he says, I had to do what I had to do, I had to protect myself, I had to do what I had to do.
So then he starts getting pushy, you know, I don't like the idea of you letting everybody know what my brother did, you know he's in Montreal, and I swear to this day I didn't know he was in Montreal. I didn't know he was up there.
But he says, you're letting these guys know where my brother is, I had to do what I had to do, and you shouldn't discuss my business and ray brother's business with them. I said what do you mean, you to do what you had to do, explain that to me. And he gets kind of flighty and bounced off my bookcase and all my books started falling,
and I grabbed him, and he starts shouting, so I push him out and throw him against the rail. The next day he came in the kitchen, we had a little kitchen set up, and he was apologizing. I know now what it was, but I knew it stunk, what he said right there, but I didn't know what it really meant. Again, another piece of the puzzle went in that fit with the documentation.

MR. WILSON: There's no concise way to ask this question, but we've forwarded now sort of past the time of the Deegan trial, but let's go back to the time when Joe Barboza seems like he's going to be cooperating and nobody's sure what's happening at the time. You told us Raymond Patriarca was very concerned that

he would somehow be implicated in something and that Barboza would testify against him. Is there anything more you can tell us about the Deegan murder prosecution and all the events that were taking place around the murder, prosecution? For example, did you have any
interactions with people like Paul Rico about what was going on at that time?

MR. SALEMME: No. Like I said before, Jim, I was not concerned with that. I mentioned my concern for Vincent Flemmi only because of Stevie Flemmi, who I thought was my friend. Teddy Deegan was a nonentity. As far as I was concerned he was a maverick. He put himself in his position. Roy and him were -- that was one thing that came up, mentioning Roy. Roy was the one that lugged him on the pretense of the score. He was one of the ones that shot him. They threatened -- that's another thing. See, it's hard to remember everything.

MR. DURHAM: When you say Roy, you're talking about Roy French, just for the record?

MR. SALEMME: Right, who I got to know very well in Walpole. He was a nice guy, but he went soft after he set up his friend. He didn't have to do that. There's a certain amount of honor you have to have even among thugs like us. If you don't have it, like me setting up Stevie would be out of the question, you know. I'd rather go down or him and I take off and go down fighting, and all the time he's given up on me . I would never do that. That was my mindset in the ', 's and's. You just didn't do those things. They got Roy to lug him, and they were going to kill Roy. That's one of the things that came up in the conversation with Jimmie Flemmi, that they were going to kill Roy, and Roy brought him in, and he thought he was going on a burglary with Roy, and the kid Stathopoulos drove them there, but Roy was one of the triggermen in the alley. Subsequently he did go a little nuts. He'd made an altar out of the toilet bowl and was blessing himself with the toilet water. We didn't see it, but we heard it from the guys. They said this guy's gone nuts.

MR. WILSON: At the time of the Deegan trial, when it was clear that there were a bunch of guys who were facing a death sentence and Jimmie Flemmi wasn't one of them, was there any talk amongst yourselves as to how Jimmie Flemmi managed to get off the hook

MR. SALEMME: No. The only talk would be with myself and Steve, you know, that Joe Barboza was his friend, was Jimmie Flemmi's friend, and he wouldn't put Jimmie in with it, he took Jimmie out of it. That part of it was all right morally, if that's such a term, gangster morals, in other words, not legitimate people or real world morals. In other words, for Jimmie to accept that, in other words, what could I do, I can't tell them to stop doing it, not that it was all right for Joe Barboza to do it. It was all right for Vincent to accept that, but he should have been a little more adamant probably in saying don't do that to them. But that wasn't him anyway, and not many guys would do that. He wasn't ratting out anybody in one sense; he was just accepting a gift of life from Joe Barboza.

MR. WILSON: From what you just said, I've concluded that Stephen Flemmi did say to you that Joe Barboza kept Jimmie out because they were friends.

MR. SALEMME: Exactly.

MR. WILSON: And that was just in various conversations you had?

MR. SALEMME: It was kind of an unspoken thing. It was obvious that he left Jimmie out of it. I know Jimmie was there because he said he was there.

MR. DURHAM: Frank, did you say earlier something about that Rico had provided a photograph showing Raymond L.S. and Peter together?

MR. SALEMME: Yes.

MR. DURHAM: When did that occur?

MR. SALEMME : During the prosecution and when he was going to put his defense on for Peter Limone . There was a photograph, it had to be an eight by ten, and it was a blown-up photograph of Peter Limone .

MR. DURHAM: Like a surveillance photograph?

MR. SALEMME: Yes.

MR. DURHAM: And who did he show it to?

MR. SALEMME: I took it down to the north end to Joe Lombardo, he was the consigliere for the family at that time, and explained that they were going to use a defense of Peter not knowing them, that they'd better not do it, here's a photograph.
Why this guy did that to build himself up to me, I don't know, but I took the photograph and went down with it. It should be a matter of record, that photograph

MR. WILSON: This is a question that goes out of chronology a little bit, but just to get a sense of Jimmie Flemmi and the gang war, you had said previously that you personally didn't care much about the gang war but Jimmie Flemmi did, and that he was involved and more interested in what was going on than some other people, yourself included, and he sort of dragged you into it. Can you give us a sense of why Jimmie Flemmi was interested in the gang war?

MR. SALEMME: First of all and most important, he was in the can with a lot of these guys. He was in the can with Buddy McLean, with Tony Dagostino, Joe McDonald, names that might ring a bell to you from your investigation. Plus, he wanted to be Mr. Macho around in the gang. He wasn't interested in like starting a business or having a business going like I was. I wanted my football business, I wanted my car business and all that stuff. I had that going. He was into the night scene, going to after hour joints, all that stuff. And he had arguments with guys from around the Dorchester Roxbury area, with Jimmie O' Toole, who was part of the McLaughlin gang. He had an argument with him. Buddy I liked very much. I might have even given him a heads up a couple of times. I'm pretty sure I did. And I wouldn't do that for the other crowd. Although I met Punchy a couple of times, he wasn't my cup of tea, and the Hughes brothers, they were dangerous guys, just enough to keep your distance, you know .

MR. WILSON: I'm going to read something that I got recently to you and see if you can help me with some of the names here, if I can find it. Let me just read this to you and see if you can help me out with some of the names. These couple of sentences come from some notes that were taken when an FBI special agent was listening to the microphone surveillance of Raymond Patriarca. He wrote stuff down by hand. This was three days before Teddy Deegan was killed on March . Jimmie tells Raymond they are having a problem with Teddy Deegan, Teddy did what he did to press some other people. Jimmie says that the kid, they're talking about Rico Sacramoni, did not have to be killed. Bobby did not, he is friendly with Rico Sacramoni, and Deegan is looking for an excuse to whack Donati. Donati thinks he's trying to set him up for Buddy McLean. This is what Jimmie Flemmi's telling Patriarca three days before Deegan gets killed.? How does this fellow Bobby Donati fit into the landscape?

MR. SALEMME: Bobby and Nicky Donati are two brothers, a street kid, a thief, you know, who was suspected in the Gardner Museum robbery, but he subsequently gets killed too, found in Revere killed in a trunk. But at the time he's a knock-around kid. He and his brother track, you know, choosing horses, all that stuff. He would be a setup guy, but he had no courage whatsoever face up, one-on-one. Nicky was a more standup guy than him. I . .....

MR. WILSON: Was Donati tied in the McLaughlin side of the gang war?

MR. SALEMME: I would say no. Donati was east Boston, Revere, so he would be on neither side. But if somebody asked him to do a favor for them, like Barboza, Cassesso, he would definitely look to - - even if he flubbed it at the end, he would agree that he would do it. That's my interpretation of him.

MR. WILSON: The other interesting thing about this exchange between Jimmie Flemmi and Patriarca, Flemmi says, and this is a quote from the notes, Deegan fills Peter Limone's head with all kinds of stories. Can you shed any light on Teddy Deegan
and any relationship he might have had with Peter Limone at the time?

MR. SALEMME: Teddy Deegan is a west end kid. Peter Limone is a west end kid. That's an Italian-Jewish section. It's now all hospitals, very little domestic housing there at all. It was all old tenement houses, three-deckers and all that. Limone had an after-hours club on Cambridge, the Harvard Gardens on Cambridge Street . Up above was his club, and everybody went there, all the late night wannabe guys. They'd all end up there or the Coliseum or one of those places. They could have been on burglaries together, too. They could have done a few burglaries together. But shortly after -- I don't know about that document, but shortly after – it was around that time Raymond L.S. -- Stevie and I both went to see Raymond L.S. I think he asked to see me. He used to go to Tom DiSilva, the trucking firm. He had a piece of Tom DiSilva, and he'd get word to me that the man George wants to see me.

MR. DURHAM: George was the code for Patriarca?

MR. SALEMME: He called him George. So we went down there, and we had a conversation, but I know the conversation we were having with him wasn't really the conversation that he wanted to see us about So when we were leaving he said Frank, he says, hold up a second, Steve. And he said Frank, I just want to explain something to Stevie here, so I was from here to the door, and I said sure, go ahead. He didn't want to say anything in front of me to embarrass Stevie. That's the protocol of that situation. He said listen, your brother's coming down here, he's coming down here with Barboza, I don't want him down here anymore, I want you to talk to him and tell him not to come here anymore, in other words showing his respect to Stevie instead of just ordering his brother out. He said tell your brother to stay out of here, and so I says I will. Probably not too long after that scene, as far as I know, I never went down there again. But it was more of a kiss-off with George. He would like kiss them off, you know, more than anything, but he was in a position he shouldn't even have accepted it, but I could never question him. And I said, what are you going to do, let these guys in? They used to buy him boxes of Cuban cigars and white stockings. He was diabetic and wore white stockings. But he used to let the guys in the office down there.

MR. WILSON: One of the documents that we've seen talks about Patriarca saying that Flemmi and Barboza should check with Angiulo before the Deegan murder, and I know we talked about this last time, but my question is: Is that in character with the way things would have worked?

MR. SALEMME: He would tell them that was part of the kiss-off, oh, don't worry about it, I'll check with Angiulo, don't worry, in other words don't come down here looking for an answer, go see Jerry, kissing it off to him, if there was even going to be an answer. And if you had the other side of it, if there was a follow-up somehow, then I'd say well, then the whole conversation was legitimate. But to me it sounds like it was just a kiss-off. And why did they go to Angiulo? I know Jimmie Flemmi used to go to Angiulo and took credit. He took credit for the Punchy McLaughlin murder and got $ off of Angiulo. Raymond L.S. said Jimmie went down. And they'd go along with it. - All he wanted to do was have notches on his gun. He was like something from the OK Corral. The more notches he had on his gun the bigger man he thought he was, but all the while these guys would be thinking what a fool you are, we know who did it. Raymond L.S. knew what was happening. He knew what I was doing and who took part in this and that, he did, but he was the only one.

MR. WILSON: Just to move back to the issue of the police reports and what was going on in law enforcement at the time of the Deegan trial, maybe if we can step back a minute. We touched upon the DiSeglio trial before and you had some concerns and didn't answer some questions about DiSeglio. If we could just move through that
fairly quickly and get a sense of what happened with the DiSeglio trial.

MR. SALEMME: Well, I didn't have concerns about the murder itself.

MR. WILSON: For the record, we had some concerns about our asking some questions at that time without the immunity order being granted.

MR. SALEMME: I don't think that would have mattered anyway, the immunity. The witnesses now are gone. I went into the courthouse, Suffolk Superior Court house, one evening. The head custodian in there was a fellow from the neighborhood, an old-timer, Benjamin Eisenstadt. His brother was a judge Tommy Eisenstadt. And Raymond L.S. -- at that time jury fixing was not beyond the realm of possibility, more so then than it is today. I knew one of the jurors, and I went in and spoke to that juror, with her husband, and got her -- her and her friend was the forelady of the jury, and they'd come back not guilty.

MR. WILSON: Now, at that time, when all these three trials are sort of percolating, there's this Angiulo prosecution for the DiSeglio murder, the Marfeo conspiracy, and the Deegan case, were you getting any feedback or information from law enforcement at the time as to what was really going on behind the scenes? ? '

MR. SALEMME: I know we were, and I can't come up with it off the top of my head right now, but I know we were getting feedback on it . I know the Marfeo trial, for instance, I think I went over this, with how Raymond was perturbed with Joe Balliro. He was supposed to put on a defense for

MR. WILSON: You had mentioned that some Marfeo family members might come and testify, and Angiulo discouraged Patriarca from going down that path, and they ended up not putting witnesses on.

MR. SALEMME: He actually discouraged Joe Balliro to go in when he talked to Raymond before the trial or when they had their conferences that this would not be a good idea and this was their opinion. And Raymond, he was furious for a long time with Jerry Angiulo.

MR. WILSON: So what about individual members of the police force, the local police force? Did you get any feedback or intelligence from them about any of the various events involving Barboza, if you can recall? Bill Stewart, for example?

MR. SALEMME: Bill Stewart would give information. He's the one that I think told us that -- I think it was Bill that said that --Linsky was the cop, Linsky was the detective that set up Joe Barboza and put the pistol in his car. He was the one that arrested him, and he said he set him up. And I'm percent sure it was Bill Stewart. But we got a lot of information, you know, plate numbers, like different guys, like Jimmie ' Toole, what he was driving. Jimmie Toole was another one of Dottie Barshad's -- he's the one that had two kids with Dottie.

MR. WILSON: I'll get back and ask a couple of questions about ' Toole in a bit, but what about Ed Walsh? Did he provide any information?

MR. SALEMME: Eddie Walsh, my understanding was he was giving information to Nick Angiulo, who was Jerry's brother, but I don't know that firsthand, and I never heard it. Bill Stewart, as a matter of fact, or one of them, might have been the ones that said that, you know, be careful when he comes down here because he goes right back to Angiulo with everything, but he was the one that kicked in Angiulo's door. He led the charge on Angiulo when the indictments came down. But there was Bill McLean. Flemmi There was a whole bunch of -- Jimmie Flemmi onetime -- what the hell was their names, the two cops -- shot a guy in the south end. Was it -- he shot one of the guys in the south end, and they witnessed the shooting. Jimmie Flemmi got out of the car and left, and they took the car and pushed it out of their division so it would be in another division and they wouldn't have to investigate it. They came down to the corner and got $, off of Steve, Steve Flemmi, so they wouldn't have to explain what they did. But that's the era that it was, anything for money, even murder. But the end justified the means. Like I think I said before to you, it wasn't considered illegal to do that kind of thing, as crazy as that may sound today.

MR. WILSON: What about police reports? At the time of the Deegan trial or the other two trials, did you or any of your friends or Patriarca have access to any of the police reports? We have them so we've seen them. There were a number of different contemporaneous police reports about the Deegan murder. Three years later, when the trial was taking place, did you have in your possession or any of your friends have in their possession these police reports?

MR. SALEMME: I don't think so. I know like the captain with the turned up plate or the guy with the bald wig, all of that came out, but I don't remember written documents. Subsequently I come to find out that there was all kinds of notification by different agencies. Chelsea certainly was informed. Revere was certainly informed. We were given a statement about who was involved initially, and that was somehow brushed aside. We found that all out afterwards, but at the time, no, I didn't see any written documents. It was all street talk.

MR. WILSON: We went over this last time, so we won't take much time, but with Stathopoulos, he was under the impression that John Fitzgerald was involved in a couple of attempts to kill him. Are you aware of any involvement between anybody in reference to kill Stathopoulos?

MR. SALEMME: No, I'm not. I'm sure that there was, but I can't think of it because he was definitely supposed to be -- he was a witness, you know, so whether it was the Barboza faction or whether he was going to cooperate now with Barboza, I can't really say. I hardly even knew the kid. I'd see him around, and that was it.

MR. WILSON: Jimmie ' Toole, you mentioned him briefly a little while ago. Do you have any information that would sort of help us out with Jimmie ' Toole? Did he have any real involvement in what was going on?

MR. SALEMME: He was a member of the McLaughlin gang. He was the one the night that Jimmie Flemmi --he was the one that Jimmie Flemmi had an argument with on the phone, one of the ones, and a short time afterwards they ambushed Jimmie Flemmi at his house. Stevie was involved, and naturally I was involved because he was my friend. He was there the night Jimmie Flemmi got shot. It was Jimmie O' Toole, Stevie Hughes, Punchy McLaughlin, and Hughes drove the car. Those threemade the attempted hit on him in Dorchester, Massachusetts.

MR. WILSON: Now, I think last time you mentioned that there was a time when there would be animosity between Fitzgerald and ' Toole. Can you tell us about that?

MR. SALEMME: Well, Fitzgerald ended up living with Dottie Bershad while he was in prison, O' Toole. Jimmie ' Toole had vowed through street talk that he was going to kill John Fitzgerald when he got out. John Fitzgerald was now living with her, and he had a wife and, I think, four kids in Westwood, Massachusetts, which was the opposite end of the universe as far as Everett, where he lived, or Maiden, I'm not sure, but they were side by side. And Westwood, it was miles apart, plus you had to go through the city to get there. So it wasn't like he could sneak up there and see her and sneak back home. He lived there.

MR. WILSON: But was there any sort of talk that you're aware of about Fitzgerald wanting to go after O' Toole?

MR. SALEMME: Positively. As a matter of fact, it came out -- that's part of the transcripts. At my trial, the in camera session, there's or or pages that I never got. I know they had an in camera session, Mulvey, Roger Donohue, F. Lee Bailey and John Fitzgerald. And for character witnesses and whatever, we were bringing in John O' Toole, who was Jimmie ' Toole's brother, Dottie Bershad was coming in, and numerous other witnesses to discredit Barboza and the mere fact that somebody else had motive and means and opportunity to kill John Fitzgerald. And in this session in the back room, this in camera session, I didn't have any idea what an in camera session was at that time, and they were in there for at least an hour and a half. And at that meeting John Fitzgerald makes a joke. Bailey says I've got to bring this up, he's going to bring in Dottie Bershad. It's right in the transcript, you hired me, you retained me to represent you, and if you killed James O' Toole I was to represent you, and if you got killed by O' Toole I was to give the money to Dottie Bershad, how do I get around that . So they're going back and forth, and Mulvey interjects, and then Fitzgerald says I'll bring up about you, and he mentions a time that F. Lee Bailey had a girl that he had some kind of a relationship with. Well, what good's that going to do? Roger Donohue got up in the middle with the judge and said let's get all this together, let's come to a decision here, I've got a jury waiting out there, what are you going to do? So they made the agreement not to bring my defense in. They threw my defense out. So when he came out, Bailey got me in a huddle and said trust me, you don't want to bring this up, you don't want to make this guy look bad. So subsequently Fitzgerald walks in and limps down the aisle, he had a walker, and he never did this much to scratch him, all because of Bailey and him, the judge and Mulvey making this agreement in the in camera session to leave this part of the defense in, but he kept giving me this, don't worry about. it, it's okay, it's okay, don't worry about it. There was an evidentiary hearing where all this came out, all this, but Judge Donohue ruled against it then on a conflict of interest, newly discovered evidence, when I filed this, and I wasn't supposed to get this, I got this by accident. I filed a motion for an evidentiary hearing in front of Roger Donohue , who was now sitting, they interchange counties up there with Superior Courts, but he went from Middlesex, where I was convicted, to Suffolk County. And we had a lengthy hearing on that along with a state police report about a fellow by the same of Sonny Calantonio that tried to assassinate John Fitzgerald out at the lounge, the Dedham Lounge at the Rotary circle. That was all stuff that I didn't know about.

MR. WILSON: When did that happen, that attempt? ?

MR. SALEMME: Probably three weeks before the bombing, three or four weeks. He used to go into this place on the way home. He was a drinker. Buddy was a ladies' man the drunker he got. So Sonny Calantonio's girl who became his wife worked as a waitress in this Dedham Lounge, and John Fitzgerald stopped there a few times and used to hit on her, for lack of a better word, and she fluffed him off and told Sonny about it. Sonny showed up one day. He comes in and makes a play, and Sonny was an ex-boxer, and punches him all over the place and knocks him out into Washington Street, the main thoroughfare out there, and gives him a good beating, booted him and everything, and he told him he was going to kill him. He gets up and gets away from there. Now cops come around and break it all up. And he says I'm going to kill you. Sonny Calantonio. Detective Sergeant Hiteman of the Massachusetts state police had this report. He goes to the Dedham police station and makes the report, John Fitzgerald, about Sonny Calantonio. That's when the state police get called in, and he makes that statement to a Detective Sergeant Hiteman, and that's the Hiteman report that I never got, but that was also turned over in discovery as newly discovered evidence that went in as part of my conflict of interest, newly discovered evidence charge that I went before Judge Donohue with. He took months and shot it down in half a paragraph.

MR. WILSON: A couple of questions about Joe Barboza. After the Deegan trial do you know if Barboza was coming back to Massachusetts?

MR. SALEMME: Definitely, yes.

MR. WILSON: And how do you know that and what do you know?

MR. SALEMME: Well, it was common talk that he was bouncing in and out. He was around the Fall River New Bedford area. That's where he was from anyway. There were kids around that would occasionally come to Boston and look to buy a car. I had a great business with legitimately buying cars at Pontiac Village, Herb Connolly Buick, luxury cars, fixing them up, and they'd come from all over the state. You'd get that kind of word that he was bouncing around from them. I think there was police -- one of the police intelligence reports, not a written report, that he had been spotted down there.

MR. WILSON: Well, outside of the documents that you might have seen, do you have any "knowledge or any recollection of Barboza doing any work for law enforcement when he came back to Massachusetts?

MR. SALEMME: Setting people up or whatever.

MR. WILSON: Well, there are various documents that go into certain things, things that Barboza allegedly was involved in that say he was brought back for various projects.

MR. SALEMME: I'm not aware of that.

MR. WILSON: What about Barboza's activities once he was resettled? Were you aware of anything that was going on with Joe Barboza once he was moved out of Massachusetts, for example in California, when he was there, the murder that he committed there?

MR. SALEMME: Most of that time I was in jail, but sometimes the word you get from the jail grapevine is faster than you get on the streets, believe me. And I knew what transpired with Barboza and the killing of that fellow in Santa Rosa or Santa Barbara or one of those places.

MR. WILSON: Santa Rosa.

MR. SALEMME: I know what transpired there. Garroway, Jim Garroway or Bobby Garroway.

MR. DURHAM: Billy Garroway.

MR. SALEMME: Right. He's the one that Barboza made this confession to that subsequently led to the grabbing of the wife of the guy that they killed out in California. That's when Harrington and Rico went out there and said he thought it was a guy -- the guy got shot in the back of the head and buried. But anyway, she did it in Montana, I believe. But that type of information, sure, there was plenty of that.

MR. WILSON: Any other sort of inside grapevine information about Joe Barboza and his possible involvement in other killings?

MR. SALEMME: Was he involved?

MR. WILSON: Yes.

MR. DURHAM: What's the time frame you're talking about?

MR. WILSON: After Barboza moved out of Massachusetts. There was the Wilson murder, and there were allegations of other murders as well.

MR. SALEMME: Romeo Martin he killed. (Martin was murdered because he was an informant in the Deegan case) Those murders, there are plenty of those. The cab driver they beat to death with a tire iron. But afterwards out in California --he ended up with a Greek kid that used to be from Lynn, Massachusetts. He ended up with him. Shamas . That's how he got jacked up, through Shamas. But Shamas, I think, was an informant. I don't know if I've heard that or if I surmised that. But anyway, he ended up with Shamas, figuring out he could do good for himself making money and shaking people down, and Shamas saw a good way to get rid of a potential nemesis, and that's when he made the call to Boston, you know.

MR. WILSON: And what do you know about that from the time, not from subsequent documents or - -

MR. SALEMME : I don't know anything about it firsthand at all. I know Joe Russo was not a participant in that crime. I know he was in Boston. Even though he pled out to it on a RICO, he was in Boston at the time of the shooting. And who the guys were, I can't say. I really can't say truthfully how or who I heard it from. I know it was not Joe Russo. He was in Boston. I know people that were with him when that murder happened in San Francisco and he was in Boston.

MR. WILSON: You know people who were with Russo at the time?

MR. SALEMME: Right. But it was definitely Shamas that set him up.

MR. WILSON: Paul Rico, we can shift our attention to him briefly. When last we spoke you talked about Ronnie Dermody, and if you could just go back through the story that you recounted the last time we talked, that would be helpful.

MR. SALEMME: Well, this call comes from Buddy McLean. Dermody was high on Buddy's hit list. He was a McLaughlin guy. He was living with Dottie Bershad again at I think the Commodore Hotel in Cambridge, Harvard Square. Dermody makes a phone call, according to Buddy, to Paul Rico, and makes a prearranged meet with Rico. Rico gets ahold of Buddy to tell him where Dermody's going to be, and Buddy goes there and kills him. He walks out, kills Dermody, gets picked up and taken to Rico's house in Belmont, that's where he's living at the time, and gets safely tucked away for a few days until the heat rolled over. This is Buddy telling me. Although I knew Paul Rico, I didn't know that Paul -- I never approached him on something like that at this time, but Paul's an all right guy, this is what he did for me, you'll find he's all right, Frank, you can trust Paul. It was all strictly from Buddy.

MR. WILSON: I think we covered this before, but I'll ask the question again just for clarity of the record. Rico's interest on the McLean side versus the McLaughlin side came from Where?

MR. SALEMME: His like for Buddy and his dislike for Punchy McLaughlin. He disliked Georgia. He was a psychopath. He was dangerous, psychopathic like, and he did not like him. He was an O'Toole, and Georgie McLaughlin, they hung together, that crazy part of the McLaughlin crowd. They had a pretty good crowd around, and he had a dislike for those guys and the way they used to come after him.

MR. WILSON: Because of the surveillance that you talked about before?

MR. SALEMME: Yes. Don't forget, Dennis Condon was a Charlestown guy, and that's where this McLaughlin crowd originated from, Charlestown, and the Knights of Columbus were over there, but in combination with the states and feds and all them, they were all from the same area, and that's how they knew each other.

MR. DURHAM: You'd mentioned earlier or made reference to the fact that at one point you and Stevie Flemmi had given Paul Rico a handgun or maybe you just said a gun. Can you describe what the circumstances were surrounding that and why you gave him a gun?

MR. SALEMME: Well, he wanted a throwaway. I'm sure he could have got a gun somewhere, but he wanted a throwaway, one that's clean, one that either had the numbers obliterated or else could not be traced. When he made the request, I had an arsenal all over the city in my garages, so I went and got him a clean . and slipped him the gun at the garage. He was in that much concern, I won't say fear, because he wasn't the type of guy that would show fear, he was a very savvy, suave type guy, but he was very concerned. And also, Georgie McLaughlin and Jimmie ' Toole
were lamsters at the time from the Georgie McLaughlin gang.

MR. DURHAM: Would you define lamster for the record?

MR. SALEMME: Fugitives from justice. I keep going back to the vernacular. You can take the boy out of Boston but you can't take Boston out of the boy, and that's not the university side of Boston, believe me. But Paul made the statement about this gun, that if he got the opportunity to bang out Georgie McLaughlin he was going to do it.
That was one of the concerns.

MR. WILSON: He said that to you?

MR. SALEMME: Right, to us, to Steve Flemmi and myself. But I got the gun and handed it to him. He said if he has an opportunity for Georgie, Georgie ' s gone. But he was concerned about, you know, about Stevie Hughes, a very capable, very dangerous guy, and Punchy McLaughlin, Eddie McLaughlin, also very dangerous.

MR. WILSON: Now, when we spoke last time you mentioned a time when a car was given to Paul Rico. If you could just tell us that story again, please.

MR. SALEMME: Paul wanted a car, and I think it was at Marshall Motors. Georgie Kauffman, my partner, was going back and forth. George bought the car for us and brought it to Marshall to have it fixed because we used to do that. I didn't want those guys coming to my garage. The more you keep away from your area, the better off you are. The normal truck thieves, that's one thing, but when this gang thing was going on, we didn't want everybody mobbed up down there. I gave George cash to let him fix the car, to buy the parts or whatever they had to do, I gave him the cash for it. I'm almost a hundred percent sure that the car was brought to Marshall and fixed up, and he made the comment afterwards thank you, that was a beautiful piece, no mention
about money. You don't mention those things. Just like when the FBI car was fixed. I mean, it was a substantial amount of damage.

MR. WILSON: It's my understanding that Paul Rico brought in a government car that was damaged and wanted you to fix it.

MR. SALEMME: It was a motor pool car. He was down at the track and somehow got rammed and had substantial damage to it, the right driver's side fender, a door, a driver's side door, not that he wasn't in the car at the time. Somebody rammed him. Maybe they did it on purpose? Who knows. We never ascertained just how it happened. But he couldn't bring it back to the motor pool, he had to get it fixed. If he had to go in with the car damaged there was going to be too many explanations or whatever. If it was true or wasn't, maybe this lady can answer When he called for it to see if we were going to be there, you know, Georgie took the phone and said, Paul's on his way up with a car, it's just a little fender, so I thought it was put a skin on the fender and maybe a skin on the door. - And when I go up and see it, jeez. He left for a while, but we didn't finish the car until : at night, and it went out of there with the paint still not even dry. But he was happy.

MR. WILSON: You mentioned before that Flemmi got informant money from the FBI for the information he was giving up, information about you in particular. Was Rico getting any of that money?

MR. SALEMME: I would have no way of knowing that, but he claimed -- when it came out in Plymouth Steve Flemmi claimed to me that he never got any money, because to me that was like the ultimate. When it came out, I said for money, you jewed this, I mean come on, I never got the money, Paul took it, Paul took it, but that's him saying it. Why would Paul take it unless he was hooked at the track or something? I don't know, but I can't believe he would be that petty, either. But it was a substantial amount of money. There was money for Patriarca, there was money for Zannino, there was money for different information that this clown was making up and turning in, some made up and some not. I never tallied it up, but it was a substantial amount, a few grand, if my memory serves me right. He claims that he never got the money, but that could very well be to make himself not look as bad, if that's possible. I mean, what's the difference whether he did or didn't? Still, in my eyes I couldn't change him from the low life that he was.

MR. WILSON: So why do you think Stephen Flemmi and Jimmie Flemmi became informants?

MR. SALEMME: Stevie Flemmi, no question, loved the -- let me back up a little bit. He may have become an informant because -- I'm convinced, knowing what I learned at these hearings, that Wimpy Bennett was an informant also. I'm convinced of it. So he was a protégée of Wimpy Bennett's. Him and Wimpy, they were together before I got into it, when they had numbers and they had their shylock. They used to be in the garage all the time with me. I was never part of their business. I didn't need it. I had my own thing. I didn't want anybody to be part of me, and I didn't want to be part of them. That was one reason. Another reason, again in retrospect, I think he was fascinated with it. It gave him a safe boundary so that he could do what he wanted, and obviously he could do what he wanted up until the time that we got indicted. It gave him that sense of security that he could continue his criminal activity, and all he had to do was give up on jerks like me and he'd be all set. As it turns out, he had a natural dislike for the LCN, that's for sure. I know he had a physical confrontation with Baione and Phil Wagenheimer, I believe at a pool room on Dudley Street.
Right down by my garage they had a physical confrontation, but that was supposedly all cleaned up, and that was part of what the association with Raymond was about. And Raymond -- and then we became friendly with Larry.

Don't forget, I didn't mention this, but Larry was very friendly with Stevie Hughes. Larry wanted to get involved in the gang war for Stevie Hughes. He was in prison with Stevie Hughes and he liked Stevie Hughes, and I never was that close with him at that time. He went to Raymond to get permission to be helpful to the McLaughlin/Hughes faction.

So when I got word from Raymond to come and see him, he explained to me what Larry had done. He said but don't worry about it, you know. And then he says, all the help you need you've got with us, you know that, don't worry about Larry. Now, Larry doesn't know whether Raymond told me or not, and he's trying to be friendly and friendly

and friendly, you know, but I never let on. Naturally I wouldn't let on what L.S. told me. But maybe that was part of the dislike that Stevie had. With Stevie, it's more personal with him. Anything against him, it's personal. He doesn't look at it, well, I know I had an argument with a guy but for the good of everybody I'll overlook it.

That wasn't him. Do you follow me? He had a very good rapport with Paul Rico, a very good rapport, you could see that. I guess I did too up until the time I had the argument with Dennis and I refused the lunch. I know he hit on me that day because I told him about it, that I can't do that.

MR. WILSON: What about Jimmie Flemmi? It seems that one traditional reason for someone to become an informant is that somebody's got something on you and you're in a bind. What about Jimmie?

MR. SALEMME: I don't know firsthand, but it's very possible that they could have had that on him. I don't know when he became an informant, but after the Deegan murder it's very possible that they held that over his head.

MR. DURHAM: Frank, did you know anything about Jimmie Flemmi having been an FBI informant for even a short period of time prior to the fairly recent disclosure of the Deegan murder?

MR. SALEMME: No.

MR. DURHAM: Would your knowledge be limited, then, to what was disclosed in some of these documents about the Deegan murder when information spilled out? Or whether Jimmie Flemmi was an informant, would it just be based on what came out fairly recently on that? You don't have any independent knowledge that Jimmie was also an informant?

MR. SALEMME: I had this knowledge, and I don't know which one of the Boston police brought it to us, but he identified the fellows that shot him when he was in the hospital. I knew that anyway, but that report came out afterwards, and I was told by, I don't know if it was Stewart or Jesus, I don't know who it was -- that he identified the --

MR. DURHAM: The people who had shot him?

MR. SALEMME: The people who had shot him. To me that's an informant.

MR. DURHAM: Sometimes the rest of us don't understand these rules, but if you know who shot you you're not supposed to say.

MR. SALEMME: Well, I got shot, I got riddled, and I didn't say who did it. As a matter of fact, they came in the ambulance with me. But Tom Spottocino was the lieutenant detective for the state police who was at my trial. He was a good guy. He sat with me at the hospital. I wouldn't say anything to him. I never said -- until this day I really never said who shot me.

MR. WILSON: How about if we take a break now?

(Whereupon, at : p.m., the proceedings in the above-entitled matter were recessed, to reconvene this same day.)

AFTERNOON SESSION

MR. WILSON: The microphone surveillance of Raymond Patriarca is of great interest to the committee. Earlier we talked about some of the handwritten notes to some of the surveillance and we had access to the tapes. If you could, tell us what you know about Taglianetti and the efforts to obtain copies of microphone surveillance transcripts.

MR. SALEMME: Well, I don't really know that Raymond gave the order for it. He didn't tell me he did, but I know from Billy Candelmo and from Louie Monacio that that was the reason, that they were part of the Rhode Island faction. There's two parts of the New England crime family, Boston and Providence. That's what caused a friction when Connecticut stepped into it. But Monacio and Candelmo were part of, although the same family, the New England crime family. At that time it was known as the Patriarca, but after the kid did what he did, they changed it back to the New England crime family. But that faction was upset that Louie Taglianetti was taken out like that. He had a young girlfriend and she was killed with him in the car. That set a very bad taste, and that was the reason for it. It could have been handled differently. That faction of the family felt that it shouldn't be done like that, that it was just vindictive on his part. In one sense you can say that. But if you're looking at it from the real side of it, Louie Fox should have known better than to have crossed him. I mean, after all, he's the representate, the boss, and he had a purpose for doing it. months is not the end of the world, and then save the girl. That's the bottom line.

MR. WILSON: Just for the purpose of the record, Taglianetti was killed because he pursued the requests to get the microphone surveillance records?

MR. SALEMME: Right, to help me get a new trial, an evidentiary hearing for a new trial on newly discovered evidence that these tapes were illegal and what was on those tapes was used to prosecute. That's my understanding. I didn't get that from Louie Fox. He was gone by then.

MR. WILSON: And you made a statement the last time we spoke about Joseph Balliro and microphone surveillance. If you could go back through that, that would be helpful.

MR. SALEMME: Joe Balliro had information that would have -- how the hell did that work now? Man, I can't think. It would have helped Angiulo and hurt Patriarca or helped Patriarca and hurt Angiulo. But he was privy to that and he didn't use it, and whoever it was was upset about it, and it should have been used. I just can't think, Jim.

MR. WILSON: Is this something that you've picked up from subsequent revelations or something you knew about at the time?

MR. SALEMME: We knew about it at the time. He had to get that from L.S., because he's the one that had the connections anyway to get it down there, connections with the Providence Journal. There was nothing in the State of Rhode Island that this man didn't have control of, including the chief justice.

MR. WILSON: And why do you say that?

MR. SALEMME: Well, he didn't want the tapes.

MR. WILSON: I'm asking specifically about the chief justice.

MR. SALEMME: Because that would have come out, that he had conversations with either the vending company or the cleaners with the chief justice and about the chief justice. That's a very close-knit community down there. Maybe in Boston the chief justice wouldn't go into it, but up in Federal Hill, it's a very, very small community, Rhode Island, very small, and I think the state is like percent Italian. They just elected an Italian governor again now. But he wanted that protection for Joe Bevilacqua.

MR. WILSON: One thing we didn't finish before, just to jump back, was the chronology after you left Massachusetts and went down to New York and Stephen Flemmi had gone off to California and come back.

MR. SALEMME: Well, we went to California before I went back to New York.

MR. WILSON: Let's go through the rest of that chronology, because we haven't touched on it today. ?

MR. SALEMME: I have him back in New York now and I'm back in New York, and we're living in Billy Candelmo's apartment until we can get put up in our own places, so I had plenty of time to talk to him about it. And that was the conversation. Was initially when he came back, it was on Poulos, and I didn't want to keep dwelling on it with him because it made him uncomfortable when I brought it up. So I thought I can't resurrect this kid, what's done is done, but I had to say something, I had to say something, why, and in his mind it was because this guy, if he ever did come in, would be a damaging witness.

MR. WILSON: Was there a concern at the time that Poulos was an informant?

MR. SALEMME: It was no concern of mine, unless he knew something about him being an informant. I don't know.

MR. WILSON: Moving forward from that time until the time that you had your encounter with John Connolly on the street, sort of walk us forward to the point where you and Connolly met up on the street.

MR. SALEMME: It was a strictly by chance meeting. I went to the Prudential Center off of the Massachusetts turnpike, which is a pretty good place to slip a surveillance if you had any. You could take turns that if somebody else took them with you, you could pick up on them immediately, and it's a good spot to go because you could leave your car and walk around. I happened to be on the phone this one particular day, and I hear Frankie, Frankie, and I look up and there's John Connolly walking up to me. I was talking to DeLuca on the phone, giving him a call back on the beeper to call me back. I said I'll call you back, that Connolly kid is calling for me, and I hung up. He struck up thing, good to see you, John. He said, you know, no hard feelings, I did what I had to do, and we shook hands. And I said no hard feelings, John, I told Walt Steffens and another agent, I can't think of who it was, when they came to my house. In other words, I knew what they were doing out there. I said I had no hard feelings with John Connolly, I knew him from when he was a kid from the L Street bath house. John Connolly, Ray Flynn, they were all over there, younger than me by a few years. I told Steffens that I liked Connolly, that I had no hard feelings. So we talked, and he said why don't you come up to my office. I said I can't go today, John. He said why don't you come up, you have an open invitation to come up to my office any time. I think it was the 9th floor. The st floor. It was up there somewhere in the Prudential Center. .... '" So we made a little more small talk. I get back on the phone, shook hands with him, and made my appointments on, Frank, Jr., and I explained to them later at lunch what happened. My son said why don't you go up, and DeLuca said yeah, go up, and I said why go up, and he said well, because you don't know what he'll say, let's see what he has to say, we're taking care of this guy after all. So the next day or the day after I went up and announced myself to the secretary, and she went inside, and out he comes, come in, come in, his arm around me, come in. We sat for a pretty lengthy conversation that day. The text of the conversation was basically -- well, he had a manuscript of a book and a movie, but the book was the big thing. He said he was writing a book, and he carries a big conversation on, and I said that's great. So he says you're going to be a big part of it . I says, me. To myself, I'm saying good thing I came up, to myself I'm saying this. And he explains to me, you were one of standup guys I ever met in my life, even when I was a kid, you went to jail like a man, blowing smoke, you know, and I said yeah, right. And he says, you know, Jules and Joe Pistone thought that I gave you a tipoff on Gill Street. And I said who's Jules and Joe Pistone, and he says they're agents from New York, and if they didn't know better they'd swear I tipped you off. And I said John, I was riddled, how could I go there, and he says I know, but that's the way it looked. It was that kind of conversation. He said he was going to make a chapter, it will be a great chapter, and it will make you out to be the person you really are. Then we get off of that. I wanted to get going, and now m giving him this with my watch because he ' s a windbag when he gets going. So he tells me, you know, that things will be all right, don't worry about it, I think things will be all right, you stay in touch with your friends and Steve, and I'll let you know when things are not good if you have to leave, much the same way Paul Rico did. But he didn't say there was anything out there because there wasn't. So I left and went down and discussed it with my son. I don't know where we went, but we went for lunch again with DeLuca, but something kept bothering me. I said I can't have this thing. I said to myself why does he have to put me in there or is he going to put in that they tipped me off to the induction ceremony. I said that's going to look like shit if I knew about it. I said I don't want that thing in the chapter.

And my son said well, he didn't say he was going to put it in the chapter, did he, and I said well, I don't want anything in there, I don't want a chapter.

Anyway, I went back up there a second time. Now they know who I am. There's no question in my mind. The girl comes out all smiles, and he comes running out. She buzzed him or went in for him, and he comes out and puts his arm around me again and took me into the office. Now there's another gentleman in there with him. He introduces me, and I thought it was Tom, but as it come out it wasn't. But anyway, he was an ADA, and I thought he said Middlesex, but as it came out it was Suffolk, but my recollection was that he said Middlesex. Maybe I had Middlesex on my brain because of the car bombing conviction over there. But anyway, he was an ADA in the Superior Court in Suffolk, and he introduces me to him, uses my right name, and the guy's like, he pulls his hand back. I have a reputation up there. I'm in the paper like seven days a week, you know, front page. Like I used to tell my son, I'm riding in a train and everybody stares at me. And he says pa, look, that's the front page of the Herald, you're on it . That's the way it was with this guy. John could not wait to introduce me as Frank Salemme, he couldn't wait. The kid was really taken aback by it. He was polite, but he excused himself. Within seconds he was out of there, you know.

But I went through with him about the chapter. Oh, no, no, I would never do that to you, I would never do that, I told you I'm going to make you look good. I said why don't you just leave me out of it. He said it will fit in, don't worry about it. This was a very short conversation compared to the last time, minutes and I was out of there. And then he paraded me right out to the elevator, right past the girl, like a dog and pony show. That was the extent of that.

MR. WILSON: Before I forget about this I should go back to New York before you got arrested, and Connolly did arrest you. We haven't done that today. I'd like to just go through that fairly quickly. If you can just sort of briefly sort of provide the chronology. You and Flemmi end up in different apartments. Correct?

MR. SALEMME: Right.

MR. WILSON: Just sort of walk us forward from there until you get arrested. Tell us what happened.

MR. SALEMME: We used to meet in Central Park. Candelmo had a little watch shop and he sold watches in Hell's Kitchen. So we went to Central Park. One day he shows up in Central Park and tells me he's leaving, he doesn't know where he's going but he's leaving. He might have even said, I might go to Montreal. But he said, I'm getting out of here, it's too hot down here. And I said well, you can't leave unless you put it on record. We got in kind of an argument about it, not an argument, but you're not supposed to do this, how come so sudden, what did you hear, did you hear something. It was too spontaneous. It didn't make sense, that two or three days before, nothing, and this day, he's going to leave. So I couldn't change his mind, decided it wasn't even going to be worthwhile to change his mind, just to let him go. You'll see some of the documents I didn't get until afterwards about Flemmi and Salemme having an argument in New York. There's only one person. That's so singular in nature. I know it came out of his file anyway, but that's what he was doing, setting the whole thing up, Jack from south Boston calling Paul Rico, and Condon was the fugitive coordinator at the time, and he was getting all this stuff, and that didn't come out of Flemmi's file, I don't believe, because he was closed in ', and he wasn't opened again until ', when he came back, and they had that meeting with Dennis Condon and Connolly and Bulger in Newton Center.

But anyway, that cemented the fact that it was time for him to move. John Connolly had transferred from San Francisco to New York, and he could identify me. Like I said, I knew him since he was a kid in L Street, along with Billy Bulger and a few more of them, but that was his purpose for being there. They knew I was there, they knew I was in that vicinity, and they couldn't go to the house without making it too singular in nature with Flemmi. They had me without going to the house, but they had to get him out of New York, and so they put the whole thing together. They got it together with Daddeico and that crew. They got the money and put their money together to save Steve and let the other guy sink. He got out of there, and it wasn't shortly after that I was bumped into by John Connolly

MR. WILSON: About how long after Steve finally left New York did it take for them to find you?

MR. SALEMME: Months. It wasn't double digit months, it was single digit months. It
wasn't long afterwards. I couldn't say truthfully. I wouldn't hit you with a figure and be a hundred percent sure of it, but I know it was single digit months.

MR. WILSON: And are you aware of any contacts between Flemmi and any law enforcement personnel after he left New York?

MR. SALEMME: Well, I'm aware of them through the documents, all kinds of them, and his own testimony, which I'm sure you have. He was jacked from south Boston. See, a lot of stuff with Rico, if we had had it at the time of his testimony, we could have ripped him apart. For instance the jai alai stuff. We got this much stuff on the jai alai after the fact. Judge Wolf gave us the option of calling him back. Why we didn't, I don't know. I think Paul Rico went on before Flemmi did, I know he did, and if we'd had Flemmi's testimony, if it was put more in a chronological order we could have done more damage than we did with Rico. He was so bad that Judge Wolf asked him if he ever heard of plausible deniability. Sure, an FBI agent never hearing of plausible deniability. The same with Dennis Condon. He disavowed the fact that he was an alternate handler for Flemmi. We didn't get the documents until afterwards, the documents that he signed on Flemmi. I didn't know at the time naturally, but I knew afterwards that he was in constant contact, and they put it together for him to come back in after I got arrested. Dennis Condon met him at the Suffolk courthouse when he got the bail put on him. He was there to give him --

MR. DURHAM: Mitchell?

MR. SALEMME: Mitchell. Dennis was there to give him the heads up, everything's going to be okay, everything's okay in Middlesex. Chronologically I may have them backwards, but I'm almost positive it was Suffolk first. Then he got bail put on him, and then he went to Middlesex and had the same bail put on him, so it was $, bail for both offenses. It was a gangland figure murder by a gangland figure, and he got bailed shortly after that and was out in the street. He tried not to come back, as I'm sure you're aware of, from Montreal.

MR. WILSON: First of all, is it correct to say that when Flemmi left New York he did not contact you?

MR. SALEMME: That's correct.

MR. WILSON: I don't know when the next contact was, but not before you were arrested.

MR. SALEMME: That's right. The next contact was years later. He went to my house and saw my first wife when he got bailed, and I never forget this, strictly the dog and pony show, he's my man, he's this and that, he broke down crying. And there I was saying, he'll do the right thing, L.S., and him telling me he's a

phony, you'll see it. But he did go to the house and make the appearance, because he knew it would get back
to me through her, and I'd take the attitude well, at least he's back, maybe he'll do something now, but nothing.

MR. WILSON: Follow that strain by he didn't want to come back from Montreal.

MR. SALEMME: Right. He didn't want to come back. He told Rico he was happy where he was at and, you know, he was working, and he would prefer to stay there for a while, he had his stuff all put together, and Rico got indignant with him, this is his testimony now, and told him that he had to come back. And he told him, you know, that we didn't put all this together for you staying in Montreal, and told him that Dennis was going to be there to put things in motion and take care of him, which he did.

MR. DURHAM: The basis of your knowledge is what Flemmi testified to in front of Wolf?

MR. SALEMME: That's right. Sure. I wouldn't have no way of knowing. If I knew that I knew he was an informant. But as it came out, then that fell right in order, when he got back and got bailed. They didn't make the meet between Connolly, Condon, and Flemmi until his cases were all resolved. They didn't make the meet. Then when it was resolved sometime in I'd like to say in the spring of ', but I'm not sure, they made a meet in Newton Center, and Flemmi and Bulger were properly introduced by Dennis Condon being the alternate.
We didn't have that. At the time Condon was on, we didn't know he was an alternate, and John Connolly was now – it was not his alternate then. Dennis was, I think, then the commissioner of public safety or something at the time maybe. I think he was out of the bureau by then. But he was the sponsor of Flemmi, he and Rico, so he could introduce him as a top echelon. A person can't say they're a member of the Cosa Nostra unless they're introduced by a member who knows them. I couldn't tell you, for instance. I could say John's a friend of ours. Otherwise, if John goes up and says I'm a friend of yours, it would be see you later. Anyway, they were introduced in a coffee shop in Newton Center, and that's when they took off together and Connolly became their primary agent, and

Nick and John -- anyway, Nick Gianturco was an alternate for them, too, I believe.

MR. WILSON: So take us back to the times that you were close to Stephen Flemmi. Jim Bulger, was he in the picture at all?

MR. SALEMME: Not at all.

MR. WILSON: Tell US, beyond what you told US, what you know about that developing relationship between Stephen Flemmi and Jim Bulger.

MR. SALEMME: I know that Steve Flemmi, I find out afterwards in a conversation with Jimmie Martorano down at Plymouth jail, whatever it's called, Plymouth --

MR. DURHAM: Correctional center.

MR. SALEMME: They're in constant contact with Steve. Ed helped put that together and put Daddeico in with the van and all that stuff.

MR. WILSON: For the record, you made a reference to the Somerville gang, and if you could in a sentence or so just wrap that up.

MR. SALEMME: Before he leaves Plymouth, Martorano wants to clear the air between him and I. Well, not clear the air. He wants to tell me he's going to inform and wants to put it on record. DeLuca comes to me and said John wants to talk. I didn't have much conversation with John Martorano.

MR. DURHAM: For the record, you're talking about Jimmie Martorano?

MR. SALEMME: Yes. But we talk, and he says, I want to tell you what I'm going through, I'm going to testify against them after what they did to us, meaning him and I, they deserve it, I'm going to testify against them. I hadn't even been approached by John and Gary at that time. This was much before that. He went what, ' or somewhere around there? But I said do what you have to do, you don't have to inform me about it, what are you telling me for, in other words you have nothing to do with me, you're not a member of my organization. To myself I'm saying that. So I say, what are you telling me for, and he says, well, after what he did to us .

It's just the way he said it, it just struck me wrong. What did he do to you was my response to him. Well, you know, he ratted us up, what did he do to you. I said forget me, I'm asking what he did to you. He said well, he, he, and he started stammering. And he said well, he said he gave you over a million dollars for the time you went away in the numbers business and the shylock business, and he said I didn't get any more than $,, and I said is that right, I wish I got $, from him when I'm in for the years and I'm his partner and boyhood pal. He said he knew you were in southern Florida, he knew you were in Boca Raton, he knew you had a house and wife, and you were still out on the day the indictments came out. John Connolly put reports in on you, you had dinner and lunch and known informants in the Boston area, and I know that because people would say it. I was in George Kauffman's house one day when you called from Boca Raton. I said, John, they saved you, what are you doing this for, in case Flemmi or Bulger or both of them decide to turn and put the finger on you, you're beating them to the Punchy. That's telling it like it is, kid. Well, I know he did worse to you than me. And I said well, I wish he did to me what he did do you, I ' d be sitting here happy as a lark right now. But he told me all about the conversations with him, the conversations with Daddeico, the large sum of money they gave Daddeico and the van, that they were taking him to a safe house in Minnesota, which I had heard anyway, and I'll explain that to you afterwards, to a lawyer out in Oregon that Mr. Daddeico went to. But I'll get to that .

MR. DURHAM: Your understanding was that George Kauffman and Johnny Martorano had put money up for Daddeico. He needed money to get a truck and have him get lost .

MR. SALEMME: Johnny Martorano and Howie Winters were the ones that gave him the money.

MR. DURHAM: And what was going to happen?

MR. SALEMME: He was not going to testify against Steve, and he was going to get off the scene so that he wouldn't be brought in to testify if he left. But I said

John, he was a federal witness. He said everything's been arranged, he's going to get off the scene and nobody's going to look for him, and that's just what happened, nobody's going to look for him. He testified against me in the bombing, and that was the last anybody ever saw of him. Now he's a federal witness. Even though he was testifying for the county, for the state, Middlesex County, he was still initially a federal witness.

And as we found out subsequently, he was approached and offered a sum of money by a federal agent like Buckley, so he's still a federal agent. I can see them not finding Bin Laden, but Bob Daddeico? Well, you met him, you know. But they didn't want him found. They wanted him off the scene. It's just as plain and nice and sweet as you can possibly imagine as you look at it.

MR. WILSON: What about Stephen Flemmi meeting with Rico? Did you have any record that from the time of the indictment and you fled to the time that Flemmi came back to Boston, when everything got taken care of, have you heard of any meetings or conversations or interaction between Rico and Stephen Flemmi?

MR. SALEMME: I heard that he went to Miami when he left New York to meet with Rico

MR. WILSON: I....

MR. SALEMME: REDACTED He had the wife and Marian Hussey, that sweet little thing he ended up killing. That was part of his harem. We didn't have a lot of this stuff coming out when Rico was on the stand. But Daddeico was living on the west coast for a while. He was approached to come in and testify against Angiulo and Zannino in those trials, and he positively refused. He said I don't want to testify against them. They said well, we can subpoena you, we'll subpoena you in, and then you'll be forced to testify, and he said, well if you subpoena me, then I'm going to tell how you people made me frame frank Salemme.

MR. WILSON: That comes from the documents, though. Correct?

MR. SALEMME: Right.

MR. WILSON: That information comes from documents, not from something you knew contemporaneously.

MR. SALEMME: Well, I'm leading up to that. He leaves from there because he doesn't want to get a subpoena. They don't touch him. And to the best of my knowledge, they don't write a document on that. Quinn doesn't write a document on that. I'll stand corrected, but he doesn't write -- and that was the part that stuck out, that they didn't write it up. How can you go, an FBI agent, two FBI agents, how can you have an interview like that and not have a document on it? That's my understanding, there's no document, and that's what stunk about it, you know, stay off of this, this kid's going to blow the whistle on it. So this makes culpability for not just one or two agents but it stretches the whole thing out. And he gets money from George Kauffman and he has to leave California because now they're going to come back and he's afraid they're going to come back and subpoena him, and he doesn't want to go back to Boston. He knows he lied and he doesn't want to get caught up in any more lies, that's my interpretation of it, he goes to Oregon, and somehow he looks up with a lawyer by the name of Royce Ferguson. He gives Royce Ferguson the story of how he framed Frank Salemme, and he wants a certain assurance that his life will be not in jeopardy if he comes back. Royce Ferguson calls F. Lee Bailey's office and talks to - - I don't know if Bailey was in the office then, but he talks to Jim Murberg, who was a junior partner or whatever with Bailey back at the time of my trial. He sat in on my trial .

Royce Ferguson runs the story by Jim Murberg. Jim Murberg gets ahold of my brother John, and he talks to Royce Ferguson by conference call, and Murberg is down in Boston on the harbor, and they talk in a conference call. He's asking Daddeico questions and he's answering them back and forth. Jim makes all the notes on it, Murberg, and

he says he'll get back to you. Royce Ferguson says, I'll call you back, I'll sort through this,

call me in a couple of days. My brother Jackie comes and sees me in prison and tells me what happened, and he's all elated. And I said what are you getting all happy

about, and I said we have no break. First of all, I have years in, and this clown wants me to give him the okay that he won't be killed. Thank God that I didn't,

because I know his kid would have come back here and Connolly would have said okay, he's back, he's going to tell this and that, and he would have got it and I would have been blamed
again. But I can't give this guy the okay. All I can do is tell them I have no animosity
personally myself, Jackie, and make sure you tell Jim Murberg, I don't know if he comes back or not, see you later. By this time I'd had it up to here with him, and who wants that. But anyway, he makes this statement, and Jim Murberg contacts Royce
Ferguson, get me some affidavits and send them, Murberg says to them. They never did, as far as I know, but I wasn't interested in them. Then he ended up going from there to
Maryland or somewhere, I don't know, and he ended up - - he ends up getting arrested a couple of times for peeping tom, voyeurism, Daddeico. Why he turned on me, I wouldn't let him in the city of Boston, you know. I told him stay over there where you come from, get out of there, and he's lucky I didn't kill him because of one thing he did to this
particular girl. He beat this girl almost senseless, and I saved him from getting a sentence on it because he shot at a cop and the rest of it, but get out of town, get over there with Winters and stay over there. And he did the same thing with Winters, with a postman's daughter. That's the kind of a pervert this guy was. He was a woman
abuser, he was a voyeur, and he was a witness against me, and I got my years. But those are things you should know in case he comes back in again. It's a matter of record. It's not something that's pulled out of blue. It's a matter of record.

MR. WILSON: A couple of last things. You've talked about Dennis Condon in a number of areas. Is there anything you know about his interaction with you or other people that you want to tell us that you haven't already asked you about.

MR. SALEMME: Dennis?

MR. WILSON: Yes.

MR. SALEMME: No. Dennis was pretty low key. Paul was the point man. Dennis was low key. That's why it was so shocking to see him come in so elated about this other thing, but that was a big case. That was a big case to get those guys convicted, as it was a big case to get Patriarca convicted. To get one and two, you knock them down, and Paul was instrumental, and Dennis too, in getting those convictions.

MR. WILSON: Condon says that he wasn't aware that Stephen Flemmi was an informant.

MR. SALEMME: Exactly. He said that in open court.

MR. WILSON: Does that strike you, based on what you know and your interactions with him, as believable?

MR. SALEMME: Absolutely false. I mean, there's documents, they've got -- this young lady will know. There's documents with him signing them, Dennis. He was an alternate. He was Flemmi's alternate.

MR. WILSON: I'm just going to jump around a little bit to finish up. But the tip that allowed Bulger to get out of Boston, yourself to get out of Boston, and of course Flemmi did not, what can you tell us about that? What do you know, aside from what you learned from documents after the fact?

MR. SALEMME: I didn't learn anything from documents beforehand. I was given the heads up sign by John Connolly when I went to his office. Now when I got a beep from my son's house, my first wife's house, and I went up there with Joe Ruggiero, who was sitting in the kitchen. ... Steve Flemmi tells me, well, we've got bad news, the indictments will be out the 5th This was January 5th. I didn't know Flemmi was
there. I got a beep. My son was sick with lymphoma and was dying and subsequently he did die, but when I got into the house I was very surprised to see Steve Flemmi sitting in the kitchen because he didn't park his car there, he parked in a wooded area.
And I went in the kitchen, and it's not a big kitchen, and Joe Ruggiero stood at the door of the kitchen and Steve told me we've got bad news, the indictments will be out the 9th. This was the 8th, I believe, January th, I believe. And he says -- I said well, how bad are they going to be, and he said there are going to be racketeering indictments. And I said John Connolly. He said John Connolly got in touch with me, and you better be out of here.

MR. DURHAM: Did he tell you Bulger had already left?

MR. SALEMME: Jimmy's already left, but he didn't know --he left before even the morning of the indictments. He just left. He knew they were coming, and he was setting things up, plenty of money, and he took his girl and went up and set up a lot of drops. I said are you going to leave. This was a Thursday, I think, or a Friday, a Thursday, I think, and the indictments were going to be out that Tuesday. He said, I'm going to leave this weekend, I'm just putting things together. He had a restaurant downtown on Exchange Street. I think it was the Exchange Restaurant and Bar, a nice place,
one of those cigar places that you can smoke in. In the meantime he's saying he didn't have any money. But he outfoxed himself. I left right from there, and I said that's it. I went down to Quincy to a restaurant on the water and I beeped DeLuca

and met him down in Rhode Island, putting things together, and I met with a couple of other guys.

I said that's it, I'm going to be leaving, I'm putting this together, putting that together, and getting out of here. I get a beep from my second wife. Steve Flemmi had got arrested. So that was the end of that. They pulled the rug out from under us. They had arrest warrants out for us. But before the indictments come down, they got the arrest warrants five days ahead figuring if we got wind of it we'd be gone, and they were right. That's how I got out of there.

MR. WILSON: Did Flemmi ever talk to you about any of Bulger's assets, the money he'd squirreled away in various places?

MR. SALEMME: No, he never did, but anything money-wise that would come up, different allegations in the paper, he'd say that was Jimmie. And Patriarca, the kid, junior, not even a junior, but Patriarca the kid said they had money with Mike

Carrauna, that Patriarca was present when they cut up $, apiece. I said what kind of money are you talking about here, Steve, and he said oh, I had nothing to do with it, and Patriarca swore they got $, apiece.

MR. WILSON: And what was that deal?

MR. SALEMME: That was with Frank LaPere, (Below) who ended up testifying against Dave Toomey, who was a police attorney.

MR. DURHAM: When he was prosecuted he had already left, hadn't he?

MR. SALEMME: He was the connection for Frank LaPere, who owned a fish processing plant and boats in Plymouth. He'd even go into Canada illegally and poach swordfish and process it at this plant. They used to have boats come in and drop bails of grass back in the 's. He had the connection with Toomey and went to bring the boats in and out. And tons -- I heard one astronomical figure and no way of verifying it, that there was a $ million loan commitment, and they had Joe Murray from Charlestown with barrels of money coming in with the trucks and took money off the boat at that time and pocketed that money and sent out garbage. When they arrested the boat over in Irish waters it had nothing on it . They pocketed over a million dollars apiece on that deal. I heard they were worth at least $ million apiece. Bulger was a squirrel, and so was Flemmi. They're not extravagant people. They're not nightlifers or boozers. They weren't gamblers and they didn't do drugs, so he had plenty of money. Flemmi made three or four, maybe a half a dozen trips that I know of to various countries. He joined an international parachute company and he jumped all over. South Africa, Thailand, Europe, Russia. He went to Russia one time. He went to Haiti one time and he went to the Grand Cayman Islands. It doesn't take much to figure out what

Bulger

he's doing there. Bulger made a lot of trips to Iowa. They probably have as strict laws Switzerland used to have, I don't know about now, but that's a good place to deposit money. And I don't know for sure, but I know that's what Flemmi was doing. He claimed to me that he was going to China, and he had a Chinese girlfriend, another one of his girls, but he said he was going to China, so you know he had money there. He went twice to Asia.

MR. WILSON: The China claim was made in , just before he was arrested.

MR. SALEMME: Right. I forget her name now. She was with him when he got arrested. He had suitcases and not all his stuff, but he had suitcases and everything in the car.

MR. WILSON: Schneiderhan, what can you tell us about Richard Schneiderhan?

MR. SALEMME: In Plymouth, Schneiderhan by name, I don't know, but in Plymouth we were trying to get from him, which he gave us, numerous names of informants. That was part of my testimony at John's trial, when Kevin Weiss came up and showed they'd been informants for the affidavits on Gill Street. That was an important notice to get,
because we wanted to attack that affidavit to attack the bug, and if we could prove that one or more of the informants was present at the induction ceremony -- I didn't care about the induction ceremony. I already had the wording and all the rest of it. What's the difference, you know? I cared about the legality of it, that from that document they t and got probable cause for another bug, probable cause for another bug after that. It was a domino theory. So if they knocked this one out maybe they could topple the rest and knock Rico to hell. Your question was what?

MR. WILSON: Well, it was just a very general question about your knowledge of Schneiderhan ' s activities. The specific question
would be him providing Stephen Flemmi with information or anybody else he shouldn't have provided information to, do you have firsthand knowledge about that.

MR. SALEMME: Well, I was paying him. It turns out it was Schneiderhan, but he's the one that got money too, and state policeman in the attorney general's office, his name to us was Lou. He had various names for different people. You might call Schneiderhan Lou to him, Pete to him.

MR. WILSON: If we can just back up, this was Stephen Flemmi obtaining information from law enforcement people, and he's giving you alias names, and you're giving him money to be passed on to those people?

MR. SALEMME: Right. "

MR. WILSON: And to the extent you know what happened, tell us all you can about that, to the extent you know that a particular thing did happen.

MR. SALEMME: Well, we took two payments off our numbers business to give to Connolly, and we took a $, payment out to give to the connection, Lou, in the attorney general's office, who used to work for the attorney general's office who gets all the is a very important thing for –

MR. DURHAM: For people in your business?

MR. SALEMME: It's the truth. If you don't have a clean phone, you're not going to stay in business very long. Plus, we were looking for him along with Connolly to get information on an informant from Rhode Island. It ended up we knew he was an informant anyway with the CS . That was important . Both ways we could have it .
Now it ' s beyond the bug stage . Now it ' s the informant stage to know what we can knock out of this racketeering indictment and what we can't. Once he got exposed down there, we could open him up pretty good. I stayed talking with him up until
the point that he took the stand and named John Morris, all the way up to the elevator from the court, from our holding cell downstairs.

MR. WILSON: This is Stephen Flemmi?

MR. SALEMME: Stephen Flemmi. He's naming John Connolly, John's going to come in, he's going to help us and so forth and so on, John Connolly, John Connolly, John Connolly. I was telling Anthony Cardinale, John Connolly was coming in, and he was saying he's giving you a story, he'd ruin himself if he came in. All the way up the
elevator he's telling me and DeLuca . He gets on the stand, and the first question was who tipped you off to the indictments, John, and I was thinking here it comes, and then he says Morris. I didn't say anything. I took him downstairs and grabbed him and
threw him against the wall and started choking him, and the marshal saw, but they didn't come in to stop it, they wanted to hear what was going on, and I said you SOB, you're doing this, you can't even tell the truth, why didn't you say John Connolly
like you were going to say. They were going to testify for you, weren't they.

Agent Connolly

MR. DURHAM: They did.

MR. SALEMME: They did? They testified? But how I could have kept myself from causing him severe -- after learning all that. Had I learned about the two little girls, Debbie Davis and especially Debbie Hussey, she was like a niece to me,

she was his stepdaughter, molesting her at and killing her at . I mean, I used to take this
kid to the beach with my daughters. But if I knew that at the time I couldn't have held back. I knew the truth. I don't know how he thought he was going to get away with it, which he didn't, but I don't know how he thought he was going to, how he held it
up, and then I hear John Morris. He wanted to get it out before I could stop him. He was convinced John Connolly was going to ride him or the Bureau was going to come through and John Connolly ride him out . He asked for Charlie Gianturco. I don't
know if Charlie ended up one of his alternates or what, I don't think so, but it was two brothers, Charlie and Nick Gianturco. Nick ran Operation Lobster that you probably read about, and Bulger saved his life because there was a guy from Charlestown, Patty McGoneghal, who was going to kill him. Even Judge Wolf picked up on that. The
operation went on for -- it was an month operation. At the the month you find out that
this guy's going to kill you. They all get commendations for it.

Bulger as a young man

You know, it stunk, but no way that was going to happen. But he asked for Charlie

Gianturco the day he got arrested. He asked Jack Smith, the marshal in the old courthouse, to call Charlie Gianturco for him, and Jack did. Jack told me. He said this guy called and asked for Charlie Gianturco. And I said well, maybe he's a friend of
Connolly's. I said who's Charlie Gianturco. He said he's an FBI agent, he and his brother Nick. I thought well, maybe he's a friend of Connolly's, I don't know, but then it all came out.

MR. WILSON: You were talking before about money that went out to people to obtain
information. Can you tell us anything more about other money that went out to law enforcement sources to obtain information? '

MR. SALEMME: There were small payments for local police and all that, but the office would take care of that, a hundred, two hundred, whatever it was. The ones I was interested in was when he'd come in and say he have to take an EX for It was a very lucrative number business, we did like $100 g, a week, like $2 million or $3 million
volume for the year, and you win like or percent of that, so numbers are a good business, it ' s a profitable business, and if it's run right it could be a good business.
But the small stuff that the office paid out, your phone man, that's something else, if he's
robbing me a couple hundred here or there, what's that. If it starts getting out of hand, you catch it. A fellow by the name of Jake Rooney used to run that for us.

(Discussion off the record.)

MR. WILSON: Going back to the Poulos murder indictment, just to characterize the
indictment, or at least there was a warrant that was issued at one point, and I'm aware of this warrant, if you could tell us what you know about the warrant that was ultimately issued for the Poulos murder.

MR. SALEMME: A warrant was issued against me, and I found out that there was one issued against Steve Flemmi also. I filed under the speedy trial act, the interstate system act. I filed in Walpole through Joe Balliro, but in the law library I did it myself, and Joe signed it, Joe's office, and I got the response back that due to the lengthy sentence of Mr. Salemme's serving that Nevada is no longer interested in interviewing him for this murder or words to that effect, not verbatim. In other words, they dropped the charges

against me because I filed that. And they weren't interested -- they certainly knew where I was, and they knew when I got discharged and all the rest of it. ?

He never filed that, because when he found out I filed it, he asked did I have one filed

for me, and I said I don't know, did you put one in, you don't file it, the FBI files it for you. But that was as far as that went. I don't know of any law enforcement interference on my behalf. I know how I got the case dropped, and I got it dropped that way. I don't know about him. He never filed for a speedy trial or anything else. He just forgot about it, and they never came or asked for an apprehension warrant or a detention warrant or something like that on it or have him extradited to Nevada. So you can assume

what you want. I know what I think, but that's only a thought. It's speculation, not anything based on fact.

MR. YEAGER: Would you care to describe what you know of Joe Salvati's role, if any, in the Deegan murder?

MR. SALEMME: Well, it was street talk that Joe Salvate was part of the murder, but I don't know if he knew that there was a score. This is strictly street talk, that he was going to be at a house, if my memory's right his aunt's house in Chelsea. Whether my I know. But he was very, very close with Cassesso and Eddie Edolino, Mike Amari . That's how he fit in. He didn't fit in in the Barboza part of the faction. I like to call it the banding of the misfits, because since they couldn't hook on anywhere else, they hooked on with themselves, and they used to hang out together, and Joe Salvati was a runner for them, a gofer for them basically.

Joe Barboza

MR. DURHAM: What did you understand Salvati's role was supposed to be that night?

MR. SALEMME: As not a crash car but as a pickup car in case they needed somebody. And I understand also that --it had nothing to do with this story that he owed $ to Joe. That's ludicrous, . That's chump change. But they held -- Joe Barboza held Ronnie Cassesso partly responsible for Tash Bratsos and Tommy DePrisco getting killed. He used to pass himself off as LCN, and he wasn't LCN, Cassesso, and he wasn't a well-liked guy at all with the LCNs. He was a wannabe, and that's why he hooked up with all these different people. But the story I heard for whatever it's worth was Joe Salvati was asked to corroborate Joe Barboza, and he refused, and Cassesso was asked and he refused, and when he refused, he said if you don't want to help me, that proves you're with them. Now, that's what came out of Cassesso's mouth to me in Walpole. I had numerous conversations with these guys. I would go and talk with Peter and Henry Tameleo mostly.

Enrico "Henry" Tameleo

MR. DURHAM: Peter being?

MR. SALEMME: Peter Limone. Not the other one.

REDACTED

There's two Peter Limones . But that's Cassesso.

MR. DURHAM: What did Cassesso tell you about Salvati?

MR. SALEMME: He wouldn't go along with him. Just that Joe wanted those two to go out and corroborate his testimony, which would have solidified the case. So when he put Salvati in the back of the car with the bald head, that was Jimmie Flemmi, a bald headed wig on or whatever it was.

MR. WILSON: What would have been in it for Salvati or Cassesso to have corroborated the testimony, if they told you?

MR. SALEMME: What would have been in it? They wouldn't have been doing life in prison. Salvati never got the death sentence. He's got a nice family, Marie and Sharon and a young boy I don't know. But Joe's a full time asshole, believe me, and that's the . He never got sentenced to the chair, and he never corrects it when he gets in conversations with reporters. He loves to give out interviews. He went to a play with Brian Dennehy at the Wang Center and went up and shook hands. It was a play about guys who get convicted wrongly. He didn't get sentenced to first degree, to life - to the chair. He got sentenced to first degree, which was bad enough, but Joe did about five years in Walpole, and when I get to Walpole he transferred to MCI Framingham

REDACTED

He got into the computers and he ran the commissary up there for MCI Framingham

REDACTED

But what gets me is don't play off like you're some kind of abused hero. You were part of that crew. I told him that in Walpole. I wasn't clairvoyant to the point that I knew what he was going to come out and say afterwards, but now he's making himself off like sure you got screwed, so has everybody, that's the life you chose, kid, you want to be a gofer, opening and closing the doors in the afterhours joints, that's the price you pay. But he spent a good percentage of his time in MCI Framingham until it got busted because they were running a numbers game on the computers up there. But he spent a lot of his time in MCI Framingham, so he wasn't so abused to the point that he was on death row for or or years. Henry died in prison. That's abuse. Louie, that's abuse. He died in prison. Even Peter Limone, that wasn't right, five years on death row. That's like years of your life gone right there. You don't know what it's like to be in that kind of a lockup, and to be there falsely accused. That's tough. I know what it's like to be falsely -- you can't do a thing about it. Who's 's going to listen to you? But Salvati had a nice woman,
Marie, and Sharon, a nice daughter, and the son, too, nice, nice people. And I could never tell them. Over the years they wanted me -- Sharon approached me a number of s, you've got to help my father, you know the story, Frank, you know my father's innocent, I know, Sharon. I had dinner with her a couple of times when she came in the restaurant, and she would ask, you've got to help my father, and I'd say I can't help him, I don't really know, Sharon, you know, it should be Flemmi. Joe Balliro had information that he couldn't divulge because of the attorney-client privilege he had with Vincent Flemmi. So I said Vincent Flemmi'

s dead, you know, I can't go to them and tell them to waive that on the son, who I thought was my friend, too, and Stephen Flemmi, I can't do that, you've got to tell your father he's got to bite the bullet, that's the life, the proverbial street life. He was abused, yes, but I think he's carrying it to the point now of being ridiculous, you know. But that's the story I got right out of Cassesso's mouth because they would not corroborate Mr. Barboza or help go along with Mr. Barboza to make that case, and he turned on them, and Barboza went to his grave thinking that Cassesso, that clown, was a made man, and he wasn't, so it cost Cassesso. .

MR. WILSON: Your conversation with Rico and Condon about Greco, you described that fully. Was there talk at the time, and I know it was part of the trial, but was there talk at the time that Greco really wasn't really in Massachusetts at the time of the murder?

MR. SALEMME: Absolutely. Every cop that came in my garage and every one you met on the street, some was sympathetic to him, some thought it was a joke, but not to the extent that Condon carried it. And Condon and Rico -- what perturbed me about it was they initiated this thing with Barboza. I didn't know they went to that extreme. I just thought Barboza gave them a story, the FBI, and they couldn't help it that they substituted people. But when he made it known that they knew he substituted people, that makes it a different ball game as far as I'm concerned.

MR. DURHAM: Why don't you just quickly describe for the record, and I know the fingers are about to fall off on Keith, but what your relationship with Greco is? What was your relationship with Greco.

MR. SALEMME: Up until that point I had never formally met Louie Greco. Him and Maxie used to hang together, Maxie Cataldo from Revere. Louie was a big tough guy, and so was Maxie. That's why they pummeled Nicky Femia down at Bennington and Saratoga Street. They gave him a serious beating. But as I met him going on, he was just a big dummy, an easy person to put in that position if you had some kind of a vendetta to go against him. He was easy because he didn't know how to talk even. But I didn't know him. It just galled me the way Dennis came on the way he came on, and it was very unusual for Dennis to show that kind of emotion, but he was elated over it. He was more laid back. You would think that it would be more Paul that came on like that, but Paul, like I said, was suave, and he was kind of -- he knew how to handle himself, Paul. He was a street guy, and obviously he was suave with the director because he was down there. I've seen pictures of him with the director.

MR. WILSON: Well, thank you very much, Mr. Salemme . Thank you very much to John Durham for coming down and being part of the process. Thanks to the Justice Department for helping organize this. Again, my apologies for what we discussed at the beginning, but thank you very much for coming.

MR SALEMME: If I might say, in the future, and you don't have to put it down if you don't want, if there's any contact, if I can get a heads up just so I can prepare myself mentally if I'm in the middle of like I am with this medical thing, I would like to get myself prepared mentally for it

MR WILSON: Absolutely. Thank you

(Proceedings concluded.)

Investigative Chronology
(Abridged)

The Committee's Report and the entries in this Investigative Chronology are supported by cases, memoranda, published books, articles, and reports, and other documents. The superscripts identify the number of the entry and generally, an associated exhibit. All exhibits that are referenced in the Committee's Report are reproduced and published in conjunction with the Report and the Investigative Chronology.

The 1940's

1945: Joseph Barboza is arrested at the age of thirteen for breaking and entering.

December 1949: The *Boston Herald Traveler* reports, "In a space of a few days in December 1949, Barboza's gang broke into 16 houses in various parts of New Bedford and stole money, watches, liquor and guns."

12–31–49: At age seventeen, Joseph Barboza is imprisoned for the first time.

The 1950's

1–29–51: Dennis Condon becomes an FBI Special Agent. He retires on May 20, 1977.4

2–26–51: H. Paul Rico joins the FBI. He retires on May 27, 1975.5

April 1952: Paul Rico is assigned to the Boston FBI Office.

7–13–53: At age twenty, Joseph Barboza leads a revolt and escapes from prison in Concord, Massachusetts.

5–19–54: Joseph Barboza is convicted of robbery by force and violence, assault and battery with a dangerous weapon, assault and battery, kidnapping, larceny of autos, and escape from prison. He is sentenced to 10–12 years, 8–10 years, 10–12 years, 2½–3 years, and 2–3 years.

1–19–56: Dr. Daniel Levinson administers a psychological exam to Joseph Barboza. Dr. Levinson concludes that Barboza's "features make him look less bright than he actually is; his I.Q. is of the order of 90–100 and he has the intellectual ability to do well in a moderately skilled occupation."

3–5–56: A personal and confidential memorandum from the Special Agent in Charge (SAC) in Boston to FBI Director J. Edgar Hoover states the following information about James "Whitey" Bulger: "This office had known Bulger because of his suspected implication in TFIS tailgate thefts. We knew of his extremely dangerous character, his remarkable agility, his reckless daring in driving vehicles, and his unstable, vicious characteristics." Agents Paul Rico and Herbert F. Briick, "undertook to develop a PCI [Possible Confidential Informant] who could and would inform on Bulger's location. . . . SA's Briick and Rico continued to contact REDACTED and ultimately developed his confidence and willingness to cooperate." The SAC recommends that Rico, who took Bulger in to physical custody, and the other agents involved in Bulger's arrest receive a letter of commendation, with particular emphasis on "the fine work of SA's Rico and Briick in cultivating the informant who made the arrest possible."

3–28–56: In a letter from FBI Director Hoover to Paul Rico, Hoover notifies Rico of his promotion to the position of Special Agent. Hoover states, "It is a pleasure to approve this promotion in view of your superior accomplishments in connection with the Bank Robbery case involving James J. Bulger, Jr., and others." Hoover also commends Rico for his outstanding work "in developing a valuable source of information" and "in developing other confidential sources of information."

3–13–58: A psychiatric report by Dr. Saltzman states that Joseph Barboza has a "sociopathic personality disturbance, anti-social reaction." He continues, "There is always a great possibility of further Anti-social behavior in the future."

7–12–58: Joseph Barboza marries Philomena Termini.

9–6–58: Joseph Barboza is convicted of possession of burglary tools and attempted breaking and entering. He is subsequently sentenced to 3–5 years.

11–14–58: Joseph Barboza is convicted of attempted breaking and entering at night with intent to commit larceny and possession of burglary tools. He is subsequently sentenced to 3–5 years.

1961

2–13–61: In a letter from Attorney General Robert F. Kennedy to the Honorable Mortimer M. Caplan, IRS Commissioner, Kennedy lists Raymond Patriarca, as one of the 39 top echelon racketeers in the country targeted for investigation and prosecution.

The Deputy Attorney General pointed up the need for the receipt of full information in order to develop a case and cautioned against too speedy action. The Attorney General took issue with this, saying that while it was necessary to develop information, nevertheless, he expected the attorneys in the Organized Crime Section to be more aggressive and get something accomplished. . . . The Attorney General concluded the meeting by reiterating that he was going to insist on action being taken by the Organized Crime and Racketeering Section and he expected something to be accomplished.
He advised he intended to hold another meeting on May 20 and by that time, those in the section would have to be in a position to report more favorably or he might have to take other action to get the job done." (This information is contained in an FBI
Memorandum from C.A. Evans to Mr. Parsons dated April 28, 1961).

6–21–61: The Top Echelon Criminal Informant Program was inaugurated. (*See* 12/7/62 entry). A letter from Director Hoover to FBI SACs states in relevant part: "To successfully complete our intelligence picture of the controlling forces which make organized crime operative, it is now urgently necessary to develop particularly
qualified, live sources within the upper echelon of the organized hoodlum element who will be capable of furnishing the quality information required. The most significant information developed to date indicating organization among the nation's hoodlum
leaders has been obtained from highly confidential sources in Chicago, New York, and Philadelphia concerning the existence of a 'commission' of top leaders of the organized hoodlum element exerting a controlling influence on racket activities in this country."
Raymond Patriarca was listed as Boston's Top Hoodlum and as a "commission" member. The letter further states that "there is an urgent need for amplifying information which will reveal full details concerning the operations of these interrelated organized criminal groups throughout the nation. Our urgent need for new
live sources strategically placed in the upper echelon of organized crime is brought into clear focus by the fact that no information regarding the 'commission' has been reported by any live criminal source to date. . . . [I]t is mandatory that the development of *quality* criminal informants be emphasized and the existing program be implemented and greatly expanded. You are again reminded that the penetration and infiltration of organized criminal activity is a prime objective of the Bureau, and to accomplish this it is necessary to give a renewed impetus to the development of *quality* criminal informants. . . . [T]he best source we could possibly obtain would be a criminal informant who is highly placed in organized crime. . . . To insure [sic] the success of this program, it is necessary to utilize Special Agents with the will and desire to employ
new approaches and means to secure the Bureau's goals." Selection of a particular criminal informant should be based on "a combination of a particular hoodlum's qualification by virtue of

his position in the organized crime hoodlum element, and upon circumstances indicating his possible vulnerability to development.
. . . To properly develop informants of this caliber, varied approaches can and should be utilized, dependent upon the individual under development. . . . Every office is being advised of this program since in the future it may be appropriate to expand it to include
additional offices. . . . This program has, as its primary purpose, the development of *quality* criminal intelligence informants. The two most important components of this program are the selection of individuals for development as informants and the designation of the Special Agents who will participate."

1962

3–6–62: The FBI installs electronic microphone surveillance at Raymond L.S. Patriarca's office at the Coin-O-Matic Distributing Company, located at 168 Atwells Avenue in Providence, Rhode Island. "[F]rom March 6, 1962 until July 12, 1965, inclusive, agents of the Federal Bureau of Investigation (hereinafter called 'F.B.I.')
maintained an electronic surveillance of the place of business of a business associate of the defendant [Louis "the Fox" Taglianetti] located at 168 Atwells Avenue, in the City of Providence, in the State of Rhode Island. The overall purpose of said surveillance was to
gather criminal intelligence with respect to organized crime. It was conducted under the direction of Mr. John F. Kehoe, Jr., a Special Agent in Boston. . . . At the end of each day said log and tape recording were mailed or delivered to Special Agent Kehoe in Boston.
. . . Special Agent Kehoe would review the log and listen to the tape recording. After doing so, he would dictate a memorandum and an airtel summarizing the contents thereof. The tape recording would then be routinely erased."

3–12–62: In an airtel from FBI Director Hoover to the SAC in Boston regarding Raymond Patriarca, FBI Director Hoover orders, "You are authorized to discontinue submission of daily teletypes in this case and in lieu of same submit summary type airtels on Tuesday and Thursday of each week. . . . This case is to continue to receive full-time attention and every effort must be made on a daily basis to develop any criminal violation which Patriarca is committing or has committed with any relevant statute of limitations period."

3–30–62: Memorandum from Director Hoover to the personal attention of the SAC in Boston. The memorandum states that on March 6, 1962, the Boston SAC activated the microphone surveillance at Raymond Patriarca's place of business in Providence,
Rhode Island. The memorandum discusses the "wealth of worthwhile information" obtained from the microphone. The memorandum authorizes the Boston SAC "to give immediate consideration to submitting recommendations for incentive awards and/or commendations for the personnel responsible for the success of this matter." (Hoover later receives recommendations to keep the surveillance in place.

4–9–62: Memorandum from Director Hoover to the personal attention
of the Boston SAC discussing "additional misur [microphone surveillance] coverage."

4–10–62: An FBI letter to Field Office SACs entitled, Criminal Intelligence Program—Necessity of Affording Protection to Highly Confidential Informants and Techniques states: "It is mandatory that our highly confidential informants and techniques are afforded complete protection at all times. When attributing information to these sources, care must be exercised in order that our operations are not impaired through the divulgence of their identities."

May 1962: Joseph Barboza is arrested for assault and battery with a deadly weapon but no disposition is given.

5–8–62: The Boston SAC prepares a memorandum to Director Hoover noting that Raymond Patriarca is one of the original forty hoodlums selected by the FBI for intensive investigation and early prosecution.

5–31–62: In a memorandum from the Boston SAC, Director Hoover is informed that since the microphone surveillance was installed on March 6, 1962, in Raymond Patriarca's office in Providence, Rhode Island, it "has furnished a wealth of worthwhile information concerning Patriarca's activities and associates." The memo further states that the microphone surveillance "has shown that Patriarca exerts real control over the racketeers and racketeering activities in Rhode Island and Massachusetts . . . and has
also shown definite connections between Patriarca and the New York City hoodlum element and has strongly indicated that Patriarca is a member of the 'commission.' " The memorandum recommends that the microphone surveillance be continued until September 5, 1962.

8–1–62: The Boston SAC prepares a memorandum to Director Hoover stating: "In accordance with Bureau instructions set forth in re[ferenced] let[ter], a complete review has been made of the entire program of inquiry concerning gambling matters in the Boston Division. This review points out that the primary target of this office has been to develop admissible evidence which would result in the prosecution of Raymond L.S. Patriarca . . . . In furtherance of this phase, Boston informant 837–C* [microphone surveillance] has been developed and this informant has indicated clearly that Patriarca is conducting activities which appear to be in violation of the ITAR statute. Intensive efforts are continuing to develop proof of his involvement. This investigation, which is being conducted, consists of surveillances to determine contacts outside his regular
place of business and to identify his lieutenants and close confidants. Informants are being utilized and where information is developed which can be disseminated, it is being furnished to other law enforcement agencies for the purpose of harassing Patriarca
and his associates with the hope that a provable violation may develop. Patriarca's activities seem to concern gambling, attempts to corrupt officials and he furnishes general aid and counsel to assorted members of the underworld. In investigating those who are identified as lieutenants or close associates of Patriarca, it is felt that some violation of which they are guilty might serve as a leverage to break through the barriers with which Patriarca has surrounded himself. Some of the persons close to Patriarca and identified to date, have been Gennaro [Jerry] Angiulo and his brothers . . . Henry Tamaleo [sic], Samuel Granito and Ted Fuccillo. . . . As the Bureau is aware, the data being made available regularly through BS 837–C* [microphone surveillance] highlights the activities of these individuals. Probing of individual situations has been and will be intensified. Wherever possible, efforts are made to so utilize this information so as to develop separate independent cases." Four examples of independent cases currently being developed against Henry Tameleo, Raymond Patriarca, Herbert Ashton
Page, Jr., and Carl L. Strobeck were discussed. The memorandum states that two of these cases will go before a grand jury soon and convictions in these cases could lead to more information on other crimes.

8–9–62: According to an FBI memorandum, IRS Agent Edgerly was paid money to "straighten out" the Nicholas Angiulo tax case.

8–14–62: Director Hoover notifies the Boston SAC that the "[r]eferenced airtel [8–9–62 Airtel from Boston SAC] sets forth information regarding Internal Revenue Service Agent Edgerly who reportedly accepted a payment of $3,000 in connection with his handling of the [Jerry] Angiulo investigation. In order that this information may be properly disseminated to the Internal Revenue Service and to the Department you should promptly furnish further identifying information regarding Edgerly, including his full name. You should also include available information regarding the actual outcome of the Internal Revenue Service case involved. . . . Note: BS 837–C* [microphone surveillance] advised that Jerry Angiulo informed Raymond Patriarca on 8–3–62 that IRS Agent Edgerly had accepted $3,000 to straighten out Nick Angiulo's case." Additional corruption is mentioned. In a letter dated November 21, 2001, the IRS informed this Committee that it "could not identify" the aforementioned Agent Edgerly. (However, see 1975 entry regarding a rogue IRS Agent.) The IRS also indicated to this Committee that it was unable to identify the Nicholas Angiulo tax case.

10–11–62: Raymond Patriarca takes a polygraph test regarding allegations of his involvement in a mail robbery.

11–15–62: Director Hoover authorizes microphone surveillance of Jerry Angiulo, the "over-all boss of rackets in the Boston area" and "chief lieutenant of Raymond L.S. Patriarca, notorious New England hoodlum," at Jay's Lounge in Boston, Massachusetts.

11–27–62: In a memorandum, Director Hoover requests of the Boston SAC: "Advise your progress in connection with the installation at Jay's Lounge, 255 Tremont Street, Boston, Massachusetts."

1963

1–9–63: The FBI commences microphone surveillance on Jerry Angiulo at Jay's Lounge, located at 255 Tremont Street in Boston, Massachusetts. The FBI assigns BS 856–C* as the reference code for the Jay's Lounge bug.

2–21–63: Dennis Condon receives a $150 cash award for his contributions to the establishment of a "highly confidential source of information" of interest to the Bureau in the criminal field regarding Jerry Angiulo. [Note: The reference to a "highly confidential source of information" is referring to microphone surveillance.

3–12–63: Microphone surveillance at Jay's Lounge picks up Jerry Angiulo speculating that Ronald Cassesso may be an informant.

4–22–63: Joseph Barboza divorces Philomena Termini.

5–9–63: During a conversation with Raymond Patriarca, Jerry Angiulo states that John Callahan had approached him and "John Callahan, Chairman of the Boston Licensing Board, Boston, Mass., stood up 100%."

8–8–63: The FBI learns from the Raymond Patriarca microphone surveillance: "On 8/8/63 the informant advised that an unman [unknown man] was of the opinion that Rocco Balliro did not kill the child in Roxbury, Mass., several months ago for which crime Balliro is now being held. He is of the opinion that the police officers who were trying to apprehend Balliro at the time were responsible for the death of the child."

John Callahan was murdered by the mob in 1982. Retired FBI agent John Connolly was convicted of second-degree murder for the death.

11–14–63: A memorandum to a top FBI official, named Belmont, from C.A. Evans, discusses a dispute between Salvatore Iacone and Jerry Angiulo. The memorandum states that a "highly confidential source" provided the following information: "In the morning hours of 11/9/63 Angiulo's car was found riddled with bullets in the vicinity
of his apartment in Boston, Massachusetts. The highly confidential source giving direct coverage of Angiulo has since furnished information indicating that Angiulo professes ignorance of the shooting. He is shown to have left his car at 3:30 a.m. the morning in
which the shooting took place and the car had not been shot at at that time. It is possible the shooting was done by some person who mistakenly believed Angiulo was still in the car or done as a warning. The highly confidential source directly covering [Raymond]
Patriarca in Providence, Rhode Island, has advised that on the day before the shooting Salvatore Iacone complained to Patriarca that Angiulo on the previous night had visited Iacone in the company of others and verbally abused him, calling him an obscene name on four different occasions during an argument over the proprietorship of the Indian Meadow Country Club of Worcester, a joint enterprise of Iacone and Angiulo. Iacone told Patriarca that he was about to kill

Angiulo for this insult but that had restrained himself because of the possibility that such action would indicate disrespect for
Patriarca. In reply Patriarca told Iacone that he should have killed Angiulo at the time the name was called and if Angiulo ever called Iacone the obscene name again Iacone had the right to kill Angiulo on the spot and no questions would be asked by Patriarca. The shooting of Angiulo's car occurred the following morning. We have had recent indications of a growing coolness in attitude by Patriarca toward Angiulo." This information came from "very sensitive valuable sources."

11–21–63: The Boston SAC informs Director Hoover by memorandum that the FBI is monitoring Jerry Angiulo's contacts with his lawyer.

12–8–63: A memorandum from Boston SAC to Director Hoover, dated 1–31–64, states that the FBI learns from the Jerry Angiulo microphone surveillance that "Jerry Angiulo complained that Suffolk County District Attorney Garrett Byrne upset the deal that he
had made in connection with the sentencing of his brother, Nick, after conviction for the aforementioned charges. He said that he had made no deal with Judge Felix Forte, but that it was Forte's idea that if Nick Angiulo brought in the two individuals who allegedly
accompanied Nick at the time of the assault on Albert Christensen, Forte would show leniency. He said that now since Garry Byrne pressured Forte, he, Forte, was backing down. Angiulo said that there was talk around that Forte had been reached by the Angiulos, but the truth of the matter was that they had not reached Forte, and Forte, according to Angiulo, did not have the guts to be a party to any deal."

In a separate airtel, Director Hoover tells the Boston SAC, "Boston should submit a weekly summary airtel to the Bureau setting forth information obtained from this source and a verbatim transcript of any significant data specifically set out." The airtel also states: "In the future your airtels setting forth the information received from BS 856–C* can be set out as you would information received from a regular informant. By doing so, it will not be necessary to submit your communications as JUNE mail and the information can be filed in the regular case file."

1964

1964: Informants report that Joseph Barboza is engaged in money lending activities. From 1964 to 1966, Joseph Barboza is employed at Shawmut Insurance Company in Boston as a salesman and a clerk. Also, he works in a public relations capacity and payroll clerk for $100 a week at the Blue Bunny Lounge and Duffey's Lounge.

5–4–64: Police find the body of Francis Regis Benjamin a couple of days after he is murdered. Vincent "Jimmy" Flemmi, who Vincent Teresa calls "Vinnie the Butcher," allegedly committed the murder.

5–7–64: The FBI installs an electronic eavesdropping device at the place of business of Joseph Modica, an associate of Raymond Patriarca's. The device is installed at the Piranha Finance Company on 85 State Street in Boston, Massachusetts. The conversations overheard at the Piranha Finance Company are reflected in memoranda, logs, and airtels. See Prosecution memorandum from Walter T. Barnes and Assistant U.S. Attorney Edward F. Harrington to Henry Petersen, Chief of the Organized Crime and Racketeering Section (June 6, 1967) **[Note: Executive privilege was claimed over this document. It is in the custody of the Justice Department]**.

5–25–64: Special Agent Dennis Condon writes in a memorandum that REDACTED was contacted on 5/22/64 and said he was in contact with Vincent "Jimmy" Flemmi. The memorandum continues, "Flemmi told him that all he wants to do now is to kill people, and that it is better than hitting banks. . . . Informant said, Flemmi said that he feels he can now be the top hit man in this area and intends to be." A letter from the Boston FBI Office to Director Hoover and the Newark SAC states: "Informant stated that it appears that [Vincent 'Jimmy'] Flemmi, a Roxbury, Mass. Hoodlum, will probably become the 'contract man' in the Boston area."

6–4–64: In a letter from the Boston Office to Director Hoover, the Director is told "[Vincent 'Jimmy'] Flemmi is suspected of a number of gangland murders and has told the informant of his plans to become recognized as the No. One 'hit man' in this area as a contract killer." The Director is further told that the informant is "presently
associated" with Vincent "Jimmy" Flemmi.

8–21–64: A memorandum from Dennis Condon states that informant advised that "[Joseph] Barboza told him that he [Barboza] heard that Jimmy Flemmi had killed Frank Benjamin and cut off his head."

9–15–64: The FBI Director is informed that the Raymond Patriarca microphone surveillance caught a conversation about Peter Limone giving Edward "Teddy" Deegan two guns.

9–28–64: Vincent "Jimmy" Flemmi throws a substance into the eyes of someone and knocks him unconscious. One week later, the victim still has not regained his sight. The informant who provides this information indicates that he thinks Vincent "Jimmy" Flemmi has committed several murders. This information is contained in a
memorandum from H. Paul Rico to the Boston SAC dated October 8, 1964.

10–8–64: Special Agent Paul Rico informs the Boston SAC by memorandum of the following: "Informant advised that **REDACTED SECTION** and [Vincent] "Jimmy" Flemmi wanted to be considered the 'best hit man' in the area."

10–17–64: Anthony Sacrimone is murdered. Edward "Teddy" Deegan is the suspected killer.

10–18–64: The FBI learns from an informant that Vincent "Jimmy" Flemmi wants to kill Edward "Teddy" Deegan.

10–20–64: The Boston SAC informs Director Hoover by airtel that Vincent "Jimmy" Flemmi asked Peter Limone about Edward "Teddy" Deegan. After Flemmi left, Limone called Deegan and told him Flemmi was looking for him concerning a $300 loan that
Flemmi claimed Deegan owed him. Deegan denied owing the loan. Limone and Deegan believed that Flemmi was out to kill Deegan.

November 1964: Stephen Flemmi is first targeted as an informant, according to a Summary Report from the FBI Office of Professional Responsibility

11–5–64: The Raymond Patriarca bug captures Raymond Patriarca telling Gennaro Angiulo that "$5,000 was paid to the Massachusetts Attorney General Edward W. Brooke to obtain the acquittal of Patriarca's associate, Joseph Krikorian" This conversation was also reported in handwritten notes taken by the FBI Special Agent listening to the microphone surveillance.

12–28–64: A letter from the Boston FBI Office to Director Hoover states that FBI Informant BS 771C was stabbed fifty times and then shot. His body is found in the South End. Vincent "Jimmy" Flemmi committed the murder, and Director Hoover was informed of this fact on the day of the murder.

1965

1965: On July 18, 1967, FBI Agent Thomas H. Sullivan writes a report describing Joseph Barboza's activities in 1965. The report states, "In 1965 it was rumored REDACTED SECTION that Barboza was under contract to be assassinated since he was tied into the Buddy McLean-George McLaughlin feud. He was reported in frequent
attendance at the Ebb Tide, Revere, Mass., with Romeo Martin and Ronnie Cassessa [sic]. In 1965, Barboza was rumored to be the killer of Joseph Francione."

1–7–65: In an airtel from the Boston Office, Director Hoover is informed that "Patriarca had told the group [on 1/4/65] that is too bad the McLeans and the McLaughlins could not settle their feud over a handshake"

1–26–65: Joseph Francione is murdered. Vincent Teresa writes in his book, *My Life In The Mafia,* that Joseph Barboza went to Joseph Francione's apartment as a favor for his friend Johnny Bullets, since Francione cut Bullets out of a deal, and shot Francione
through the back of the head.

An airtel from the Boston Office to Director Hoover indicates that the Patriarca microphone surveillance revealed that a man named Frankie told Raymond Patriarca that "all the people are getting scared of Jimmy (apparently referring to [Vincent] James
Flemmi) and asked Raymond [Patriarca] to talk to Jimmy and impress upon him that there should be no more killings in Boston." The surveillance further revealed that Louis Taglianetti met with Patriarca and expressed concern that the FBI had an interest in
him, Taglianetti. Taglianetti also told Patriarca of an illegal scheme that he has been involved in for the past two years.

2–2–65: The Boston SAC apprises Director Hoover by airtel that the Raymond Patriarca microphone surveillance overheard Henry Tameleo say that Joseph Barboza killed Joseph Francione in Revere, Massachusetts.

2–24–65: Raymond Patriarca is told that "Ronnie" and Louis Greco are in Florida.

2–25–65: Dennis Condon receives a $150 incentive award for his outstanding work investigating and apprehending top ten fugitive George Patrick McLaughlin, the subject of an unlawful flight to avoid prosecution for murder.

3–3–65: A memorandum from the Boston FBI Office to Director Hoover dated 3–10–65 states: "BS 837–C* advised on 3/3/65 that unman ["unknown man"] contacted Patriarca and stated he had brought down Vincent ["Jimmy"] Flemmi and another individual (who was later identified as Joe Barboza from East Boston, Mass.)
It appeared that Frank Smith, Boston hoodlum, was giving orders to Flemmi to 'hit this guy and that guy.' Raymond Patriarca appeared infuriated at Frank Smith giving such orders without his clearance and made arrangements to meet Flemmi and Barboza in

a garage shortly thereafter. He pointed out that he did not want Flemmi or Barboza contacting him at his place of business."

The following additional information obtained by the FBI took place between 3–3–65 and 3–10–65, and was sent to Director Hoover: "Angiulo told Patriarca that Vincent ["Jimmy"] Flemmi was with Joe Barboza when he, Barboza, killed Jackie Francione in Revere, Mass. Several months ago. It appeared that Frank Smith, Boston hoodlum, had ordered the 'hit.' Patriarca again became enraged that Smith had the audacity to order a 'hit' without Patriarca's knowledge. Patriarca told Angiulo that he explained to Flemmi

that he was to tell Smith that no more killings were to take place unless, he Patriarca, cleared him. Jerry explained that he also had a talk with Flemmi. He pointed out that Patriarca has a high regard for Flemmi but that he, Patriarca, thought that Flemmi did

not use sufficient common sense when it came to killing people. Angiulo gave Flemmi a lecture on killing people, pointing out that he should not kill people because he had an argument with him at any time. If an argument does ensue, he should leave and get word to Raymond Patriarca who, in turn, will either 'OK' or deny the 'hit' on this individual, depending on the circumstances."

3–4–65: Handwritten notes of the Patriarca microphone surveillance state as follows for 11:20 a.m.: "UNMAN [unnamed man] in to see [Patriarca]—says he saw Henry Tameleo last night in Boston. He says he brought down Flemmi and another guy—since [illegible word] and involvement he should know about—Frank Smith is going around giving orders to hit this guy & that guy. R.P. [Patriarca] wants to know where they are. Man says in [illegible word] Parking Lot. R.P. [Patriarca] then says since they are here

I'll see them. He tells Richie—office worker to go with man and show them where Badway's Garage is—he tells man I'll see you over there." Patriarca came back to his office at 12:15 p.m

3–5–65: Handwritten notes of the Patriarca microphone surveillance cover a discussion between Gennaro Angiulo and Raymond Patriarca about how Angiulo was trying to influence clerks to Judge Ford. The names of the clerks are provided, so it can be determined whether they were discussing Judge Ford or Judge Forte. Angiulo also states that a certain Assistant United States Attorney is "his boy." The notes make it seem that a man named "Flemming" or "Fleming" is a part of the conversation. A comment in the margin states "Flemmi with Barbosa [sic] when whacked Francione." States that Sacrimone was with McLean and that Deegan, who killed Sacrimone, was with McLaughlin.

3–5/7–65: In a memorandum from the Boston SAC to Director Hoover dated 3–10–65, Hoover is notified of the following, which appears to have taken place between 3–5–65 and 3–7–65: "According to Patriarca, another reason that REDACTED came to Providence to contact him was to get the 'OK' to kill Eddie Deegan of Boston who was with **REDACTED SECTION**. It was not clear to the informant whether he received permission to kill Deegan; however, the story that **REDACTED** had concerning the activities of Deegan in connection with his, Deegan's, killing of [Anthony] Sacrimone was not the same as **REDACTED SECTION**." (*See* 3–10–65's second entry) [Note:

Due to Justice Department redactions, it is impossible to determine when the request to kill Deegan actually took place. However, a reasonable reading of the document seems to indicate that the request took place between March 5–7, 1965. *On April 25, 2002,* the

Department of Justice released portions of this document to the Committee in unredacted form. That document also revealed that "another reason that [Vincent 'Jimmy'] Flemmi came to Providence to contact him was to get the 'OK' to kill Eddie Deegan of Boston who was 'with the McLaughlin,' Top 10 Fugitive." In addition, the unredacted document revealed that Flemmi's story "concerning the activities of Deegan in connection with his, Deegan's, killing of [Anthony] Sacrimone was not the same as Jerry Angiulo's."]

3–9–65: Handwritten notes made by an FBI Special Agent while listening to the conversation indicate that Henry Tameleo told Patriarca that "Brownie (ph) is coming today—they have been talking about Deegan (ph)." Later, the notes continue: "Unman
[unnamed man] says Jimmie (ph) is coming in today. They only want the stuff that is signed and the bearer bonds. The other stuff from Boston they don't want. (This probably refers to hot bonds Henry had.) Unman says Jimmie has a guy with him who is a real desperado." The handwritten notes continue to describe the conversation between Raymond Patriarca and Joseph Barboza and Jimmy Flemmi: "Jimmie tells Raymond they are having a problem with Teddy Deegan (ph). Teddy did what he did to press some other people. Jimmie says that the kid [Rico Sacrimone] did not have to be killed. . . . Bobby Donati is friendly with Rico Sacrimone and Deegan is looking for an excuse to whack Donati. . . . Deegan thinks Donati is trying to set him up for Buddy McLean. Jimmie says Deegan is an arrogant, nasty sneak. Deegan fills Peter Limone's head with all kinds of stories. Raymond asks if they have discussed this matter with Jerry—They have. Raymond instructs them to check out Deegan and get more information about him." Later, Patriarca states that: "the happiest days of his life were when he was on the street clipping."

A report by Charles Reppucci regarding the Raymond Patriarca microphone surveillance, and dated July 20, 1965, reads, "[The microphone surveillance] advised on 3/9/65 that James Flemmi and Joseph Barboza requested permission from Patriarca to kill Edward 'Teddy' Deegan, as they are having a problem with him. Patriarca ultimately furnished this 'OK.'"

On March 12, 1965, the Boston Office informs Director Hoover and the SACs of the FBI offices in Albany, Buffalo, and Miami by airtel that "**REDACTED** advised on 3/9/65 that [Vincent "Jimmy"]

James Flemmi and Joseph Barboza contacted [Raymond] Patriarca, and they explained that they are having a problem with Teddy Deegan and desired to get the 'OK' to kill him. . . . Flemmi stated that Deegan is an arrogant, nasty sneak and should be killed.
Patriarca instructed them to obtain more information relative to Deegan and then to contact Jerry Angiulo at Boston who would furnish them with a decision." "Investigation into Allegations of Justice Department Misconduct in New England," Hearings Before the Comm. on Govt. Reform, 107th Cong. at 132 (May 11, 2002).70 [**On April 25, 2002, the Department of Justice released this document to the Committee in unredacted form. The unredacted document revealed that the portion redacted was "BS 837–C*"—the Patriarca microphone surveillance.**]

According to a memorandum from the SAC in Boston to Director Hoover, "Vincent Jimmy Flemmi, aka 'Jimmy' Flemmi, is being designated as a target in [the Top Echelon Criminal Informant Program]." The document further states that "Flemmi also is believed to be involved in the murders of the following individuals: **REDACTED
SECTION**." The document also states that Flemmi was the subject of an "Unlawful Flight to Avoid Prosecution" for armed robbery investigation.

3–10–65: Special Agent Paul Rico writes in an FBI memorandum dated 3–15–65, "Informant advised [on 3–10–65] that he had just heard from 'Jimmy' Flemmi that Flemmi told the informant that Raymond Patriarca has put out the word that Edward 'Teddy' Deegan is to be 'hit' and that a dry run has already been made and that a close associate of Deegan's has agreed to set him up."

A Boston airtel apprises Director Hoover that "REDACTED told [Raymond] Patriarca that REDACTED was with Joe Barboza when he, Barboza, killed REDACTED in Revere, Mass. several months ago. . . . "According to Patriarca, another reason that REDACTED came to Providence to contact him was to get the 'OK' to kill Eddie Deegan of Boston who was with REDACTED SECTION. It was not clear to the informant whether he received permission to kill Deegan; however, the story that REDACTED had concerning the activities of Deegan in connection with his, Deegan's, killing of [Anthony]
Sacrimone was not the same as REDACTED SECTION."
[On April 25, 2002, the Department of Justice released this document to the Committee in unredacted form. That document revealed that Jerry Angiulo told Patriarca that Vincent "Jimmy" Flemmi was with Barboza when Barboza killed Jackie Francione. That document also revealed that "another reason that [Vincent 'Jimmy'] Flemmi came to Providence to contact him was to get the 'OK' to kill Eddie Deegan of Boston who was 'with the McLaughlin,' Top 10 Fugitive." In addition, the unredacted document revealed that Flemmi's story "concerning the activities of Deegan in connection with his, Deegan's, killing of [Anthony] Sacrimone was not the same as Jerry Angiulo's."]

3–12–65: Vincent "Jimmy" Flemmi is assigned as an informant to Special Agent Paul Rico. This information is contained in an FBI memorandum dated 6–10–65 from Inspector H.E. Campbell to Boston Special Agent in Charge James L. Handley.
Edward "Teddy" Deegan is killed in a Chelsea, Massachusetts, alleyway between 9:00 P.M. and 11:00 P.M. Statement of Joseph Kozlowski states: "About 10:P.M. went to
Fourth St. Chelsea and saw a red car with motor running with three men sitting in it, two in the front and one in the rear seat. This car was parked about the second meter from Broadway between Broadway and Luther Place on the side near the P.A.V. I
walked behind the car and saw the rear number plate Mass. Reg. # 404 - - - with the right half of plate folded towards the center obstructing the other three digits. I then went to the drivers [sic] side of the car and rapped on window motioning the driver to lower the window. As I did this the driver took off at a fast rate of speed and took a screeching turn to the right on Broadway. I observed that the man in the back had dark hair with a bald spot in center of head."

3–13–65: The same informant from the March 10 memorandum tells Special Agent Paul Rico in detail who killed Edward "Teddy" Deegan and how. The informant said Vincent "Jimmy" Flemmi contacted the informant and said that Deegan was lured to the finance company to be killed. The memorandum states: "Informant advised that [Vincent] 'Jimmy' Flemmi contacted him and told him that the previous evening Deegan was lured to a finance company in Chelsea and that the door of the finance company had been left open by an employee of the company and that when they got to the door
Roy French, who was setting Deegan up, shot Deegan, and Joseph Romeo Martin and Ronnie Cassesa [sic] came out of the door and one of them fired into Deegan's body. While Deegan was approaching the doorway, he (Flemmi) and Joe Barboza walked over towards a car driven by Tony 'Stats' [Anthony Stathopolous] and they were going to kill 'Stats' but 'Stats' saw them coming and drove off before any shots were fired. Flemmi told informant that Ronnie Cassesa [sic] and Romeo Martin wanted to prove to Raymond Patriarca they were capable individuals, and that is why they wanted to 'hit' Deegan. Flemmi indicated that they did an 'awful sloppy job.' This information has been disseminated by SA Donald V. Shannon to Capt. Robert Renfrew (NA)

of the Chelsea, Mass. PD." Special Agent Paul Rico memorializes this information in a March 15, 1965, memorandum to the Boston SAC.

3–14–65: A Boston Police Department report on the Edward "Teddy" Deegan murder, likely written by Detective William W. Stuart, contains the following information: "From a reliable informant the following facts were obtained to the [Deegan murder]: Informant states that the following men were Joseph Barron aka Barboza, Romeo Martin, Freddie Chiampi, Roy French, Ronnie Cassesso, Tony Stats. (Greek) Chico Amico[.] . . . Informant states that they were over lounge in Revere when they received the call from French that everything was OK then they all left together. . . . Romeo Martin is a former informant but since hanging in the North End hasn't been to [sic] helpful. . . . Informant states that the reason for the killing of Deegan was that Barren [sic] claims that he is with the Hughes brothers and McLaughlins and he felt that Deegan was a threat to his friends in Roxbury (Flemmi & Bennett)."

The Chelsea Police also received evidence about who murdered Edward "Teddy" Deegan. Lieutenant Thomas Evans of the Chelsea Police Department writes an undated report containing meticulous details of the Teddy Deegan murder. In the report, Lieutenant Evans states, "I received information from Capt. Renfrew that a[n] informant of his had contacted him and told him that [Roy] French had received a telephone call at the Ebb Tide at 9 P.M. on 3–12– 65 and after a short conversation he had left the cafe´ with the following men: Joseph Barboza, Ronald Cassesso, Vincent Flemmi, Francis Imbruglia, Romeo Martin, Nicky Femia and a man by the name of Freddi who is about 40 years old and said to be a 'Strong arm.' They are said to have returned at about 11 P.M. and Martin was alleged to have said to French, 'We nailed him.' " There is no mention whatsoever of Joseph Salvati, Peter Limone, Henry
Tameleo, or Louis Greco in the report.

3–15–65: Detective Lieutenant Inspector Richard J. Cass of the Massachusetts State Police writes a report to Captain of Detectives Daniel I. Murphy regarding the homicide of Edward "Teddy" Deegan. The report states that Chelsea Officer James O'Brien was
the routeman for the area where Deegan was found. Officer O'Brien checked the alley around 9:00 P.M. and turned the lights on; he returned around 10:59 P.M., found the alley lights out, explored the alley, and found Deegan's body. The report continues by
stating that during the evening of Friday, March 12, Joseph Barboza was at the Ebb Tide with Francis Imbruglia, Ronald Cassosa (sic), Vincent Flemmi, Romeo Martin, Nick Femia and man known as "Freddy." At about 9:00 P.M., Roy French received
a phone call, and the above group left the Ebb Tide with him. According to the report, Chelsea Captain Joseph Kozlowski was around Fourth Street at about 9:30 P.M. and saw a red car withthe motor running and three men inside. The rear license plate
was obstructed. [This was Romeo Martin's car. See 10–25–65 entry.] Officer Kozlowski approached the driver and the driver sped off. Officer Kozlowski described the driver as Romeo Martin. The man in the back seat was "stocky with dark hair and a bald spot
in the center of his head." In addition, the report states that the Massachusetts State Police received information three weeks ago indicating Deegan pulled a gun on Barboza at Ebb Tide, forcing Barboza to back down. Inspector Cass writes in his report:
"Unconfirmed information was received that Romeo Martin and Ronald Cassessa [sic] had entered the building and were waiting just inside the rear door. [Anthony] Stathopoulos was waiting on Fourth Street in a car and French and Deegan entered the alley. Deegan opened the rear door. He was shot twice in the back of the head and also in the body. The information at the

time was that three guns were used. Lieutenant John Collins of Ballistics confirmed the report of three guns being used at a later time. Two
men approached the car in which Stathopoulos was waiting and he took off."

Special Agent Paul Rico writes in a memorandum to REDACTED SAC that SA Donald Shannon allegedly provided information about the Edward "Teddy" Deegan murder to Captain Robert Renfrew.

3–16–65: Director Hoover instructs the Boston SAC: "At the earliest possible time that dissemination can be made with full security to BS 837–C* [Patriarca microphone surveillance], you should advise appropriate authorities of the identities of the possible perpetrators of the murders of [Anthony] Sacrimone and [Edward "Teddy"] Deegan. Advise the Bureau when this has been done.

3–19–65: The Boston SAC advises Director Hoover by airtel: "Informants report that Ronald Casessa [sic], Romeo Martin, Vincent James Flemmi, and Joseph Barboza, prominent local hoodlums, were responsible for the killing. They accomplished this by having Roy French, another Boston hoodlum, set [Edward "Teddy"] Deegan up[.] French apparently walked in behind Deegan when they were gaining entrance to the building and fired the first shot hitting Deegan in the back of the head. Casessa [sic] and Martin immediately thereafter shot Deegan from the front. Anthony Stathopoulos was also in on the burglary but had remained outside in the car. When Flemmi and Barboza walked over to Stathopoulos's car, Stathopoulos thought it was the law and took
off. Flemmi and Barboza were going to kill Stathopoulos also. . . .

Efforts are now being made by the Chelsea PD to force [Anthony] Stathopoulos to furnish them the necessary information to prosecute the persons responsible. It should be noted that this information was furnished to the Chelsea PD and it has been established by the Chelsea Police that Roy French, Barboza, Flemmi, Casessa
[sic], and Martin were all together at the Ebb Tide night club in Revere, Mass. and they all left at approximately 9 o'clock and returned 45 minutes later. It should be noted that the killing took place at approximately 9:30 p.m., Friday, 3/12/65. Informant also
advised that REDACTED had given the 'ok' to Joe Barboza and 'Jimmy' Flemmi to kill REDACTED SECTION who was killed approximately one month ago."

3–23–65: An FBI memorandum from Special Agent REDACTED to the Boston SAC, dated 4-6-65, states the following: "On 3/23/65, PCI [Potential Confidential Informant] advised that Joe Barbosa [sic] is from East Boston and an ex-fighter, was very friendly with Romeo Martin, Ronnie Cassessi [sic] and REDACTED SECTION. PCI
stated that Barbosa [sic] was supposed 'to have hit' Francione from Revere and Eaton. He stated that Barbosa [sic] reportedly killed Eaton with a Magnum gun. PCI stated that Barbosa [sic] was in prison with Benjamin who was murdered after he left prison and
beheaded. He stated that Barbosa [sic] is a Portuguese kid who would otherwise
be accepted into La Cosa Nostra except for his nationality. He stated that Barbosa [sic] claims that he had shot [Edward] Teddy Deegan with a .45 caliber gun. PCI related that Barbosa [sic] indicated that Roy French was with Deegan and another individual
when Deegan was shot by Barbosa [sic] and two other individuals, one of whom informant believed was Romeo Martin. REDACTED SECTION. Informant stated that he had heard Barbosa [sic] indicate that one of the guys with Deegan whom they had
planned to kill along with Deegan ran off when the law showed up and fled.

PCI stated that rumors have it that Roy French actually set up Deegan to be killed.
PCI stated that he had heard that Joe Barbosa [sic] was extremely friendly with Jimmy Flemma [sic] from Dudley Street. He stated that Barbosa [sic] had tried to reach Jimmy Flemma [sic] a short time ago and wanted to know if Flemma [sic] has gone to
Providence to see Raymond (Patriarca). PCI subsequently determined from a source that Jimmy Flemma [sic] had gone to Providence, R.I. earlier on the day that Barbosa [sic] had tried to contact Flemma [sic]. PCI stated that Jimmy Flemma [sic] had gone to Providence just before Teddy Deegan was slain in Chelsea. REDACTED SECTION. REDACTED SECTION. REDACTED SECTION. PCI further advised that
about a week ago, there was a big party for Romeo Martin at the Ebtide [sic] Restaurant and Bar in Revere and that [Edward] Wimpy Bennett, Jimmy Flemma [sic], REDACTED SECTION, Roy French, Joe Barbosa [sic], Ronnie Cassessi [sic] and REDACTED SECTION were in attendance. He stated that this party was in honor
of the recent marriage of REDACTED SECTION." [The informant information
provided is categorized as "very good."]

3-24-65: An airtel from the Boston SAC to Director Hoover discusses the Edward "Teddy" Deegan murder: "In connection with the information furnished by BS 837–C* relative to the possible perpetrators of the murders of Anthony Sacrimone and Edward
Deegan, Capt. Robert Renfrew (NA), Chelsea, Mass. PD, was advised of the same information, as furnished by REDACTED. This informant also furnished basically the same information as did BS 837-C* relative to the murder of Edward Deegan [this appears to be an error because Sacrimone was killed on 10/17/64] on 10/17/64.
This information was furnished to Inspector Henry Doherty of the Everett, Mass. PD on 10/18/64." The memorandum continues by stating: "The Chelsea Police at that time had no knowledge of the murder; however, when the body was discovered, they immediately
started to look for Roy French. French told them he was at the Ebb Tide night club, Revere, Mass., all night and their investigation has indicated that French got a telephone call about 8:45 p.m. After the phone call he left the Ebb Tide with Joseph Barboza, Vincent Flemmi, Ronnie Casessa [sic], Romeo Martin, and Frank [Francis] Imbruglia. Further investigation reflected that they all returned about 45 minutes later. The time of the murder was approximately 9:30 p.m., 3/12/65. Romeo Martin's car was identified by a Chelsea Police Officer as being parked with two men in it in the vicinity of the murder. When the police officer approached the car, it sped off."

3-26-65: Special Agent Dennis Condon drafts a memorandum that was completely redacted when released to this Committee.

4-5-65: The first reported contact between Vincent "Jimmy" Flemmi as an informant and Special Agent Paul Rico occurs. Rico contacts Flemmi as an informant four times prior to Flemmi being closed on September 15,

4-8-65: A memorandum from the Boston SAC to Director Hoover and the New York SAC dated 4-13-65 states: "Informant [BS 837– C*] also advised [on 4-8-65] that [Jerry Angiulo told Raymond Patriarca that] Angiulo is of the opinion that Edward 'Wimpy' Bennett and [Vincent] James Flemmi are 'stool pigeons.' " This memorandum
also discusses how Vincent "Jimmy" Flemmi was paid $1,500 for disposing of the body of a girl. The handwritten notes prepared by Special Agent Murphy while listening to the microphone surveillance indicate that Flemmi also cut the body into pieces. In addition, the memorandum stated that Flemmi "admitted that he was very friendly with Det. William Stewart [sic]."

4–9–65: An FBI Memorandum reflects information provided to Special Agent Paul Rico by Jimmy Flemmi.

4–18–65: Raymond Patriarca is told that "[Boston Police Department employee] Stuart must be getting info from the Feds." Gennaro Angiulo was also told that "Stuart + Flemmi went to NYC on $100,000 of AMEXCO check (counterfeit) 5 or 6 months ago[.]" Patriarca is also told that Stuart and Flemmi were at a New York grand jury.

5–3–65: FBI informant Vincent "Jimmy" Flemmi, on his way to meet Joseph Barboza, is shot at by two individuals with shotguns. Flemmi is wounded.

Director Hoover is informed that the Raymond Patriarca microphone surveillance captured Patriarca questioning Jimmy Flemmi about his association with Detective William Stuart of the Boston Police. The summary notes that Patriarca "was concerned with Flemmi being a 'stool pigeon' for Stewart [sic]." The surveillance also captured Patriarca giving Flemmi permission to "finish off" Frank Smith.

5–5–65: The Raymond Patriarca microphone surveillance gathers the following information: "[I]nformant advised that Patriarca had been approached by Joseph Barboza, Ronald Cassessa [sic], and James Flemmi in order to obtain permission to kill Sammy Linden of Revere, Mass. The reason for this killing was that Linden was
furnishing a considerable amount of money to the McLaughlin group in their efforts to kill various individuals of the McLean group. Subsequently the informant stated that Patriarca had not given a definite 'OK' for the killing, but Barboza and his group was
of the opinion that he did. Linden heard of the fact that he was marked for a 'hit' and went to Joseph Lombardo of Boston, Mass. Lombardo, in turn, sent word to Patriarca, and after explaining the situation the 'hit' was called off." [This information is contained in report prepared by Special Agent Charles Reppucci on 7–20–65.]

Also on this day, Henry Tameleo contacts Raymond Patriarca and tells him that Joseph Lombardo told Tameleo that he had heard that Barboza, Vincent "Jimmy" Flemmi and Ronald Cassesso received permission to kill Linden. Lombardo also told Tameleo to
instruct Barboza and Flemmi not to kill Linden.

5–7–65: The Boston SAC sends an airtel to Director Hoover and the SACs in New Haven, Connecticut, New York and Washington. The airtel cites the BS 837–C* [Patriarca microphone surveillance] as the source for the following: "A . . . lengthy discussion took place wherein Joe Lombardo was very perturbed because Cassessa
[sic] and Joseph Barboza were associating with the Flemmi brothers; and further, that information had been put out to the effect that Barboza was with Flemmi when they killed Edward Deegan."

5–12–65: By memorandum, Director Hoover informs the Attorney General Nicholas Katzenbach of microphone surveillance at Jay's Lounge, located at 255 Tremont Street in Boston, Massachusetts.

5–18–65: The Boston SAC notifies Director Hoover by airtel of the following developments concerning Raymond Patriarca: "Joe Barboza requests permission from Patriarca to kill some unknown person. This person lives in a three-story house but Barboza has never been able to line him up to kill him. Barboza told Raymond that he plans to pour gasoline in the basement part of the house and set it afire and thus either kill the individual by smoke inhalation or fire, or in the event he starts to climb out a window, Barboza would have two or three individuals there with rifles to

kill him as he started to step out a window or door. Upon questioning by Patriarca, Barboza said that he had planned to cut the telephone wires so that the individual could not call for assistance and also to ring false alarms in other sections of the city so that the engines could not respond quickly. He also explained that the third floor apartment was vacant but the first floor apartment was apparently occupied by the intended victim's mother. This apparently caused no concern to Barboza who stated it was not his fault that the mother would be present, and he would not care whether the mother died or not. Patriarca told him that he did not think it was a good idea to effect the killing in the above manner and attempted to dissuade Barboza from this type of killing as innocent people would probably be killed. It was not clear to the informant whether

Barboza accepted Patriarca's objections, but Patriarca indicated very strongly against this type of killing."

6-4-65: An airtel from the Boston SAC to Director Hoover states that the previous day "[REDACTED] went into detail concerning the killing of Edward [Teddy] Deegan which had been previously reported, and the fact that the Attorney REDACTED of Everett, Mass, was called by Deegan's accomplice at the time Deegan was killed." The airtel later states "Taglianetti discussed a yard which he contemplates using in order to make a 'hit.' Informant did not know who Taglianetti was referring to, but possibly Willy Marfeo, which information had been disseminated previously. This group has been attempting to kill Marfeo for over one year, but has not been successful, as yet."

In a memorandum from Director Hoover to the Boston SAC, Hoover requests the following regarding BS 919 PC [Jimmy Flemmi]: "Advise Bureau by 7/1/65 [the] status of your efforts to effect the development of the above-captioned target."

6-8-65: Special Agent Paul Rico advises Vincent "Jimmy" Flemmi "of the FBI's jurisdiction and of his confidential relationship with the Bureau. Flemmi was told he was not a Bureau employee and that he was to furnish information only to the Bureau.

He also was told that any payments he received are to be considered as income and he is not to contact the office personally." In response, Flemmi states that "he is willing to aid the Bureau, as he can help put away the individuals who attempted to kill

him."

6-9-65: The Boston SAC writes a memorandum to Director Hoover, in response to Director Hoover's inquiry five days earlier: "It is known through other informants and sources of his office that this individual has been in contact with Raymond L.S. Patriarca

and other members of La Cosa Nostra in this area, and potentially could be an excellent informant. Concerning the informant's emotional stability, the Agent handling the informant believes, from information obtained from other informants and sources, that BS-919-PC [Vincent "Jimmy" Flemmi] has murdered (REDACTED), (REDACTED),

(REDACTED), (REDACTED), Edward 'Teddy' Deegan, and (redacted), as well as a fellow inmate at the Massachusetts Correctional Institution, Walpole, Mass., and, from all indications, he is going to continue to commit murder. . . . Although the informant

will be difficult to contact once he is released from the hospital because he feels that REDACTED SECTION will try to kill him, the informant's potential outweighs the risk involved." [102]

6–10–65: An FBI document indicates that James Vincent Flemmi was assigned to Special Agent Paul Rico on March 12, 1965

6–14–65: The Boston SAC is advised in an FBI Memorandum from Correlator Helen Hatch, that on 3–9–65 "James [Vincent "Jimmy"] Flemmi and Joseph Barboza contacted [Raymond] Patriarca, and they explained that they were having a problem with [Edward] Teddy Deegan, and desired to get the 'OK' to kill him. . . . Flemmi stated that Deegan is an arrogant, nasty sneak and should be killed. Patriarca instructed them to obtain more information relative to Deegan and then to contact Jerry Angiulo at Boston who would furnish them a decision." The memorandum also states that "Joe Lombardo was very perturbed because Cassessa [sic] and Joseph Barboza were associating with the Flemmi brothers; and further, that information had been put out to the effect that Barboza was with Flemmi when they killed Edward Deegan."

7–9–65: Romeo Martin is shot and killed. In his 1973 book, *My Life In The Mafia*, Vincent Teresa writes that Joseph Barboza killed Martin. Teresa provides the following account of the Martin murder: "In the time I knew him [Barboza], he handled more than twenty-three murders, most of them on his own—I mean, they weren't ordered by the Office. Romeo Martin is a typical example of what I mean. This was in 1965 [sic], in July. I'd been out all day with Castucci and Romeo playing golf. Romeo was planning to leave for Florida the next day with his wife. He'd just gotten married and was going to Florida for sort of a honeymoon. After we'd played golf, I told Romeo to come over to the Ebbtide for a steak dinner and a couple of drinks. While we're talking, he said that heand Barboza, after busting up a club, had had an argument. He said he'd shaken the owner down for more money than he was supposed to and had held out on Barboza. Barboza had found out and threatened to kill him. . . . When he [Martin] went outside, Barboza and Cassesso were waiting for him. They grabbed him, took him someplace, and pumped five slugs into him before dumping his body. When the cops found him, [Henry] Tameleo blew his top at me. . . . [H]e said[,] 'Why didn't you get a hold of Joe [Barboza] and stop it?' . . . [I responded,] 'Christ, Henry [Tameleo], they were supposed to be friends. Who knows this animal is going to kill him?' That's how treacherous Barboza was. The slightest thing, the slightest word and he'd want to kill you."

7–12–65: The microphone surveillance on Raymond Patriarca is discontinued.

7–20–65: A report by Charles Reppucci of the Boston FBI Office discusses the Raymond Patriarca microphone surveillance. The report reads, "[The microphone surveillance] advised on 3/9/65 that James Flemmi and Joseph Barboza requested permission from Patriarca to kill Edward 'Teddy' Deegan, as they are having a problem with him. Patriarca ultimately furnished his 'OK.' "

7–27–65: Special Agents Paul Rico and Raymond Ball author a memorandum to the SAC regarding BS 919–PC (Vincent "Jimmy" Flemmi) stating, "Informant advised that he himself is still recovering from wounds after being shot by Jimmy O'Toole and two other unknown individuals, whom he believes were Stevie Hughes and Edward 'Punchy' McLaughlin. . . . Informant also advised his biggest regret is that he did not kill George McLaughlin . . . before he became sought for murder."

9–10–65: An FBI memorandum indicates that advised that Joseph Barboza had been arrested Friday night, September 10, 1965, for beating a policeman with a gun at the Ebb Tide in Revere, Massachusetts.

9–15–65: According to a memorandum from the Boston Office to Director Hoover, Vincent "Jimmy" Flemmi is closed as an informant after being charged with "Assault with a Dangerous Weapon with Intent to Murder," after shooting John Cutliffe. The memorandum further states that Flemmi failed to appear in court on September 3, 1965. The memorandum continues, "In view of the fact that informant [Jimmy Flemmi] is presently a local fugitive, any contacts with him might prove to be difficult and embarrassing. In view of the above, this case is being closed."

10–20–65: Edward J. "Punchy" McLaughlin is killed by Joseph Barboza and Chico "Joseph" Amico.

11–3–65: The Boston SAC notifies Director Hoover by memorandum of a potential addition to the Top Echelon Criminal Informant Program, stating, "Stephen Joseph Flemmi, FBI REDACTED is being designated as a target in this program." The Boston SAC continues, "Although the LCN [La Cosa Nostra] in this area has not actively
taken part in this gang war, there is every possibility that they may move into the picture in the near future and since Flemmi is in contact with the leaders of the different groups that are against the remaining McLaughlin faction, and that all these groups are
very aware of the possibility of LCN moving in to support the McLaughlin group, it is felt that Flemmi will be in a position to furnish information on LCN members in this area."

11–15–65: Joseph Barboza murders Ray DiStasio, a member of the McLaughlin mob, and John B. O'Neil, an innocent bystander. In his book, *My Life in the Mafia,* Vincent Teresa writes, "Barboza went into the club [searching for a member of the McLaughlin mob named Ray DiStasio] and caught DiStasio cold. The trouble was, a poor slob named John B. O'Neil, who had a bunch of kids, walked in to get a pack of cigarettes. Barboza killed them both because he didn't want any witnesses. DiStasio got two in the back of the head and O'Neil got three. It was a shame. I mean, this O'Neil was a family man—he had nothing to do with the mob. Barboza should have waited. That's why he was so dangerous. He was unpredictable. When he tasted blood, everyone in his way got it."

11–19–65: Vincent "Jimmy" Flemmi is convicted of armed assault with intent to murder. He serves his time at the Massachusetts State Prison at Walpole and is discharged on March 28, 1969.

11–30–65: The *Boston Globe* reports that Joseph Barboza attended a bail hearing with his attorney, F. Lee Bailey. Assistant District Attorney for Suffolk County Jack Zalkind said he had three East Boston policemen in court who knew of three attempts
to kill Barboza. Ed Burns and Gordon Hillman

1966

1966: Informants report that Barboza split with Connie Frizzi in loan sharking to go into partnership with Arthur Bratsos.

1–14–66: The United States Attorney's Office in Boston, Massachusetts, receives a Boston gangland murder report that includes a summary of the Deegan murder. The report, entitled

"Boston Gangland Murders; Criminal Intelligence Program" was prepared by John Kehoe Jr. and is dated January 14, 1966. It covers the investigative period between November 15, 1965, and January 11, 1966. This report was approved by Boston SAC James Handley and contains a section entitled "Informants" that is completely redacted except for the following sentence: "REDACTED is BS 955–PC [Stephen Flemmi], contacted by SA H. Paul Rico." The synopsis of the report reads: "This report contains information concerning the various gangland murders that have occurred in Boston and vicinity from 5/4/64 through 11/15/65." The report states the following about the Deegan murder: "*Method of Killing* Teddy Deegan's body was found in a doorway in the alley off Fourth Street, Chelsea, Massachusetts, behind the Lincoln National Bank, at 10:59 PM, Monday, March 12, 1965. Shot in head and body with three different guns, one a .45 caliber and two .38 calibers. *Background* Edward Deegan was born January 2, 1930, Boston, Massachusetts, and was employed spasmodically as a laborer. His record consisted of 'Larceny, Breaking and Entering, Felonious Assaults, Armed Robbery, Accessory After the Fact to Assault with a Dangerous Weapon, and Automobile thefts.' REDACTED advised that James Flemmi has told him that Deegan was lured to a finance company in Chelsea, Massachusetts, where the door of the finance company had been left open by an employee. At that time he was accompanied by Roy French who was actually setting Deegan up to be killed, Joseph Romeo Martin, and Ronald Cassessa [sic]. All of these individuals hung out at the Ebb Tide restaurant in Revere, Massachusetts, and were close associates of Henry Tameleo, top lieutenant of Raymond L.S. Patriarca. While Deegan was approaching the doorway, James Flemmi and Joseph Barboza, hoodlums who were in the immediate vicinity, walked over to the car driven by Tony 'Stats' Stathopoulos who had brought Deegan to the scene of the proposed burglary. Barboza and Flemmi were going to kill 'Stats'; however, 'Stats' saw them coming and immediately drove off before any shots were fired. Flemmi told informant that Ronald Cassessa [sic] and Romeo Martin wanted to prove to Raymond Patriarca they were capable individuals and that is why they wanted to 'hit' Deegan. Flemmi indicated that they did an awful sloppy job. It should be noted that prior to the time Deegan's body was found, 'Stats' apparently immediately proceeded to the offices of Attorney John Fitzgerald, thinking that the two individuals who approached him while waiting for Deegan to come out of the finance company were Police Officers. After telling Fitzgerald the story, Fitzgerald called the Chelsea, Massachusetts Police Department requesting information concerning Deegan. The Police Officer suggested that Fitzgerald come to the Police Department for the information, which Fitzgerald did. When he came the Police Officers, having no knowledge of the escape or shooting, and having not, as yet, found the body, talked to Fitzgerald at the station and commenced looking for the break. At this time they came upon the body of Deegan behind the finance company. The above information was furnished to the Police Department. However, as yet, they have not obtained sufficient evidence to warrant production against any of the above individuals."

3–9–66: Vincent "Jimmy" Flemmi goes to prison in Massachusetts for 4–6 years for armed assault with intent to murder.

3–31–66: According to Special Agent Paul Rico's FBI personnel records, Rico is rated excellent with comments that he had been assigned exclusively "to the development of Top Echelon informants and had worked primarily on this important program." The comments further state that Rico "had exceptional talent in his ability to develop informants and his participation was considered outstanding."

6–15–66: Rocco DiSeglio is murdered.

7–13–66: William Marfeo is shot and killed. Vincent Teresa writes in his book, *Vinnie Teresa's Mafia*, the following account of William Marfeo's murder: Butch Micelli's "gang handled . . . the hit on Willie Marfeo, a bookie who tried to operate on his own on
Federal Hill in Providence. Raymond [Patriarca] called [Joe] Paterno [from New Jersey] for outside talent to whack out Marfeo because Marfeo knew all our assassins. Butch paid a visit to the office in Providence, and two days later [July 13, 1966] Marfeo was
shot while he was eating a pizza in the Korner Kitchen Restaurant in Providence."

9–23–66: Stephen Hughes and Samuel D. Lindenbaum are murdered. Vincent Teresa writes in *My Life In The Mafia* that "Barboza and Chico Amico knew that Hughes and Lindenbaum were heading for Lawrence to take over some numbers and lottery
action" and "dropped Hughes and Lindenbaum right in their seats."

10–6–66: After receiving a letter from Joseph Barboza, *Boston Herald* reporter James Southwood writes, "Barboza was arrested at gunpoint in downtown Boston with Nicholas F. Femia, 27, Patrick J. Fabiano, 24, both of East Boston, and Arthur C. Bratsos, 33, of Medford. Police said the car the three were in had in it an Army
M–1 rifle, a loaded .45 caliber automatic pistol and a knife. At the time, Barboza and Femia were out on bail in connection with a stabbing three months earlier. Because of the pending court action and a new charge of illegal possession of firearms, the bail set on Barboza was high—$100,000."

11–1–66: According to Dennis Condon's personnel file, he is "involved in a substantive error write-up case when a review of an informant file assigned to him disclosed an instance of failure to properly disseminate information obtained from the informant."
The informant had reported that an individual who was a suspect in another FBI case had a machine gun in his possession and was "crazy." Condon did not disseminate this information to the Treasury Department in accordance with the provisions of Manual of Instructions. Condon explained that he inadvertently failed to make the appropriate dissemination because the suspect was under active investigation by the FBI. The SAC initialed the serial for filing with the belief that the appropriate dissemination would be made in a separate communication. No administrative action was taken against Condon.

Arthur Bratsos and Thomas J. DePrisco are found dead. The *Boston Herald* reports, "Bratsos [32 of Medford] and Thomas J. DePrisco, 27, of Roslindale, . . . friend[s] of Barboza, went out and tried to raise bail for [Barboza, who was in jail on a gun-carrying
charge.] They started shaking down the wrong people and on Nov. 1, 1966[,] Bratsos and DePrisco were found in a black Cadillac in South Boston. They were dead. And the money was gone."

On January 25, 1967, Barboza is found guilty of the gun-carrying charge and is sentenced to four to five years at Walpole. Nick Femia and Patrick Fabiano are sentenced with him

11–7–66: The U.S. Supreme Court issues its landmark decision regarding electronic surveillance in *Black* v. *U.S.*, 385 U.S. 26 (1966). The Court finds that the listening "device monitored and taped conversations held in the hotel suite during the period the
[alleged criminal] offense was being investigated and beginning some two months before and continuing until about one month after the evidence in this case was presented to the Grand Jury. During that period, 'the monitoring agents,' the Solicitor General advised overheard, among other conversations, exchanges between petitioner and the attorney who was then representing him (Black) in this case." Thus, the Court holds, "In view of these facts it appears that justice requires

that a new trial be held so as to afford the petitioner an opportunity to protect himself from the use of evidence
that might be otherwise inadmissible."

12–7–66: Joseph Barboza's partner Chico Joseph Amico is killed while Barboza is incarcerated in Charles Street Jail.

12–22–66: Director Hoover advises the Acting Attorney General by memorandum: "The installation of the eavesdropping device placed in Jay's Lounge was made under the general authority of Attorney General Robert F. Kennedy. By memorandum of May 12, 1965, Attorney General Katzenbach was advised that the device had been in operation since January 9, 1963, and he authorized its continuance. It was discontinued on July 12, 1965." This document was copied to the Deputy Attorney General and the Assistant Attorney General of the Criminal Division.

1967

1–25–67: Joseph Barboza, Nick Femia, and Patrick Fabiano are all found guilty on possession of weapons charges and immediately sentenced to prison. Barboza is sentenced to 4–5 years for having a gun in an automobile, and 4–5 years for a similar charge involving a knife. These sentences will run concurrently. Barboza also is sentenced to 4–5 years probation following his prison term on a receiving stolen property charge. The *Boston Globe* reports, "Extraordinary precautions were taken with the transport of Baron and Femia to state prison. . . . [P]recautions were taken because of 'the climate in the underworld today.' In the past two years, 42 persons have been slain in gangland warfare."

2–7–67: According to the Justice Department, Stephen Flemmi began to work for the FBI as a Top Echelon Criminal Informant. (Interview with Assistant United States Attorney John Durham

2–14–67: Stephen Flemmi is approved as a Top Echelon Informant, according to an FBI Office of Professional Responsibility Report

3–8–67: Special Agents Paul Rico and Dennis Condon interview Joseph Barboza at Walpole State Prison. Barboza says he will talk to the agents as long as they do not testify against him for what he tells them. The say they will respect his confidence. Barboza advised that "as a matter of fact, he used to see Raymond Patriarca and get an 'OK' before he made most of his moves." Barboza "made statements that he was going to kill several" people who killed three of Barboza's friends (Thomas J. DePrisco, Arthur C. Bratsos, Joseph W. Amico) and stole $70,000 from him. The agents learn that Barboza "knows what has happened in practically every murder that has been committed in this area. He said that he would never provide information that would allow James Vincent
['Jimmy'] Flemmi to 'fry' but that he will consider furnishing information on these murders." [There appears to be a REDACTED SECTION immediately following this quote.] 131

3–21–67: Joseph Barboza is interviewed in Boston by H. Paul Rico and Dennis Condon. John Fitzgerald was present. (*See* 3–28–67 entry).

A teletype from the Boston Office to Director Hoover reads, "REDACTED SECTION. Boston 'Record American' received call from someone at Walpole Correctional Institution, Walpole,

Mass., that Barboza was taken out by federal authorities and headlines in this afternoon's paper stated that U.S. Government opened its war on
crime by bringing gang leader from Walpole for appearance before federal grand jury."

3–28–67: The Boston SAC informs Director Hoover by memorandum of an interview of Joseph Barboza conducted on March 21, 1967. This interview was a follow-up to an interview conducted on March 8, 1967. Special Agents Paul Rico and Dennis Condon conducted the interview at the Federal Building in Boston. Barboza conferred with his attorney, John Fitzgerald, at one point, received some advice, and then continued the interview. [Information obtained by the Committee from the FBI indicates that Fitzgerald's girlfriend may have been an FBI informant.] Barboza said he would talk to the agents, but he would not testify to any information that he was furnishing at this time. Barboza stated that since the last time he talked to the agents, he had concluded that they have a common enemy in the "Italian organization." He would like to help the FBI in its efforts to obtain evidence against the "Italian organization." Barboza said he hopes Suffolk County District Attorney Garrett Byrne appreciates Barboza's assistance and gives him a break on his two cases pending in Suffolk County. Barboza said
he also discussed his last interview with the agents with Vincent "Jimmy" Flemmi, and he told Flemmi that he was considering having Patrick Fabiano cooperate with the FBI. Flemmi thought that was an excellent idea. Barboza was informed that he could be making a very serious mistake in talking to any other inmate concerning his interview with the FBI. Barboza told the agents that Edward "Teddy" Deegan had been causing some problems and had been "out of order" at the Ebb Tide Restaurant. This document further states, "This office is aware of the distinct possibility that Barron [Barboza], in order to save himself from a long prison sentence, may try to intimidate Fabiano into testifying to something that he may not be a witness to." Joseph Barboza says he does not know who killed William Marfeo, and he had nothing to do with the murder.

3–31–67: In a performance appraisal, Special Agent Dennis Condon receives an excellent rating. It is noted that he handled complicated matters in an able and capable fashion. It is further noted that he is dependable, enthusiastic and showed a great interest in the Bureau's work. The appraisal also states that he has an outstanding knowledge of the hoodlum and gambling element in the Boston area and is considered to be an outstanding investigator. In particular, his participation in the informant program is considered outstanding. However, according to the appraisal, Condon is not interested in administrative advancement.

4–18–67: Police informer Joe Lanzi is killed by three of Jerry Angiulo's enforcers—Benjamin DeChristoforo, Carmine Gagliardi, and Frank Oreto. (VINCENT TERESA, MY LIFE IN THE MAFIA

4–24–67: Joseph Barboza is convicted for unlawfully carrying a weapon and a dagger in a motor vehicle. He is subsequently sentenced to not more than 4–5 years for the first charge and 4–5 years for the second charge. Both sentences are to be served concurrently.

4–27–67: FBI Special Agents Paul Rico and Dennis Condon interview Joseph Barboza at Barnstable County Jail.

5–16–67: FBI Special Agents Paul Rico and Dennis Condon contact Ronald Cassesso at the U.S. Attorney's Office prior to his appearance before a federal grand jury: "Cassessa [sic] was told that if he would cooperate in the investigation of organized crime, and, if he was of material help, his assistance would be brought to the attention of local authorities and his degree of cooperation would also be made known to the Parole Board. Cassessa [sic] said that he had nothing to worry about and did not plan to furnish any information before a Grand Jury."

5–19–67: Chief Judge Edward Day of the U.S. District Court in Providence, Rhode Island, releases the "Taglianetti Logs" to Louis Taglianetti and his attorneys. The logs are summaries of wiretapped conversations recorded by the Raymond Patriarca microphone surveillance. (CLARK R. MOLLENHOFF, STRIKE FORCE: ORGANIZED
CRIME AND THE GOVERNMENT 124 (1972)).139

5–24–67: Director Hoover instructs the Boston SAC by airtel that "a review of the Bureau records reveals that no investigation of Barron [Barboza] has ever been conducted by your office. In view of the current circumstances, the Bureau should be cognizant of all background information. Therefore, you should submit to the Bureau
an investigative report per instructions set out under the Criminal Intelligence Program containing all background and identifying data available."

6–6–67: A memorandum from Walter T. Barnes and Assistant U.S. Attorney Edward F. Harrington to Henry Peterson, Chief, Organized Crime and Racketeering Section. The memorandum is typed by Harrington, dated June 6, 1967, and discusses proposed
prosecutions of Raymond Patriarca, Henry Tameleo and Ronald Cassesso. Joseph Barboza is an unindicted co-conspirator. The following are important points made in this memorandum. Numbers in parentheses coincide with page numbers in the memorandum.[Note: The original memorandum is not appended to the Committee's
chronology and is retained in Justice Department files.] "[T]here has . . . been excellent cooperation between United States Attorney Paul Markham, District Attorney Garrett Byrne, and the F.B.I. District Attorney Byrne has, at our request, held off calling
Baron before a local grand jury until we have concluded our investigation."
(3) There is a short redacted section. (3) "Lastly, with respect to Baron's willingness to talk, he is, of course, desirous of obtaining some favorable consideration in connection with the local charges still pending against him." (3) Patriarca, in the presence of
Henry Tameleo, told Baron and Cassesso that he wanted Willie Marfeo "whacked out." (4) "Patriarca told Baron and Cassesso that he would give all the help he could in aiding them to kill Willie Marfeo." (4) "Patriarca explained to Baron that he was angry because
Marfeo's crap game had been creating a lot of "heat" on Patriarca's crap game and on his booking operations." (4) Shortly thereafter, Patriarca called off the proposed murder. (5) Seven or eight months later, Tameleo told Barboza that "Marfeo got it."
Tameleo explained the details of Marfeo's murder to Barboza. (5–6) "The establishment of the agreement will not be based on circumstantial evidence or inferences arising therefrom but rather the very agreement itself will be testified to by one of the individuals who was to participate in its execution. The overt acts which took
place in Massachusetts are especially appropriate in a case involving a gangland assassination in that it has always been one of the essential factors in perpetrating a successful "hit" that the contract be given to an out-of-state "torpedo" as a means of minimizing the chance of detection of the assassination and thus lessening the risk
that the individual who planned the assassination be traced." (13) There is a short redacted section that appears to discuss a discrepancy in dates. (13) In a section discussing weak points in the government's case, it is noted that the electronic surveillance of Barboza proves that "his testimony is true[,]" and this is "of special

significance[.]" (15) "Raymond Patriarca was the subject of an F.B.I. electronic surveillance by means of an electronic eavesdropping device installed by trespass at his place of business, 168 Atwells Avenue, Providence, Rhode Island, during the period
March 6, 1962 to July 12, 1965." (16) "Walter Barnes . . . and Edward F. Harrington reviewed 26 volumes of FBI logs, memoranda and airtels in the Boston office of the FBI." (16) "It is clear that we will have to disclose all of the material pertaining to the FBI electronic surveillance of Patriarca since the device was in his place
of business and some of the overheard conversations are clearly relevant. Some of this material has already been disclosed in connection with the income tax case against Louis Taglianetti of Providence, Rhode Island." (16) "We were also informed that an other [sic] associate of Patriarca's namely Joseph Modica, was the subject
of an electronic surveillance by means of an electronic eavesdropping device installed by trespass at his place of business, the Piranha Finance Company, 85 State Street, Boston, Massachusetts, during the period May 7, 1964 and July 12, 1965. The overheard
conversations are reflected in logs, memoranda and airtels." (16) There is a six page section titled "Pertinent Excerpts from the Logs of the Electronics [sic] Surveillance at 168 Atwells Avenue, Providence, Rhode Island." (17) "January 28, 1965—Henry Tameleo tells Patriarca that Joseph Barboza "hit" the guy in Revere." (17)
"March 4, 1965—An unman contacts Patriarca and states that he has brought down Flemmi and Joseph Barboza. Patriarca is infuriated at Frank Smith for allowing Flemmi and Barboza to come to see him without prior authorization. Patriarca makes arrangements to meet with Barboza and Flemmi in a garage shortly thereafter,
as he does not want to meet these two individuals at his place of business." (17) "March 5, 1965—Jerry Angiulo states to Patriarca that Vin [Jimmy] Flemmi was with Joseph Barboza when Barboza killed Jackie Francione in Revere, Massachusetts, several
months ago." (18) "March 9, 1965—James Flemmi and Joseph Barboza contact Patriarca and during the meeting explain to Patriarca that they are having a problem with Teddy Deegan and desire to get an "okay" to kill him. Flemmi and Barboza tell
Patriarca that Deegan is looking for an excuse to "wack [sic] out" Bobby Donati who is friendly with Rico Sacrimone. Patriarca instructs Flemmi and Barboza to obtain more information relating to Deegan and then to contact Jerry Angiulo at Boston who would furnish them with a decision whether they could kill Deegan."
"May 3, 1965—James Flemmi, Ronald Cassessa, and Joseph Barboza contact Patriarca and discuss "hitting" an unnamed individual." (19) "May 5, 1965—Henry Tameleo tells Patriarca that Joe Lombardo of Boston told Tameleo that he had received information
that Barboza, Cassessa and Jimmy Flemmi had received the "okay" to kill Sammy Linden for the reason that Linden was on the side of the McLaughlin group and had been furnishing them with considerable money so that they could continue in their efforts to kill individuals connected with the McLean group. Patriarca tells
Tameleo to contact Barboza and Flemmi and to instruct them to forget the "hit" on Sammy Linden in that "he is connected with one of our group." Tameleo tells Patriarca that Joe Lombardo was perturbed because Cassessa and Barboza were associating with the Flemmi brothers and information had been put out to the effect that Barboza was with Flemmi when Teddy Deegan was killed; that Lombardo had expressed concern that the Italian group, because of Barboza's and Cassessa's associations might be drawn into
the McLaughlin-McLean feud, and because of this, Lombardo had told Barboza and Cassessa to stay away from the Flemmis." (19) "May 10, 1965—An unman mentions that Barboza had previously talked with Patriarca regarding unknown topic and that Flemmi

had told Barboza that Patriarca had given him an "okay" to kill Linden." "May 13, 1965—Cassessa and Barboza and Henry Tameleo contact Patriarca. Barboza discusses his prospective killing of an individual by the name of O'Toole and the means by

which he is to carry out the murder." (19) The June 22, 1965, entry is a very long detailed recitation of the plan to murder Willie Marfeo. Patriarca is clearly the principal involved in planning the murder. "The killers are named as Barboza and Cassessa. . . .

Patriarca states that he would love to kill Marfeo himself." (20) "The Bureau monitor overheard the conversation between Patriarca, Tameleo and Baron on June 22, 1965, in which Patriarca hired Baron to kill Marfeo and recorded it in the log. However, the

conversation was not picked up on the tape recorder through some inexplicable mechanical failure. Accordingly, the Bureau supervisor in Boston who regularly reviewed the logs and tapes, in noting that the tape had failed to record the conversation, did not incorporate the information in any memoranda, airtel, or Bureau report, nor did the Bureau supervisor disseminate the information to other agents." (23) Information about an attempt by someone other than Barboza to kill Marfeo was disseminated to Paul Rico and Dennis Condon. (23) "It should also be noted that Special Agent Rico of the F.B.I. did receive information on July 1, 1965, from a live informant,

that Patriarca had hired Joe Baron to "hit" Willie Marfeo."

"On January 12, 1967, the I.R.S. informant furnished information to [REDACTED] that in view of the fact that the Boston organization had killed several of Baron's criminal associates, Baron might be willing to talk." This information was given to Walter Barnes, who gave it to U.S. Attorney Markham and Henry Peterson.

Peterson then requested Barnes to arrange an interview with Barboza at "the earliest opportunity." (24) Barnes found that Barboza was on trial in local court for illegal possession of firearms. "It was inappropriate to interview Baron at this time so Mr.

Barnes returned to Washington and was later advised that Baron had been convicted and sentenced to four to five years on January 25, 1967, and was immediately incarcerated in Walpole Prison. Mr. Barnes returned to Boston in February, 1967, at which time Barnes requested Special Agents Rico and Condon of the F.B.I. to

interview Baron at an appropriate time and place." "It should be noted again that Special Agents Rico and Condon were, as a matter of fact, never made aware of the information overheard by a Bureau monitor on June 22, 1965, and which forms the basis of this indictment. As mentioned above, Special Agent Rico received information from a live source on July 1, 1965, that Patriarca had hired Baron to kill Marfeo."

6–20–67: By memorandum, the Boston SAC recommends to Director Hoover that Special Agents Paul Rico and Dennis Condon receive quality salary increases. The memorandum discusses Rico and Condon's handling and development of Top Echelon Criminal Informants in the Boston Office, including informant BS 955 C–TE

[Stephen Flemmi], and praised their efforts and results. The memorandum

also describes Barboza as a murderous ruffian: "BS 955 C–TE [Stephen Flemmi] was developed by [Rico and Condon] and via imaginative direction and professional ingenuity utilized said source in connection with interviews of Joseph Baron, a professional assassin responsible for numerous homicides and acknowledged

by all professional law enforcement representatives in this area to be the most dangerous individual known. SAs Rico and Condon contacted Baron in an effort to convince him he should testify against the LCN [La Cosa Nostra]. Baron initially declined to testify but through utilization of BS 955 C–TE [Stephen Flemmi], the agents were able to convey to Baron that his present incarceration and potential for continued incarceration for the rest of his life, was wholly attributable to LCN efforts directed by Gennaro [Jerry] Angiulo, LCN Boston head. As a result of this information received by Baron from BS 955 C–TE [Stephen Flemmi], said individual said he would testify against the LCN members." This memorandum also states: "The indictments against Patriarca, Tameleo and Casesso are the first major blow to the LCN in New England. Patriarca, as LCN boss and possible Commission member, and his top lieutenant, Henry Tameleo, were felt to be beyond prosecution by top state and local police officials based on what for years resulted in frustration in securing witnesses who would testify. . . . SAs Condon and Rico were assigned to develop a prosecutable quality case against top LCN members in New England. They have done so via highest devotion to duty, requiring personal sacrifices, in time, on a continuing basis." [This document is heavily redacted.] 141 [Note: Dennis Condon later told the Committee that he was not involved in the development of Stephen Flemmi as an informant.]

A federal grand jury indicts Raymond Patriarca on charges that he and two others had conspired to engineer the murder of William Marfeo over a competitive gambling enterprise Marfeo was running. (CLARK R. MOLLENHOFF, STRIKE FORCE: ORGANIZED CRIME AND THE GOVERNMENT 124 (1972)).142

6–22–67: Between June 22, 1967 and July 3, 1967, Officer Robson talked to Anthony Stathopoulos on several occasions. While Stathopoulos was incarcerated with Patrick Fabiano at Deer Island, Fabiano said the "beef" between Barboza and Stathopoulos had been cleared up. Stathopoulos told Officer Robson that on the night Edward "Teddy" Deegan was murdered, he actually saw Ronnie Cassesso with a gun in his hand and Romeo Martin. "He did not see the others involved." Stathopoulos also said that Vincent "Jimmy" Flemmi met with him, Deegan, and one other at a restaurant to discuss "arrangement to silence" Anthony Sacrimone because Sacrimone was too talkative about the Populo theft. Shortly after this meeting, Flemmi was shot and unable to complete the job.

6–23–67: J.H. Gale, the Boston SAC, writes a memorandum to Cartha DeLoach recommending incentive awards for Paul Rico and Dennis Condon. The memorandum states, "SA Rico through a resourceful and diligent effort in October 1964, obtained the cooperation of REDACTED SECTION. Based upon development of this source, the Boston Office was able to determine the basic reasons for the numerous gangland slayings in the Boston area and the identities of many of the individuals involved in these murders. . . . As a direct result of the shrewd guidance given the informant by SAs Ricoand Condon, REDACTED SECTION. This information has been vitally important in establishing the Interstate Transportation in Aid of Racketeering violation against [Raymond] Patriarca and his chief LCN [La Cosa Nostra] henchman, Henry Tameleo, who were arrested this week by Bureau Agents. REDACTED SECTION. SAs Condon and Rico also developed another top echelon informant, BS 955–C–TE [Stephen Flemmi]. He [Stephen Flemmi] was most effectively utilized to convince Joseph Barboza, the professional assassin, that he should testify against Patriarca and his associates. The informant's efforts with skillful interviews of REDACTED by SAs Rico and Condon resulted in REDACTED appearance before a Federal Grand Jury and the indictments of Patriarca and Tameleo. The arrest of Patriarca and Tameleo by Bureau Agents received extensive publicity and constituted a major blow against LCN. These noteworthy achievements were brought about by the development and handling of top echelon informants by SAs Rico and Condon." The document continues, "SA Rico's resourcefulness and diligent efforts to obtain cooperation of an informant, REDACTED SECTION resulted in receipt of much accurate and authentic data regarding gangland slayings in the Boston area. SAs Rico and Condon thereafter shrewdly guided him, which, REDACTED SECTION. They developed still another top echelon informant and their efforts culminated in the arrest of Raymond Patriarca, La Cosa Nostra leader in New England, and Henry Tameleo, his chief henchman." This memorandum also indicates that Rico and Condon were censured.

6–27–67: The Government files a memorandum and places logs of the Raymond Patriarca surveillance conducted at 168 Atwells Avenue in Providence, Rhode Island, in the custody of the U.S. District Court for the District of Massachusetts.

7–3–67: According to letters from Director Hoover to Paul Rico and Dennis Condon, the agents each receive a $150 incentive award for the "developing and skillful handling of several confidential sources of great concern to the Bureau in the criminal field"

An FBI Memorandum from S.R. Burns to Mr. Walsh, dated October 22, 1975, states that Dennis Condon received a $150 incentive award on this date (7–3–67) "in recognition of his developing and handling several confidential sources of much interest to the Bureau in the criminal field. (Re: BS 868 C–TE, BS 954 C–TE, BS 955 C–TE [Stephen Flemmi])." 147

7–9–67: James Southwood writes in the *Boston Herald:* "A few months ago, Barboza was transferred from the state prison to the Barnstable County House of Correction on Cape Cod—for the obvious reason of removing him from the company of men still loyal to the Cosa Nostra. He was placed in isolation there and only the two FBI agents [presumably Rico and Condon] can get in to see him."

7–18–67: Thomas Sullivan from the Boston FBI Office reports on Joseph Barboza per instructions from Director Hoover (*See* 5–24–67 entry). Sullivan's report reads, "Enclosures to Bureau—Original and one copy of a letterhead memorandum characterizing informants used in this report." The section on informants is completely redacted. A large portion of the text under the heading *Administrative* is also redacted. That portion reads as follows: "REDACTED SECTION. REDACTED SECTION that Ronnie Cassessa [sic] and Joe Barboza were responsible for the shooting of Romeo Martin in Revere, Massachusetts. REDACTED SECTION. REDACTED SECTION that Joseph Barboza was the individual who shot and killed Di Stasio and O'Neil at the Mickey Mouse Lounge in Revere, Massachusetts, the previous weekend. The informant stated that Barboza had been in the Mickey Mouse Lounge a couple of weeks ago and after he left, someone took several shots at him and Barboza suspected that Di Stasio had set him up with the McLaughlin crowd. As a result of this, Barboza returned and killed Di Stasio and O'Neil. REDACTED SECTION that Joseph "Chico" Amico and Guy Frizzi are always together and were usually with Joe Barboza before Barboza went to jail. The informant stated he heard reports that Barboza and Guy Frizzi were the ones who "bumped off" [Edward] Teddy Deegan a few months ago in Chelsea, Massachusetts. REDACTED SECTION that while Joe Barboza was on trial in Suffolk Superior Court he decided to make one more "hit." He was trying to hit "Indian Al" from Medford, Massachusetts. At the time Barboza made his move against "Indian Al," he was in the company of "Chico" Amico, Rick [sic] Femia, and Guy Frizzi. REDACTED SECTION that Joseph

Barboza, Romeo Martin and Ronnie Cassessa [sic] are frequently in attendance at the Ebb Tide in Revere, Massachusetts.

REDACTED SECTION that Joe Barboza is very frequently with Romeo Martin, Ronnie Cassessa [sic], and Frank [Francis] Imbruglia. Barboza was supposed to have "hit" Francione of Revere, Massachusetts, and also "hit" Eaton. He also stated that Barboza was in prison with Benjamin, who was murdered after he left prison. The informant stated that Barboza is a Portuguese kid who would otherwise be accepted into the LCN [La Cosa Nostra] except for his nationality. Barboza claims that he shot Teddy Deegan with a .45 caliber gun. Barboza indicated that Roy French was with Deegan and another individual when Deegan was shot by Barboza and two other individuals, one of whom the informant believes was Romeo Martin. The informant stated he heard that Joe Barboza was extremely friendly with Jimmy Flemmi. The informant added that

Barboza tried to reach [Vincent] Jimmy Flemmi a short time ago and wanted to know if Flemmi had gone to Providence, Rhode Island, to see Raymond Patriarca. REDACTED stated that he had heard that Joe Barboza made the statement that Roy French was

on the way out. Informant stated that French hangs around the Ebb Tide in Revere and appears to be friendly with Barboza, Ronnie Cassessa [sic] and other individuals." REDACTED SECTION. REDACTED SECTION. This case is being placed in a closed status inasmuch as all information developed from interviews of Barboza by

SA Dennis M. Condon and SA H. Paul Rico is being placed in Boston File 166–629 entitled 'Raymond L.S. Patriarca,

Thomas Sullivan from the Boston FBI Office files an additional report regarding Joseph Barboza. A large portion of the text under the heading *Activities* is redacted. That portion reads as follows: "REDACTED SECTION advised that Joseph Barboza had been arrested Friday night, September 10, 1965, for beating a policeman with a gun at the Ebb Tide in Revere, Massachusetts. REDACTED SECTION. REDACTED SECTION stated that the general rumor REDACTED SECTION was that Joseph Barboza of Revere was under contract to be assassinated since he was tied into the McLean—McLaughlin feud. REDACTED SECTION stated that Joseph Barboza split with Connie Frizzi in loansharking and was then in partnership with Arthur Bratsos. Informant added that Barboza had plenty of money and had just purchased a new home in Swampscott, Massachusetts. REDACTED SECTION advised that he had been frequenting

the Ebb Tide in Revere, Massachusetts, that it was being operated by Richard Castucci and Nicholas Junior Ventola. Informant added that Joseph Barboza, Romeo Martin and Ronnie Cassessa [sic] were frequently in attendance at the Ebb Tide. REDACTED SECTION stated that Joseph Barboza had married[.] . . .Informant added that the subject frequently visited the Ebb Tide and it was rumored that Barboza was the killer of Joseph Francione in Revere. REDACTED SECTION stated that Guy Frizzi and Joseph Barboza, who hung around at North Station, occasionally were there to see Johnny Bats who worked for the Boston Garden Corporation. Informant added that Bats was associated with Frizzi and Barboza in the money lending activities. REDACTED SECTION stated that on May 3, 1965, Joseph Barboza and Ronnie Cassessa [sic] were looking for [Vincent] Jimmy Flemmi REDACTED SECTION and returned in the evening of May 3, 1965. Informant further stated that it was later during the evening of May 3, 1967 [sic], that Flemmi was shot when he left his home on Adams Street, Dorchester, Massachusetts. REDACTED SECTION."

8–9–67: A memorandum from the Boston SAC to Director Hoover advises, "In statement to press, District Attorney Byrne stated that this tremendous penetration into the La Cosa Nostra and the hoodlum element was effected through the outstanding investigative efforts of the FBI and his office. As a matter of information, this entire

case which was presented to the grand jury by DA Byrne was developed through the efforts and able handling of Barboza by SA H. Paul Rico and Dennis M. Condon of the Boston office. They also cooperated fully with DA Byrne in the preparation of this matter
for the grand jury. I know that this indictment would not have been possible in any sense of the word if it were not for the efforts of these agents and the FBI at Boston. . . . I further recommend that Supervisor John F. Kehoe who supervised this entire program
and was involved deeply in the developments and the planning relative to Barboza and the matters attendant to this indictment be strongly commended for his excellent supervision."

8–14–67: In a letter from Director Hoover to Special Agent Paul Rico, Hoover commends Rico for his "splendid services in a phase of the investigation of Raymond L.S. Patriarca and others" Dennis Condon also receives a letter of commendation from the FBI for his excellent performance in connection with the investigation of the Interstate Transportation in Aid of Racketeering case involving Raymond L.S. Patriarca and others.

8–28–67: "On [this date] August 28, 1967, BS 955–CTE [Stephen Flemmi] furnished the following information to SA H. Paul Rico: The informant advised that Larry Baione asked the informant to contact [Vincent] "Jimmy" Flemmi on behalf of Gennaro [Jerry]
Angiulo to see what Flemmi can do to keep Nick Femmia from testifying against anyone and to see if Flemmi can find some way to destroy Joe Barboza's testimony against [Raymond] Patriarca and [Jerry] Angiulo. The informant advised that this puts Jimmy
Flemmi in a very bad position because Jimmy Flemmi owes Angiulo over $10,000, and is therefore indebted to him. The informant knows that Jimmy Flemmi would just as soon see Patriarca and Tameleo get hurt but that he has always looked down on
Angiulo as a source of money for him and he feels that Flemmi would want to help Angiulo. The informant advised, however, that he will, when he is talking to Flemmi point out to him that Barboza could end up seriously hurting him, Jimmy Flemmi, if he,
Flemmi, did anything to attempt to discredit Barboza. Informant further advised that he has learned that Larry Baione and Peter Limone have received information that Joe Barboza is going to testify for Suffolk County on the murder of [Edward] Teddy Deegan
and that they in all probability attempt to make sure that Anthony Stathopoulos will not be around to corroborate Barboza's testimony. The informant advised that he believes Stathopoulos' life is in danger."

9–8–67: Detective John Doyle of the Suffolk County District Attorney's
Office interviews Joseph Barboza at the Barnstable County Jail in Barnstable, Massachusetts, in the presence of FBI Special Agents Paul Rico and Dennis Condon.

Boston police take Anthony Stathopoulos to the Barnstable County Jail where he talks with Joseph Barboza. Barboza and Stathopoulos talk about the events of the day of the Deegan murder, March 12, 1965, and about testimony that he and Barboza
were going to give before a grand jury about the night of the Deegan murder. Stathopoulos asks Barboza about Vincent "Jimmy" Flemmi. Barboza tells Stathopoulos that he is going to keep Flemmi out of it because Flemmi is a good friend of his and is the only one that treated him decently. (*See* 1–5–71 entry).

9–9–67: The Boston SAC writes a memorandum to Director Hoover containing the following information: "[T]he Bureau was advised that Joseph Baron has furnished information relative to subject Limone's involvement in the gangland killing of one Edward ["Teddy"] Deegan."

9–11–67: John Doyle prepares a report of the September 8, 1967, interview with Joseph Barboza conducted at Barnstable County Jail. Barboza stated that he was approached by Peter Limone during the first week of February 1965. Deegan's death was desired because of his participation in the robbery of an Angiulo bookmaker.

Limone told him that Henry Tameleo had approved the murder. Barboza then confirmed this with Henry Tameleo. Barboza stated that he had been in Florida until around March 8, 1965. When Barboza was told by Roy French that there would be another man with him and Deegan on a "score." Barboza allegedly said that another $2500 would be paid if the other man were also killed. Jimmy Flemmi is not mentioned in the six page report.

9–12–67: Sergeant Detective Frank Walsh and Detective John Doyle, of the Suffolk County District Attorney's Office, interview Barboza in the presence of FBI Special Agents Paul Rico and Dennis Condon at the Barnstable County Jail regarding the Edward "Teddy" Deegan murder. A six page statement was prepared. It states that Barboza came back from Florida the first week of March. Barboza said that "[a]nother reason for them wanting Deegan out of the way was the fact that John Fitzgerald went to a gas station and, with Deegan, got a $1000.00 off of Peter Limone for George McLaughlin." Barboza explained that Limone was angry because he thought that McLaughlin was "shaking him down." Barboza also stated that Chiampa and Imbruglia left the Ebb Tide the same time that he did, but that they had "no part in the
thing."

9–14–67: Special Agents Paul Rico and Dennis Condon contact Joseph Barboza at the Barnstable County Jail. Barboza tells Rico and Condon that his attorney, John Fitzgerald, called him the previous evening and told him that "a good many people were going to be picked up" and that Baron "was going to be going to court." The agents and Barboza also briefly discuss transferring Barboza out of Barnstable. Barboza states that he would welcome a transfer since he fears for his life.

9–15–67: In an airtel to Director Hoover, the Boston SAC describes the weekly developments: Anthony Stathopoulos turned himself in to the Suffolk County District Attorney's Office for protection. The airtel also informs that during the latter part of last week, an attempt was made to kill Stathopoulos. Joseph Barboza had previously advised that Stathopoulos' life was in jeopardy. In addition, Stathopoulos furnished information relative to the Edward "Teddy" Deegan murder.

9–16–67: From jail, Joseph Barboza calls Dennis Condon at home. Barboza is concerned that he may appear before the grand jury the next day. He is also greatly concerned about his safety because he is still at Barnstable County Jail.

9–18–67: Special Agents Paul Rico and Dennis Condon contact Joseph Barboza at the U.S. Marshals Office in Boston while he is in the process of transferring from Barnstable County Jail.

Barboza is placed in the custody of the U.S. Marshals Service by Order of U.S. District Judge Ford. Judge Ford's Order issued in the federal trial of Raymond Patriarca, Henry Tameleo and Ronald Cassesso for the murder of William Marfeo, also indicates that the
government filed transcripts of the logs obtained from the Patriarca microphone surveillance on June 27, 1967.

In a handwritten order, Judge Ford "ordered that the [Patriarca] logs be impounded and placed in the custody of the Clerk, and the inspection of said logs is restricted to counsel for the defendants, namely Messrs. [Joseph] Balliro, Curran and [Ronald] Chisholm." Attorneys Balliro and Chisholm will later represent two of the same defendants in the William Marfeo murder trial as they represented in the Edward "Teddy" Deegan murder trial. (Judge Ford held a hearing regarding these transcripts on June 27, 1967.) 164

9–19–67: Joseph Barboza is transferred from Barnstable County Jail, Massachusetts, to federal custody. Barboza is taken to Thatcher Island in Gloucester, Massachusetts. He is later taken to a private estate in Gloucester.

9–21–67: Special Agents Paul Rico and Dennis Condon contact Joseph Barboza at Thatcher Island and inquire about his physical welfare. During this contact, Barboza states that Detective Walsh observed him at the Florentine Café on Boston's Hanover Street in the past with Ronald Cassesso, Henry Tameleo and possibly Roy Thomas. Barboza said that Detective Walsh should be able to testify to these observations.

10–6–67: Special Agents Paul Rico and Dennis Condon contact Joseph Barboza at Thatcher Island.

10–10–67: Ronald Chisholm, attorney for Ronald Cassesso, discusses the Raymond Patriarca logs in federal court

10–16–67: Detective Sergeant Frank Walsh and Detective John Doyle interview Joseph Barboza at Thatcher Island in the presence of Special Agent Paul Rico. According to Barboza's statement on the Edward "Teddy" Deegan murder, he told the detectives that Peter Limone said to Barboza, "I'll give you a contract for $7,500.00" to murder Deegan." Barboza also stated that Vincent "Jimmy" Flemmi was with Barboza in the Ebbtide on the night of the Deegan murder. Special Agent Paul Rico notifies the Boston SAC by memorandum that an informant learned that Raymond Patriarca "has told everyone that is to be indicted on the [Edward "Teddy"] Deegan murder to surrender when the indictments are returned rather than fleeing[.]"

10–25–67: Joseph Barboza testifies before the Suffolk County Grand Jury regarding the Edward "Teddy" Deegan murder. Barboza testifies that they used Romeo Martin's maroon Oldsmobile convertible as a getaway car for the Deegan murder. According to Barboza's testimony, Ronald Cassesso bent back the rear license plate on the car so only the numbers "404" were showing. (122) Barboza also testifies that no promises were made to him in exchange for his testimony. (103) He also testifies that Peter Limone offered him a total of $10,000 for killing both Deegan and Anthony Stathopoulos. (112) Further, Barboza's testimony implicates Henry Tameleo as agreeing to the killing. Barboza also testifies that he left the scene before the murder and got the details later in a meeting in a back room at the Ebb Tide.
According to Barboza's testimony, Roy French told him that French shot Deegan first in the head with a .38, and Romeo Martin told him that Martin shot Deegan in the chest and Louis Greco shot Deegan with a .45 in the stomach (126). [An FBI memorandum
dated 4–6–65 refutes the veracity of this testimony. This memorandum states that Barboza told a PCI (Potential Confidential Informant) that he "shot Teddy Deegan with a .45 caliber gun." *See* 3–23–65 entry.] Barboza also testified that Peter Limone gave him the money he promised (131). In addition, notwithstanding the fact that Barboza told Detective Sergeant Frank Walsh, Detective John Doyle and FBI Special Agent H. Paul Rico in an interview on 10–16–67 that Vincent "Jimmy" Flemmi was in the Ebbtide on the night of the Deegan murder, Barboza does not mention Flemmi as
being one of the individuals at the Ebbtide on the night of the Deegan murder in his grand jury testimony. (118) (*See* 10–16–67 entry).

The Boston SAC notifies Director Hoover by memorandum of the following: "REDACTED SECTION testified before the Suffolk County Grand Jury this date in connection with the gangland murder of Edward Deegan on March twelve, sixty five. REDACTED SECTION as a result of REDACTED testimony before this Grand Jury, indictments were rendered against Henry Tameleo, Peter Limone, Ronald Cassesso, Roy French, "Joe the Horse" Salvati, Louis Greco and Joseph Baron." 172 Joseph Salvati is arrested.

November 1967: Edward "Wimpy" Bennett is murdered. In Vincent Teresa's book *My Life In The Mafia,* Teresa claims that "it was a cop that was responsible for the murder of Wimpy Bennett." Henry Tameleo told Teresa that Wimpy's "a stoolie. We got the information straight from our man on the Boston Police Department."

Teresa further describes the circumstances surrounding Wimpy's murder: "Tameleo's warning was clear as a bell. I didn't go near Wimpy. Then in November 1967, Wimpy disappeared.

Steve Flemmi and Frank Salemmi [sic] handled the job. They're a couple of assassins for [Raymond] Patriarca. Both of them are missing, either whacked out or in hiding. They're wanted in a murder case, for killing Wimpy's brother, Billy. They hit Wimpy and

dumped him in lye in a construction site that's now part of Route 93. After the mob hit Wimpy, they had to hit his three brothers. Walter ran a nightclub in Boston, and when Wimpy disappeared, Walter began talking about hitting Patriarca. He disappeared, too,

without a trace. They found Billy in the Dorchester section of Boston on December 23, 1967. They indicted Daddieco, Salemmi [sic], a kid named Peter Poulos, and another kid named Richie Grasso for the murder. Grasso was talking, so he was hit about six days after Billy Bennett got his. They found Poulos' body later on in the desert in Nevada. After that they whacked out the two other Bennett brothers. That's six guys that died all because a cop on the take fingered one man for the mob."

11–1–67: Paul Rico, Dennis Condon, U.S. Attorney Paul Markham and U.S. Marshal Robert Morey contact Joseph Barboza at Thatcher Island in Rockport, Massachusetts. They discuss Barboza's physical well-being, and Markham discusses the possibility
of moving Barboza to a new location in the near future.

11–4–67: The Boston Globe reports that Assistant Suffolk County District Attorney John J. Pino told a Superior Court judge that the government made no promises, offers or inducements to Barboza in return for his Grand Jury testimony.

11–6–67: Special Agents Paul Rico and Dennis Condon contact Joseph Barboza at Thatcher Island in Rockport, Massachusetts.

11–8–67: Notes on the Edward "Teddy" Deegan murder are taken from Joseph Barboza in the presence of Detective John Doyle and Special Agents Paul Rico and Dennis Condon.

11–9–67: Paul Rico, Dennis Condon, Detective John Doyle, and Sergeant Detective Francis Walsh of the Suffolk County District Attorney's Office contact Joseph Barboza at Thatcher Island in Rockport, Massachusetts. Rico and Condon check on the physical
well-being of Barboza and his family. Walsh briefly discusses the Edward "Teddy" Deegan murder with Barboza.

11–14–67: Louis Greco, defendant in the Edward "Teddy" Deegan case, takes a polygraph examination regarding Deegan's murder. The polygraph indicates that Greco responded truthfully when he said he did not shoot or kill Teddy Deegan. According to the polygraph, Greco truthfully says that he was in Florida on March 12, 1965, and not in Chelsea, Massachusetts. Harold Lokos, the Director of the Polygraph Unit of the City of Miami Police Department, conducts the examination.

11–15–67: Special Agents Paul Rico and William J. Welby interview Joseph Barboza's attorney. According to the write-up, "John E. Fitzgerald, Jr. was interviewed in a restaurant across the street from the Dorchester District Court, Washington Street, Dorchester, Massachusetts. He advised that he has learned that his law partner,
Alfred Paul Farese, has decided to testify as a defense witness against his client, Joe Barboza, if he is indicted federally for 'Obstruction of Justice.' Fitzgerald advised that Farese has in his possession a letter that Joe Barboza had sent to Joseph 'Chico' Amico
after Tommy De Prisco and Arthur Bratsos had been murdered, and in this letter Barboza allegedly tells of the movements of Larry Baione, Gennaro [Jerry] Angiulo, and others. In addition, Farese has in his possession three by five cards on which he has recorded conversations he has had with Barboza.
Fitzgerald advised that some time ago Guy Frizzi came up to his law office and he had made some threatening statements to the girl running the office; he said that he had killed before and he would kill again; he would not stand for this, and he was referring to something that had gone wrong with his income tax that was supposed to have been handled by his Attorneys. Fitzgerald advised that he went down to the Bat Cove on Friend Street, Boston, and he walked up to the person who seemed to be in charge and introduced himself as Attorney John Fitzgerald, and this individual introduced
himself as Larry Baione. Fitzgerald said that he was looking for Peter Limone, and Larry said he was sitting right over here, and he called Peter over to Fitzgerald. Fitzgerald said he told Limone how Guy Frizzi had been up to his office threatening this 45 year-old woman and how Frizzi has been telling everyone that he is Peter Limone's partner, and he wondered if Peter could do anything about this. Limone said he could stop Frizzi from going up to his law office, if that is what he wanted.
Fitzgerald advised that last week he got a telephone call at his office from Larry Baione. Larry wanted to talk to him. Fitzgerald advised he would agree to meet Baione at Howard Johnson's Restaurant on Route 1 in Dedham, Massachusetts. Before he made the meet with Baione, he notified someone that he was going to have this meet. He advised that Baione arrived by car and the person that was with him in the car remained in the car. Fitzgerald believes this party was Phil Waggonheim. Baione told Fitzgerald that he understood that he was going to be indicted on information furnished
by Joe Barboza, and he wanted to know what Fitzgerald could do to help him. Fitzgerald said that he told him that there was nothing he could do; that he does not influence Joe Barboza; that he is only his legal counsel, and Baione said that it would be worth money to him if he could tell him everything he could about Joe and everything he could find out. Fitzgerald claimed that he told Baione that he does not discuss these matters with Joe and could not be of any help to him. Fitzgerald advised that, shortly thereafter, his girlfriend, Dorothy Barchard, received a telephone call in which the caller indicated that if she did not stop associating 'with that guy,' that she and her children could be killed. Fitzgerald advised that, in addition, his wife received a telephone call in which the caller told his wife about how he, Fitzgerald, was 'keeping' Dorothy Barchard. Fitzgerald stated that he also had been told that if he would help them weaken Joe Barboza, they would have Jimmy O'Toole killed at Concord where O'Toole is presently incarcerated. Fitzgerald was asked who made this statement to him, and he said, 'I am not going to divulge the identity of this person, but I have given the identity of this party to Jimmy O'Toole, and he will probably be in trouble when O'Toole comes out of jail.' Fitzgerald

also advised that when he was checking around as to who made the telephone calls to this wife and to Dorothy Barchard, 'the office' tried to lead him to believe that it was Jimmy O'Toole's friends; that he checked with O'Toole, and this was not so. Fitzgerald said that recently, while he was out of the office, two men came up to the office and asked if 'Joe Barboza's braintrust' was there? Fitzgerald said that his secretary told him that one of the men was about 5'7", paunchy and in his late 50's, and the other one was

about 6', about the same age and was smoking a cigarette held in a cigarette holder, and that both of these individuals had accents and were not from this area. Fitzgerald later had ascertained that one of these individuals was Henry Tamelo's brother. Fitzgerald

stated that he blamed Al Farese for causing some of his problems and he made some statements to Farese concerning what he was going to do to Raymond Patriarca and other individuals for the trouble they are causing him, and he feels sure that, for this reason, he is now "on the hit parade."

11–24–67: Detective John Doyle and Detective Robson of the Suffolk County District Attorney's Office contact Roberta Grimes, a former waitress at the Ebb Tide who worked the night Edward "Teddy" Deegan was killed. She identifies pictures of the following

persons as being present at the Ebb Tide on the night Deegan was murdered: Joseph Barboza, Ronald Cassesso, Joseph Salvati, Nick Femia, Frank [Francis] Imbruglia, Freddie Chiampi, Romeo Martin, and Roy French. According to the interview summary, Grimes was aware that these men left the Ebb Tide at approximately 9:00 p.m. in groups of three or four at a time and returned within two hours. Grimes, however, refused to testify at the Deegan trial because her husband prohibited it, and she feared her family in Chelsea would be in danger. Barboza is contacted at Thatcher Island. Special Agents Rico and Condon are there to check on the "physical well-being" of Barboza and his family; Frank Walsh and John Doyle have a brief discussion with Barboza about some points concerning the Deegan murder.

11–30–67: Deegan defendants file a motion to obtain "Police Department reports" and information regarding "promises, rewards or inducements." Detective John Doyle and Investigator Joseph Fallon of the Suffolk County District Attorney's Office, along with Special Agents Paul Rico and Dennis Condon, meet with Joseph Barboza in

Gloucester, Massachusetts. Doyle and Fallon review with Barboza information regarding the gangland murder of Rocco Di Seglio.

12–7–67: Special Agents Paul Rico and Dennis Condon check on the physical well-being of Joseph Barboza in Gloucester, Massachusetts.

12–14–67: Assistant District Attorney John Pino and Investigator Joseph Fallon of the Suffolk County District Attorney's Office, meet with Joseph Barboza in the presence of Special Agent Dennis Condon in Gloucester, Massachusetts. Pino and Fallon review with

Barboza information regarding the gangland murder of Rocco Di Seglio in preparation for trial.

12–20–67: Special Agent Paul Rico, in addition to Assistant District Attorney John Pino and Investigator Joseph Fallon of the Suffolk County District Attorney's Office, meet with Joseph Barboza in Gloucester, Massachusetts. Pino prepares Barboza for trial.188

12–23–67: William "Billy" Bennett's bullet-riddled body is thrown from a moving car on Harvard Street in Dorchester, Massachusetts. Stephen Flemmi and Francis "Frank" Salemme are later indicted for Bennett's murder. (Shelley Murphy, *Playing Both Sides Pays Off,* BOSTON HERALD, Apr. 23, 1993).189

12–27–67: Special Agents Paul Rico and Dennis Condon check on the physical well-being of Joseph Barboza in Gloucester, Massachusetts.
190

1968

1–3–68: Special Agents Paul Rico and Dennis Condon meet with Joseph Barboza in Gloucester, Massachusetts. They tell him that he will probably be required to testify in Suffolk County Superior Court during the week of January 8, 1968, in connection with the gangland murder of Rocco Di Seglio. Barboza says that he is ready to testify and hopes good arrangements have been made for his protection since "the organization" will do everything possible to prevent him from testifying.

1–8–68: Special Agents Paul Rico and Dennis Condon contact Joseph Barboza and advise him that he would be called to testify in Suffolk County Superior Court within the next few days regarding the gangland murder of Rocco DiSeglio.

1–18–68: Jerry Angiulo, Benjamin Zinna, Marino Lepore and Richard De Vincent are found not guilty in a jury trial in Suffolk County Superior Court of the gangland murder of Rocco Di Seglio.

1–25–68: Special Agents Paul Rico and Dennis Condon check on the physical well-being of Joseph Barboza in Gloucester, Massachusetts.

1–30–68: John E. Fitzgerald loses one leg and part of the other when a car bomb explodes in his car. Francis "Frank" Salemme and Stevie Flemmi allegedly planted the bomb. Salemme and Flemmi are indicted on October 10, 1969. Salemme is convicted on
the basis of testimony from Robert Daddieco and ultimately serves 17 years; Flemmi flees on H. Paul Rico's advice. *See United States* v. *Salemme,* 91 F.Supp. 2d 141, 151 (1999). "Law enforcement officials said Mr. Fitzgerald was targeted for death because he was the lawyer for a famed Cosa Nostra soldier-turned-informer, Joseph
Special Agents Paul Rico and Dennis Condon check on the physical well-being of Joseph Barboza. Dennis Condon files a report indicating that he will maintain contact with Joseph Barboza.

1–31–68: Cartha DeLoach telephones and speaks with Director Hoover four separate times over the course of one hour and thirteen minutes. The first call is placed at 9:15 am.964 The log of Hoover's telephone calls lists no other business calls for the day. There also appears to be no other day over a two year period where there is a similar pattern of telephone calls from DeLoach or any other aide.

2–2–68: Special Agents Paul Rico and Dennis Condon check on the physical well-being of Joseph Barboza.

2–9–68: Special Agents Paul Rico and Dennis Condon check on the physical well-being of Joseph Barboza.

2–19–68: Special Agent Paul Rico, Sergeant Detective Frank Walsh, and Assistant District Attorney Jack Zalkind meet with Joseph Barboza in Gloucester, Massachusetts. Zalkind reviews with Barboza the details of the Deegan murder in preparation for trial
in Suffolk County Superior Court.

2–21–68: Special Agent Paul Rico, Sergeant Frank Walsh, and Assistant District Attorney Jack Zalkind interview Joseph Baron about the Deegan murder. Barboza tells them that he got the okay to "hit" Deegan from Henry Tameleo.

3–5/6–68: Joseph Barboza testifies in the Raymond Patriarca, Henry Tameleo and Ronald Cassesso case in federal court, involving the murder of William Marfeo.

3–6–68: The *Boston Globe* reports that Ronald Cassesso's attorney, Ronald Chisholm cross-examined Joseph Barboza, in the trial of Cassesso, Raymond Patriarca, and Henry Tameleo for conspiracy to murder William Marfeo. Barboza was asked if he said that
Cassesso was present when he first told Special Agents Paul Rico and Dennis Condon about the alleged conspiracy. When Barboza said he could not recall, Barboza was shown a piece of paper that he said refreshed his memory. Barboza then said he did not tell Rico and Condon who went with him to Rhode Island.

3–8–68: Raymond Patriarca, Ronald Cassesso, and Henry Tameleo are convicted in federal court of conspiring to kill William Marfeo. Joseph Barboza testified against the defendants. (Barboza was an unindicted co-conspirator, whom they allegedly tried to hire as the "hitman" to kill Marfeo. With regard to Barboza's testimony, U.S. Attorney Paul Markham said, "The case in the main depended on his [Barboza's] credibility. The jury obviously believed him, believed him 100 percent. It was a significant victory." Asked how the outcome of the case would affect the
government's battle against organized crime, Markham said, "To put it in a negative way, if we didn't win it, it would be all over." Walter T. Barnes, an attorney on Markham's staff, declared, "We can't overemphasize the importance of this case." Another attorney on Markham's staff, Edward Harrington, commented, "Because of these convictions there may be more information coming to us, and because of this there may be further cases developing."

3–12–68: Special Agents Paul Rico and Dennis Condon check on the physical well-being of Barboza where he is in the protective custody of the U.S. Marshals Service.

3–15–68: Dennis Condon receives a $150 incentive award "in appreciation
for his noteworthy performance in the investigation of the Interstate Transportation in Aid of Racketeering-Gambling case involving Raymond L.S. Patriarca and others." Condon is acknowledged for skillfully handling an important Government witness
whose cooperation was vital to the conviction of Patriarca and his two associates.

3–19–68: According to a memorandum by Special Agents Paul Rico and Dennis Condon, Joseph Barboza is contacted where he is in the custody of the U.S. Marshals and a check is made of his physical well-being. Barboza indicates that he is very disappointed in the attorneys who handled the Raymond Patriarca prosecution:
Paul Markham, U.S. Attorney; Edward Harrington, Assistant U.S. Attorney; and Walter Barnes, Departmental Attorney; for not immediately coming down to personally thank him for his contribution to convicting Patriarca. Barboza is told that U.S. Attorney
Markham had gone to Washington for, possibly, matters relating to Barboza. Barboza responded, "While these people don't want to show their appreciation, I am sure that Joe Balliro, the chief attorney for the defense, would show his appreciation in me, and I am sure that if things don't work out, that I can at least end up with $150,000 from Balliro." Special Agents Paul Rico and Dennis Condon contact attorney John Fitzgerald at Massachusetts General Hospital where Fitzgerald is recovering from injuries sustained in the bombing of his car. Fitzgerald says he has

come in contact with or has knowledge of many criminals, whom he believes are all now his enemy. Fitzgerald
tells the agents that he is about to write a letter to Joseph Barboza telling Barboza that because he lost a leg in this bombing, Barboza should turn on these people and provide testimony that will send them to jail. Rico tells Fitzgerald that Rico would prefer
that Barboza testify about whatever he could, without Barboza being pressured into testifying against specific individuals. Rico summarizes, "If we feel that at a later date that Baron is 'holding out,' we then may ask Fitzgerald's assistance, but we do not want
Baron to be motivated by [Fitzgerald's] revenge.

3–20–68: In a letter from Attorney General Ramsey Clark to Director Hoover, Clark states the following: "The recent conviction of New England Cosa Nostra leader, Raymond Patriarca, and two of his cohorts is one of the major accomplishments in the Organized Crime Drive Program. I have been advised by the Organized Crime
and Racketeering Section and Mr. Paul Markham, the United States Attorney in Boston, that without the outstanding work performed by Special Agents Dennis Condon and H. Paul Rico these convictions could not have been obtained."

3–21–68: Special Agents Paul Rico and Dennis Condon check on the physical well-being of Joseph Barboza where he is being held in the protective custody of the U.S. Marshals Service. Assistant District Attorney Jack Zalkind and Detective Frank Walsh both of the Suffolk County DA's Office are also present. Barboza discussed some aspects of the Edward "Teddy" Deegan murder, including the involvement of Louis Greco.

3–28–68: Assistant District Attorney Jack Zalkind, Sergeant Frank Walsh, and Detective John Doyle interview Joseph Barboza about the Deegan murder.

3–29–68: Special Agents Paul Rico and Dennis Condon contact attorney John Fitzgerald at the hospital where he is recovering from the car bomb. Fitzgerald tells them that he told Assistant District Attorney Jack Zalkind that he will testify in the Edward "Teddy" Deegan trial if his testimony is the difference between convicting
these people and letting them go free, but he does want to testify unless his testimony is critical. By memorandum, the Boston SAC recommends to Director Hoover
that Special Agent Paul Rico receive a quality salary increase: "Through his intensive and most skillful efforts, SA Rico developed four Top Echelon informants, namely, REDACTED SECTION BS 955 C–TE and REDACTED SECTION. The Top Echelon informants have furnished the day-to-day activities of Raymond L.S. Patriarca, LCN
[La Cosa Nostra] boss from Providence, Rhode Island, and LCN hierarchy in the New England area.... Through the careful, selective use of the information derived from these informants, SA Rico was able to exploit same and develop Joseph Baron, aka Joseph Barboza, to a point where he testified against Raymond L.S. Patriarca; his underboss, Henry Tameleo; and LCN member, Ronald Cassesso. This resulted in the conviction of above-named individuals and also, the indictment of LCN members Ralph Lamattina and Peter Limone in the gangland slaying of Edward Deegan"

3–31–68: In his performance appraisal, Dennis Condon receives an "excellent" rating and is considered outstanding in his knowledge of the hoodlum element and La Cosa Nostra (LCN) activities in the Boston area. Condon is recognized for being particularly
adept in the development of informants and was instrumental in obtaining a conviction of Raymond Patriarca and several other LCN members. The appraisal also notes that five informants are assigned to Condon. He is also considered an "outstanding probative-type investigator." The

review further states that Condon handled the most complicated matters, such as his handling of the Government witness in the Patriarca case. He is also considered dependable and resourceful.

4–2–68: Special Agents Paul Rico and Dennis Condon contact Joseph Barboza in Gloucester, Massachusetts, to check on his physical well-being. Barboza also stated that he spoke to United States Attorney Paul Markham.

4–4–68: While in custody of the U.S. Marshals Service, Joseph Barboza is contacted by Special Agent Paul Rico, Detective Frank Walsh, and Assistant District Attorney Jack Zalkind. Walsh and Zalkind review aspects of the Edward "Teddy" Deegan murder with
Barboza.

4–5–68: Sergeant Frank Walsh and Detective Edward Walsh interview Geno Cognato, a bartender at Stella's Restaurant, on Boston's Fleet Street. Cognato states that he knew Ronald Cassesso and Joseph Salvati. Cognato did not know Joseph Barboza but had seen him on a few occasions. Cognato tells the detectives that Cassesso and Salvati were frequent customers of Stella's, but he never saw Peter Limone or "any of the others" in
the restaurant. Cognato has no recollection of the night of Deegan's murder, and he does not recall seeing any of the men on the list in Stella's on the night of Deegan's murder.

4–9–68: Special Agents James D. McKenzie, Paul Rico, and Dennis Condon check on the physical well-being of Joseph Barboza at the location where he is in the protective custody of the U.S. Marshals Service.

4–17–68: Special Agents Paul Rico and Dennis Condon check on the physical well-being of Barboza at the location where he is held in custody of the United States Marshals Service in Gloucester, Massachusetts.

4–18–68: The motions made by the Deegan defendants for police reports are denied.

4–20–68: Rudolph Marfeo and Anthony Melei are shot to death while shopping at a market in Providence, Rhode Island. *State v. Patriarcha,* 308 A.2d 300, 305 (R.I. 1988).221

4–24–68: Special Agents Paul Rico and Dennis Condon check on the physical well-being of Joseph Barboza where he is held in the protective custody of the U.S. Marshals Service in Gloucester, Massachusetts.

Special Agent Dennis Condon reports the following on Joseph Barboza: "Baron contacted on 3/21/68 and 4/4/68 by representatives of the Suffolk County District Attorney's Office in preparation for the murder trial involving the gangland death of Edward Deegan.
[Attorney John] Fitzgerald also in contact with Suffolk County authorities
relative to Deegan case. *Subject should be considered armed and dangerous.*" 223
Special Agent Dennis Condon reports that he will maintain contact with Joseph Barboza

4–26–68: Sergeant Detective Frank Walsh, Detective John Doyle, and Assistant District Attorney Jack Zalkind interview Joseph Barboza about the Deegan murder.

4–29–68: Special Agent Dennis M. Condon met with FBI Director J. Edgar Hoover in Washington, D.C.965 J.B. Adams writes an FBI memorandum to Mr. Callahan regarding Dennis Condon stating, "He developed Joseph Baron, aka Joseph

Barboza, described as the most vicious criminal in New England and one whom law enforcement generally felt could never be compromised to testify against La Cosa Nostra's head, [Raymond] Patriarca, and Patriarca's associates. SA Condon directed Baron to the point where Baron testified for the Federal Government. The
trial was finalized with the conviction of Patriarca, his underboss, Henry Tameleo, and La Cosa Nostra member Ronald Cassesso in U.S. District Court, Boston, in March 1968." 226

5–8–68: An FBI memorandum describes a letter written by Joseph Barboza to Senator Robert Kennedy, complaining about his treatment since being in federal custody.

5–9–68: Assistant District Attorney Jack Zalkind interviews Joseph Barboza on the Deegan murder. Sergeant Frank Walsh takes notes of Barboza's statements.

5–13–68: Special Agents Paul Rico and Dennis Condon check on the physical well-being of Joseph Barboza where he is being held in the protective custody of the U.S. Marshals Service in Gloucester, Massachusetts. The FBI summary reads, "Baron advised that United States Attorney Paul Markham and Departmental Attorney Walter Barnes had contacted him with Attorney General De Simone from Rhode Island and Colonel Walter Stone of the Rhode Island State Police. De Simone was trying to ascertain if Baron would be willing to testify against [Raymond] Patriarca in the State of Rhode Island. Baron said he listened to what they had to say but gave them no definite answer. He said he would be very much concerned for his personal safety if he had to go to Rhode Island and testify against Patriarca."

5–17–68: Assistant District Attorney Jack Zalkind interviews Joseph Barboza on the Deegan murder, with Sergeant Walsh taking notes.

5–20–68: Special Agents Dennis Condon and James D. McKenzie check on the physical well-being of Joseph Barboza where he is in the custody of the U.S. Marshals Service in Gloucester, Massachusetts. Barboza expresses concern that Assistant District Attorney Zalkind is not spending enough time with Barboza in preparation
for his court appearance in Suffolk County. Barboza is advised that this matter would be brought to the attention of Zalkind and John Doyle of the District Attorney's office.

4–29–68: Special Agent Dennis Condon personally meets with Director
Hoover in Washington.

5–21–68: According to the *Boston Globe,* Joseph Barboza "pleaded guilty Monday to two counts of [c]onspiracy to murder at the outset of the Suffolk Superior Court trial of seven men in connection with the gangland slaying of Edward 'Teddy' Deegan."

5–23–68: Director Hoover's office is informed who will testify in the Deegan trial. "Special Agents Condon and/or Rico regarding witness Baron first mentioning Deegan murder to them, referral of matter to District Attorney's office, no promises made, etc." (Document retained by the Department of Justice).233 [Subsequently at trial, SA Condon testifies that Barboza was not shown papers or reports. Condon further testifies that no facts about Deegan's death were communicated to Barboza. Moreover, Condon testifies that it was not fair to say that he and Rico were "major figures, so to
speak, with regard to the investigations surrounding the information furnished by Mr. Baron." He further testified that he was very careful not to impart any information to Barboza. *See* 7–19–68 entry.] Assistant District Attorney Jack Zalkind, Sergeant Detective Frank Walsh, and Joseph B. Fallon meet with Joseph Barboza. Zalkind discusses Barboza's testimony before the Grand Jury

with Barboza. Barboza read personally prepared handwritten notes relative to matters that Zalkind had previously discussed with him to Zalkind.

5-27-68: The Edward "Teddy" Deegan murder trial begins.

5-28-68: Special Agent Paul Rico notifies the Boston SAC by memorandum that an informant advised that Jerry Angiulo and Larry Baione are very concerned about the Deegan trial that recently commenced; they have tried "to reach" prospective jurors
and defense witnesses, and they are going to try and reach Assistant District Attorney Jack Zalkind. The informant indicated to Rico that Angiulo said that they are going to offer Zalkind $200,000 for a guaranteed "not guilty."

5-31-68: Special Agent Dennis Condon checks on the physical well-being of Joseph Barboza where he is being held in the protective custody of the U.S. Marshals Service in Gloucester, Massachusetts. In his memorandum, Condon states, "Baron advised that
there have been a number of occasions when Assistant District Attorney for Suffolk County, Jack Zalkind, notified him that he was going to meet with Baron in preparation for the pending Deegan murder trial in Suffolk County and then Zalkind called him to cancel the meeting. He complained that he did not feel Zalkind was spending adequate time with him in preparation for the case. However, he was advised that this would be brought to the attention of Mr. Zalkind and that Zalkind would take the matter up with
him."

6-5-68: Special Agents Paul Rico and Dennis Condon check on the physical well-being of Joseph Barboza where he is being held in the protective custody of the U.S. Marshals Service in Gloucester, Massachusetts.

6-12-68: Special Agents Paul Rico and Dennis Condon check on the physical well-being of Joseph Barboza where he is being held in the protective custody of the U.S. Marshals Service in Gloucester, Massachusetts. According to the report, Barboza advises that "he has been in touch with Suffolk County authorities and hopes to testify in the near future in the Edward 'Teddy' Deegan murder case. Baron advised that he knows that the Rhode Island authorities want him to testify against [Raymond] Patriarca in State proceedings but he had not made up his mind whether he wants to do this as he would be concerned for his protection if he had to go to the State or Rhode Island where Patriarca had had so much influence for so many years."

6-19-68: Special Agents Paul Rico and Dennis Condon check on the physical well-being of Joseph Barboza where he is being held in the protective custody of the U.S. Marshals Service in Gloucester, Massachusetts.

6-24-68: Special Agent Dennis Condon prepares a memorandum regarding Joseph Barboza, describing him as "armed and dangerous."

6-28-68: Special Agent Dennis Condon contacts Joseph Barboza at the Suffolk County Superior Court in Boston. Barboza is being held at the Court prior to his appearance to furnish evidence in the Edward "Teddy" Deegan murder trial. Condon writes that no matters of any pertinence are discussed.

7-2/11-68: Joseph Barboza testifies at the Edward "Teddy" Deegan murder trial that he did not shoot Deegan, nor did he did see who shot Teddy Deegan. [An FBI Memorandum dated 4-6-65

contradicts this testimony. According to this memorandum, Barboza told a PCI ("Potential Confidential Informant") that he
"shot Teddy Deegan with a .45 caliber gun." *See* 3-23-65 entry.] Barboza also testifies that hours before the perpetrators left the Ebb Tide for the Deegan murder Barboza told Joseph Salvati to "go outside and put Romeo's car down the far end of the parking lot."
(3363–64). Barboza also testifies that he told Salvati that when Salvati saw him and the others come out the back door of the Ebb Tide to "blink your lights once to let us know where you are, in what direction in the back of the parking lot you are." (3364).
Barboza further testifies that Salvati wore a disguise consisting of glasses, a moustache and a wig that made him look bald. (3367, 3370, 3372). Barboza testified that once they were in the car "I could see Joe [Salvati] putting on this wig and the snapping of the
elastic. . . . [The wig] had hair around this way and it had few strands over here. It gave you a very high—there's a few strands in front that went back here and you were bald." When asked what the wig looked like from the back, Barboza responded, "You were
bald." (3391–92). Barboza also testifies that Salvati was sitting in the back of the car. (3388). Barboza tells the Court that he is testifying in part to get "a break." Barboza explains, "I am hoping that in regards to a break that what I give before this Court would be taken into consideration[.] . . . And the only promise that has been made in regards to that is that the FBI will bring it to the attention of the Judge and it shall rise and fall, in regards to the cooperation that I gave, to the Court." Yet, Barboza claims that his "hoping for a break" has nothing do with his testimony. Barboza further testifies that he was promised that his wife and child would be protected.

7–19–68: Special Agent Dennis Condon testifies in the Edward "Teddy" Deegan murder trial. Condon states that he did not show Joseph Barboza any reports or papers concerning the death of Deegan. He further testified that he communicated no facts about Deegan's death to Barboza. Condon denies that it is fair to say that he and Rico were "major figures" in the investigations surrounding the information furnished by Barboza. Agent Condon again testifies that he was "very careful not to impart any information" about the case to Barboza.

7–29–68: In his closing argument, Joseph Salvati's attorney, Chester Paris, emphasizes that the only evidence inculpating Salvati came from "the lips of Joseph Barboza, uncorroborated in every respect." In his closing argument, Robert Stranziani, attorney for Peter Limone, quotes from a letter Barboza wrote to his girlfriend, " 'I don't care whether they're innocent or not. They go."
In the prosecutor's summation at the Deegan murder trial, he made the following argument to the jury: "Can you believe Joseph Baron? I suggest to you, ladies and gentlemen, Joseph Baron—and this would apply to anyone who took the stand—that in order for that person to tell a story such as Joseph Baron told in this case, he would have to have the cooperation of the FBI, the Chelsea Police Department, the District Attorney's Office, the Federal Bureau of Investigation, the United States Attorney's Office

7–31–68: Joseph Salvati, Ronald Cassesso, Louis Greco, Henry Tameleo, Roy French, and Peter Limone are convicted of the murder of Edward "Teddy" Deegan. The jury deliberated for more than seven hours over a two-day period. Vincent "Jimmy" Flemmi was neither prosecuted, nor convicted for the Deegan murder. Furthermore, Joseph Barboza received no additional time beyond what he had already been sentenced for a firearms conviction. Romeo Martin and Chico Amico, also allegedly involved in the Deegan murder, were murdered in 1965 and 1966 respectively. By teletype, the Boston FBI Office informs Director Hoover of the convictions and sentences for the Edward "Teddy" Deegan murder. Joseph Salvati and Roy French are sentenced to life. Louis Greco, Ronald Cassesso, Peter Limone and Henry Tameleo are sentenced to death.

The teletype notes that Paul Rico and Dennis Condon were instrumental in developing Barboza and recommends they receive letters of commendation.

8–1–68: In a letter to Director Hoover from Congressman John W. McCormack, Congressman McCormack recommends John J. Connolly, Jr., for the FBI's favorable consideration.

8–2–68: An FBI memorandum from SA (redacted) in the Boston Office to the Boston SAC advises that an informant said Francis "Frank" Salemme was very angry with the verdict in the Edward "Teddy" Deegan trial and stated that (REDACTED) was trying to make an empire for himself (REDACTED) and that something should be done regarding (REDACTED). He further indicated that it was too bad that they did not finish the guy that they wheeled into court

[John E. Fitzgerald, Barboza's attorney at the Deegan trial, was injured in a car bomb in Jan. 1968. Fitzgerald used a wheelchair sometimes in court.] Salemme indicated that the DA's office had lied, the witnesses in the trial had lied and also the Feds had lied and according to the informant, the only ones that did not lie were the defendants. Informant stated that he considered Frankie Salemme one of the worst and most treacherous individuals in the Boston area. He stated that he is constantly with Larry Baione and has made a statement that he did not care about the results of the verdict in the Deegan murder case except for the verdict against Peter Limone and Henry Tameleo. "On August 2, 1968, District Attorney Garrett H. Byrne was informed of the above information by SA H. Paul Rico."

8–5–68: Director Hoover commends Paul Rico and Dennis Condon by letter for their work "in the investigation of a local murder case involving Roy French and others."

8–12–68: Special Agents Paul Rico and Dennis Condon check on the physical well-being of Joseph Barboza, who is in the protective custody of the U.S. Marshals Service in Gloucester, Massachusetts. Barboza advises the agents that his wife had given birth a few days ago to a healthy baby boy.

8–14–68: Special Agents Paul Rico and Dennis Condon contact Joseph Barboza, who is in the protective custody of the U.S. Marshals Service in Gloucester, Massachusetts, and check on his physical wellbeing. Though Barboza understands that he is going to be moved from his protective custody location within the next few days, he hopes to remain in contact with Special Agents Rico and Condon even if moved from the area.

8–15–68: In a letter from the FBI, Dennis Condon is commended for "the excellent fashion in which he performed in the investigation of a local murder case involving Roy French and others."

10–4–68: The Special Investigative Division of the Department of Justice requests an "interview of Boston hoodlum Baron [Barboza] by 2 Boston Agents [Rico and Condon] who developed Baron as a cooperative witness which resulted in the conviction of six hoodlums in connection with gangland slaying in that area. . . . Department advises Baron has indicated having additional information to discuss with Boston agents Condon and Rico who developed his cooperative attitude."

11–15–68: J.H. Gale writes a memorandum to F.B.I. Deputy Director Cartha DeLoach "to set forth the FBI's views with reference to the Department of Justice—'Task Force' (also called 'Strike Force') concept on organized crime." The memorandum notes that a "principal objection [to the Task Force concept] is that the FBI's accomplishments would be submerged in the claiming of credit by the Task Force beyond its actual contribution, and they will wind up grabbing the lion's share of favorable publicity." The memorandum mentions the Boston prosecutions as primary examples of "prosecutive achievement," and states "as a result of FBI investigation, in State court in Boston, Massachusetts, six more were convicted in the 1965 slaying of Edward Deegan. La Cosa Nostra members Henry Tameleo, Ronald Cassesso, Peter Limone, and Louis Greco were all sentenced to death while two confederates were given life sentences."

1969

1969: Special Agent Paul Rico tells Stephen Flemmi that he and Francis "Frank" Salemme will soon be indicted for the attempted murder of John Fitzgerald, Joseph Barboza's attorney. Rico suggested that Flemmi and Salemme flee; they heed his advice. While a fugitive, Flemmi stays in touch with Rico. Yet, Rico does not share this information with the fellow FBI agents responsible for finding Flemmi. [The FBI apprehends Salemme on December 4, 1972, and he is convicted in June 1973. Salemme serves 12 years in prison.
."

3–28–69: After serving three years for armed assault with intent to murder, Vincent "Jimmy" Flemmi is released from prison. He receives a good conduct discharge from Massachusetts Correctional Institute at Walpole. Flemmi was incarcerated for this crime on March 9, 1966. "Joseph (Baron) Barboza 36, self- admitted hired gun was granted freedom . . . on the condition that he leave the state and never return. Baron . . . was released . . . after a special hearing of the state Parole Board at Charles street jail. He was taken under guard to Logan Airport and put aboard a plane for a secret destination. Baron was paroled from a four to five year state prison sentence for carrying a gun. Earlier in the day, Superior Court Judge Felix Forte suspended a year-and-a-day sentence for conspiracy to murder. Also hanging over Baron's head had been habitual criminal indictments carrying sentences up to 70 years. These were dropped by Suffolk County District Atty. Garrett H. Byrne after Baron kept his promise to testify against his former gangland associates."

3–31–69: In a performance appraisal, Special Agent Dennis Condon is rated excellent. He is considered outstanding in dependability, loyalty and enthusiasm, and he is "capable of handling the most complicated investigative matters with a minimum degree of supervision." The evaluation notes that Condon is not interested in administrative advancement.

April 1969: Joseph Barboza is moved from Fort Knox, Kentucky, to Santa Rosa, California, by federal authorities.

6–5–69: Special Agent Paul Rico meets with John "Red" Kelley at the Charles Street Jail, where Kelley was incarcerated. Subsequently, Rico meets with Kelley on several occasions (June 6, June 25, July 8, July 9, July 10, and July 17) before Kelley testifies before the grand jury on August 14.

8–11–69: In a prosecution memorandum from Mr. Gerald E. McDowell, Organized Crime Strike Force, Boston, Massachusetts, to Mr. Thomas Kennelly, Deputy Chief, Organized Crime and Racketeering Section, U.S. Dept. of Justice, Washington, D.C., McDowell recommends prosecuting Raymond Patriarca for his role in the Rudolph Marfeo and Anthony Melei murders. This memorandum states that this case is "remarkably similar" to the Willie Marfeo case. The memorandum also indicated that there could be concurrent state and federal prosecutions.

8–14–69: John "Red" Kelley appears before a Grand Jury to answer questions regarding the murders of Rudolph Marfeo and Anthony Melei.276 Kelley is granted immunity in exchange for his testimony. Indictments are filed, ordered, and issued for defendants Maurice "Pro" Lerner, Robert E. Fairbrothers, Rudolph Sciarra, John Rossi, Luigi Manocchio and Raymond Patriarca for the murders of Rudolph Marfeo and Anthony Melei. In particular, an indictment charges Lerner with two counts of murder and one count of conspiracy to murder.278 [Note: Two published opinions, *State* v. *Lerner,* 308 A.2d 324 (R.I. 1973) and *State* v. *Patriarca,* 308 A.2d 300 (R.I. 1973), both state that indictments were returned against Lerner and Patriarca on June 2, 1969.]

9–29–69: Francis "Frank" Salemme and Stephen Flemmi allegedly murder Peter Poulos, in the desert outside of Las Vegas. Poulos is shot three times in the head with a .38 caliber pistol. Poulos could have tied Salemme and Flemmi to the William Bennett murder. (*See* November 1967 entry). Chuck Lee, the homicide detective who investigated the Poulos slaying and built the case against Flemmi and Salemme learned that Poulos was a Boston police informant who decided to flip. Someone tipped Flemmi and Salemme off and Poulos was killed. The *Las Vegas-Review Journal* reported, "It was obvious to Lee early on that the investigation was officially being hampered, and after a few months the FBI took control of the case." Despite the fact that the Court issued murder warrants, Lee said that " 'everything came to a sudden stop.' " The local police were not allowed to interview the suspects, and there was no move to extradite them.

10–10–69: Indictments are returned against Stephen Flemmi and Francis "Frank" Salemme for their roles in bombing John Fitzgerald's car, severely injuring Fitzgerald.

Peter Poulos' body is discovered near Las Vegas, Nevada. The identity of the body is unknown at this time. A tentative identification was made on January 30, 1970, and a positive identification was made on February 2, 1970.

1970

1–8–70: Vincent "Jimmy" Flemmi is arrested for assault with intent to murder James Abbout. This incident occurred when Flemmi accused Abbout of being an informant for the Boston Task Force on counterfeit money. Flemmi is subsequently convicted on March 20, 1970.

1–19–70: The Boston FBI reports that Boston police detectives suspect that Vincent "Jimmy" Flemmi is collecting shylock money for his brother, Stephen "The Rifleman" Flemmi, who along with Francis "Frank" Salemme and Peter Poulos are currently the subjects of an unlawful flight investigation.

1–30–70: The Las Vegas FBI Office notified the Clark County Sheriff's Department that it had received information from the Boston FBI Office that the Boston P.D. had established tentative identification of the murder victim found near Las Vegas on October 10, 1969, as being Peter J. Poulos.

2–2–70: The unknown murder victim found on October 10, 1969, near Las Vegas is positively identified as Peter J. Poulos using the victim's fingerprints. Sergeant Frank Walsh of the Organized Crime Section of the Boston Police Department is contacted by the Clark County Sheriff's Department regarding the Peter Poulos murder. Walsh stated that Poulos, known to be a loan shark and racketeer, was wanted by the Boston Police Department, along with Stephen Flemmi and Francis "Frank" Salemme, for the murder of William Bennett. All three were indicted for the Bennett murder on September 11, 1969. Flemmi, Salemme and Poulos disappeared from Boston on that date. Walsh also indicates that these three men are suspected of several more murders in the Boston area. Walsh states that it is common knowledge that Flemmi and Salemme considered Poulos to be a "weak link" and would eventually kill him.

2–3–70: Sergeant Detective Frank Walsh of Boston's Organized Crime Section writes a letter to Detective Charles Lee of the Clark County Sheriff's Office. On a night prior to the September 11, 1969, William Bennett murder indictment, the letter states that "Peter [Poulos] received a telephone call from a person who stated to Mrs. Katherine Poulos [Peter's mother] that it was very important for Peter to get in touch with Steve [presumably Flemmi]. This message was given to Peter when he came home on Monday, September 8, 1969[,] and he stated to her that he was going to Cape Cod for a couple of weeks vacation. He took some clothes in a paper bag and left [in his car]. . . . On September 15, 1969, Katherine Poulos notified the office of the Organized Crime Section [of the Boston Police Department that [Peter's] car was now parked outside of her home. . . . She stated that the vehicle was put there sometime during the night by person(s) unknown. . . . Further examination of the right front fender of the vehicle disclosed what appeared to be blood." The department chemist determined that the blood was
human blood. The letter advises that William Fopiano is a known criminal who may have been in the Las Vegas area recently. The letter concludes, "There is a strong possibility that this man may be involved in this matter[.]"

2–27–70: Maurice "Pro" Lerner's trial for the murders of Rudolph Marfeo and Anthony Melei begins.

3–3–70: Henry E. Petersen, Deputy Assistant Attorney General of the Criminal Division, authors a memorandum to William Lynch, Chief of the Organized Crime and Racketeering Section. With regard to Joseph Barboza, Petersen writes, "The memoranda submitted by Walter Barnes do not in my judgment support the expenditure of Nine Thousand Bucks. . . . The additional $4,000 requested to make up the total of Nine, obviously has no support. I
am bothered by the thought on this score that Baron, if my recollection is correct, expected a $10,000 payment at the time his testimony was concluded."

3–9–70: John "Red" Kelley takes the stand at the Maurice "Pro" Lerner trial. Under direct examination by Assistant Attorney General Richard Israel, Kelley testifies that no law officer or any prosecutor of any jurisdiction made any promises to Kelley before he testified and no one promised Kelley that he would receive any consideration for his testimony. Kelley testifies that he was granted immunity from prosecution for crimes related to the Marfeo/Melei murders in Rhode Island and he hopes "that my testimony will be in cooperation with and brought to the attention of the other jurisdiction [Massachusetts] in the final outcome of [the Brink's Robbery] case."

3–10–70: Ronald J. Chisholm, attorney for defendant Maurice "Pro" Lerner, cross-examines John "Red" Kelley at the Rudoph Marfeo and Anthony Melei murder trial. In the exchange, Kelley states that Special Agent Paul Rico and Robert E. Sheehan "couldn't promise but they'd bring any testimony that I would give to the attention of the proper authorities, that's all they said." Moreover, without giving any detail, Kelley testifies that the Government (presumably the FBI) promised him protection. Kelley then adds that there were no other promises, "none whatsoever." In particular, Kelley states that he was not promised a new identity, saying agents of the U.S.

Government "didn't promise me anything." He also testifies that the U.S. Government made "no promises at all" to relocate Kelley to another part of the world. In addition, Kelley tells the Court, "I refused to testify unless I was given immunity" for his acts in relation to the Marfeo and Melei murders. Under cross-examination by Robert S. Ciresi, attorney for defendant Robert Fairbrothers, John "Red" Kelley states that he was not being supplied with income from the U.S. Government.298

3–11–70: Clark County Sheriff Ralph Lamb sends Clark County District Attorney George Franklin a case summary on the Peter Poulos murder, which was compiled by Detectives Jim Duggan and Charles Lee. The case summary concludes, "[I]t becomes apparent that victim Peter J. Poulos and suspects Stephen J. Flemmi and Francis P. Salemme left Boston, Massachusetts on or about 9/11/ 69, traveling to Los Angeles, California. On 9/18/69, [an apartment] was rented by one of the subjects, using the name 'Paul J. Andrews.'
On or about 9/27/69 victim Poulos and suspects Flemmi and Salemme left the apartment in Los Angeles en route to Las Vegas. . . . Suspects Flemmi and Salemme shot and killed victim Peter J. Poulos leaving his body alongside the highway where it was subsequently discovered. This Department has been unable to find any evidence to indicate that victim Poulos ever arrived at Las Vegas . . . To date no trace of either suspect has been found. . . . [Sgt. Frank Walsh] can . . . testify to the fact that [Poulos, Flemmi, and Salemme] were, and are now under indictment for murder, and that Poulos was a potential witness against them." The Detectives request that murder warrants and complaints be issued for Flemmi and Salemme for the murder of Poulos.

3–12–70: A warrant for the arrest of Stephen Flemmi and Francis "Frank" Salemme is issued in Clark County, Nevada. Judge Roy Woofter signs the warrant charging Flemmi and Salemme for the murder of Peter Poulos.

3–13–70: Special Agent Paul Rico testifies at the Maurice "Pro" Lerner trial for the murders of Rudolph Marfeo and Anthony Melei. Prosecutor Richard Israel conducts the direct examination of Rico. The following exchange takes place:

Q: Now, in the course of any of your conversations with Mr. Kelley, did you make any promises to him regarding his making statements in your presence, any promises regarding the statements he might have made in your presence?
A: I made no promises to him.
Q: Now, regarding any testimony which he might give, did you make any promises to him regarding any testimony he might give?
A: I made a statement to him.
Q: You made certain statements to him?
A: Yes, I did.
Q: Regarding what?
A: I told him than any cooperation that he gave to the United States Government will be brought to the attention of the proper authorities.
Q: Now, did you make any statements to him regarding testimony that he might give in Rhode Island?
A: No, I did not.
Q: Did you make any promise or any statements to him as to what might happen if he were to make statements to authorities from Rhode Island?
A: I made no such statements. Rico also testifies that he told Kelley that the U.S. Government, meaning the U.S. Marshals Service, would give him personal security,

but Rico did not describe to Kelley the kind of personal security and protection that Kelley might expect to receive. Rico is then cross-examined by Ronald J. Chisholm, attorney for defendant Lerner. During the examination, Rico states that neither he nor anyone in his presence told Kelley that he would be provided with a new identity. Rico also testifies that he did not tell Kelley that he would be relocated to another part of the world. When asked what members of the U.S. Government were going to provide Kelley with personal security, Rico responds that the U.S. Marshals Service agreed to provide such security. Yet, Rico tells the Court that he spoke with "Theodore F. Harrington" of the Department of Justice—not a representative of the U.S. Marshals Service—about Kelley's security. Rico also states that he promised Kelley that he would bring any cooperation Kelley gave to the attention of the proper authorities. The proper authorities Rico was referring to were Walter Barnes, of the Strike Force in New England and Garret Byrne, Suffolk County District Attorney.

3–16–70: Vincent "Jimmy" Flemmi's trial for assault with intent to murder James Abbout begins. Joseph Balliro represents Flemmi.

3–19–70: Vincent "Jimmy" Flemmi leaves the courthouse, where he is on trial for the James Abbout case, and becomes a fugitive.

3–20–70: Despite his absence, the jury returns a guilty verdict against Vincent "Jimmy" Flemmi for assault with intent to murder James Abbout. Flemmi is apprehended and arrested on October 28, 1970. (*See* 10–28–70 entry).305

3–27–70: Maurice "Pro" Lerner is convicted of murdering Rudolph Marfeo and Anthony Melei and conspiracy to murder. John "Red" Kelley, an FBI cooperating witness handled by Special Agent Paul Rico, provides crucial testimony against Lerner. The jury also returns verdicts convicting Robert Fairbrothers, John Rossi, Rudolph Sciarra, and Raymond Patriarca only of conspiring to murder Marfeo and Melei. These defendants are later sentenced to ten years in prison. As for the indictments charging these defendants with the murders of Marfeo and Melei, the jury is unable to reach a verdict

3–30–70: The Boston SAC sends an airtel to Director Hoover recommending incentive awards for Special Agents Paul Rico and Robert Sheehan "for their outstanding accomplishments in the development of and handling of John J. ["Red"] Kelley." Kelley was "the star witness" in the prosecution of Raymond Patriarca, Rudolph Sciarra, Maurice "Pro" Lerner, Robert Fairbrothers, and John Rossi. Kelley will also be a witness in several other Federal cases. According to the airtel, "The handling of Kelley posed numerous problems on a day-to-day basis as he has always been a professional thief and 'standup guy' and the idea of being a witness against many of his associates was repulsive to Kelley but all this was overcome by the patience, diligence and intellectual approach of SAs Rico and Sheehan. Both Rico and Sheehan were in close contact with the Attorney General's Office in Providence concerning the testimony of Kelley, the preparation of the case and both appeared as witnesses in corroboration on the part of Kelley's testimony."

3–31–70: In an FBI memorandum to Mr. DeLoach, J.H. Gale writes, "With the murder conspiracy conviction of New England Mafia boss Raymond Patriarca and four other racket figures in Rhode Island on 3/27/70, it is believed appropriate to bring to your attention the truly remarkable record established by SA [Paul] Rico in organized crime investigations during recent years. The achievements in question primarily involve SA Rico's development of highlevel organized crime informants and witnesses, a field in which he is most adept. SA Rico's development of Boston mobster Joseph Barboza, a vicious killer and organized crime leader in his own right, set off a chain of events which have seen the surfacing of a number of additional racket figures in New England as cooperative witnesses during the past few years. Making use of compromising information he had received from other top echelon informants he had previously turned, Rico brought Barboza to the point where he testified against Patriarca and two of his La Cosa Nostra (LCN) subordinates in a[] . . . [g]ambling case resulting in [the] conviction of all three in Boston Federal Court on 3/8/68. . . . SA Rico also induced Barboza to testify as the state's key witness in Massachusetts in the gang slaying of hoodlum Edward Deegan. In this case, Rico was additionally instrumental in developing a second witness, attorney John Fitzgerald, resulting in the 7/31/68 murder convictions of LCN members Henry Tameleo, Ronald Cassesso and Peter Lamone [sic], who were sentenced to death; one additional death sentence for another hoodlum, and life sentences for two others also convicted in this case. Following the above major achievements, Rico was instrumental in the development and handling of notorious Boston hoodlum John ["Red"] Kelley as an informant and witness. Kelley was the state's principal witness in the recently concluded trial of Patriarca and four others in Rhode Island for the murder of Rudolph Marfeo. Patriarca and four others were convicted of murder conspiracy while Maurice "Pro" Lerner, the gunman, was convicted of first-degree murder. This is considered an achievement of major dimension causing telling disruption at organized crime's top-level in New England. At the Director's approval, this has been called to the Attorney General's attention by memorandum of 3/31/70. . . . Further, SA Rico's development of Boston gang leader REDACTED SECTION as an informant resulted in the obtaining of a wealth of information regarding high-level organized crime activities in New England including a number of murders.
REDACTED SECTION. SA Rico's overall performance has also contributed materially to the development REDACTED SECTION and were induced to cooperate following Kelley's defection." The memorandum states that La Cosa Nostra plotted to kill Rico and Kelley in August 1969 "for the disruption Rico had caused in La Cosa Nostra circles through his development of informants and witnesses." Appropriate precautionary measures were taken to prevent harm to Rico. The memorandum recommends the following: "In recognition of SA Rico's superior performance which has resulted in the murder convictions of Patriarca and four of his racket associates, it is

recommended that SA Rico be granted an incentive award in an amount to be decided by the Administrative Division. SA Rico's efforts have virtually decimated the Mafia's top-level structure in New England and his proven ability to develop organized crime in formants and witnesses would be of significant value to the Bureau in an area such as Miami, which is his first office of preference."

Special Agent Paul Rico's performance rating report for the period of April 1, 1969, to March 31, 1970, states the following: "During the rating period, SA Rico has been assigned exclusively to the development of criminal informants and investigations of LCN [La Cosa Nostra] members and their associates. He is considered outstanding
in this category and is responsible for the development of several PCs and informants who have been converted into Government witnesses, the most outstanding one of whom is John J. ["Red"] Kelley, notorious armored car robber in this country.
Through his resourcefulness, ingenuity, and aggressiveness, he developed Kelley which at this time, has resulted in the conviction of Raymond L.S. Patriarca, LCN boss, New England area, and other members of the LCN and their close associates. . . . Also indicted through the efforts of SA Rico have been Gennaro [Jerry] Angiulo, acting boss, LCN, Boston, and other prominent hoodlums in this area. His knowledge of duties and the know-how of application both in investigative matters and development of informants is outstanding. . . . During the rating period, SA Rico has handled REDACTED top echelon criminal informants all of whom are considered to be outstanding, and also REDACTED PCs. He is considered outstanding in this regard."

4–1–70: Director Hoover sends a congratulatory letter to Special Agent Paul Rico: "It is with considerable pleasure that I commend you and advise that I have approved an incentive award of $300.00 for you in recognition of the excellence of your services in developing and handling sources of information of great importance to the Bureau in the criminal field. A check representing this award will be sent to you at a later date. It is obvious that you have not only fulfilled your duties with a high degree of professional skill but have approached your assignments with a dedication that truly serves as an inspiration to your associates. I want you to know how much I appreciate your valuable contributions to our work which have enabled us to fulfill our vitally important obligations."

5–4–70: The *Boston Globe* reports that Boston police detective William W. Stuart said last week that he believed Henry Tameleo, Louis Greco and Peter Limone were innocent of the Edward "Teddy" Deegan murder.

6–24–70: A memorandum from Director Hoover to SAC REDACTED attaches a letter dated June 17, 1970, from John E. Fitzgerald, Jr. In the letter, Fitzgerald wrote, "In all my dealings with [Paul Rico] I have never found him making unethical promises or
deals or undertaking committments [sic] which he could not fulfill. . . . In closing, although I lost a leg in the so called 'war against organized crime,' if I had to do it over again I would follow the same road, and my motivations would largely be the result of the integrity, professionalism, and the high traditions of your organization as exemplified in my eyes by Paul Rico."

July 1970: Joseph Barboza is told by Dennis Condon that his life was in danger on this date (July 1970) while he is in California. Based on information furnished to Condon from confidential sources of the FBI, Condon concluded that Barboza's life was in
"serious jeopardy." Condon further testifies "that in January of 1970 we received information that two individuals were coming to the San Francisco area to either kill or do bodily harm to an individual in this area. We did not know at that particular time the

identify of the intended victim but as a precautionary measure, I did advise Mr. Baron about those people coming to the area."

7–5–70: Joseph Barboza kills Clay Wilson.

7–11–70: While at a friend's (Larry Hughes) house back East, Joseph Barboza talks with attorney F. Lee Bailey. Barboza testifies at the Clay Wilson murder trial that a retainer was paid to Bailey by Frank Davis "on behalf of Raymond Patriarca." When Barboza and Bailey are alone, Bailey hands Barboza an envelope containing $800 and says, "Somebody left it in my office. I don't know who left it for you." Barboza and Bailey discuss his "Mafia testimony" and
that Bailey would arrange to see him. Barboza gives Bailey his address and telephone number in Santa Rosa, California.

7–17–70: Joseph Barboza is arrested in New Bedford, Massachusetts, on narcotics and firearms charges. Once informed of his arrest, the Massachusetts Parole Board revokes his parole. Barboza is held on $100,000 bail and taken to the Bristol House of Correction
after pleading innocent in New Bedford Municipal Court. He had been free for 16 months. [While in prison, Barboza apparently tells William Geraway about the Clay Wilson murder. Later, Geraway is able to recount to police that Barboza said he killed Dee Mancini's husband, and that there were two female witnesses (one to the killing and one to the burial). *See* 10–5–70 entry.

7–21–70: Joseph Barboza is housed in Massachusetts' Walpole State Prison for violating parole. From July 21, 1970, until September 25, 1970, Joseph Barboza shares the same Walpole cell blocks as William Geraway.

7–22–70: Director Hoover writes a memorandum to the Attorney General that describes how Joseph Barboza was a significant government witness and yet was arrested on July 17, 1970, in New Bedford, Massachusetts. The memorandum further states, 'On July 20, 1970, the charges against Barboza were nolle-prossed by the District Attorney's Office in that Barboza's rights had been violated as he was not represented by counsel. Barboza was released; however,
the parole board revoked his parole and returned him to the Massachusetts Correctional Institution, Walpole, Massachusetts, where he is supposed to stay until October 5, 1970." This memorandum is copied to the Deputy Attorney General and the Assistant Attorney General of the Criminal Division.

7–30–70: According to the *Boston Globe,* Raymond Patriarca attorney Charles Curran "filed an affidavit by [Joseph Barboza] Baron, which asserted that Baron was ready to present testimony 'which will exonerate' Patriarca, [Henry] Tameleo and Ronald Cassesso in the death of William Marfeo."

According to the *Boston Globe,* Peter Limone files a motion for a new trial. Accompanying the motion is "an affidavit signed by police detective William W. Stuart of Mattapan, stating that he (Stuart) has information that Limone and three co-defendants are innocent of the Deegan killing." Henry Tameleo filed a similar motion yesterday on the basis that Joseph Barboza wants to recant his testimony. (*Limone Files Appeal of Deegan Slay Conviction,* BOSTON

8–3–70: The Boston SAC notifies Director Hoover by airtel that the Deputy Chief of the Strike Force Edward Harrington met with Suffolk County District Attorney Garrett Byrne and Assistant District Attorney Jack Zalkind. At this meeting, Byrne said the affidavit signed by Barboza and filed with the motion for a new trial was not sufficient to warrant a hearing as it simply contains a general statement. District Attorney Byrne is going to confer with the judge in the Edward "Teddy" Deegan murder trial, Judge Felix Forte, and request that the motion is denied on this basis. The District Attorney also plans to confer with John Fitzgerald who testified in the Deegan case. [Note: Assistant District Attorney Zalkind meets with John Fitzgerald on August 7, 1970. See 8–7–70 entry.] The airtel also states, "Boston informant reports that Baron had been seeking $250,000 from the defense on the promise of helping them out." Attorney Fitzgerald advised that Barboza wanted him to contact Joseph Balliro to obtain money from him for changing Barboza's testimony. During the last week, Attorney F. Lee Bailey called Barboza's wife and told her not to pick up a Western Union money order that had been forwarded to her because other funds would be sent to her.

8–7–70: In New York City, Attorney John Fitzgerald, Assistant District Attorney Jack Zalkind, and Detective William Powers of the Suffolk County District Attorney's Office meet to discuss a 1969 meeting in Massachusetts between Fitzgerald, Joseph Barboza, and James Southwood, which Channel 5 in Boston filmed for the purpose of a television special. According to the transcript of the New York City meeting, Barboza claimed to Fitzgerald that he had 50 pages of material that if he left out, would overturn three cases without Barboza being charged with perjury. Barboza also allegedly told Special Agent Paul Rico that a guy named Jimmy was missing and buried at the Cape. Fitzgerald says Barboza was trying to leave the impression that he killed someone. Fitzgerald relates a discussion he had with Barboza where Barboza felt he could return to the streets of Boston by contacting Joseph Balliro. Barboza said, "I got enough that will convince any Court that I was lying, so we will change the testimony and we will pick up a bundle of dough and everything will be straighten" Southwood allegedly
told Edward Harrington that Barboza was willing to say Louis Greco was innocent, which upset Barboza. Barboza said his testimony was that Ronald Cassesso and he went to Peter Limone, and that Romeo Martin never had any dealings with Limone. Later, Barboza supposedly told Harrington that he never said any of the men were innocent, according to Special Agent Dennis Condon.

8–20–70: The *Boston Globe* reports, "Superior Court Judge Joseph Ford signed an application in Suffolk Superior Court yesterday authorizing the issuance of a warrant charging underworld informer Joseph (Barboza) Baron with violation of his probation. The Probation Department of Suffolk is seeking to have the probation revoked and have Baron serve a four to five year suspended sentence he received on various charges in 1967."

10–12–70: Santa Rosa police find the buried body of Clay Wilson. Special Agent Ahlstrom and Lieutenant Brown of the Sonoma County Sheriff's Office contact Dee Wilson who denies any knowledge of her husband Clay's murder.

10–13–70: In a teletype, the San Francisco FBI Office notifies Director Hoover of the following: "Chief of Police Melvin Flohr, Santa Rosa, Calif., just advised that Paulette Ramos, Santa Rosa, under questioning by local authorities, disclosed that Joseph Baron shot and killed Clay Wilson, local Santa Rosa hoodlum, several months ago. Ramos admitted assisting Baron with disposal of [the] body by burying in wooded area several miles outside Santa Rosa. Ramos led local authorities to said area and a body has been recovered. Chief Flohr states body being examined today; however, due to badly decomposed condition, positive identification has not been made."

In a memorandum from Gerald E. McDowell to File, McDowell states that Joseph Barboza made a collect call to Walter Barnes, and McDowell made notes of their conversation. According to McDowell, Barboza states the following: "The only lie detector test I ever agreed to take had to do with my gun charge.' " Barboza also adds, "As far as the Deegan trial coming up I stand on the transcript as being the gospel truth."

10–16–70: A teletype from the San Francisco FBI Office to Director Hoover and the Boston Office informs that Dee Mancini witnessed Joseph Barboza shoot Clay Wilson in the presence of Paulette

10–28–70: Vincent "Jimmy" Flemmi is arrested. He was convicted on December 1, 1970, in Suffolk Superior Court for attempted murder and subsequently sentenced to fourteen to eighteen years at the Walpole State Prison.

11–18–70: Judge Felix Forte of Suffolk County Superior Court dismisses motions for a new trial in the Edward "Teddy" Deegan murder case, according to an airtel from the Boston SAC to Director Hoover.367 Five defendants were seeking new trials: Peter Limone, Henry Tameleo, Ronald Cassesso, Louis Greco, and Joseph Salvati. The sixth defendant, Roy French, did not seek a new trial.

12–1–70: Vincent "Jimmy" Flemmi is convicted in Suffolk Superior Court for attempted murder. He is subsequently sentenced to 14 to 18 years at Walpole State Prison.

1971

1–5–71: Anthony Stathopoulos executes an affidavit that states in part: "Officer [John] Doyle told me that [Joseph Barboza] Baron had told him that [Louis] Grieco [sic] was in the alley shooting [Edward "Teddy"] Deegan.

2–24–71: Joseph Barboza is due to arrive in California to stand trial for the Clay Wilson murder.

2–25–71: The *Boston Herald Traveler* reports, "Federal authorities sought [Joseph Barboza] Baron's parole as a reward for his cooperation[.] . . .

3–1–71: Joseph Barboza pleads not guilty to the murder of Clay Wilson.

Spring 1971: According to a July 11, 1995, affidavit by Joseph Barboza's former biographer James Southwood, "[I]n the spring of 1971, Mr. Barboza said: 'Louis Greco wasn't in the alley!' I have previously made this known to Mr. Louis Greco's then attorney. To this end, Mr. Barboza apparently sent a message to Raymond Patriarca, boss of the New England Mob, who was presently in jail as a result of Mr. Barboza's testimony, that the writer, James Southwood, was in possession of the Grand Jury minutes of the so called 'Teddy Deegan Murder' case. Among those convicted in this case was Louis Greco. Mr. Barboza told me that the Grand Jury minutes would prove that he lied in the courtroom. He instructed me to return the Grand Jury minutes to Attorney Joseph Balliro. To the best of my knowledge, the Barboza copy of the Grand Jury minutes was given to Attorney Balliro in the summer of 1971."

3–26–71: The State of California formally charges Joseph Barboza for the murder of Clay Wilson.

3–27–71: In a letter from Barboza to Ted Harrington, Barboza writes, "[I]f I still have my sanity by the time trial come around I'll see you Denny [Condon], [John] Doyle and Paul [Rico]."

3–29–71: William Geraway's affidavit states, "[O]ne of the men against whom [Barboza] gave perjured testimony was a man named Joseph Salvati[.] That Salvati was entirely innocent of participation or complicity in the crime[.] That he had testified at trial that when a witness or witnesses had described one of the men in the getaway vehicle as bald or balding, he stated that this man was Joseph Salvati, when in reality it was a man named Joseph Romeo Martin[.] He said his motive for placing Salvati on the scene of the murder was a personal feud[.] Baron stated that Salvati had no part in the crime whatsoever, nor any knowledge that it was to happen."

4–30–71: The Boston SAC informs Director Hoover by airtel that since the filing of Raymond Patriarca's "Motion to Vacate," Walpole inmate William Geraway advised that he was furnishing a false affidavit for Ronald Cassesso in an attempt to free Cassesso in the Edward "Teddy" Deegan murder. In return, Geraway was supposed to receive $10,000, given by Cassesso's relative to Geraway's sister on the evening of 4/29/71.

5–13–71: James "Whitey" Bulger is opened as an informant by Special Agent Dennis Condon. Bulger is closed on 9–10–71 due to "unproductivity."

6–4–71: A *Press Democrat* article states that two FBI agents visited Joseph Barboza in his California prison cell last week. The agents returned to the East Coast with affidavits signed by Barboza affirming his testimony, which resulted in the convictions of several Mafia figures in 1968.400

6–9–71: The *Peabody Times* (Essex County Newspapers) reports that according to inmate Kenneth Landers, Anthony Stathopoulos testified that Louis Greco was at the Edward "Teddy" Deegan murder scene out of fear for his life, believing that Roy French would kill him. Stathopoulos testified for the state to put French safely behind bars.

9–10–71: James "Whitey" Bulger is closed as an informant due to "unproductivity." John Connolly later reopens Bulger on 9–18–75.

10–19–71: The Clay Wilson murder trial in California begins.

11–8–71: Special Agent Paul Rico is subpoenaed to testify for Joseph Barboza in the Clay Wilson murder trial on November 18,

12–13–71: Joseph Barboza pleads guilty to the second degree murder of Clay Wilson.

1972

1972: Joseph Barboza and author Bob Patterson sign a contract to collaborate on a book called *In and Outside the Family*. Barboza is obligated to supply documents, memos, and photographs to Patterson. James Chalmas (aka Theodore Sharliss) is under written contract with Barboza to pay advances to Patterson.

In his book, *Strike Force, Organized Crime and the Government,* Clark R. Mollenhoff writes in relevant part the following regarding the Raymond Patriarca tapes: "The Federal Bureau of Investigation bugged the office of New England's crime boss, Raymond Patriarca, from March 1962 until July 1965. Monitoring of conversations . . . was stopped on orders from President Lyndon Johnson who told the public he was against obtaining evidence in this way. . . . The Johnson Administration's decision to assure 'fair play' for Fred Black, Jr., had repercussions throughout the country. Since by disclosing the complete bugging file on Black the Department of Justice had enabled him to avoid a federal prison term, it had to apply the same rule now in similar cases. . . . The decision threatened to overturn the conviction of Louis (The Fox) Taglianetti, who had been convicted of federal income-tax evasion in 1966. . . . Under the new 'Black' rule, Taglianetti had to be given access to any government information that dealt even remotely with him while he was under investigation. In May 1967, Justice Department lawyers delivered the airtels of the bug in the Patriarca office to Chief Judge Edward Day of the United States District Court in Providence. Judge Day reviewed them all, and concluded that only ten had to be made available to Taglianetti and his lawyers. Those ten airtels appeared in the federal court record, and a tremor went through the East Coast Cosa Nostra and the entire political-criminal world of New England. (p.119–20). . . . Many of the conversations related to gangland murder victims: Samuel Lindenbaum and Steven Hughes in Middleton, Massachusetts; Joseph Francione, gunned down in Revere; and Henry Reddington, killed in his Weymouth home. Patriarca was told 'Joe Barboza of East Boston' killed Francione. (p. 123). . . . The so-called 'Taglianetti logs' were made public by Judge Day on May 19, 1967. . . . On June 20, 1967, a federal grand jury indicted Patriarca on charges that he and two others had conspired to engineer the murder of William Marfeo over a competitive gambling enterprise Marfeo was running. . . . Named as a coconspirator, but not as a defendant, was the man they had tried to hire in 1965 as the 'hit man' to kill Marfeo. Joseph (Barboza) Baron, named in the tapes by [Henry] Tameleo as the man who had murdered Joseph Francione, had decided to cooperate with the Attorney General's office in April, immediately before the revelation that Patriarca's office had been bugged. (p. 124). . . . The tapes gave federal and local investigators reason to join forces in developing the Joseph (Barboza) Baron testimony. So long as the case originated from Baron's discussion and not from the FBI eavesdropping it could be used to prosecute. Baron voluntarily furnished a statement to agents of the FBI in April of 1967 concerning the offense in 1965. (p. 125). . . . Bob Blakey had been a Special Prosecutor in the Organized Crime and Racketeering Section of the Justice Department from August 1960, until June 1964. He declared that the Taglianetti airtels were far and above the best information that he had obtained. [I read] . . . investigation reports that were the product of the use of normal investigative methods. There is just simply no comparison in the two kinds of reports. In light of this, I find it nothing short of incredible that Mr. Clark and others would seriously suggest that the use of electronic- surveillance techniques is "neither effective nor highly productive. (p. 129). Louis the Fox thought he was sly when he had his lawyers request the disclosure of all FBI eavesdropping records. (p. 130). . . . Though the bugging of Patriarca's headquarters in Providence had taken place when the results were not admissible evidence in state or federal courts, the revelation of the ten airtels in connection with Taglianetti's income-tax case produced the example that Professor Blakey needed to demonstrate that Ramsey Clark didn't know what he was talking about.

March 1972: FBI Supervisory Special Agent John Morris is assigned to the Boston FBI Office until approximately November 1991.

Morris

3–7–72: Attorney General Robert Quinn writes a letter to Massachusetts State Senator Joseph Ward regarding allegations made by William Geraway to Senator Ward about Barboza. Quinn writes that he inquired into the allegations and was told investigations (presumably about Barboza) were underway by the District Attorneys of Suffolk and Norfolk Counties, and the FBI. Therefore, Quinn writes, "to avoid any interference with current investigations, no direct action has been undertaken by this office with regard to Mr. Geraway's allegations."

3–8–72: A letter from Edward Harrington, Attorney in Charge of the Boston Strike Force, to T.R. Fahey, Correctional Counselor of the California Department of Corrections states in relevant part: "Thank you for your letter dated February 25, 1972[,] relating to Joseph [Barboza's] conversation with members of your screening committee. This information is of great value to the federal government. . . . I greatly appreciate your taking the time to keep us informed of this matter."

5–2–72: FBI Director J. Edgar Hoover dies.

5–17–72: In a letter from Edward Harrington to Joseph Barboza, Harrington states that he received Barboza's letter dated May 7, 1972, and indicates that he will be "very happy" to talk to the person writing Barboza's book. Harrington promises to introduce the writer to "other individuals who would have background information relating to your career."

5–24–72: Joseph Barboza testifies before Representative Claude Pepper's Select Committee on Crime about organized crime's involvement in sports, specifically horse racing. Barboza reportedly testified under heavy guard because he had been given special protection since his testimony against Raymond Patriarca.

The Boston FBI Office advises the Acting Director by teletype that Edward Harrington advises the FBI that Joseph Barboza is in Washington D.C. on subpoena from Claude Pepper's Select Committee and is to appear before the Committee the following day, Thursday, May 25. The teletype states, "Baron will reportedly give testimony re[garding] race fixing and organized crime. Justice Department was not aware of Baron's subpoena and is not in agreement with his appearance before [the] Committee."

5–26/29–72: U. S. House of Representatives investigator Roy Bedell conducts an interview of Joseph Barboza, a part of which was recorded. Barboza describes the Edward "Teddy" Deegan murder in detail and makes no mention of Joseph Salvati.

6–1–72: A Montana state prison report states: "Rec'ed from U.S. Marshall [sic] Wash D.C. PC will receive all PC Privileges. 'Any questions' concerning this man will be referred to Lt. King." [The word "confidential" is crossed out.]

6–2–72: A letter from R.E. Coyle, Assistant Director, Law Enforcement Liaison, California Department of Corrections, to Chris Nolde, Associate Counsel, Select Committee on Crime, states in relevant part: "[P]rior to [Barboza's] transfer to Washington, he alerted other inmates at the institution where he was housed that he was en route to Washington to testify." The letter continues, because of Barboza's "inability to keep his identity and activities limited, . . . I [must] take very stringent action to insure his protection. . . . Effective this date, I have directed that he is a protective custody case. . . . He will not under any circumstances come in contact with other inmates."

6–4–72: Raymond Patriarca is found not guilty at a second jury trial of charges alleging he was an Accessory to Murder. During the trial, John "Red" Kelley again testified about the alleged meeting that took place in front of the Gaslight Restaurant.

6–13–72: Joseph Barboza receives a letter from Edward "Ted" Harrington. In a letter from Joseph Barboza to Marteen Miller, Barboza says that the writer of his book will interview Edward Harrington, Dennis Condon, John Doyle, Col. Walter Stone, Superintendent of the Rhode Island State Police and others who have consented.

6–15–72: Joseph Barboza sends a letter to Edward "Ted" Harrington at the U.S. Post Office and Courthouse in Boston, Massachusetts.

6–16–72: Joseph Barboza sends a letter to Edward "Ted" Harrington at the U.S. Post Office and Courthouse in Boston, Massachusetts.

6–19–72: Edward Harrington's letter to Joseph Barboza states, "You are well aware, I know, that there is no requirement for you to testify in any new cases in order for the Dept. of Justice to bring to the attention of the Parole Board at the appropriate time the contribution which you have already made to the government's campaign against organized crime."

6–20–72: A memorandum from Folsom State Prison, Represa, Associate Warden H. Morphis, to the Visitor Processing Officer grants "approval to Mr. and Mrs. Sharliss of San Francisco to visit [Barboza].

6–21–72: In a letter from Joseph Barboza to a friend, Barboza shows his gratitude for her work on putting together his biography. He writes, "But if in some way through this book that it should cause and add to the public awareness of the diabolical menacing foothold which the mafia is embracing this country so that at least one person will stand up and fight then your work . . . and my endeavorments [sic] will not entirely in the least be in vain!"

6–22–72: A letter from William Geraway to Joseph Barboza says that policeman Bill Stuart "gave a police report to Gerry [Angiulo] on Romeo Martin giving him information on the [Edward "Teddy"] Deegan murder; Gerry then ordered Romeo killed

6–28–72: Joseph Barboza receives a letter from the Department of Justice in Washington, DC.

July 1972: According to William Geraway, in July of 1972, Congressional Investigator Roy Bedell from the Select Committee on Crime, visits him at the state prison in Walpole. Geraway claims that it was clear to him that Bedell "intended to utilize the interviews as a screen to get into the record from me 3 points which would allow Joseph Barboza Baron freedom: 1) That Baron had killed Wilson in self-defense, which is absurd; 2) That Baron's testimony against men in Massachusetts had not been perjury; 3) To get into the record from my own lips that Baron does not have a second body in Sonoma County."

7–9–72: Folsom State Prison Correctional Lieutenant F. Gaul writes a memorandum to J. Campoy, Correctional Captain. The memorandum informs that Mr. Sharliss came to visit Joseph Barboza and was denied entry because of lack of personal identification.
Mr. Sharliss was extremely agitated and hostile towards the Corrections Lieutenant. Sharliss even tacitly threatened the Lieutenant, explicitly stating that he "would be sorry [that he] did not show [Sharliss] more respect and courtesy and take more responsibility
on my own."

NOTE ON THE TEXT: Twenty-five years later it was revealed that Ted Sharliss was an FBI informant and that the government "was aware Barboza was to be killed prior to the murder taking place."

7–24–72: A letter from Joseph Barboza to a friend, states that "I learned to cook Chinese food while cooking aboard ship to the orient and I know a lot of secrets to their cooking. But I hurt my back in Kowloon [and] collected $18,500, strange how well my back feels now?"

11–2–72: Joseph Barboza requests the following people be allowed to visit and correspond with him in Montana State Prison: Ted Sharliss and his wife; Greg Evans; Edward Harrington; and Dennis Condon. A letter from Joseph Barboza to a friend regarding Edward "Ted"
Harrington states, "Did you send Greg a photo stat of that news clipping? Tell him to send you the letter from Ted Harrington and make sure he photo stated a copy for himself! Also to inform you about the answer he received from Boston regarding Nepco's *hold,* ask him to explain that to you."

11–13–72: Joseph Barboza's letter to a friend regarding his belonging states, "So you haven't gotten my belongings yet that I sent you. Well you will and please list what was sent you, I have my reasons. Give the Greek back his electric razor, I never used it. Give the pants and white shirt to some stumble bum, Folsom gave me those to wear! Blah! Keep the yellow jacket and blue one. Here is a clipping my brother sent me, I am inserting the clipping with this letter." Barboza also explains that "the part of the manuscript that was stolen was the part that I gave Ted that was typed up, I do not have the rest, that was handwritten because I gave it to you through Ted to type up. I also have the same amount hand written in a vault in Washington, D.C." Later he also tells the friend that "I've now wrote to Coyle in Sacramento, Greg, Bodell in Wash., Harrington in Boston, Colonel Stone in Rhode Island, let's see if I get any news. I am most anxious to hear whatDoubleday's offer was since they have had the book 1 week now."

12–14–72: Francis "Frank" Salemme is apprehended in New York City by FBI Special Agent John Connolly.

12–21–72: Special Agent John Connolly is recommended to receive a group incentive award for his effort in identifying Francis "Frank" Salemme, a badly wanted fugitive, whom Connolly and two other agents "observed walking on a street in New York City."

1973

Vincent Teresa writes in his book, *My Life in the Mafia,* the following about Joseph Salvati: "One of the first to go was a guy named Edward Teddy Deegan. Deegan was with the McLaughlin group. He and two of his friends, Harold Hannon and Wilfred Delaney, had been holding up some of [Jerry] Angiulos' bookmakers, and it was costing the Office a lot of money. . . . On March 12,1965, Barboza hit him on orders from Pete Limone, Angiulo's right arm. . . . There was one bad thing about that hit. Two guys went to jail for murder that had nothing to do with setting it up: [Henry] Tameleo and Joe the Horse Salvucci [sic][.] . . .Tameleo didn't authorize the hit. Barboza said Tameleo did, but that wasn't true, according to Tameleo. Tameleo said he found out about it the next morning when he read it in a newspaper. I don't know if he was telling the truth, but I guess in a way it's justice. Tameleo set up a lot of other people and got away with it. The guy I really feel sorry for is Joe the Horse. He wasn't a bad guy, and
he was just a flunky. What Barboza did wasn't right. After that, Barboza became the top gun for the McLeans and the Office. He handled more hits than any one guy during the war. On October 20, 1965, he and Chico [Joseph] Amico caught Punchy McLaughlin alone at the Spring Street Metropolitan Transit Authority turnaround in West Roxbury. Punchy had been shot twice before during the war, in November 1964 and in August 1965, but he'd survived
both. He didn't survive this one. Barboza cut him down for good."

Vincent Teresa also writes that Barboza "handled more than twenty-three murders, most of them on his own—I mean, they weren't ordered by the Office. Romeo Martin is a typical example
of what I mean." Regarding the Romeo Martin murder, Teresa says, "This was in 1965 [sic—1966], in July. I'd been out all day with Castucci and Romeo playing golf. Romeo was planning to leave for Florida the next day with his wife. He'd just gotten married and was going to Florida for sort of a honeymoon. After we'd played golf, I told Romeo to come over to the Ebbtide for a steak dinner and a couple of drinks. While we're talking, he said that he and Barboza, after busting up a club, had had an argument. He said he'd shaken the owner down for more money than he was supposed to and had held out on Barboza. Barboza had found out and
threatened to kill him. . . . When he went outside, Barboza and Cassesso were waiting for him. They grabbed him. Took him someplace, and pumped five slugs into him before dumping his body. When the cops found him, [Henry] Tameleo blew his top at me.
. . . [H]e said[,] Why didn't you get a hold of Joe and stop it?' . . .[I responded,] Christ, Henry [Tameleo], they were supposed to be friends. Who knows this animal is going to kill him? That's how treacherous Barboza was. The slightest thing, the slightest word and he'd want to kill you."
Teresa also comments that "Barboza was a stone killer with a terrible temper." Vincent Teresa writes in his book, *My Life In The Mafia,* the following: "McLean had his own mob, but he had some friends that worked on the fringes with the Office, like Joe Barboza, Steve [The
Rifleman] Flemmi, and his brother, Vinnie the Butcher [Vincent "Jimmy" Flemmi]. Vinnie got that nickname because he got his kicks out of cutting his victims up."

Vincent Teresa writes in his book, *My Life In The Mafia,* the following: "Barboza went into the club [searching for a member of the McLaughlin mob named Ray DiStasio] and caught DiStasio cold. The trouble was, a poor slob named John B. O'Neil, who had a bunch of kids, walked in to get a pack of cigarettes. Barboza killed them both because he didn't want any witnesses. DiStasio got two in the back of the head and O'Neil got three. It was a shame. I mean, this O'Neil was a family man—he had nothing to do with the mob. Barboza should have waited. That's why he was so dangerous. He was unpredictable. When he tasted blood, everyone in his way got it."

Vincent Teresa writes in his book, *My Life In The Mafia,* the following: "Then there was one by Vinnie the Butcher. He killed a guy called Francis Regis Benjamin was a holdup artist who was also a friend of some of the McLaughlin mob. Anyhow, Vinnie and Benjamin got into an argument at Walter's Lounge. The Butcher got hold of a gun—it was a cop's gun—and shot Benjamin. He took the body out to a housing project in South Boston, cut the head off, and cut up the rest of the body."

Vincent Teresa writes in his book, *My Life In The Mafia,* that Barboza went to Joseph Francione's apartment as a favor for his friend, Johnny Bullets. Francione had cut Bullets out of a deal, so Barboza shot Francione through the back of the head. Vincent Teresa writes in his book, *My Life In The Mafia,* that "Barboza and Chico Amico knew Hughes and Lindenbaum were heading for Lawrence to take over some numbers and lottery action" and "dropped Hughes and Lindenbaum right in their seats."

Vincent Teresa writes in his book, *My Life In The Mafia,* that Barboza was not a made member and he did not "live by the same rules that made people do." He further stated that "[Barboza] killed for the hell of it whenever he lost his temper."

Vincent Teresa writes in his book, *My Life In The Mafia,* the following: "In 1962 the Federal Bureau of Investigation slipped an illegal electronic bug into [Raymond Patriarca's] office on Atwells Avenue in Providence. Between 1962 and 1965, the FBI listened daily to Patriarca's conversations with such men as Henry Tameleo and Vincent Teresa. And on October 6, 1966, the mortal blow was struck. It was on that date that Joseph (The Animal) Barboza and three colleagues were arrested by police in the heart of Boston. In Barboza's car, police found a fully loaded Army M-1 rifle and a .45 caliber pistol. The law then began applying a squeeze that was to force Patriarca to make fatal mistakes. Barboza was a violent, uncontrollable enforcer "

Vincent Teresa writes in his book, *My Life In The Mafia,* that the story that has been going around about the two individuals, Thomas DePrisco and Tashe [Arthur] Bratsos, who supposedly raised seventy thousand dollars for Barboza's bail, was not true. According to Teresa, DePrisco and Bratsos went all over Boston shaking down bookies and nightclubs to raise the bail Barboza needed. The last place they went on the shakedown trail was the 416 Lounge, also called the Nite Lite Café. They entered the Lounge like "Gangbusters" and asked for money to help Barboza out. The patrons, who included Larry Baiona, [sic] Ralphie Chong, Joe Black, and Phil Waggenheim, refused to help. DePrisco and Bratsos then proceeded to hold them up with a gun and demanded them to empty their pockets, stating, "We'll take what we want." DePrisco and Bratsos were then killed and "the mob took [only $12,000] from their pockets," not [$70,000]. Teresa continues, "Now what Baiona, [sic] Chong and Waggenheim didn't know was that there was a police informer in the place, a guy by the name of Joe Lanzi.
He was a bartender and part-time owner of the Four Corners bar and he was in the joint at the time Bratsos and DePrisco came barging in." Teresa further states, "Then on April 18, 1967, they

caught up with the informer, Lanzi. Three of [Jerry] Angiulo's enforcers—Benjamin DeChristoforo, Carmine Gagliardi, and Frank Oreto—were driving through Medford at four in the morning. In the front seat of their car was Lanzi, who they'd just shot." Once Barboza heard about what was going on, "He got a message to Chico [Joseph] Amico, who was his closest friend, and gave him orders to whack out Waggenheim. The mob found out, and they hit Chico right outside Alfonso's Broken Hearts Club, where he'd been trying to put an arm on some people to help Barboza. Barboza went wild when he heard what happened. He called Patriarca a fag, and he promised he'd hit everyone in sight for killing Chico.

. . . [Henry] Tameleo said, '[G]o see Butch [Frank Miceli of the New Jersey assassination squad] and get a supply of shotguns and rifles. Barboza's got to get hit." Teresa also writes, "It wasn't long after that that Barboza found out he was going to be killed. I guess [District Attorney] Byrne told him, and two FBI agents who were working on him, Paul Rico and Dennis Condon, told him. They convinced him that Patriarca had double-crossed him and was going to have him killed. Barboza was frantic. He didn't want to die, and he didn't want to be an informer. He hated informers."

Vincent Teresa writes in his book, *My Life In The Mafia,* that Raymond Patriarca told him and Henry Tameleo that Joseph Barboza is "gonna get killed in or out of the can." Patriarca continued, "You send the word to him—and that's all there is to it."

Vincent Teresa writes in his book, *My Life In The Mafia,* that after he listened to Raymond Patriarca's tirade regarding Joseph Barboza, Teresa told Barboza's friend Al that Patriarca said, "[W]herever [Barboza] is, he's gonna get it. That's all I can tell you. Now you can tell Joe." According to Teresa, "About a week later the FBI agents met with Barboza again, and he began talking. What the hell could the guy do? Patriarca had shoved his back to the wall. It was the dumbest play Patriarca ever made. If he'd done what [Henry] Tameleo wanted him to do—convinced Barboza everything was forgiven and then, when he got out of jail, whacked him, there wouldn't have been any trouble. But when Barboza started talking, there was hell to pay. First Barboza claimed that Patriarca, Tameleo and Ronnie Cassesso had conspired with him to kill Willie Marfeo. That was true." As a result of Barboza's testimony, "They were all convicted, even though the actual murder was handled by the New Jersey assassination squad. Barboza wasn't through talking, though. He accused Tameleo, Cassesso, Roy French [an Angiulo enforcer], Lou Grieco [sic], Pete Limone, and Joe the Horse Salvucci [sic] of planning and carrying out the Teddy Deegan murder. I told you before how that was done. . . . I still don't think Tameleo was in on that one. . . . Joe the Horse was just an innocent sucker who Barboza didn't like, but he's doing life because of what Barboza said. He never had anything to do with the hit."

Vincent Teresa writes in his book, *My Life In The Mafia,* the following regarding Barboza's involvement in the Witness Protection Program: "The FBI, unable to handle the job alone, called in an elite, trusted contingent of sixteen deputy U.S. marshals, headed by Deputy Marshal John Partington, an experienced law officer with the highest credentials. For the next sixteen months, the marshals would have the task of living with Barboza and his family, keeping them safe and in a proper frame of mind for the trials that were to come. During those sixteen months, Hoover would often call personally to determine how the Barboza protection detail was progressing and what problems were faced."

Vincent Teresa writes in his book, *My Life In The Mafia,* the following regarding John Partington of the U.S. Marshal's Service: "Partington was the man in charge of 95 percent of all the protection details the deputies moved me on, whether it was to New England or Florida, New York or Washington. He's what they call a security specialist, and there are only ten like him in the country. He headed the detail that protected Joe Barboza long before the federal government ever came up with the Witness Protection Program. He lived for sixteen months with Barboza, day and night. . . . He's protected every top mob witness from Barboza to [John] Red Kelley to me and Bobby Daddieco as well as scores of others."

1–19–73: In a letter from Edward "Ted" Harrington to Joseph Barboza, Harrington lists 57 individuals who are either killed or missing. Harrington provides the information because it "might be valuable to [Barboza] in the preparation of [his] book."

2–20–73: FBI Special Agent John J. Connolly, Jr., is assigned to the Boston FBI Office, where he stays until December 1990.

6–1–73: Edward F. Harrington writes in a letter to Robert Miles, Director of the Parole Board, Montana State Prison at Deer Lodge: "I have been requested by Joseph Bentley, who will appear before the Montana Parole Board on June 26, 1973, to testify as a witness in his behalf. I am the former Attorney in Charge of the Department of Justice's Organized Crime Strike Force for New England and am extremely knowledgeable of Bentley's contribution to law enforcement in its efforts against organized crime. Bentley was the chief federal government witness in the prosecution which resulted in the conviction of Raymond L. Patriarca . . . Henry Tameleo . . .
and Ronald Cassesso[.] He was also the chief State of Massachusetts witness in the Boston gangland murder trial of Edward Deegan . . . which resulted in the conviction of first-degree murder of six major underworld figures, including . . . Joseph Silvati [sic][.] The conviction of Patriarca is considered by knowledgeable law enforcement officials to have been the most important organized crime case in the history of New England law enforcement.
Government witnesses John J. 'Red' Kelley, alleged mastermind of the Plymouth mail robbery, and Vincent C. Teresa, who were developed by the United States subsequent to Bentley and whose testimony resulted in the conviction of many major syndicate leaders in the New England area have advised that one of the reasons that they decided to cooperate with the federal government was on account of the fact that Bentley had first broken the syndicate's 'code
of silence' and had survived the underworld's reprisal. Bentley's defection from the organized underworld and his decision to become a government witness against his former associates constitutes the single most important factor in the success of the federal government's
campaign against organized crime in the New England area. Bentley's significant contribution to law enforcement as the pivotal figure in the government's effort to combat organized crime
should be weighed when his eligibility for parole is considered. Please advise me if the appearance of witnesses before the Montana Parole Board is in conformity with your practices."

6–11–73: The Francis "Frank" Salemme trial begins. The trial ends on June 15, 1973, with Salemme being convicted.

7–20–73: The Rhode Island Supreme Court sustains Raymond Patriarca's conviction of conspiracy to murder Rudolph Marfeo.

8–30–73: The *Boston Globe* reveals that Joseph Barboza was "in protective custody at the State Prison in Deer Lodge, Mont. He was moved from a California prison after his life was threatened." The article also states that Barboza is seeking parole from his life sentence.

9–6–73: In a letter from Joseph Barboza to Greg Evans, Barboza expresses a great deal of self-pity. He says he realized he is going back to Folsom State Prison, and states, "one week today since the story broke [.]" [Barboza is referring to articles in the *Boston Globe,* 8–30–73, and the *Boston Herald,* 8–31–73, indicating that he is now in protective custody at the state prison in Deer Lodge, Montana. *See* 8–31–73 entry.]

12–17–73: Joseph Barboza is reportedly involved in an incident at the Deer Lodge Prison in Montana where a guard's jaw was broken.

1974

1974: Stephen "The Rifleman" Flemmi returns to Boston on Special Agent Paul Rico's advice after being a fugitive since 1969 for the Fitzgerald car bombing. As Rico promised, Flemmi was released on bail and the attempted murder charges against him were dropped.

1–29–74: According to an airtel from the Butte SAC to the FBI Director, Joseph Barboza is interviewed at his request by the FBI at the Missoula County Jail in Missoula, Montana, where he is completing his incarceration for a second-degree murder conviction in California. According to the memorandum, "Baron advised that he desired the Justice Department be informed of the fact that he is willing to furnish new testimony against Raymond Patriarca and his henchmen concerning the murder of Romeo Martin, who was shot and killed in July, 1966. He stated that his motives for doing this were that he has a grudge against Patriarca and his lieutenants and wishes them to remain in jail and also because of the fact that Patriarca and the 'New England Family' have a contract for his death outstanding in the amount of $100,000.00." Barboza states that Romeo Martin was shot and killed for two reasons: First, Martin furnished information to Suffolk County, Massachusetts, Detective Billy Stewart, who was on Patriarca's payroll, concerning the shooting and death of Edward "Teddy" Deegan; and, Second, prior to providing information regarding the Deegan murder, Martin attempted to buy into and control a penny arcade in which Patriarca was interested, without advising his lieutenant or Patriarca. Barboza claims to have set up Martin, with William Geraway's assistance, by advising him by telephone that Martin was to meet with Ronald Cassesso and Joseph Dimico. Barboza further claims that his "assignment during [the Martin] murder was to drive a back-up car, and immediately prior to the meeting, he made the last phone call to Martin giving him the time of the meeting and thus setting him up." Barboza stated that "the murder was ordered by Raymond Patriarca, and the plans for it were formulated by his lieutenants, Henry [Tameleo] and Jerry [Angiulo]." Barboza also indicates that he is afraid of being returned to California in light of the contract Patriarca has issued for him. Barboza also states that he wants Rhode Island Attorney General Israel, who was actively investigating the Martin murder to receive the foregoing information.

2–1–74: Joseph Barboza is transferred back to California from Montana after striking a prison guard. Barboza is in San Quentin, California, by February 2, 1974.

2–11–74: An airtel from the FBI Director to the SACs in Butte and Boston states, "He now appears to be bargaining for a quick release and has furnished information concerning the murder of a New England hoodlum, Romeo Martin, July, 1965. Baron's [Barboza] information concerning the Martin murder has been furnished to Massachusetts officials and they have concluded that Baron would not make a credible witness and William Geraway, who is presently

incarcerated in Massachusetts and whom Baron has stated would corroborate his information, is also considered by Massachusetts officials as a pathological liar. The Boston office
sees no useful purpose to be served in detailed interviews of Baron at this time, and Butte has been so advised by Boston airtel dated 2–5–74."

2-14-74: Lieutenant John S. Regan of the Massachusetts State Police and Richard Hoffman, Assistant District Attorney at the Norfolk Complex in Massachusetts interview Joseph Barboza at San Quentin Prison. (*See* Airtel from SAC, San Francisco, to Director, FBI (Mar. 28, 1974)).599 The purpose of this interview is to obtain information and possible testimony from Barboza against William Geraway regarding the murder of David Sidlauskas. Regan
and Hoffman believe Geraway may have told Barboza about the murder while they were in prison at Walpole State Prison.

5-28-74: The *Boston Globe* reports, "[Anthony] Stathopoulos now says in an affidavit that [Joseph Barboza] Baron told him he lied during the trial by omitting the name of a participant out of friendship. Boston Police Officer William Stuart in an affidavit stated that the late Romeo Martin, one of the alleged participants in the Edward "Teddy" Deegan slaying, said that [Louis] Greco and [Joseph] Salvati were not involved. Writer James Southwood, who was
planning a book about Baron, said Baron told him that Greco was not in the Chelsea alley the night Deegan was shot."

11-13-74: The William Bennett murder charges against Stephen Flemmi are dismissed, as they had already been against Francis "Frank" Salemme.

1975

1975: Vincent Teresa writes in his book, *Vinnie Teresa's Mafia,* that he is "responsible for putting fifty guys away in trials and maybe another three hundred guys because of information I gave to police in various states." (p.4). He further states that "right now . . . there are more than seven hundred guys under federal protection. All of them have squealed on the mob. They're talking because the government is providing them with something that they
can't get anymore from their own: protection, real protection."

Vincent Teresa writes in his book, *Vinnie Teresa's Mafia,* that "the only guy who had the guts to say it was all up to me, that I had no obligation to [testify in a case in Newark since I fulfilled
all my promises or] do any more if I didn't want to, was Ted Harrington."

Vincent Teresa writes in his book, *Vinnie Teresa's Mafia,* the following regarding Claude Pepper's congressional committee and the committee's hearing on horse race fixing: "That committee didn't know what time of day it was. [T]hey had Joe Barboza testify about
fixing races, and Joe never fixed a race in his life. He was an enforcer, a mob assassin, not a moneymover."

Vincent Teresa writes in his book, *Vinnie Teresa's Mafia,* the following regarding bugging devices: "Another thing that has shaken the mob real bad has been bugs [the electronic listening devices that the FBI placed on mafia bosses around the country]. That really hurt. A lot of secrets became common knowledge to the FBI. . . . I remember when Raymond learned he'd been bugged. He was half out of his mind to think it could happen to him. He blamed
everybody but himself[.]" (p. 101).

Vincent Teresa writes in his book, *Vinnie Teresa's Mafia,* the following regarding Joseph Barboza: "Take Joe Barboza. He was one of the toughest enforcers around in New England before he became a federal informer. He had a reputation on the street of being a violent, violent guy with a terrible temper. The cops were afraid of him, street people were scared of him, even me—as close as I was to the guy, I'd never so much as cross a bridge alone with him in a car. You never knew what would set the guy off. There was one incident I remember in particular involving Joe. This happened on Bennington Street in East Boston. It was about one in the afternoon, and I was standing on the corner. Barboza was in a car with Guy Frizzi, a street guy that Joe was close with at the time. They were driving along Bennington Street when some poor guy with his wife and two little kids cut Barboza off by accident. Joe went wild. He started chasing this guy, blowing the horn and yelling out the window: 'You mother . . . you son-of-a-bitch . . . I'll get you[.]' Finally, Joe caught up with the guy and cut him off. The driver was smart enough to lock all his windows and doors. Barboza and Frizzi pounded on the windows and then jumped up on the hood of this guy's car, smashing at the windshield. At the same time Barboza was yelling nasty things he planned to do to the guy's wife. I remember seeing the poor little kids, crying their eyes out, hanging on to their father while their mother is screaming her head off. Now, while all this was happening, there was a cop standing on a nearby corner, just watching. Finally, the cop turned away and walked down the street. He was scared to death of Barboza himself. Joe wasn't through though. He ran back to his car and got out a baseball bat and started pounding on the car. He smashed the fenders, the windows, everything. He almost destroyed the car before some cops finally came over and tried to calm Joe down. While they were trying to cool Joe, they told this poor driver who's sitting there in his smashed-up car to get the hell out of the area fast and forget about the damage. I was standing there all the time watching it, laughing my head off. At the time it was funny. Now I think back and it ain't so funny. The driver would have been killed if Joe had got his hands on him, and all because he accidentally cut Joe off in traffic." (p.111–113).

Vincent Teresa writes in his book, *Vinnie Teresa's Mafia,* that Louis Greco had an ongoing feud with Benny Zinna and, in fact, attempted to kill Benny Zinna by firing two shots at him. He further states that "Grieco [sic] himself was a vicious, vicious guy. He was always losing his temper. He was six-two, weighed about two twenty, and he had hands on him like Virginia hams. He could kill you with his bare hands. He never had to do much fighting because everyone was afraid to tangle with him. He was a bumbling idiot and he had a gimp. His close friends used to call him The Gimp, but nobody else dared. Grieco [sic] had feuds with a lot of guys." (p.119–122).

Vincent Teresa writes in his book, *Vinnie Teresa's Mafia,* the following regarding an IRS agent: "There was one guy in particular in New England who was a big [Internal] Revenue [Service] hotshot. He was way up the ladder. He was supposed to be a big racketbuster while he was on the street. He'd hit the after-hours joints, the gambling spots. He made all kinds of noise. The only thing that no one knew was when he was going to raid the Coliseum; he used to call Nick Giso up. 'Hey, Nicky,' he'd say. Sure enough, he'd come busting in and they wouldn't find a thing. He tipped a lot of the boys off when he was raiding them. Sometimes they'd have stand-ins there to take a bust to make it look good. Then he got out of the IRS. That's when he started making really big money. He had a lot of connections with IRS bosses, and he had the confidence of the mob. He could fix almost anything."

5–27–75: Special Agent Paul Rico retires from the FBI. He became an FBI agent on February 26, 1951. Shortly after retiring from the FBI, Rico becomes Director of Security for World Jai Alai.

9–18–75: James "Whitey" Bulger again opened as an FBI informant. which states that Bulger was opened as an informant on September 30, 1975, but which does not recognize that FBI Special Agent Dennis Condon had already opened Bulger as an informant four years earlier).

9–19–75: An FBI Memorandum from the San Francisco, California, Office states, "By LHM . . . Boston advised Bureau that information received from reliable source indicating members of Boston LCN [La Cosa Nostra] family [are] interested in making determination as to where [Joseph] Barboza [is] located upon his parole in order [that] they could kill him. Information received that member of organization located in Boston area stated sizeable amount of money available to [a] person who sets up Barboza from organization in order that he be killed. Above LHM based on information developed by REDACTED. Referenced report indicates that REDACTED advised on REDACTED the De Sciscio and/or Russo had advised while in San Francisco area that a $100,000 contract on Barboza or $25,000 available for 'lining him up.' REDACTED SECTION." 625 An airtel from the Boston SAC to the FBI Director states, "Enclosed for the Bureau are four copies of an LHM setting forth info received from sources indicating [that] the LCN [La Cosa Nostra] is interested in locating" Joseph Barboza and killing him. This memorandum also states that Barboza's murder "would represent a lethal blow to the Witness Protection Act and would serve as a deterrent for future potential witnesses in the Boston area." 626

A U.S. Government Memorandum states that an official from the DOJ advised that Joseph Barboza will be paroled soon and "the word on the street in Boston is that the bad guys know [Barboza's] name and they plan on publicly executing him." The DOJ official requests that we offer technical assistance to the State of California if needed, such as documentation or employment. The "FBI have [sic] already requested help in [the] form of job assistance. This is being done."

10–30–75: Joseph Barboza is "quietly paroled" from Sierra Conservation Camp in California where he served four years for the murder of Clay Wilson. Two underworld figures, one being J.R. Russo, were reportedly in California in August and said to be looking for Barboza.

A San Francisco Police Report notes that Barboza was paroled to San Francisco and is residing with a friend. The report further states that Barboza works as a cook at the Rathskeller Restaurant.

11–1–75: Joseph Barboza lives at Ted Sharliss' residence from this date until November 15, 1975.

1976

1976: Stephen Flemmi provides information that allows Special Agent John Connolly to turn a co-conspirator into a cooperating witness who identified Joseph Russo as Barboza's killer. Russo pleads guilty in 1992.

James "Whitey" Bulger, Stephen Flemmi, and John Martorano meet Back Side restaurant owner Francis X. Green at his restaurant and threaten his life unless he repays a $175,000 debt. Green then contacts Edward Harrington and asks what he should do. The case is turned over to the FBI. The FBI supposedly interviews Green and later denies that an interview took place.

About a year later, the case is dropped because of Green's supposed reluctance to testify against Bulger.

1–26–76: Frank Walsh, the Boston Police Sergeant responsible for investigating Joseph Salvati's involvement in the Edward Deegan murder, recommends a commutation of Salvati's sentence.

1–27–76: The Massachusetts Parole Board votes unanimously to deny Joseph Salvati's petition for a hearing.

2–11–76: Joseph Barboza (a.k.a. Joe Donati or Denati—after release from Wilson murder; Bentley, Baron) is murdered in San Francisco. According to an FBI Memorandum from the San Francisco, California, Office dated June 8, 1978: "[A]t about 3:40 PM, Baron was shot and killed as he attempted to enter his personal automobile parked at the intersection of 25th Avenue and Moraga Street, San Francisco, California. Baron had just departed residence of Theodore James Sharliss, 1717–25th Avenue. Baron was visiting Sharliss for several hours and was returning to his apartment where he was residing with his girlfriend. Baron walked to his vehicle, a 1969 Ford Thunderbird, two door, parked on Moraga Street. As Baron reached the driver's door, a white 1972 Ford Econoline van pulled up and stopped beside Baron and his automobile.
The cargo door on the right side of the van was thrust open and several shots were fired. A white male American wearing a red ski cap, pointed at the top, was observed by witnesses firing a shotgun out of the right side of the van. The van drove off at a high rate of speed and was abandoned some five blocks from the murder scene."

4–9–76: Gerald Alch, a former employee of F. Lee Bailey, signs an affidavit based on interviews with Joseph Barboza at Walpole State Prison in July and August 1970. Alch states that Barboza said all allegations made by him at the Edward "Teddy" Deegan
trial with regard to the involvement of Peter Limone in the crime were false. Barboza said that during his conversation with prosecutors he was interrogated in regard to Limone's involvement in such a way as to cause him to believe that by incriminating Limone, he would be strengthening his position with regard to the promises made to him by the authorities. Since Barboza believed the authorities were not keeping their promises, he had no obligation to adhere to his false implication of Limone. Barboza indicated that he had in his possession notes which he utilized for testimony preparation which had in their margins handwriting on Limone's alleged implication. As a result of these interviews, an affidavit was prepared for Barboza's signature, which "to the best of my recollection, was brought to him . . . by my then associate Colin W. Gillis, Esquire, before whom he acknowledged the contents thereof to be true and did execute said affidavit."

May 1976: Hank Messick writes an article in the *Boston Globe* about Joseph Barboza and his book. Messick writes, "In time he [Barboza] smuggled out the manuscript. [Barboza's friend] typed it and, on the recommendation of former Boston Strike Force chief Edward F. Harrington, brought it to me to make into a book."

5–16–76: An FBI teletype from Boston to the Director and the San Francisco Office states, "BS 1544–CTE [Whitey Bulger] advised that he heard that Jimmy Charlmis [Ted Sharliss], formerly from Boston and currently residing [in] San Francisco, is the individual who set up Joe Barboza to be killed by the 'outfit' and the 'outfit' people are discussing taking [Sharliss] out because he is considered a weak link to their involvement in the 'hit' on Barboza."

5–19–76: According to an FBI teletype from Boston to the Director and the San Francisco Office, "Joseph M. Williams, Jr., Supervisor, Investigation Unit, Commonwealth of Massachusetts Parole Board, advised FBI, Boston, that source close to REDACTED SECTION advised [Ted Sharliss] former associate of Joe Barboza prior to his [Sharliss'] leaving the Boston area years ago, is the individual who set up Barboza to be killed and now they (LCN) intend to kill [Sharliss] to insure [sic] he never talks. Strike Force Chief, New England area, has had continuing interest in developments surrounding Barboza killing due to serious impact on witness program and has continually expressed interest in use of FGJ in event evidence developed regarding individuals responsible for hit. Strike Force Chief advised of above informant information and has expressed intent in having Sharliss subpoenaed before FGJ, Boston."

5–24–76: An FBI teletype from Boston to the Director and the San Francisco Office informs, "REDACTED SECTION advised that the 'outfit' is going to eliminate Jimmy Charlmis [Ted Sharliss] who helped them line up Baron for a 'hit' on the west coast. They don't want to take a chance on him folding up." The teletype continues, "[O]n REDACTED SECTION advised that the Italian outfit had Joseph Baron 'taken out.' They also 'took out' [Patrick] Fabiano because of his connections with Joe Baron. Fabiano had been holding the outfit up over the years, example: getting money from them, etc., because he would not corroborate Baron in Court. They were waiting until they got Baron to 'take out' Fabiano."

5–25–76: FBI teletype from the San Francisco Office to the Director and Boston regarding Joseph Barboza states, "Bureau and Boston office should be alert to the fact that during recent contact with TE [(Top Echelon Informant)], he has furnished some information concerning REDACTED SECTION. TE stated that he would in the near
future furnish extensive information concerning these two areas of criminal activity; however, desired to give the matter further thought and noted that REDACTED SECTION. At time of last contact, TE indicated that he would consider testifying if his testimony became necessary in the above matters. On REDACTED it was determined
that REDACTED SECTION."

5–27–76: An FBI Memorandum from the San Francisco Office states that Ted Sharliss was interviewed by the San Francisco FBI Office. Sharliss is told that he is going to be eliminated. Sharliss denies any involvement or knowledge concerning the Barboza murder.

5–28–76: According to an FBI Memorandum from the San Francisco Office, Ted Sharliss is re-interviewed by the San Francisco FBI Office. The memorandum states, "He admitted that during November, 1975, he furnished LCN [La Cosa Nostra] figure Joseph Russo of Boston, information as to Sharliss' address at San Francisco
and that [Joseph Barboza] Baron was visiting with him on a daily basis. Sharliss admitted subsequent thereto he was in telephonic contact with Russo on other matters, including contacts a day or two prior to the murder. On practically each contact Russo
inquired as to whether or not Baron was still in the area and maintaining contact with Sharliss. He stated that he always advised Russo that he was. Sharliss emphatically denied any involvement in the murder of Baron other than the fact that he furnished Russo the whereabouts of Baron. He admitted that by furnishing this information
to Russo he had 'given Baron up.' Sharliss stated that he believes Russo was responsible for Baron's murder, however, denied knowing who handled the hit. He denied receiving any money, consideration, or favors."

June 1976: Special Agent John Connolly accepts a diamond ring from James "Whitey" Bulger and Stephen Flemmi, according to Connolly's Indictment.

Theodore James "Ted" Sharliss is interviewed concerning information he had regarding the Barboza murder. Sharliss informs that Barboza lived at Sharliss' residence from November 1 to November 15, 1975. Barboza later moved to an apartment with his girlfriend. Barboza visited with Sharliss on a daily basis. On February 11, 1976, Barboza was murdered just outside Sharliss' residence at 1710—25th Avenue, San Francisco. According to the interview summary, "Sharliss advised that during the latter part of 1975, he received a telephone call at his residence from Joseph Russo, a Boston La Cosa Nostra (LCN) Lieutenant and well known 'outfit' hit man. Russo asked Sharliss to meet an individual in the lobby of the Hilton Hotel in Downtown San Francisco. . . . [T]he individual . . . at the Hilton Hotel was none other than Russo. Russo asked Sharliss if he 'would like to make some big bucks'. Sharliss immediately knew that Russo wanted him to kill or handle the contract on Baron. Russo talked of $25,000 for the contract
and Sharliss reiterated that he wanted nothing to do with killing Baron and that he wanted to take a 'neutral position.' Russo became extremely mad and pointed out to Sharliss that he had made friends with a 'lying bum' who testified about 'George' and a number of other guys that he put on Death Row. Sharliss noted that when Russo mentioned 'George' he was referring to Raymond Patriarca, head of the New England LCN. Russo calmed down, left the hotel, and told Sharliss 'keep your mouth shut,' don't say anything to him (Baron) or anybody else." Sharliss also states that he had no other personal contact with Russo, but did talk with Russo by telephone on a number of occasions after the November 1975 contact including a day or two before the Baron murder. During those calls, Russo asked Sharliss if "that lying bum [is] still out
there." (FBI Memorandum, Dec. 16, 1976).648

8–20–76: A teletype to the FBI Director regarding Joseph Barboza states: "For information of Las Vegas, Joseph Barboza was a well-known hoodlum figure and 'hitman' in the Boston area who testified against Raymond Patriarca, New England La Cosa Nostra (LCN) Leader, and numerous other hoodlum figures during 1967–
1968."

October 1976: A San Francisco FBI Office memorandum states, "John Frederick Loewe, bookmaking associate and confidant to Sharliss, provided information to the San Francisco FBI that during January 1976, he accompanied Sharliss to the Hilton Inn, San
Francisco International Airport (SFIA). Sharliss related to Loewe that he (Sharliss) was to meet with Larry Baione, the number two man in the Boston La Cosa Nostra (LCN). Loewe believes Sharliss mentioned the name of the other individual from Boston who was with Baione. Loewe did not recall this individual's name. Loewe believes Sharliss mentioned at this time or it may have been at a later date that Baione and his associate had discussed the hit on Baron with him. During late March or early April, 1976, Sharliss told Loewe he met with the same two individuals at the SFIA Hilton Inn. Loewe, who was arriving from Las Vegas on April 2, 1976, was met by Sharliss. On the drive home from the airport Sharliss told Loewe that he had been to the airport at least once, possibly twice that morning. After dropping Loewe off at his residence,
Sharliss returned to the airport to meet with the previously mentioned individuals from Boston. The purpose of the meeting was for Sharliss to collect $5,000 for 'lining up' Baron. Hotel registration records at the SFIA Hilton . . . and others . . . in the airport complex were checked for the time period in question with negative results.
REDACTED SECTION." (FBI Memorandum, Oct. 26, 1977; *seealso* FBI Memorandum, Dec. 16, 1976, for virtually the same synopsis of facts). [Note: According to the December 16, 1976,

memorandum, Sharliss later told Loewe that he did not get the $5,000 and has never received any money.]

11–3–76: John Frederick Loewe takes a polygraph exam. The results provide that "no specific, consistent significant psychological responses were detected which indicate[s] deception when Loewe answered relevant questions." (FBI Memorandum, Oct. 26, 1977). The San Francisco FBI Office writes a memorandum stating that they administered a polygraph examination of an individual whose name is redacted.

11–15–76: Suffolk County District Attorney Garrett Byrne opposes a commutation of Joseph Salvati's sentence.

11–29–76: A memorandum from Joseph M. Williams, Jr., Supervisor of the Massachusetts Parole Board's Investigation Unit, to the Board of Pardons, Special Attention Board Member Wendy Gershengorn indicates that [Joseph] Salvati associated with a number of Italians tied to organized crime. "The 'word' from reputable law enforcement officers was that [Salvati] was just thrown in by Barboza on the murder because he hated subject, that Joseph Barboza was asked by people was this true and that Barboza denied this."

12–17–76: John Loewe is unable to positively identify Larry Baione from a spread of representative photographs. REDACTED SECTION. (FBI Memorandum, Oct. 26, 1977).

12–29–76: Richard Castucci, a nightclub owner and bookmaker associated with the Winter Hill Gang, is murdered after Special Agent John Connolly tells James "Whitey" Bulger that Castucci is an FBI informant, according to John Connolly's Indictment.

1977

2–28–77: The Massachusetts Parole Board denies Joseph Salvati's second petition for a commutation hearing because Salvati had served an insufficient amount of time to warrant a hearing.

5–20–77: Special Agent Dennis Condon retires from the FBI.

August 1977: Edward Harrington serves as the U.S. Attorney for Massachusetts from August 1977 until October 1981.659

8–9–77: Phillip Sumner contacts the San Francisco FBI Office and relays the following: "On the evening of August 5, 1977, Sumner viewed a television news special dealing with the February 11, 1976, murder of [Joseph Barboza] Baron. In brief, Sumner related that he was incarcerated at Soledad Prison, California, during 1973–1974. Sumner had occasion to meet Red Hogan, a fellow inmate who told Sumner that he was originally from Boston, Massachusetts. Hogan related to Sumner that he served time at Walpole State Prison, Boston, Massachusetts, with Joe Barboza. Hogan also showed Sumner letters received by him from Barboza using the name of Joe Bentley at a prison facility in Montana, believed to be Deer Lodge. The letter writing continued between September 1973 to September 1974. Because of his close association with Hogan and statements by Hogan that he was going to kill Barboza, Sumner feels convinced that Hogan is definitely involved in the Barboza murder."

The memorandum states that Sumner's information, in part, has been verified and investigation continues to further identify and locate Hogan. (FBI Memorandum, Oct. 26, 1977).

10–13–77: FBI Special Agents Thomas Daly and Peter Kennedy interview Francis X. Green about his loan of $175,000 from James "Whitey" Bulger's associates and Bulger's threat on Green's life if he did not repay the loan. (Shelley Murphy, *Cases Disappear as FBI Looks Away,* BOSTON GLOBE, July 22, 1998).

10–26–77: An FBI memorandum states, "Investigation concerning the murder of Joseph Baron in San Francisco, California, on February 11, 1976, continued and eventually focused on Baron's closest personal friend and associate in San Francisco, Theodore James Sharliss."

12–21–77: Florida Attorney Richard Barest states the following in an affidavit: "I was contacted and retained by Mr. [Louis] Greco to attempt to prove his innocence to a murder charge that he felt he was being 'set up' on involving the alleged murder of one [Edward] Teddy Deegan, which was approximately two years old. He advised me of things to check out because he felt he could prove he was in Florida at the time the offense was committed, and that he was 'totally' innocent of that offense, and that he would be willing to take a lie detector test on that specific crime. Pursuant to
his request, my investigator set up an examination with a respected polygraph operator who was then working as the official police polygraph operator for the City of Miami Police Department. I gave my approval of the test, with the only specific instructions
to the polygraph operator was that he confine his questions strictly to the Teddy Deegan homicide, and that he could ask anything he desired about that case with reference to Louie [sic] Greco's alleged participation therein. My recollection is that Mr. Greco's responses were truthful and that he did not participate in the Teddy Deegan
homicide." (*See* 11–14–67 entry).

1978

4–29–78: A report of Special Agent John Morris' performance rating for the rating period of 1/15/78 to 4/15/78 states, "He is imaginative, innovative and extremely industrious and has no hesitation in tackling major projects or complicated which place a heavy demand on his time, often to the detriment of his family. SA Morris possesses all the necessary attributes to be an outstanding Bureau executive."

5–8–78: William Geraway writes to a Justice Department official: "I testified in a Florida murder trial that was contracted out of Boston[.]" This trial was *State v. John Sweet* in 1967. The trial focused on the killing of Charles Von Maxcy which had "been arranged or procured through the Boston area."

5–16–78: Handwritten notes from Butch Carlstadt indicate that Tim Brown taped conversation between Barboza and Ted Sharliss. The notes further indicate that there are twelve 7" reel-to-reel tapes, which were in the possession of Rick Oliver at (707) 527–2127. He appears to be a local homicide detective.

10–11–78: Louis Greco takes two polygraph examinations. The results of Louis Greco's first polygraph examination are determined to be inconclusive. In the second polygraph, the examiner finds that Greco was truthful when he said he was not in Massachusetts when Edward "Teddy" Deegan was killed; not present when Deegan was killed; and was not in Massachusetts on March 12, 1965.

10–16–78: According to an F. Lee Bailey affidavit, Bailey was contacted in about July 1970 by a party whose name was Frank, who had been in recent communication, through intermediaries, with Joseph Barboza, and that Barboza wished to set the record
straight as to certain perjured testimony he had given in state and federal courts. A meeting was set in New Bedford, Massachusetts. Barboza told Bailey that Roy French and Ronnie Cassesso were in fact involved, but Cassesso indirectly. Henry Tameleo and Peter Limone were not involved, but Barboza implicated them because he was led to understand by various authorities that in order to escape punishment on charges pending against him, he would have to implicate someone of "importance." Barboza told Bailey the story he told at court was in very large measure a fabrication. He implicated
Louis Greco because of a personal grudge. The authorities generally assured him that a conviction was unlikely. He stated that because he had become a government witness he would not expect to live more than a day if he were committed to the general
population in Walpole, as he feared. He authorized Bailey to advise counsel for some of the defendants as to his intent, and as to what he hoped to accomplish, and further authorized Bailey to publish his revised version of the Edward "Teddy" Deegan murder (in which he had admitted personal involvement), so long as he would not wind up in jail. Subsequently, Barboza was arrested in New Bedford. After his arrest, he told Bailey that he had been informed by persons in authority, whom he did not name, that federal agents would arrange for his release provided he discharge Bailey and terminate
his efforts to recant his trial testimony. Prior to this time, Barboza had agreed to take a polygraph test. Subsequent to his incarceration he informed Bailey that he had been told that if he submitted to such a test he would spend the rest of his years behind
bars.

10–19–78: Attorney Al Farese's affidavit states that Farese reviewed John Fitzgerald's testimony at the Edward "Teddy" Deegan trial where Fitzgerald said that Joseph Barboza had two pending indictments against him, one involving the stabbing of Arthur
Pearson where Barboza is charged as a habitual criminal. Farese said Fitzgerald told him "[t]hey are willing" to have Arthur Pearson say that Chico Amico stabbed him and that Nick Femia and Joseph Barboza came over to help Pearson. Barboza would then not
be guilty of a habitual criminal charge. If that were not enough, Fitzgerald said Greco would "whack out Pearson." In addition, Fitzgerald said they would give Barboza $25,000 not to testify. Farese stated that at no time was Fitzgerald present with Greco in his house and this conversation he testified to had never taken place. Farese said in April or May 1973, he received a telephone call from Fitzgerald, who was in South Dakota. Fitzgerald told Farese that he was going "to clear the guy with the gimpy leg," meaning Greco, because he was innocent.

10–27–78: Theodore Sharliss is indicted for conspiring to violate Joseph Barboza's civil rights.

10–28–78: The *Press Democrat* reports that a federal grand jury indicted Theodore J. Sharliss in the murder of Joseph Barboza. Sharliss allegedly set Barboza up to be murdered in San Francisco in 1976. Sharliss is indicted on conspiracy to violate Barboza's civil rights. (*Indictment Returned in Slaying,* PRESS DEMOCRAT (Santa
Rosa, CA), Oct. 28, 1978).671

10–31–78: Edward F. Harrington files an affidavit to be used against Louis Greco's Motion for New Trial.

11–3–78: In a Massachusetts Superior Court Order denying a new trial for Louis Greco, the judge states the Commonwealth's submitted materials include an affidavit by U.S. Attorney Edward Harrington. The judge chooses to rely on Joseph Barboza's testimony in the Clay Wilson case and the Harrington affidavit to evaluate Barboza's testimony in the Edward "Teddy" Deegan murder case.

11–6–78: The Massachusetts Parole Board unanimously denies Peter Limone a commutation hearing.

11–13–78: John E. Bates, the Superintendent of Framingham Correctional Institute where Joseph Salvati has been imprisoned for over five years, recommends to the Massachusetts Parole Board that Salvati's sentence be commuted.

1979

1979: The FBI assigns Special Agent in Charge Lawrence Sarhatt to the Boston office. (*U.S.* v. *Salemme,* 91 F.Supp. 2d 141, 203 (D. Mass. 1999)).676 An FBI report reflects what was said at a dinner between James "Whitey" Bulger, Stephen "The Rifleman" Flemmi, and FBI agents. (The Court found that the dinners were held to celebrate milestones. Although FBI procedures require that all contacts with informants
be documented, there was only one, a 1979 report reflecting matters discussed at these dinners. There was no record of the gifts exchanged.) (*U.S.* v. *Salemme,* 91 F.Supp. 2d 141, 149, 150 (D. Mass. 1999)).

January 1979: Special Agents John Connolly and John Morris tell U.S. Attorney Jeremiah O'Sullivan that James "Whitey" Bulger and Stephen "The Rifleman" Flemmi are informants. (DICK LEHR & GERARD O'NEIL, BLACK MASS 65 (2000).677

1–24–79: Theodore Sharliss enters a guilty plea to the charge of violating Title 18 U.S.C. § 241, Civil Rights—Murder and Conspiracy, for setting up Joseph Barboza's murder. (This information is contained in an FBI Memorandum from San Francisco to Director dated June 6, 1979.) Sharliss agrees to testify against the killers. (*Man Gets 5 Years for 'Mafia Killing,* PRESS DEMOCRAT (Santa Rosa, CA), Mar. 1, 1979).678

1–29–79: A prosecution memorandum from Gerald E. McDowell, Attorney in Charge of the Boston Strike Force, and Jeremiah T. O'Sullivan, to Gerald T. McGuire, Deputy Chief of the Organized Crime and Racketeering Section, recommends the indictment of
twenty-one individuals for their involvement with Anthony Ciulla in a five-state pari-mutuel thoroughbred horse race fixing scheme. The following are important points made in this memorandum. Numbers in parentheses coincide with page numbers in the memorandum. [Note: The original memorandum is not appended to the Committee's chronology and is retained in Justice Department files.] "The Boston Strike Force recommends the indictment of the twenty-one individuals listed below, including the principals of the Winter gang, for their involvement with Anthony Ciulla in a multistate
pari-mutuel thoroughbred horse race fixing scheme involving race tracks in five states." The net profits were almost two million dollars. (1) Ciulla and Barnoski met with Howard Winter "and six of his associates" in late 1973 to discuss a race fixing scheme.

"Winter and his partners would provide the money necessary to carry out the scheme." (4) The six associates included Bulger and Flemmi. The memo states that after the initial meeting with Winter, Ciulla and Barnoski met with Winter's other partners in the scheme—John Martorano, Joseph McDonald, James Sims, John Martorano, James Bulger and Stephen Flemmi. Bulger and Flemmi "would help find outside bookmakers to accept the bets of the group." (4) "Ciulla and the Winter group then began to fix races at tracks around the country." The scheme lasted for 2 years and more than 200 races were fixed. (5) "James L. Sims—The case against Sims rests solely on Ciulla's testimony." (55) Suggests that Bulger and Flemmi be further investigated. Indicates that they not be indicted because "the cases against them rest, in most instances, solely on the testimony of Anthony Ciulla." Suggests that the cases against Bulger and Flemmi (and others) might become stronger if indictees cooperated. (62) There are redacted sections with no indication of the reason for the redaction.

2–1–79: Joseph Salvati files his third petition for a commutation hearing with the Massachusetts Parole Board.

2–2–79: Indictments are handed down in the Anthony Ciulla racehorse-fixing case. James "Whitey" Bulger and Stephen "The Rifleman" Flemmi war John Martorano and Joe McDonald, and Martorano flees. (DICK LEHR & GERARD O'NEIL, BLACK MASS 67– 68 (2000)).

2–16–79: The Massachusetts Parole Board denies Joseph Salvati's petition for a commutation because "this petition has been presented too soon following conviction of Murder-First Degree."

2–27–79: Theodore Sharliss is sentenced to five years in prison for setting up Joseph Barboza's murder. (*See Man Gets 5 Years for 'Mafia Killing*, PRESS DEMOCRAT (Santa Rosa, CA), Mar. 1, 1979).

3–12–79: Jack Zalkind, the Assistant District Attorney in charge of prosecuting Joseph Salvati for the Edward Deegan murder, recommends that Salvati's sentence be commuted for a second time.

3–15–79: Frank Walsh, the Boston Police Sergeant responsible for investigating Joseph Salvati's involvement in the Edward Deegan murder, recommends that Salvati's sentence be commuted for a second time. Walsh says he had "never become aware that Mr. Salvati has been even remotely connected with firearms or physical violence."

3–28–79: A memorandum from the Boston SAC to the FBI Director states, "Caption matter [Joseph Baron] contains information that has enduring investigative value beyond the established destruction period and is essential to our investigative needs. In view of the foregoing, this file will be retained until such a time as these criteria no longer apply. An annual review will be conducted by the Boston Division and when this file is no longer essential for investigative reference it will be destroyed and FBIHQ properly notified."

3–31–79: A memorandum from the Boston SAC to the FBI Director states that under John Morris' direction, "Operation Lobster has been broadly acclaimed as one of the most successful law enforcement endeavors in the history of the Boston area. Also during this rating period [4/16/78 through 3/31/79], Supervisor Morris directed and provided leadership to several Agents on his squad in bringing to a successful conclusion a 'bust out' case, an east coast horse race fixing scheme and the indictment of several subjects under the RICO Statute for local burglaries and drug dealing. All of these cases received considerable notoriety in the Boston area and were of significant impact against Organized Crime in the Boston area."

4–16–79: The FBI Director informs the San Francisco Office by teletype of the following: "The Bureau is aware of the sensitivity of the informant issue in this matter and the FBI's obligations. However, the informant and the contacting agent should be aware that REDACTED SECTION unless the informant's complete knowledge REDACTED in this case is known. Unless the informant chooses to provide all relevant information to the FBI regarding his knowledge REDACTED in this investigation, it will be very difficult REDACTED SECTION as it appears he has chosen not to recall vital information. San Francisco attempt to resolve this matter with the informant prior to his scheduled appearance before the federal grand jury in order that such appearance can be avoided if possible."

5–15–79: An airtel from the San Francisco SAC to the FBI Director regarding a San Francisco telephone call to Special Agent John Connolly on May 14, 1979, states: "San Francisco continuing efforts to obtain a prosecutable case against Joseph Anthony Russo and any Boston LCN [La Cosa Nostra] associates for the murder of Barboza."

7–6–79: Defendant Luigi Manocchio appears on a warrant for the murders of Rudolph Marfeo and Anthony Melei and is arraigned. Manocchio pleads not guilty.Vincent James "Jimmy the Bear" Flemmi dies in prison.

12–7–79: San Francisco Strike Force Attorney Michael Kramer requests that Special Agent John Connolly of the Boston FBI Office testify on January 10, 1979, in San Francisco regarding Connolly's interview of Ted Sharliss.

12–20–79: An FBI airtel from the San Francisco SAC to the FBI Director indicates that Joseph Russo's FBI Number is 677 979

1980

1980: James "Whitey" Bulger and Stephen "The Rifleman" Flemmi start giving the FBI evidence against Jerry Angiulo, Boston mafia boss for the Raymond Patriarca family. (*U.S.* v. *Salemme,* 91 F.Supp. 2d 141, 152 (D. Mass. 1999)).

Kenneth "Bobby" Conrad, a prime witness in a Boston murder, disappears. James "Whitey" Bulger and Stephen "The Rifleman" Flemmi associates tell authorities that Conrad is buried in Nova Scotia. (Jonathan Wells, Jack Meyers and Maggie Mulvihill, *Whitey Gang Victims May be Buried in Canada,* BOSTON HERALD, Dec. 11, 2000).

Stephen "The Rifleman" Flemmi provides Special Agent John Connolly with information regarding the murder of Federal Judge James Wood by major drug dealers. Connolly later tells superiors that the contacts Flemmi made in the investigation, at Connolly's direction, may have created the false impression that Flemmi was
involved in drugs. (*U.S.* v. *Salemme,* 91 F.Supp. 2d 141, 205 (D.Mass. 1999)).695

3–28–80: The *Press Democrat* reports that Federal authorities have reopened the Joseph Barboza murder case because of new information. The article says that the Department of Justice wants to find Barboza's killer because his murder threatened the success of the Witness

Protection Program. Jerry Angiulo, Ilario Zannino, J.R. Russo and others were reportedly subpoenaed to appear before a grand jury. (*Jury May Probe Hit Man's Death,* PRESS DEMOCRAT (Santa Rosa, CA), Mar. 28, 1980).696

4–12–80: According to Brian Halloran's statements to the FBI, on this date he drove Louis Litif to Triple O's in South Boston for a meeting with James "Whitey" Bulger. Halloran later witnesses Bulger and an associate bring Litif's body out of the back door of the South Boston bar and put it in the trunk of Litif's new Lincoln.

July–August 1980: Agent John Morris tells Special Agent John Connolly that the Lancaster Garage was bugged; Connolly, in turn, tells James "Whitey" Bulger and Stephen "The Rifleman" Flemmi, two targets of the investigation

7–2–80: Joseph Salvati submits his fourth petition for a commutation hearing with the Massachusetts Parole Board.

September 1980: Special Agent John Connolly reopens Stephen "The Rifleman]] Flemmi as an FBI informant.

11–18–80: Special Agents John J. Cloherty, Jr., and Robert R. Turgiss meet with Massachusetts Department of Corrections officials to discuss allegations that Joseph Salvati was using Framingham Correctional Institute's canteen as a conduit for drugs into the institution. At this meeting, the FBI also alleges that Salvati was operating a gambling ring using the prison's telephones and computer equipment. (*But see* 12–30–82 entry stating that Salvati was found not guilty of these charges).701 On this same day, the Massachusetts Parole Board votes to deny Salvati a commutation hearing.

11–28–80: An FBI airtel from the San Francisco SAC to the FBI Director informs, "On 11/25/80, the enclosed REDACTED was located, which places Russo in San Francisco prior to the murder and corroborates the Sharliss testimony. The whereabouts of Russo, at this time, is unknown. As a result of this finding, San Francisco will now seek an indictment against Russo. San Francisco Strike Force Chief requests that an expedite latent fingerprint and handwriting analysis be conducted by the Bureau Laboratory."

December 1980: SAC Lawrence Sarhatt decides to continue using James "Whitey" Bulger and Stephen "The Rifleman" Flemmi as informants.

12–2–80: In an FBI Memorandum justifying the use of James "Whitey" Bulger as an informant, Special Agent John Connolly falsely credits Bulger with breaking open the Joseph Barboza murder case. Connolly claims that the FBI had "no positive leads" in the Barboza slaying until Bulger offered a helping hand.

1981

1981: Supervisory Special Agent John Morris tells superiors that Stephen Flemmi's information has been used in six successful applications for electronic surveillance, including the two highest priority organized crime investigations in Boston, one being 98 Prince Street.

Early 1981: Assistant Special Agent in Charge Robert Fitzpatrick meets with James "Whitey" Bulger. Fitzpatrick later testifies that he had misgivings about continuing to use Bulger and

Stephen Flemmi as informants because they were not sufficiently productive, and they engaged in serious criminal activity.

January 1981: According to Brian Halloran, he is summoned to a meeting with James "Whitey" Bulger, Stephen "The Rifleman" Flemmi, and John B. Callahan, former head of World Jai Alai and Winter Hill Gang associate and financial adviser.

1–9–81: With the help of James "Whitey" Bulger and Stephen "The Rifleman" Flemmi, the FBI wiretaps Jerry Angiulo's headquarters at 98 Prince Street in Boston.

1–26–81: An FBI Memorandum from J.M. Jones to Mr. Stames states, "Subject [Ted] Sharliss has stated that he met with Joseph A. Russo in 1975 and Russo offered a murder contract on [Joseph Barboza] Baron to him for $25,000.00."

February 1981: The FBI is told that James "Whitey" Bulger and Stephen "The Rifleman" Flemmi were involved in cocaine distribution with Brian Halloran. The FBI is also told that bookmakers are required to pay Bulger and Flemmi to operate in South Boston.

March 1981: Roger Wheeler, Sr., decides to sell the Hartford fronton of World Jai Alai to break its ties with the New England mafia. Edmund H. Mahony,

5–26–81: The Massachusetts Parole Board unanimously denies Peter Limone a commutation hearing.721

5–27–81: Roger Wheeler, Sr., owner of World Jai Alai, is shot dead at Southern Hills Country Club in Tulsa, Oklahoma. John Martorano shoots Wheeler, and Joe MacDonald is the getaway driver. Others implicated are James "Whitey" Bulger, Stephen "The Rifleman" Flemmi and H. Paul Rico.

July 1981: Tulsa and Connecticut investigators get a tip from Boston that the Winter Hill Gang is involved in the Wheeler murder.
723

Late July 1981: H. Paul Rico is brought out of retirement to investigate allegations of corruption by then-U.S. District Judge Alcee Hastings of Florida. He poses as a Mafioso in an FBI "sting" of Hastings.

7–29–81: Kenneth Conrad's daughter, Elizabeth Conrad Parent, learns from Special Agent John Connolly about her father's death. "When [Parent] expressed her desire to retrieve her father's body, she said Connolly told her not to pursue it and to keep quiet about the murder. 'This is an ongoing investigation and I'd appreciate it if you didn't do anything about it for a while,' Parent recalled Connolly saying. 'We've got informants. You could jeopardize them.'
Connolly did not identify the informants, Parent said. In a telephone conversation two years later, Parent said she thanked Connolly for helping her collect on her father's life insurance
Policy

9–11–81: H. Paul Rico signs an indemnification agreement with the FBI to assist the FBI in furtherance of its investigation of alleged misconduct by then-U.S. District Court Judge Alcee Hastings.

1982

3–29–82: The Massachusetts Parole Board unanimously denies Peter Limone a commutation hearing.

April 1982: Supervisory Special Agent Morris informs Special Agent John Connolly, who in turn informs James "Whitey" Bulger and Stephen "The Rifleman" Flemmi, that Brian Halloran is giving the FBI information about Bulger and Flemmi's participation in the Roger Wheeler murder.

Early May 1982: The FBI denies Brian Halloran's request to be placed in the Witness Protection Program and tells him his relationship with the FBI is terminated.

5–11–82: Brian Halloran and Michael Donahue are murdered. Jimmy Flynn is arrested for the murder and acquitted. The FBI is involved in the investigation and arrest of Flynn. [Jimmy Flynn later appeared as a judge in the movie *Good Will Hunting*.] According to Special Agent John Connolly, he filed reports prior to Brian Halloran's death noting that James "Whitey" Bulger claimed the Mafia was going to kill Halloran.

May–June 1982: Supervisory Special Agent John Morris is sent to Georgia for a training program. He asks Special Agent John Connolly for money to bring his secretary-girlfriend along. Connolly gets $1000 in cash from James "Whitey" Bulger and Stephen "The Rifleman" Flemmi and gives it to Morris. Morris knows that the money came from Bulger and Flemmi.
Special Agent John Connolly informs James "Whitey" Bulger and Stephen "The Rifleman" Flemmi that John Callahan is being sought as a witness in the Wheeler investigation.

6–30–82: A performance appraisal report of Supervisory Special Agent John Morris for the rating period of July 7, 1981, to June 30, 1982, states, "In the area of informant development and direction, he was directly involved in the development of one of the most valuable and highly placed Top Echelon Organized Crime informants. . . . As a direct result of Supv. Morris' managerial skills, he has developed and sustained, a program, the results of which are potentially the most significant fight against the LCN [La Cosa Nostra] in the New England area, even in the United States in recent history."

7–16–82: In a letter from FBI Director William Webster to Paul Rico, Webster thanks Rico for his role in the Alcee Hastings investigation.

8–4–82: John Callahan is found dead in his trunk in Miami. Callahan had apparently been dead for weeks.

9–23–82: Administratively, Stephen "The Rifleman" is closed as an informant, but Flemmi is not told.

11–3–82: The *Hartford Courant* reports that the Justice Department organized a meeting of all involved federal and state agencies in Tulsa to trade information. Participants say nothing happened and it seemed as if federal officials were trying to learn what evidence the state and local agencies possessed. The Justice Department then asked for any information on Paul Rico because he was being called out of retirement to help in an undercover investigation of a federal judge in South Florida (Alcee Hastings). Everyone balked at the request for information on Rico.

12–30–82: In a memorandum from Tammy E. Perry, Assistant to the Director, to the Massachusetts Advisory Board of Pardons, Perry reports that Joseph Salvati was found not guilty of charges that he was operating an illegal gambling ring inside Framingham Correctional Institute

1983

1–3–83: The Massachusetts Parole Board grants Peter Limone a commutation hearing.

1–27–83: Supervisory Special Agent (SSA) John Morris' letter, written by SSA James Ring, to Massachusetts Parole Board Chairman Brian Callery states the following about Peter Limone: "Current law enforcement intelligence reflects that Peter Limone continues to be considered an important cog in the Boston Organized Criminal element. Should Mr. Limone be released, he would enjoy a position of elevated status within the Boston Organized Crime Structure." Morris' letter is a response to Callery's December 7, 1982, letter regarding Limone.

Feb. 1983–May 1986: In this time period, records show 46 contacts between Stephen "The Rifleman" Flemmi and the FBI, even though Flemmi was administratively closed as a source in September 1982.

February 1983: James "Whitey" Bulger is elevated to Top Echelon informant status.

April 1983: Oklahoma City authorities seek permission from the FBI Director to interview James "Whitey" Bulger and Stephen "The Rifleman" Flemmi about the Roger Wheeler murder. Assistant Special Agent in Charge Robert Fitzpatrick denies the request by saying he already interviewed Bulger concerning the Wheeler and John Callahan murders.

John and Mary Callahan

4–22–83: Massachusetts Parole Board Investigator Joseph Williams submits a report regarding Peter Limone to the Parole Board. The report states that Williams "would clearly call him [Limone] a member of the 'Family' of organized crime here in Boston."

4–25–83: Suffolk County District Attorney Newman Flanagan writes to Brian Callery, Chairman of the Massachusetts Parole Board, to urge against clemency for Peter Limone. Flanagan says he is informed that Limone was, is, and will continue to be a close associate of organized crime figures.

4–27–83: Roy French executes an affidavit that states, "I am stating for the record that Louis Greco and Henry Tameleo, Peter Limone were not in fact involved with me directly or indirectly in the shooting death of 'Teddy Deegan,' on March 12, 1965."

May 1983: Special Agent John Connolly urges the Boston SAC to reopen Stephen "The Rifleman" Flemmi as an informant because he voluntarily continues to provide high quality information.

5–9–83: Jury selection begins in defendant Luigi Manocchio's trial for the murders of Rudolph Marfeo and Anthony Melei.

5–24–83: Assistant Attorney General for the State of Rhode Island David Leach signs an affidavit stating that he met with John J. "Red" Kelley on May 21, 1983, and that Kelley told him that certain portions of Kelley's prior testimony regarding the Marfeo/Melei murders were false.

Such false portions include: (1) his prior testimony regarding promises, rewards, or inducements; (2) his prior testimony regarding the cutting down of the murder weapon; and
(3) his prior testimony regarding the meeting outside the Gaslight Restaurant. (Leach Affidavit, May 24, 1983).761 According to a newspaper article, "Leach says in his affidavit that Kelley has said several times before that the only thing he was promised in exchange for his testimony 'was that his cooperation would be brought to the attention of the appropriate authorities.' But Kelley said last Saturday, according to Leach's affidavit, that the FBI 'told him that he would be taken care of for life, and that he was bitter that that in fact was not done.'"

Detective Urbana Prignano signs an affidavit stating that he met with John J. "Red" Kelley on two occasions. He first met with Kelley in the presence of Leach. At that time, the three discussed certain discrepancies briefly, such as the Gaslight issue, Mr. Vendituoli's automobile, etc. Prignano also met with Kelley on May 23, 1983, at an undisclosed location. The following are relevant portions from the affidavit of that meeting: "[I] said to Mr. Kelley, 'You're supposed to be such a sharp person in planning criminal activities. I cannot believe that you would make such an error in saying that you met with people when you knew this building burned.'

He then stated to me emphatically that he never knew that the Gaslight had burned. . . . He [Kelley] then rose from his seat and said to me, 'I'm going to tell you something, but I'm going to deny I ever said it to you. I'll call you a liar.' He said, 'The FBI suggested that I put Raymond [Patriarca] in front of the Gaslight the evening that I met with him.' I said, 'I don't believe it.' He said, 'I'm telling you the truth. Mr. [Paul] Rico, the FBI agent, suggested this to me.' I said, 'Well, why did you go along with it?' He said, 'Well, my life was in their hands', and he said, 'What would you do?' And I did not answer that question. I then asked him, 'Did the

meeting ever take place?' He said, 'Yes, it did take place.' I said, 'Where?' He said, 'It took place near a Brink's building.' I said, 'I know of a Brink's counting place which is on Carpenter Street.' He also stated there was a large parking lot in that vicinity where he said, 'I'll even tell you the car that Raymond pulled up in.' He said he came in a Lincoln Continental with a driver. I said, 'Did you see the driver?' He said no. He said, 'What happened down at the Gaslight

actually happened in the vicinity of this Brink's building in a large parking lot.' We then went to other subject matters that were pertaining to this trial. I said, 'John, what about the controversy over the weapons?' He said to me, 'I have an armorer, Appleton. Does that answer your question?' I said, 'Yes. I understand what you're telling me.' We left that subject matter, and I went back again to the Gaslight. I said, 'I can't understand why the FBI agent would tell you that you met Raymond at the Gaslight.' He said, 'I'll, give you my opinion why. I believe Rico wanted to show an affiliation between Raymond and the Gaslight.' " He also stated that Rico's boss stated that the Government had spent 14 to 15 million dollars up to this period of time and came up with a big zero, and he indicated with his finger. He also said that Rico told him to say that he and Raymond went into the Gaslight for a drink; but he stated to me, 'I do not remember if I stated that in the Grand Jury or not.' "

6–1–83: In the trial of *State* v. *Manocchio*, under direct examination by Rhode Island Assistant Attorney General David Leach, John J. "Red" Kelley testifies that in exchange for his testimony at the Maurice "Pro" Lerner trial, he was to receive and did in fact

receive a new identity, relocation to another part of the country, and subsistence allowance. Kelley admits to lying at the Lerner trial in 1970 and again at the [Raymond] Patriarca trial in 1972 about being promised a new identity, relocation and subsistence allowance.Kelley states that the reason he lied was because "Agent [Paul] Rico told me I shouldn't tell all of these things because it looked like I was being paid; that I should just do as he said, and everything would come out all right." Kelley also testified at the

Lerner trial that he cut down a shotgun for use in the murders. However, at the Manocchio trial, Kelley admitted that his armorer actually "cut down" the weapon. Kelley said Rico told him not to mention the armorer's role in the murders because the armorer was an important FBI informant that Rico wanted to keep on the streets in an effort to dismantle the Boston group of the Patriarca crime family. In addition, Kelley testified at the Lerner trial that the gang had a key meeting with Patriarca prior to the murders at a particular restaurant. However, at the Manocchio trial, Kelley admitted that the meeting did not take place at the restaurant he previously named. Kelley stated that Rico wanted him to put the meeting at that particular restaurant to establish a phony connection between Patriarca and the owner of the restaurant, effectively assisting Rico in his investigation against the restaurant owner.

According to Kelley, the FBI had invested millions of dollars in trying to tie the owner of the restaurant to Patriarca, but up to that point, their investigation had not been successful. Rico apparently believed that Kelley's testimony about that particular restaurant would produce valuable circumstantial evidence against the restaurant

owner. The Supreme Court of Rhode Island later grants a new trial to Lerner because of perjury.

6–2–83: Under cross-examination at the Luigi Manocchio trial by Manocchio's attorney Martin K. Leppo, John J. "Red" Kelley testifies that Paul Rico promised Kelley a new identity, that Kelley would be relocated to another part of the country, and that Kelley would be given a subsistence allowance from 1970 to 1981. He also testifies that Rico kept all of these promises. However, Kelley did testify that Rico did not follow through with his promise that he would continue to give Kelley a place to live. Kelley also testified that Rico promised him that he would be taken care of for the rest

of Kelley's life and Rico did not follow through on that. Kelley admitted to lying before the Grand Jury on more than one occasion and to other tribunals in the State of Rhode Island at the insistence of Rico. *U.S.* v. *Salemme*, 91 F.Supp. 2d 141, 183 (D. Mass. 1999).766 The Boston FBI Office sends a teletype to the FBI Director, marked to the attention of the Public Affairs Office of the Office of the Public Responsibility, Organized Crime Section. The message states that FBI cooperating witness John J. "Red" Kelley testified at the trial of Luigi Manocchio, who is allegedly involved in the Rudolph

Marfeo/Anthony Melei murders, that he lied at the behest of Special Agent Paul Rico at the prior trials of the other defendants involved in the Marfeo/Melei murders regarding promises made to Kelley in exchange for his testimony. Kelley also lied about the locationof where an alleged meeting took place. The message further states that substantial news media attention is being given to the fact that Kelley lied in court at the behest of Rico. Handwritten notes on the message state: "No action for OPR at present—former employee allegedly involved. J. CID should handle."

6–15–83: In a memorandum from the Boston SAC to the FBI Director, the SAC recommends that Supervisory Special Agent John Morris be censured for losing four FBI serials. The communications were teletypes entitled "Narcotics Policy Matters; Implementation of Federal Task Force." 769

7–1–83: In a letter from U.S. Attorney William Weld to Brian Callery, Chairman of the Massachusetts Parole Board, Weld urges the rejection of Peter Limone's commutation petition. Weld refers to communications from the FBI and Suffolk County District Attorney's office "which you have already received." Weld cites the fact that the "best information" indicates that Limone will assume control of the Boston Organized Crime's day-to-day operations if released.

7–12–83: James F. Ring, a legal assistant at Bingham, Dana & Gould, finishes *World Jai Alai: A Chronology*. This 196 page report takes the position that the World Jai Alai organization had been treated unfairly by a variety of investigators.

7-15-83: Maurice "Pro" Lerner files an application for post-conviction relief in Rhode Island Superior Court based on John "Red" Kelley's perjurious testimony at Lerner's trial in 1970, claiming in part that Kelley "admitted under oath that he testified falsely at [Lerner's] trial and that he knew, and the FBI, through its agent, knew that his testimony at [Lerner's] trial was false and perjurious."

7-25-83: A letter from Clyde Groover, Jr., Assistant Director of the Admin. Services Division, to Supervisory Special Agent John Morris states, "Careful consideration has been given to the information furnished concerning the loss of FBI documents which were charged to your custody. It is apparent that you failed to exercise sufficient care to adequately safeguard this Government property. In the future, you will be expected to be more careful in handling
Bureau property entrusted to you so that there will be no recurrenceof a dereliction such as this."
772

8-1-83: In a 5-2 vote, the Massachusetts Parole Board votes to grant a commutation to Peter Limone. The two dissenting members, Brian Callery and Michael Magruder, vote against Limone's commutation because the Suffolk County District Attorney's Office, the U.S. Attorney's Office, and the FBI reported that Limone is and will continue to be an important member of organized crime.

8-24-83: Luigi Manocchio is sentenced for a period of two consecutive life sentences, plus ten years, in the custody of the Warden of the Adult Correctional Institutions

8-25-83: A prosecution memorandum from Jeremiah T. O'Sullivan to David A. Margolis Chief of the Organized Crime and Racketeering Section of the Department of Justice in Washington,
D.C, requests permission to indict Jerry Angiulo and his principal associates (five Angiulos, Zannino and Granito), including three Capo Regimes, for their role in several murders, including the murders of Walter Bennett, William Bennett and Joseph Barboza. The
following are important points made in this memorandum. Numbers in parentheses coincide with page numbers in the memorandum.
Discusses indictment of five Angiulos, Zannino and Granito.
Two pages on the Bratsos/DePrisco murders were redacted.
Discusses the Walter and William Bennett murders. Walter Bennett held Larry Zannino responsible and was going to kill Zannino with the assistance of Flemmi and Salemme. The memorandum further states, "Unfortunately for Bennett, Flemmi and Salemme were secretly aligned with Patriarca and the L.C.N. and were under orders to kill Bennett when he made a "move" on Zannino." (14) Flemmi, Salemme and Patriarca, along with Richard Grasso, Robert Daddieco and Hugh Shields, were listed as unindicted co-conspirators in the William Bennett murder. (14) The memorandum continues, "While it is widely known that the Boston L.C.N., through Salemme and Flemmi, were responsible for [Richard] Grasso's murder,
there does not exist at this time sufficient proof to allege it as a predicate offense." (15) The memorandum also states, "Francis Salemme and Stephen Flemmi were charged with being accessories and co-conspirators to this murder [William Bennett]. However, at the time of the state trial, they were fugitives. Daddieco subsequently refused to testify against Flemmi and the charges were then dismissed." (105) The memorandum mentions a wiretapped
telephone call from Stephen Flemmi to Gennaro Angiulo where Flemmi indicates he was present at the murder of William Bennett. (108) The memorandum continues, "Barboza was placed inthe witness protection program under the name Joseph Bentley and relocated to the San Francisco,

California, area in 1969. . . . Barboza was removed from the witness protection program when indicted on the murder charge." (117) The William Bennett murder was prosecuted in Suffolk County in the early 1970s. Daddeico testified against Hugh Shields and William Stuart (and Grasso, who was already dead). Flemmi and Salemme were charged, and Daddeico later refused to testify against Flemmi. Intercepted conversations were redacted—for example, at page 106. [Note: There are numerous sections redacted for "witness not previously identified." This makes it very difficult to review the documents.] Chuck Hiner was prepared to testify that in July of 1976 he and Sharliss agreed to record a telephone call between Sharliss and Russo.

9–12–83: In a letter from U.S. Attorney William Weld to Governor Michael Dukakis, Weld urges the rejection of Peter Limone's commutation request. Weld writes, "Confirming our conversation of earlier today, it is the understanding of this office and of the Boston Organized Crime Strike Force that top-level members of organized crime in Boston desire to have Peter Limone assume charge of the day-to-day operations of organized crime in this area[.] The Federal Bureau of Investigation, the Suffolk County District Attorney, and [the U.S. Attorney's Office] all submitted letters to the Massachusetts Parole Board regarding Mr. Limone's petition."

November 1983: FBI Special Agents Montanari and Brendan Cleary interview James "Whitey" Bulger and Stephen "The Rifleman" Flemmi about the Roger Wheeler and John Callahan murders. Bulger and Flemmi deny any involvement, but refuse polygraphs and object to be photographed.

1984

January 1984: The *Boston Globe* reports that James "Whitey" Bulger, Stephen "The Rifleman" Flemmi, and Kevin Weeks forced Stephen and Julie Rakes to sell them the Rakes' liquor store in South Boston for $67,000.

Joseph Lundbloom of the Boston Police Department tells Special Agent John Connolly of the extortion of the Rakes family. Connolly says the FBI would probably not act unless Rakes agreed to wear a wire. Connolly fails to report the information he learned from Lundbloom. Several days after Lundbloom speaks to Connolly, Bulger allegedly tells the Rakes that he knew of their contact with the FBI and told them to "back off."

1–11–84: In a letter from FBI Director William Webster to Supervisory Special Agent John Morris, Webster commends Morris for his "significant achievements in connection with the 'Bostar' investigation" and encloses an incentive award for his achievements.: "Bostar" refers to the bugging of 98 Prince Street in Boston, which targeted Jerry Angiulo and the top tier of Boston's Mafia.

2–12–84: An informant tells the FBI that Bobby Daddeico called Stephen "The Rifleman" Flemmi and told him that two "Feds" had visited him and wanted him to be a witness against the Angiulos and Larry Baione. Daddeico said he "would not testify under any circumstances and if he was brought back he might have some things to say which the authorities would not want to hear." The write up of the FBI document goes on to say that "he [Daddeico] has a lot of guilt over what he did to Frankie Salemme even though Frankie had it coming." He also said that he would not hurt Flemmi.

Charges against Flemmi were dropped when a key government witness, Robert Daddeico, disappeared. Daddeico's disappearance also forced the government to drop murder charges against Salemme and Flemmi for the gangland slaying of William 'Billy' Bennett of Mattapan."

1985

1985: At a dinner at Supervisory Special Agent John Morris' home, Morris, in Special Agent John Connolly's presence, tells James "Whitely" Bulger and Stephen "The Rifleman" Flemmi that they would not be prosecuted for anything on the 98 Prince Street tapes. In addition, Morris tells them, "[Y]ou can do anything you want as long as you don't 'clip' anyone.

8–6–85: Luigi Manocchio's judgments of conviction are vacated.

10–13–85: The *Press Democrat* reports that in preparation for Gennaro Angiulo's trial, his attorney Anthony Cardinale, tells the press that federal authorities were trying to link Angiulo to the assassination of Joseph Barboza

11–12–85: Specialist Russell Davey gives latent print testimony in federal court in Boston. According to an FBI memorandum regarding Ted Sharliss and Joseph Barboza, "Davey testified that two latent fingerprints developed on . . . a Hilton Hotel Registration card[,] are the finger impressions of Joseph Anthony Russo

1986

1–6–86: The Massachusetts Parole Board grants Joseph Salvati a commutation hearing.

2–26–86: Jerry Angiulo is found guilty on RICO charges.

April 1986: A federal indictment is returned against John McIntyre, seventeen months after his disappearance.

7–15–86: State prosecutor [Name REDACTED by Committee] gives Bobby Daddeico $500.

12–1–86: Seven members of the Massachusetts Parole Board vote to deny Joseph Salvati's petition for a commutation hearing. All seven point to the receipt of information from the FBI that Salvati met with Frank Oreto as the reason for their denial.

1986 or 1987: Supervisory Special Agent John Morris accepts $5000 cash from James "Whitey" Bulger and Stephen "The Rifleman" Flemmi, with Special Agent John Connolly's involvement.

FBI Special Agent James J. Lavin III testifies that he ignored evidence that city workers erected guardrails on private property outside the South Boston liquor store controlled by James "Whitey" Bulger after Special Agent John Connolly reminded him that Bulger was an indispensable informant.

1987

1987: Nadine Pellegrini, Assistant Massachusetts Attorney General, writes a memorandum to Sydney Hanlon, Chief of the Narcotics Division on an unknown date, presumed to be in 1987. The memorandum concerns the upcoming Peter Limone commutation hearing stating, "[T]he FBI and State Police have informant information which is 'fairly solid', according to [Jeremiah] O'Sullivan, that Limone continues his loan sharking operations from prison with the help of his brother. Limone and his family continue to receive income from this operation. O'Sullivan further indicated that there would be no problem using such information as a basis for a public statement."

The Massachusetts Parole Board votes a second time on Louis Greco's commutation request. Jack Curran, who voted against commutation for Greco the first time, approves a commutation this time. Robert Gittens, who allegedly said he would recommend a commutation to Governor Dukakis when he served as the Governor's Deputy Legal Counsel in 1984, now, as a member of the Board, votes against Greco's commutation.

1-15-87: Associate Justice Bulman of the Superior Court of Rhode Island issues an opinion denying Maurice "Pro" Lerner's application for post-conviction relief. In denying Lerner's application, "[T]he Court finds that witness John J. Kelley committed perjury in the 1970 trial of the captioned indictments before this Court: 1. In failing to disclose, when asked, the full extent of the promises made him by federal agent Rico[;] 2. In claiming he alone altered the murder weapons[;] 3. In describing the meeting outside the Gaslight Restaurant[;] and[,] 4. As to the color of Vendituoli's automobile."

March 1987: James "Whitey" Bulger tells South Boston realtor Raymond Slinger that someone hired him to kill Slinger. Bulger tells Slinger he will not kill him if Slinger gives Bulger $50,000. Agents John Newton and Roderick Kennedy fail to document or follow up on realtor Raymond Slinger's claim.

4-6-87: Under a harmless error analysis, judgments of conviction are vacated for Luigi Manocchio. (Below)

June 1987: The Massachusetts Parole Board votes to grant Peter Limone a second commutation hearing.808

8–28–87: A commutation hearing is scheduled for Peter Limone. Barbara D. Johnson, Pardons Coordinator, sends a letter to Massachusetts Attorney General James Shannon inviting him to attend or submit his viewpoint.

10–19–87: Boston SAC James Ahearn writes a letter to John J. Curran, Jr., Chairman of the Massachusetts Parole Board, regarding Peter Limone. The letter details Limone's contacts with members of organized crime. Ahearn's letter is a response to Curran's request for information concerning Limone.

10–28–87: Boston SAC James Ahearn writes a second letter to John J. Curran, Jr., Chairman of the Massachusetts Parole Board, regarding Peter Limone. This letter provides additional information about Limone's contacts with members of organized crime that was previously under seal and impounded by the U.S. District Court.911

11–16–87: The Massachusetts Parole Board unanimously denies Peter Limone executive clemency.

1988

1-20–88: When being considered for the federal bench, Judge Edward F. Harrington writes to Delaware Senator Joseph Biden, Chairman of the Senate Judiciary Committee. He states, "As a public prosecutor, I developed such significant accomplice witnesses as Joseph Baron, Vincent Teresa, 'Red' Kelley, William Masiello and many others whose use as witnesses I always made available to local prosecutorial authorities. Cooperation with local law enforcement was my hallmark." 813

1-29–88: Edward Harrington writes a second letter to Delaware Senator Joseph Biden stating, "I never used an accomplice witness unless I was convinced that he was telling the truth and his testimony had been corroborated to the fullest extent possible. Nor did I ever condone any wrongdoing on any witness' part."

1988–89: Winter Hill member Joseph Murray approaches the FBI and implicates James "Whitey" Bulger and Patrick Nee in the Brian Halloran and Michael Donahue murders. Murray also alleges that Agents John Connolly and John Newton and others are selling information on law enforcement activities to Bulger and Stephen Flemmi. (*U.S.* v. *Salemme*, 91 F.Supp. 2d 141, 256–58 (D. Mass. 1999)).815

1988: At Special Agent John Connolly's request, Stephen Flemmi begins to provide information on Francis "Frank" Salemme, who was just released from prison for the John Fitzgerald car bombing. (*U.S.* v. *Salemme*, 91 F.Supp. 2d 141, 153 (D. Mass. 1999)).

Supervisory Special Agent John Morris warns James "Whitey" Bulger and Stephen Flemmi that the FBI has tapped the phone of a Roxbury bookmaker, John Baharoian, who worked for them. Indictments result from the wiretap, but do not include Bulger or Flemmi. (Shelley Murphy, *Cases Disappear as FBI Looks Away*, BOSTON GLOBE, July 22, 1998).817

Agent James Blackburn testifies that he never pursued allegations that James "Whitey" Bulger was shaking down a South Boston drug dealer after Special Agent John Connolly told him it was not true. (Shelley Murphy, *Cases Disappear as FBI Looks Away,* BOSTON GLOBE, July 22, 1998).

Francis "Frank" Salemme was "made" in the Mafia after his release from prison, reportedly achieving the rank of Capo Regime, or Underboss, in the Patriarca family.

June 1988: Supervisory Special Agent John Morris learns of a federal wiretap on telephones used for illegal gambling activity and tells Special Agent John Connolly. Connolly arranges a meeting between himself, Morris, James "Whitey" Bulger, and Stephen Flemmi so Morris could directly advise them of the wiretap.

6–10–88: The Rhode Island Supreme Court vacates Maurice "Pro" Lerner's conviction. The Court held "that Kelley's perjury at Lerner's trial relating to the extent of promises made to Kelley by the FBI in exchange for his testimony and Special Agent Rico's corroboration of that perjury were material to Kelley's credibility and
therefore to the issue of Lerner's guilt." The Court ruled that "Kelley's perjury, elicited by the FBI, constituted material exculpatory evidence withheld in violation of the applicant's due process rights." *See Lerner v. Moran,* 542 A.2d 1089, 1091, 1093 (R.I. 1988).821

8–8–88: The Massachusetts Parole Board writes a letter to Boston SAC James Ahearn requesting an update on the status of the FBI's investigation of the contacts between Frank Oreto and Joseph Salvati.822

10–17–88: Joseph Salvati applies for a commutation hearing with the Massachusetts Parole Board.

1989

3–14–89: The Massachusetts Parole Board votes six to one in favor of granting Joseph Salvati a commutation hearing.

3–29–89: The *Boston Globe* reports, "Seven persons, including prominent Boston defense attorney Joseph J. Balliro, have been indicted by a federal grand jury on charges of conspiring to conceal millions of dollars of a Mafia drug kingpin's profits from the Internal Revenue Service in false companies established in the Bahamas, Panama and the United States. The 37-page indictment was handed down last Thursday," March 23, 1989, and is unsealed today. (Elizabeth Neuffer, *Balliro Among Seven Indicted,* BOSTON GLOBE, Mar. 30, 1999).825

March 1989: A warrant issued for the arrest of Stephen Flemmi and Francis "Frank" Salemme for the murder of Peter Poulos is recalled.

June 1989: Agents Edward Clark and Edward Quinn interview Joseph Murray, but do not ask about the allegations he made that: (1) FBI Agents John Connolly and John Newton were selling information regarding wiretaps, to James "Whitey" Bulger and Stevie Flemmi; and (2) James "Whitey" Bulger and Pat Nee murdered Brian Halloran and Bucky Barrett. (*see* 1988–89 entry). However, a subsequent memorandum drafted from Assistant SAC Dennis O'Callahan to FBI headquarters states that Murray's allegations were unsubstantiated. Murray's information is not provided to agents working on the Brian Halloran investigation. (*U.S.* v. *Salemme,* 91 F.Supp. 2d 141, 256–58 (D. Mass. 1999)).827

6–7–89: In a letter from Leonard J. Henson, Assistant District Attorney of Suffolk County and Chief of the Organized Crime Division, to Supervisory Special Agent James Ring, Henson advises Ring of the upcoming commutation hearing for Joseph Salvati.
Henson asks the FBI for "any information that your office has with regard to Mr. Salvati's involvement with the Deegan murder as well as his past and present status with organized crime elements in the area." A notation at the bottom states that information previously had been submitted to the Board of Pardons by Special Agent Ring.

6–16–89: Connecticut crime boss William Grasso is murdered. Many experts on the Mafia say that Grasso, who was found shot to death along a bank of the Connecticut River outside Hartford, would not have been killed without the authorization of the New
York families. Grasso was considered to be the second highest ranking Mafioso in New England behind Raymond Patriarca, Jr. Yet, some believe Grasso was the real power while Patriarca serves mainly as titular head.

7–14–15–89: Special Agent Paul Rico testifies at a Senate Impeachment
Trial Committee hearing on the articles of impeachment filed against U.S. District Court Judge Alcee Hastings. Rico testifies about his involvement in the Hastings' investigation.

8–14–89: Former Suffolk County Assistant District Attorney Jack Zalkind recommends commuting Joseph Salvati's sentence for a third time. He refers to his earlier letter of March 12, 1979.

8–15–89: Retired Boston Police Detective Frank Walsh recommends commuting Joseph Salvati's sentence for a third time. He refers to his earlier letter of March 15, 1979.

8–16–89: Suffolk County District Attorney Newman Flanagan opposes commuting Joseph Salvati's sentence

8–21–89: Joseph Salvati appears before the Massachusetts Parole
Board in a commutation hearing.

9–18–89: A prosecution memorandum from Diane M. Kottmyer, Chief Attorney, Boston Strike Force, to David Margolis, Chief, OC&RS Criminal Division, discusses a proposed indictment of Russo, Carrozza, Baione, Ferrara, LePore, Mercurio and Tortora. The following are important points made in this memorandum. Numbers in parentheses coincide with page numbers in the memorandum. [Note: The original memorandum is not appended to the Committee's chronology and is retained in Justice Department files.] The memorandum charges an array of criminal activity. The memorandum states, "In exchange for protection and a new identity, Barboza agreed to become a government witness." (60) The memorandum continues, "Following his testimony Barboza entered the witness protection program and was relocated to San Franciscounder the name of Joseph Bentley. Barboza was expelled from the
program when he was indicted in 1970 on murder charges." Sharliss will testify at trial that Russo offered him $25,000 to kill Barboza.

10–29–89: Raymond Patriarca, Jr., presides over a Mafia induction ceremony held in Medford, Massachusetts. The induction ceremony is secretly tape recorded by the FBI pursuant to a court order. (*Former Patriarca Boss Sentenced to an Eight-Year Term*, PR NEWSWIRE, June 17, 1992). The tape, believed to be the first ever recording of a mafia induction ceremony, is the cornerstone in the racketeering case against reputed organized crime boss Raymond Patriarca, Jr., and six other defendants. The tape is secretly recorded in a clapboard house at 34 Guild Street in Medford, where four inductees take a blood oath to kill anyone who violated the organization's secrecy, federal authorities say.

11–30–89: The Massachusetts Parole Board informs Boston SAC James Ahearn that a hearing was held on Joseph Salvati's commutation. The Board states that Salvati's relationship with Frank Oreto was a question at the hearing and that the Board was aware of contacts between Salvati and Oreto in 1986. The Board requests information from the FBI about Salvati's relationship with Oreto.

12–1–89: James Ahearn, the Boston SAC, writes a letter to John Curran, Chairman of the Massachusetts Parole Board, in response to the Board's November 30, 1989, letter requesting information about a relationship between Joseph Salvati and Frank Oreto.
Ahearn writes that Salvati was intercepted on telephone lines seven times from January 1985 to January 1986. Ahearn also writes that Marie Salvati met with Oreto on November 9, 1985. The FBI concludes that Salvati had no ownership or managerial relationship with Oreto's loanshark business and that Marie Salvati probably met with Oreto to borrow money.

12–8–89: The Massachusetts Parole Board votes 5–0 to approve clemency for Joseph Salvati.

1990

1990: A raid by the DEA, Suffolk County Organized Crime Squad, and the IRS on the South Boston Liquor Mart extorted from the Rakes by James "Whitey" Bulger and Stephen Flemmi reveals a receipt indicating the FBI bought liquor there at discount prices for its Christmas party. The receipt indicates that the liquor was bought by Agent "Dick Baker (friend of John Connolly)." (Shelley Murphy, *Cases Disappear as FBI Looks Away*, BOSTON GLOBE, July 22, 1998).

3–26–90: The *Boston Globe* reports, "In what federal authorities called an 'unprecedented assault' on the leadership of the New England Mafia, federal authorities have indicted alleged Mafia boss Raymond J. (Junior) Patriarca and 20 reputed members of the
Patriarca crime family in three states on charges including racketeering, illegal gambling, extortion, drug trafficking and murder. The indictments, unsealed [on March 26], effectively accuse almost all of the Patriarca crime family's reputed top leaders, charging alleged Patriarca underboss Nicholas L. Bianco, consigliere, or adviser,
Joseph A. (J.R.) Russo and four of the organization's six reputed lieutenants with a pattern of crimes that span the past 15 years. Federal authorities said . . . that the indictments resulted from five years' worth of investigation that utilized federal undercover agents, electronic surveillance and cooperating witnesses. (Elizabeth Neurer, *Indictment Aimed at Mob Net Patriarca, 20 Others*, BOSTON GLOBE, Mar. 27, 1990).840

4–9–90: Joseph J. Balliro is acquitted in federal court by Judge Edward Harrington of helping a fugitive and reputed mobster evade income taxes. The *Boston Globe* reports that "Balliro had been charged with helping Salvatore Michael Caruana, whom he

sometimes represented, evade federal income taxes by helping him invest in the Islander Hotel in the Bahamas." (Paul Langner, *Balliro Cleared of Aiding Tax Evasion; Charge Dismissed Against Lawyer,* BOSTON GLOBE, Apr. 10, 1990). According to Balliro's attorney, Richard M. Egbert, his successful representation of fellow
defense attorney Joseph Balliro was his "proudest moment." Matthew Brelis, *Lawyer Defends His Choice of Clients,* BOSTON GLOBE, Dec. 12, 1993.841

6–25–90: The Massachusetts Parole Board unanimously denies Peter Limone a commutation hearing.

8–16–90: A memorandum from Weldon Kennedy to FBI Director Sessions states that Supervisory Special Agent John Morris received a letter of censure, one-year's probation, and fourteen days suspension without pay for his involvement in the unauthorized disclosure of information to the *Boston Globe*. Special Agent John
Connolly receives a letter of censure for the same offense. Morris' discipline is based on the conclusion that he had made unauthorized disclosures of information to a local newspaper reporter and failed to be forthright on certain related issues. With regard to
Connolly, Connolly had imposed upon Morris to initiate an unauthorized contact with Morris' *Boston Globe* reporter.

December 1990: Special Agent John Connolly retires from the FBI.

1991: Seventeen months after approving Joseph Salvati's clemency petition, the Massachusetts Parole Board forwards its recommendation to Governor William Weld.

November 1991: Supervisory Special Agent John Morris leaves the Boston Office. (*See* March 1972 entry).

11–25–91: Agent Jean F. Wynn writes a memorandum the Boston SAC regarding Angelo Marotta, Joseph Salvati's first cousin. Wynn observed Marotta standing near a window, making phone calls, and seeming very alert to others walking by to the "extent
of seeming 'surveillance conscious.' " Wynn notes that Salvati is a first cousin of Marotta and that during a letter writing campaign Marotta was able to obtain a favorable letter from State Department of Corrections Official Michael Fair. In 1989, Fair was hired
as president of Marotta Companies.

December 1991: Raymond Patriarca, Jr., whose father founded the New England Patriarca crime family, pleads guilty to conspiracy and racketeering charges. (*Reputed Mobsters Admit Racketeering,* TULSA TRIBUNE, Jan. 23, 1992).848

1992

1–22–92: Joseph Russo pleads guilty to the murder of Joseph Barboza. Five accused members of New England's largest crime family plead guilty in Boston to racketeering, kidnapping and murder charges but deny that they belonged to the Mafia. On the day
their trial is to start, a daylong change of plea hearing is held and guilty pleas are offered by Joseph Russo, Vincent Ferrara, Robert Carroza, Dennis LePore, and Carmen Tortora. Russo receives a sentence of sixteen years imprisonment and must forfeit $758,000.
Vincent Ferrara receives twenty-two years and wins immunity from prosecution for murder and attempted murder. He is ordered to pay $1.1 million. Robert Carrozza is given nineteen years and

ordered to pay $878,200. Dennis Lepore receives fourteen years and will have to pay $766,700. Finally, Carmen Tortora is given thirteen
years and will have to pay $2,000. (*See Nation Briefly,* ANGE COUNTY REGISTER, Jan. 23, 1992; *U.S.* v. *Salemme,* 91 F.Supp. 2d 141, 151–152 (D. Mass. 1999)).849

6–17–92: The former Boss of the Patriarca Family is sentenced to an eight-year term of imprisonment following his plea of guilty to charges of racketeering and violations of the Travel Act. Judge Mark L. Wolf sentences Raymond Patriarca, Jr., to a 97-month
term of incarceration followed by a three-year period of supervised release and a $50,000 fine. (*Boss Sentenced to an Eight-Year Term,* PR NEWSWIRE, June 17, 1992).

9–1–92: Dugald F. Cameron, private investigator of Massachusetts, signs an affidavit stating that he and John Cavicchi met with Robert Gittens, Assistant Legal Counsel to Massachusetts Governor Michael Dukakis, on February 15, 1984, about Louis Greco.
Gittens told Cameron and Cavicchi that he would recommend that the Governor commute Greco's sentence.

1993

1993: Frank Walsh's affidavit states that Joseph Salvati was never a suspect until Joseph Barboza mentioned him.

In his book *The God Son, A True-Life Account of 20 Years Inside the Mob,* Willie Fopiano writes the following: "It went like this: A petty thief named Teddy Deegan was suspected of killing Anthony Sacramone [sic], a cousin of Rico Sacramone [sic]. Rico [Sacrimone] wanted revenge, and got the rest of the Barboza gang to help him
carry it out" [Nick] Femia, Romeo Martin, Chico Amico, Ronnie Cassesso and, of course, Barboza himself. Romeo Martin knew Deegan a little and won him over by telling him about an easy score at a finance company. When Deegan and Martin drove up to
the back door of the place, Barboza, Femia, Amico, and Cassesso were waiting. Barboza ran up and shot Deegan five times. That was in March 1965. It was known even then who shot Deegan and why, but twenty-six months later Barboza ratted on Ronnie Cassesso and also put the finger on five other men: Henry Tameleo, Peter Limone, Louis Grieco [sic], Roy French, and Joe "the Horse" Salvati. Tameleo was an important man in the family. Along with Limone, Grieco [sic], and Cassesso, he was sentenced to the chair, and spent almost five years on death row before capital punishment was thrown out. Salvati and French drew life sentences. Of all of them, only Cassesso had anything to do with the crime. The others were innocent. . . . Salvati, who was just a doorman at an after-hours joint, wouldn't swat a mosquito. . . . He was also behind in shylock payments to Barboza. . . . The prosecutor, Jack Zalkind, today is in private practice and I've heard from reliable sources that even he now thinks that some of the men—especially Joe Salvati—might be innocent." (127–28). Fopiano also writes that
"Joe Barboza [was] known as 'the Killing Machine.' " (115) (Willie Fopiano, The Godson, A True-Life Account of 20 Years Inside The Mob 127–128).853

1–19–93: Governor Weld denies Joseph Salvati's commutation citing the "seriousness of the crime" and Salvati's long criminal record. Weld also denies Louis Greco's request for a commutation.

7–30–93: Detective Sergeant Bruce A. Holloway writes a memorandum to Lieutenant Detective James T. Curran regarding an interview with former State Police Lieutenant Richard

Schneiderhan. Holloway writes, "Lt. Schneiderhan stated that sometime after the murder of Edward T. Deegan he recalled overhearing a conversation between, then Assistant Attorney General Donald Con and Attorney John Fitzgerald who represented JosephBarbosa [sic], whereby Attorney Fitzgerald advised Attorney Con that his client, Joe Barbosa [sic] threw Joseph Salvadi [sic] into the mix because of a dispute over money. Fitzgerald went on to state that Joe Salvadi [sic] owed Joe Barbosa [sic] some money and that when Barbosa [sic] associates Arthur Bratsos and Richard DePrisca made an attempt to collect from Salvadi [sic], he refused to pay as did many others; however when Salvadi [sic] refused, he also said words to the effect, 'I'm not going to pay, and you ain't going to see daylight.' This angered Barbosa [sic] which prompted him to retaliate by throwing Joe Salvadi [sic] into the mix."

8–2–93: Joseph Balliro's affidavit states in relevant part: "I represented a co-defendant, Henry Tameleo, in the trial of the Commonwealth of Massachusetts against Joseph Salvati, and others, that concluded with a conviction on July 31, 1968. With respect to the overall conduct of the trial I served in the role that is generally
referred to as lead counsel. Joseph Salvati was represented at the trial by Attorney Chester Paris, who at the time was a young but competent trial lawyer, and associated with me in practice at my office. . . . Without Barboza's testimony the case could not have gone to the jury—and if the jury were to disbelieve Mr. Barboza as to the identity of any one of the participants there simply was no other evidence on which to base a conviction. From the outset of the preparation for the defense of Joseph Salvati, it was the strong belief of all the defense lawyers that Mr. Salvati was not only innocent, but that Joseph Barboza had substituted Mr. Salvati as a participant for some other individual, who had actually participated, and who Mr. Barboza was seeking to protect. At the time of the trial I did not know who that other person was. . . . I have recently (within the past three weeks) been furnished a three page police report that purports to be a statement by Thomas F. Evans of the Chelsea Police Department. . . . I have carefully reviewed the three page police report authored by Lieutenant Thomas F.
Evans and can categorically state that I was not aware of the existence of that report or its contents until the last few weeks; nor, am I aware that any other counsel, including Chester Paris who represented Joseph Salvati had any awareness of the report or its contents. . . The failure of the Commonwealth to provide the defendants with the report of Lieutenant Evans seriously undercut the ability of the attorneys to conduct a proper investigation and prepare an adequate defense."

8–3–93: In an affidavit, Jack Zalkind states that if he had seen the Chelsea police report sooner, he would have ordered an "intensive investigation" into Joseph Salvati's involvement.

8–19–93: Sergeant Detective Bruce A. Holloway writes a memorandum to Lieutenant Detective James T. Curran regarding a follow- up investigation with former State Police Lieutenant Richard Schneiderhan. The letter states that Schniederhan told Holloway
that "he does not believe that the group involved in the [Edward 'Teddy' Deegan] murder would have allowed Joe Salvati to participate in such an event. More importantly he does not believe they would have allowed him to hang around with them at all."

10–1–93: Lieutenant Detective James T. Curran and Sergeant Detective Bruce A. Holloway of the Massachusetts Office of Special Investigations interview Roberta Grimes, who police placed in the Ebb Tide as an employee to collect information on some of the characters who frequented the place. Grimes recalls a visit by two M.D.C. police detectives who showed her a photo array. She also recalls the names and faces of Joseph Barboza and Roy French.

10–4–93: Sergeant Detective Bruce A. Holloway writes a memorandum to Lieutenant Detective James T. Curran regarding a discussion Holloway had with Judge John Fitzgerald. Holloway writes the following about this discussion: "Judge Fitzgerald does recall hearing the rumors about Joseph Salvati and others not being involved [in the Edward 'Teddy' Deegan murder] and that Joe Barbosa [sic] was owed money. However, he stressed that at no time did he inquire of Barbosa [sic] anything relative to these rumors. Additionally, he stated that Barbosa [sic] never told him of a plan to frame anyone relative to the Deegan case and he never supplied him with any information which he, Judge Fitzgerald, deemed to be exculpatory."

10–12–93: James M. McDonough, legal assistant in the Suffolk County District Attorney's Office, signs an affidavit stating, "I was aware and saw a report that had been authored by Lieutenant Thomas Evans of the Chelsea Police Department about the Deegan murder. . . . [T]o the best of my memory and belief the copy of the
report is the same copy that was in the prosecutor's file during prosecution of the defendant's case."

10–27–93: Robert J. McKenna, Jr., Assistant District Attorney for Suffolk County, writes a letter to Jack Zalkind regarding Joseph Salvati. Zalkind apparently requested a meeting with McKenna to discuss the affidavit Zalkind executed for *Commonwealth* v.
Salvati, et al. McKenna says he talked with Robert Gittens and Jack Cinquegrana and is denying Zalkind's request because the case is presently before the Superior Court.

12–1–1993: A hearing on a Motion for a New Trial for Louis Greco, represented by John Cavicchi; Joseph Salvati, represented by Victor Garo; and Peter Limone, represented by Robert Sheketoff, takes place. Robert McKenna represents the State of Massachusetts and Judge Banks presides.

1994

12–23–94: Former Special Agent John Connolly informs James "Whitey" Bulger and Stephen Flemmi that they would soon be arrested. (Connolly Indictment at 15).864

1995

January 1995: Stephen Flemmi informs Francis "Frank" Salemme that an indictment would be coming down on him shortly. (Connolly Indictment at 15–16).865

1–5–95: Stephen Flemmi is arrested for conspiring to extort bookmaker Burton Krantz; James "Whitey" Bulger and George Kaufman are also charged.

1–9–95: The FBI admits to the U.S. Attorney's Office that James "Whitey" Bulger is an informant.

1–10–95: James "Whitey" Bulger, Stephen Flemmi, and Francis "Frank" Salemme are indicted on multiple charges of federal racketeering, extortion, and other crimes.

1–29–95: The *Boston Globe* reports that Jerry Padalino, Special Agent in Charge of U.S. Customs, publicly stated in 1995 that Customs officials considered John McIntyre a fugitive, affirmatively stating, "We have no proof that he is dead." (Kevin Cullen, *IRA
Man Tells a Tale of Betrayal,* BOSTON GLOBE, Jan. 29, 1995).869

7–11–95: John Cavicchi, attorney for Louis Greco, signs an affidavit stating that Cavicchi read in a February 17, 1994, news article that Joseph Balliro represented Joseph Barboza and "one Flemmi." Jimmy Flemmi was one of those named in the informant's statement as being involved in the Edward Deegan murder.

Cavicchi obtained an affidavit from Richard Barest, a former Florida judge who represented Greco when he surrendered to authorities in Florida. Barest said he pleaded with the Massachusetts lawyers to let him fight the extradition of Greco, but stated they were more interested in reading *Time* than listening to what he had to say. Barest specifically mentioned "Joe Bellino," but Cavicchi knew that he meant Joe Balliro. The affidavit states, "I returned to Massachusetts and asked Balliro for the Florida investigation of Greco. [Balliro] told me it had been shredded. In October or November
1994, I visited Greco at the Bay State Correctional Center. He stated that Balliro told him to waive his extradition hearing."

James Southwood's affidavit states, "In the course of making preparations to write a book for Joseph Barboza Baron about his life as an assassin for the New England Mafia and while a reporter for the *Boston Herald Traveler,* Barboza, in early 1969, gave me
scrapbooks about the Boston Gang War and numerous documents pertaining to three major trials at which he testified against New England Mafia bosses and others. Subsequently, at a time in 1970, when he claimed to me that the U.S. Justice Department had betrayed him by breaking promises made in exchange for his court
testimony, he said that he was recanting his testimony that sent men to Death Row. At this time, a date I believe to be in the spring of 1971, Barboza said: 'Louie [sic] Greco wasn't in the alley!' To this end, Barboza apparently sent a message to Raymond Patriarca [that] Southwood was in possession of the grand jury minutes of the so-called Teddy Deegan murder case. . . . Barboza told me that the Grand Jury minutes would prove that he lied in the courtroom. He instructed me to return the grand jury minutes to Joseph Balliro. To the best of my knowledge, the Barboza copy of the grand jury minutes was given to Balliro in the summer of 1971." John Cavicchi is the notary.

7–24–95: Louis Greco's affidavit states, "In 1968, when I was waiting for my hearing in Florida on the murder charges, . . . [Joseph] Balliro came to Florida. I did not ask for Mr. Balliro, nor did I know who sent him. Mr. Balliro said that I should come back to
Massachusetts. He told me that things would turn out allright [sic]. As a result of his advice, I signed some papers and returned to Massachusetts. He never told me that he represented [Joseph] Barboza-Baron, nor did I know. He never told me, nor did I know
that he represented Flemmi. He did not tell me, nor did I know that he was representing Henry Tameleo. Had I known the above, I would have remained in Florida. In Massachusetts, I was represented by Attorney Lawrence O'Donnell and his office. I have
since learned that during the handling of this case, his office also represented Henry Tameleo, Roy French, and Ronald Cassesso, codefendants in this case. Had I known this, I would have had a different lawyer. To the best of my memory, none of the evidence regarding my difficulty in walking, and inability to run was presented
at trial." John Cavicchi is the notary.

12–30–95: Louis M. Greco dies in prison.

12–31–95: Supervisory Special Agent John Morris retires from the FBI.

1996

4–3–96: In a letter from James D. Herbert, Assistant U.S. Attorney of the Organized Crime Strike Force, to Ralph Martin, Suffolk County District Attorney, Herbert writes that Assistant U.S. Attorney Brian T. Kelly recently debriefed Anthony Ciulla. Ciulla was friendly with Barboza and was his driver. Ciulla has no personal knowledge of the Edward "Teddy" Deegan murder. However, Ciulla claims Barboza discussed the Deegan murder in Ciulla's presence. According to the letter, "Ciulla believes Salvati is innocent because Barboza never mentioned Salvati when he described the Deegan murder. According to Ciulla, Barboza did mention the other individuals convicted in the case . . . as well as Vincent 'The Bear' Flemmi."

12–18–96: Governor William Weld writes to the Executive Council, recommending that Joseph Salvati's sentence be commuted, subject to their advice and consent.

1997

1–7–97: Governor William Weld writes to the Executive Council, recommending that Salvati's sentence be commuted, subject to their advice and consent.

1–15–97: Retired Boston Police Detective Frank Walsh recommends a commutation of Salvati's sentence for the fourth time.

1–22–97: Former Suffolk County Assistant District Attorney Jack Zalkind recommends a commutation of Salvati's sentence for the fourth time.

2–5–97: Governor William Weld writes to the Executive Council, recommending that Joseph Salvati's sentence be commuted, subject to their advice and consent.

The Governor's Executive Council unanimously votes 8–0 to commute Joseph Salvati's sentence. Massachusetts Governor William Weld commutes the sentence of Joseph Salvati.

3–27–97: Special Agent John Connolly sends a letter to Judge Mark Wolf purporting to be from three unnamed members of the Boston Police Department. The letter says the Massachusetts State Police, FBI, and DEA are guilty of prosecutorial misconduct in the investigations of James "Whitey" Bulger, Stephen Flemmi, and Francis "Frank" Salemme. The letter states that Boston Police Detective Frank Duwan, the Massachusetts State Police, DEA, FBI, and the Justice Department Organized Crime Strike Force furnished or relied on false information in efforts to prosecute Bulger and Flemmi. (Connolly Indictment at 16).883

6–3–97: James "Whitey" Bulger's identity as an FBI informant is made public. In response to the May 22, 1997, Federal Court's order, the government disclosed that Bulger had been a government informant. (*U.S.* v. *Salemme*, 91 F.Supp. 2d 141, 309 (D. Mass. 1999)).884

6–24–97: The *Boston Globe* reports that while William Weld was a U.S. Attorney, he learned that James "Whitey" Bulger was an informant. Weld requested surveillance on Bulger and was told that the FBI did not tap active informants. The article also states that Bulger secretly tape-recorded "years' worth" of conversations with FBI agents.

7–3–97: The Deputy Attorney General directs the Department of Justice and the FBI to initiate an Office of Professional Responsibility investigation to determine whether any Government official committed criminal acts in connection with investigations into the New England La Cosa Nostra and the Winter Hill Gang.886

7–8–97: The Office of Professional Responsibility (OPR) investigation to determine whether any Government official committed criminal acts in connection with investigations into the New EnglandLa Cosa Nostra and the Winter Hill Gang begins on this date. The investigation concludes on August 14, 1997 (with a report published as Appendix I to the Report). The OPR anticipates—but does not conduct—a second phase of investigation. The investigation
"uncovered no evidence that any potentially criminal acts were part of a continuing crime which would bring the acts within the statute of limitations. In addition, we examined and found a number of violations of FBI rules and regulations which would have warranted administrative action if those employees were still employed by the FBI. However, no current FBI employees were found to be in violation of FBI policies." 887

September 1997: Stephen Flemmi files an affidavit in court claiming that "he was told by [Robert] Daddeico some 12 years ago after the bombing charges against Flemmi were dropped that Daddieco had set up [Frank] Salemme for the [John] Fitzgerald bombing and had lied about Flemmi's alleged involvement."

9–29–97: Sergeant Kevin Manning writes a letter on behalf of Sheriff Jerry Keller, Las Vegas Police Department, to Deputy U.S. Marshal Tom Bezanson. Keller states that the Department is reviewing the murder case of Peter Poulos and would like to interview Stephen Flemmi and Francis "Frank" Salemme for possible prosecution. [Note: According to Dave Hatch, Las Vegas Police Department, Cold Case Review, he was later informed that Flemmi and Salemme could not be interviewed regarding the Poulos murder while under federal indictment.] 889

1998

1998: Joseph "J. R." Russo, the person who killed Joseph Barboza, dies of natural causes in prison.

1–6–98: The *Boston Herald* reports on the hearing before U.S. District Court Judge Mark L. Wolf. The *Herald* writes, "Winter Hill wiseguy and FBI informant Stephen Flemmi said he was rewarded for his work for the agency with a free pass on murder, attempted murder and fugitive charges in the mid-1970's, defense lawyers alleged. . . . The lawyers are trying to get racketeering charges against Flemmi, New England Mob boss Francis P. 'Cadillac Frank' Salemme, 64, and wiseguys Robert DeLuca and John Martorano thrown out of court on a variety of legal bases. . . . Flemmi claimed he was warned of the indictments by his FBI 'handler,' agent H. Paul Rico, and allowed to flee. But in 1974, Rico told him it was safe to come back and that the murder and attempted murder charges would be taken care of. [Attorney Anthony] Cardinale said Flemmi's chief accuser in the case, Robert Daddieco, was an FBI cooperating witness who had also been developed by Rico. Rico made sure his promise to Flemmi was kept, Cardinale said. 'What happens? Daddieco changes his testimony and says Flemmi was not with him (at the [John] Fitzgerald bombing) and that he lied to the grand jury,' Cardinale said. 'They control Daddieco and he changes his testimony to get Flemmi off the hook.' The murder charges against Flemmi were dropped when Daddieco disappeared. Flemmi was also never prosecuted as a federal fugitive per Rico's promise, Cardinale said."

Early 1998: In preparation to testify in pretrial hearings in *U.S.* v. *Salemme,* Stephen Flemmi informs Special Agent John Connolly through an intermediary that he will testify that Supervisory

Special Agent John Morris—not Connolly—alerted him to the indictments coming against James "Whitey" Bulger and Flemmi. In return, Connolly tells the intermediary to inform Flemmi to testify that Morris learned of indictments through Washington, which received a "pros memo."

April 1998: John Morris, Organized Crime Squad Supervisor in the FBI's Boston Office from 1977–1983, testifies under immunity that he believes an intentional leak from his squad led to the killing of Brian Halloran. Before Halloran's murder, Morris told Special Agent John Connolly, handler for James "Whitey" Bulger and Stephen Flemmi, that Halloran was incriminating them in Roger Wheeler's murder. Morris fully expected Connolly to relay this information to Bulger and Flemmi. Robert Fitzpatrick, Assistant Agent in Charge of the Boston FBI Office during the early 1980s, testifies that he also thought James "Whitey" Bulger was a suspect in Roger Wheeler murder, but his superiors decided to keep him as an informant.

5–5–98: During a criminal hearing in federal court, Condon testifies that he "spent two years in the early 1970's trying to hunt down [Francis "Frank"] Salemme and associate Stephen 'The Rifleman' Flemmi. But Condon insisted that, at the time, he had no idea Flemmi was an FBI informant—even though FBI documents show that another agent he worked closely with, H. Paul Rico, had recruited Flemmi five years earlier. In fact, one 1967 document even shows Condon had been designated as Flemmi's 'alternate contact agent' for times when Rico was out of town. Condon was also the handling agent for James Bulger, who he had opened as an informant on May 13, 1971. Condon, however, insisted that he never saw the document and that Rico never told him he had been designated as Flemmi's alternate handler." At the hearing, Salemme's attorney, Anthony Cardinale, tried to show that Flemmi received preferential treatment because he had been feeding the FBI information. The *Boston Globe* writes, "But under cross-examination by Assistant U.S. Attorney James D. Herbert, Condon said he had no 'specific information' on where Flemmi could be found, and said neither he nor any other agent hindered the search for Flemmi. Condon said he had no contact with Flemmi while he was a fugitive, had never taken a phone call from him, and had not interceded with state prosecutors to get the charges against Flemmi dropped."

June 1998: The Justice Department appoints John Durham to head a task force investigation into whether Boston FBI agents obstructed the investigation of the jai alai-related murders or otherwise broke the law during their relationship with James "Whitey" Bulger and Stephen Flemmi.

December 1998: Raymond Patriarca, Jr., is released from prison.

1999

1999: John Martorano, a Winter Hill Gang hitman, begins cooperating with federal investigators. Martorano admits to killing twenty people, including Roger Wheeler, Sr. Martorano said Whitey Bulger and Stephen Flemmi told him to kill Wheeler. Martorano
says that former FBI Special Agent Paul Rico, through a third party, provided him with information he used to locate and kill Wheeler in Tulsa.

7–12–99: Agent Daniel M. Doherty debriefs John Martorano.

7–14–99: John Durham and Gary Bald meet with Victor Garo about Garo's concern that FBI agents engaged in improper, and possibly criminal, conduct in the investigation, prosecution, and confinement of Joseph Salvati.

8–23–99: John Durham and Gary Bald write to Victor Garo asking for another meeting concerning the role of the FBI in Joseph Salvati's case.

9–9–99: The Justice Department task force reaches a plea agreement with John Martorano, a Winter Hill Gang hitman. The plea agreement states, "In exchange for a 12½ year prison term, Martorano has agreed to plead guilty to 10 murders in Massachusetts, along with one in Florida and another in Oklahoma. He will also provide investigators with details on eight other murders that took place in Massachusetts as far back as 1965." Martorano is expected to admit to killing Roger Wheeler, Sr., and John Callahan at the instruction of James "Whitey" Bulger and Stephen Flemmi.

9–14–99: Agent Daniel M. Doherty debriefs John Martorano.

9–15–99: District Court Judge Mark L. Wolf issues a 661-page opinion sharply criticizing the FBI's handling of James "Whitey" Bulger and Stephen Flemmi. Judge Wolf concludes that someone in the FBI probably tipped James "Whitey" Bulger and Stephen Flemmi that Brian Halloran was informing on them, which led to Halloran's murder. Judge Wolf concludes that Special Agent Paul Rico helped Stephen Flemmi escape the country before being prosecuted for a car bomb planted in defense attorney John Fitzgerald's car. Fitzgerald lost a leg but survived. Judge Wolf writes that it appeared Rico arranged to have the charges against Flemmi dropped.

9–21–99: Linda Reardon, a Bell Atlantic employee, allegedly tells her father, Edward G. Duff, about electronic surveillance by the FBI on certain South Boston telephone lines. Duff allegedly tells Richard Schneiderhan who tells Kevin Weeks. Weeks allegedly tells one of the targets of the electronic surveillance.907 John Martorano pleads guilty to killing ten people in the 1970's
on behalf of a racketeering enterprise. The *Boston Globe* reports, "A plea agreement calls for his cooperation against Bulger, Flemmi
and any former FBI agents being targeted in an ongoing corruption probe. Martorano also agreed to plead guilty to second-degree murder charges in Oklahoma and Florida, two states with the death penalty, with assurances that he'll only face a 15-year prison term.
He's also confessed to another 8 murders . . . for which it appears he will never be charged." U.S. District Judge Mark Wolf accepts Martorano's plea but postpones any decision on whether he will go along with a government recommendation to sentence Martorano to 12½ to 15 years imprisonment

12–9–99: Francis "Frank" Salemme reaches a plea agreement on racketeering, loansharking, and extortion. In exchange, murder charges were dropped. He is sentenced to eleven years in prison. As part of the plea agreement, he agrees to testify against former FBI Special Agents John Connolly and Paul Rico, and Winter Hill gang leaders James "Whitey" Bulger and Stephen Flemmi.

12–13–99: Stephen Flemmi signs an affidavit stating the following: "(1) For many years, including the 1980's, I acted as a confidential informant for the FBI; (2) My FBI handler was Special Agent John Connolly; (3) In or near 1987, I reported to John Connolly about information I knew concerning a number of meetings involving Anthony St. Laurent of Rhode Island and other members of the LCN [La Cosa Nostra] regarding the 'shakedown'
of a Las Vegas bookmaker; (4) At some point, I received reliable information that an associate of the Las Vegas bookmaker was planning to assassinate Anthony St. Laurent because St. Laurent had threatened the bookmaker's 15 year old daughter; (5) I immediately gave this information to

Connolly. At that point, Connolly told me that St. Laurent was also a confidential informant for the FBI. Connolly asked me to intercede and stop the attempted assassination. I was able to accomplish this task."

12–22–99: Former FBI Special Agent John Connolly is arrested and charged along with James "Whitey" Bulger and Stephen Flemmi for racketeering, racketeering conspiracy, obstruction of justice, and conspiracy to obstruct justice. Flemmi is also charged with passing classified information to Francis "Frank" Salemme.

2000

1–14–00: John McIntyre's remains are found, after Bulger gang lieutenant Kevin Weeks, who faced racketeering charges in late 1999, cut a deal with investigators and led them to the grave.
(Bulger and Flemmi allegedly killed McIntyre after McIntyre offered to cooperate with the authorities. According to U.S. District Judge Mark Wolf, "There is circumstantial evidence to suggest that [FBI Agent Roderick] Kennedy may have told [FBI Special Agent John] Connolly about McIntyre's cooperation . . . and reason to be concerned that Connolly may have told Bulger and Flemmi."

1–21–00: In a letter from John Cavicchi, Peter Limone's attorney, to John Durham, Cavicchi apparently encloses a file on a redacted case and says the only published opinion on the F. Lee Bailey affidavit

1–28–00: Agent Daniel M. Doherty debriefs John Martorano

2–10–00: Agent Daniel M. Doherty prepares a Report of Investigation. He indicates he interviewed "CS–00–098739" on July 12, 1999, and January 28, 2000, and that the confidential source told him that Joseph Barboza and Vincent James Flemmi admitted to
killing Edward "Teddy" Deegan's murder. The report states, "The CS (Confidential Source) also stated, that either just prior to or immediately after the time period that Barboza began cooperating with law enforcement, that he, Barboza, told the CS to mind it's own business and not to intervene, because 'They' (the LCN) screwed me and now I'm going to screw as many of them as possible. Barboza further stated, that he was not interested in guilt or innocence. Barboza again reiterated to the CS that the CS should just stay out of it. Barboza told the CS that the CS was a friend and that he, Barboza, would not bother the CS."
Agent Daniel M. Doherty writes a memorandum to Fred Wyshak, Assistant U.S. Attorney, stating that John Martorano advised that he was a close associate to Joseph Barboza in the mid-1960s. Martorano said that subsequent to the Edward "Teddy" Deegan murder, Barboza admitted to Martorano that he, Barboza, killed Deegan. On a separate occasion, Vincent "Jimmy" Flemmi told Martorano that he, Flemmi, killed Deegan. Just prior to or immediately
after the time period that Barboza began to cooperate with law enforcement, Barboza told Martorano to mind his own business and not intervene. Barboza said La Cosa Nostra screwed me and now "I'm going to screw as many of them as possible." Barboza further said he was not interested in innocence or guilt

3–20–00: The government waits until this day, two months after John McIntyre's body was discovered, to dismiss the indictments against McIntyre in *United States* v. *Murray et al.*917

5–25–00: Less than six months after learning sufficient facts to verify both the government's wrongful conduct and John McIntyre's fate, the McIntyre Estate presents a duly authorized Notice of Tort Claim, pursuant to the Federal Tort Claims Act, 28 U.S.C. § 2671 *et seq*. The tort claim gives notice to the FBI of McIntyre's injuries and wrongful death caused by the negligent or wrongful acts or omissions of certain employees of the Boston FBI Office. The plaintiff files the complaint on March 2, 2001. Among other things, the Estate's administrative claim and complaint allege that former agents of the FBI conspired to protect and shield James "Whitey" Bulger and Stephen Flemmi from prosecution in exchange for their agreements to provide information to aid the FBI in its prosecution of La Cosa Nostra. The complaint also alleges that the Boston FBI Office ignored the Attorney General's Guidelines; that the individual agents knew or should have known that Bulger and Flemmi were committing violent crimes, including the murder of informants cooperating with law enforcement; that despite this knowledge the agents failed to prosecute and blocked investigations into Bulger and Flemmi; and that as a direct and proximate cause of the negligence of these agents, Bulger, Flemmi, and Weeks murdered McIntyre after he agreed to become an FBI informant in 1984.918

6–20–00: Peter Limone files a Motion for a New Trial.919

7–2–00: Peter Limone's counsel moves to intervene in *United States* v. *Stephen J. Flemmi et al.*, Crim. No. 94–10287–MLW (D. Mass.), before U.S. District Court Judge Mark L. Wolf. Judge Wolf denies intervention but indicates that certain documents might be discoverable in this proceeding. Judge Margaret Hinkle, Justice of the Superior Court, thereafter gives notice to the U.S. Attorney's Office of Limone's request for discovery of matters relating to the motion. The local U.S. Attorney's Office agreed to review its files.

7–27–00: Francis Imbruglia says in an affidavit, "I am stating under oath and of my own personal knowledge that Peter Limone, Henry Tameleo, and Louie [sic] Greco had nothing to do with . . . the murder of Teddy Deegan."

8–30–00: In a letter to John Cavicchi, who is Peter Limone's attorney, Roy French writes, "[M]y affidavit was right on the money with the exception of Joseph Salvati. . . . For the record, I have no memory of Joseph Salvati being a part of my involvement with the shooting death of 'Teddy Deegan.' He in no way aided me directly or indirectly . . . to truly defeat the testimony of Tony Stathopoulos. [Stathopolous testified that he saw Louis Greco come out of the alley.] [T]here is enough evidence to support that any stride of walking or slowly running or hurriedly walking, was an impossibility to perform by Louie [sic] Greco.

9–19–00: Peter Limone files a Motion to Vacate Conviction and Dismiss Indictments.

9–28–00: In an unsealed indictment, James "Whitey" Bulger, Stephen Flemmi, and several underlings are indicted on 21 murders, extortion, distribution of drugs, obstruction of justice, racketeering, and money laundering.

10–11–00: Former Special Agent John Connolly is indicted on a range of charges, including providing tips to James "Whitey" Bulger and Stephen Flemmi to eliminate threats to their operations and misleading grand jury investigations in the Winter Hill Gang extortions.

11–14–00: Joseph Balliro, counsel for Henry Tameleo at the Edward "Teddy" Deegan trial, submits an affidavit attesting that he received a memorandum from F. Lee Bailey, and "it obviously exculpates Mr. Limone from being in any way responsible for the

death of Mr. Deegan." Balliro says he never represented Stephen Flemmi or Nick Femia. He has no knowledge of any information that Freddie Chiampa or Frank [Francis] Imbruglia had about the Deegan murder. He represented Joseph Barboza and Vincent
"Jimmy" Flemmi 35–40 years ago on matters unrelated to the Deegan matter, and he never received any information from Barboza about the Deegan murder. Balliro says he did receive information about the Deegan murder from Vincent "Jimmy" Flemmi. Balliro says Flemmi's information is exculpatory for Limone and others charged and convicted of the murder. Balliro says he would divulge the information upon court order. (*Commonwealth* v. *Limone*, Cr. No. 32367, 69–70 (Suffolk Cty. Sup. Ct., Nov.
14, 2000)).

11–15–00: An indictment of former Massachusetts State Police Officer Lieutenant Richard J. Schneiderhan, Edward G. Duff, and Linda Reardon is handed down for conspiracy to obstruct justice, obstruction of justice, and aiding and abetting. Schneiderhan and Duff are related through marriage as brothers-in-law. Duff is
Reardon's father. The indictment states that Schneiderhan maintained a personal friendship with Stephen Flemmi since the 1950s; Schneiderhan maintained a personal, non-law enforcement relationship with John Martorano from the late 1960s to about 1978; and Schneiderhan helped James "Whitey" Bulger escape capture by informing him that certain Boston telephone lines were tapped.

12–19–00: John Durham, Special Assistant U.S. Attorney, writes a letter to John Cavicchi, attorney for Peter Limone, regarding the disclosure of FBI documents relating to the March 12, 1965, murder of Edward "Teddy" Deegan. The letter states in relevant part: "Joint Task Force's [JTF] search first determined that around the time Deegan was murdered, Vincent James Flemmi was an FBI informant. According to the file maintained in support of efforts to develop Flemmi as an informant, focus on Flemmi's potential as a source began on about 3/9/1965. The first reported contact with
Flemmi was by FBI Boston Special Agent H. Paul Rico on 4/5/1965. The informant file was officially opened and assigned to SA Rico on 4/15/1965 and reflects that Flemmi was contacted a total of five times as an informant, each time by SA Rico. The dates of contact were 4/5/1965, 5/10/1965, 6/4/1965, 7/22/65 and 7/27/1965. Flemmi's
file was closed on 9/15/1965 after Flemmi was charged with a crime, unrelated to the Deegan murder." John Durham makes 26 pages of FBI documents available to Joseph Salvati and Limone relating to the Deegan murder. However, Judge Margaret Hinkle
notes that the documents produced are "heavily redacted."

2001

1–2–01: Ronald Cassesso attorney Ronald Chisholm reveals that Cassesso admitted to participating in the Edward "Teddy" Deegan murder and that four of the six convicted were innocent, but were convicted by Barboza's false testimony. Cassesso told Chisholm
that he was approached by Special Agent Paul Rico in 1967 while awaiting trial. Rico told Cassesso that he could escape prison by corroborating Barboza's testimony—Cassesso refused.

Joseph Balliro executes an affidavit stating that in the summer of 1967, Vincent "James" Flemmi told Balliro that Joseph Barboza planned the Edward "Teddy" Deegan murder and Flemmi participated in it. Flemmi also stated that Barboza substituted Joseph

Salvati for Flemmi because Salvati disrespected Barboza. Flemmi also stated that Henry Tameleo and Peter Limone did not arrange the murder, and Louis Greco was not a participant, but Barboza implicated them because they also disrespected

1-5-01: Judge Hinkle's Order granting Peter Limone a new trial states, "[T]he jury would likely have reached a different conclusion by this previously UNDISCUSSED evidence for two reasons. First, the new evidence [Durham's Dec. 19, 2000, disclosure of 26 pages of FBI documents] casts serious doubt on Barboza's credibility in his account of Limone's role. Second, the new evidence reveals that Vincent James Flemmi, a participant of some sort in the Edward "Teddy" Deegan murder, was an FBI informant around the time of the murder."

1-30-01: The Suffolk County District Attorney's Office signs a non-prosecution motion stating, "Now comes the Commonwealth in the above-captioned matter [*Commonwealth v. Salvati*] and respectfully states that it will not prosecute Indictment No. 32368 [regarding Joseph Salvati] any further. As ground therefor, the Commonwealth respectfully states as follows: (1) There exists newly discovered evidence—various FBI documents disclosed to the Commonwealth and the defendant for the first time on December 19, 2000—which significantly undermines (a) the credibility of the Commonwealth's principal witness at the defendant's first trial, Joseph Barboza, and (b) the Commonwealth's theory of the defendant's role in the murder of Edward Deegan, as presented at the defendant's first trial[;] (2) Joseph Barboza was shot and killed on February 11, 1976[;] (3) The Commonwealth has conducted a comprehensive review of the facts and circumstances surrounding the arrest, trial, and conviction of the defendant for his alleged role in the murder of Edward Deegan, including the impact of the contents of the newly discovered FBI documents[;] (4) In addition, the Commonwealth has carefully and thoroughly evaluated the nature,
quality, and sufficiency of the alleged evidence against the defendant[;] (5) As a result of that review and evaluation, the Commonwealth has concluded that it does not now have a good faith basis—legally or ethically—to proceed with any further prosecution
of the defendant."

A non-prosecution motion is also filed and signed by the Suffolk County District Attorney's Office stating that the Office will not prosecute Peter Limone for his alleged involvement in the Edward "Teddy" Deegan murder.

2-15-01: The *Boston Globe* reports that Charles Prouty said: "The FBI was forthcoming. We didn't conceal the information. We didn't attempt to frame anyone." As support for that statement, Prouty cited the document from 3-16-65 that indicates information was provided by the FBI to local law enforcement.

3-2-01: The McIntyre Estate files a complaint alleging misconduct on behalf of certain employees of the Boston FBI Office. In particular, the filing says that the FBI ignored overwhelming evidence that James "Whitey" Bulger and Stephen Flemmi were killers.
Plaintiff is seeking $50 million in damages. (*See* 5-25-00 entry).935

3-12-01: Francis "Frank" Salemme agrees to be a witness against James "Whitey" Bulger, Stephen Flemmi, and FBI Special Agents Paul Rico and John Connolly. (*Salemme Claim of FBI Frame-up Draws Criticism from Prosecutors,* Associated Press
Newswires, Mar. 24, 2001).

Francis "Cadillac Frank" Salemme files a habeas corpus prisoner petition "asking the judge for whatever relief he finds appropriate." Salemme's attorney, Anthony P. Cardinale, claims that "[t]he government literally suborned perjury in order to frame [Salemme] in the state case.
In said petition, "Salemme claims the FBI pressured a witness [Robert Daddeico] to lie in order to protect [Stephen] Flemmi, an informant, and make sure he went to prison."

3–13–01: The Estate of Michael J. Donahue files suit against the FBI, including Special Agent John Connolly, Supervisory Special Agent John Morris, Boston SAC Lawrence Sarhatt, Assistant SAC Robert Fitzpatrick, James "Whitey" Bulger, and Stephen Flemmi. The *Donahue* case centers on: (1) the May 11, 1982, murder of Michael J. Donahue, an innocent bystander to the intentional murder of Brian Halloran; (2) the systemic wrongful acts and practices of the FBI which directly and proximately caused this murder; and (3) the FBI's intentional and pervasive effort to conceal its role in the murder. Allegations include that FBI Supervisory Special Agent John Morris and Special Agent John Connolly provided confidential law enforcement information to James "Whitey" Bulger, a known crime figure, and that Brian Halloran was cooperating with law enforcement and was providing information that Bulger was involved in the previous murder of Roger Wheeler. It is alleged that they did so knowing that Bulger was a dangerous criminal and would kill Halloran. It is also alleged that as a direct result of the information provided by Connolly and Morris, Bulger and members of his Group murdered Brian Halloran, killing Donahue as an innocent bystander. Donahue and Halloran were neighbors and when the murders occurred, Donahue was giving Halloran a ride home in the course of errands to plan for a family fishing trip. As causes for Michael Donahue's death, the Donahue Family points to the intentional acts of line and supervisory FBI agents, the persistent reckless and intentional indifference of the FBI and its supervisory agents to the wrongdoing of its agents and informants, and the environment created and maintained at the FBI which allowed and encouraged this wrongful conduct. The Donahue Family seeks $36 million in compensatory damages.

May 2001: Stephen Flemmi agrees to a plea bargain with the U.S. Attorney's Office on extortion, money laundering, and obstruction of justice charges. Flemmi is sentenced to ten years. In return, prosecutors drop charges on three murders Flemmi and James "Whitey" Bulger allegedly committed in the 1960s.

5–3–01: FBI Director Louis J. Freeh issues a statement discussing the goals of an independent Justice Task Force led by Special Attorney John Durham that is charged with investigating law enforcement corruption arising out of the FBI's handling of criminal informants James "Whitey" Bulger and Stephen Flemmi. Specifically, he states the Joint Task Force's ongoing Deegan inquiry is focused on: "Whether the FBI's assistance to local authorities in this murder investigation was designed, at least in part, to protect Vincent James Flemmi from being prosecuted; Whether the FBI's motivation linked to Flemmi's status as a former FBI informant and/or the informant status of his brother, Stephen Flemmi; and, Whether the FBI properly disseminated potentially exculpatory information to local investigators/prosecutors."

The U.S. House Committee on Government Reform holds its first hearing to explore federal law enforcement initiatives in Boston over the last three decades. The first hearing focuses on the case of Joseph Salvati, who spent 30 years in prison for a murder he did not commit. The convictions were primarily based on the testimony of notorious Boston mobster killer turned FBI witness, Joseph "The Animal" Barboza. Documents obtained by the Committee prior to the hearing show that not only was the prosecution of Joseph Salvati and three others questionable, but that federal and state law enforcement authorities had information indicating that they were sending the wrong men to the death chamber or prison for life.

5–4–01: In a letter to the Government Reform Committee from the Mayor of Springfield, Massachusetts, Michael Albano writes that the FBI conspired to keep Joseph Salvati, Louis Greco, Henry Tameleo, and Peter Limone in prison.

5–16–01: FBI Director Louis Freeh testifies before the House Committee on Appropriations: Subcommittee on Commerce, Justice, State and Judiciary. When asked by Florida Representative Dan Miller "[i]s there anything you can say on [the Joseph Salvati] case and on behalf of the FBI and the Salvati family," Freeh states
that the Salvati case is "obviously a great travesty, a great failure, disgraceful to the extent that my agency or any other law enforcement agency contributed to that." He further states, "What I would say certainly to the family and any victim in such a situation is there is nothing worse that can happen under a system of law that
an innocent person is either charged or in this case punished for that period of time. It's a travesty, it's a disgrace, it shouldn't happen. I don't believe it happens frequently under our system, but it does. And when it does, it is of the gravest concern." When Rep.
Miller asks Freeh "[i]s there someone in the FBI who should have been more proactive in trying to help him through the process," Freeh responds that "we came into the situation, unfortunately, too late, but we did develop—as I understand it, we developed all the evidence which has gone now to his exoneration, with a lot of other people in the U.S. Attorney's office, but we're the ones who picked those pieces back up. It should have never gotten to that point."

7–3–01: John Fitzgerald dies in South Dakota

7–17–01: Stephen Flemmi pleads not guilty to ten charges of murder. (John Ellement, *Mobster Pleads Guilty to 10 Counts of Murder*, BOSTON GLOBE, July 18, 2001).

Stephen Flemmi's alleged murder victims in Boston include: John McIntyre, Edward Connors, Thomas King, Arthur "Bucky" Barrett, Richard Castucci, James Sousa, Debra Davis, and Deborah Hussey. (J.M. Lawrence, *Flemmi Vows Innocence as Case Heads to Trial*, BOSTON HERALD, July 18, 2001).

7–30–01: Linda Reardon takes a plea bargain on obstruction of justice charges before Judge Edward Harrington. Reardon admits telling her father, Edward G. Huff, about the existence of FBI pen registers on the phones of Billy Bulger and John "Jackie" Bulger.
Huff passed the information to his brother-in-law Richard Schneiderhan, who passed the information in a note to Kevin Weeks.

8–2–01: The Estate of Brian Halloran files suit against the United States, acting through the FBI and DOJ, and others. The *Halloran* suit centers on the May 11, 1982, murder of Brian Halloran. Halloran, at the time, was providing information to the
FBI due to murder charges that he himself was facing. In the course of his cooperation, Halloran provided information implicating James Bulger and the Winter Hill Gang in the murder of Roger Wheeler. Halloran had indicated that Bulger and others offered
him the contract to kill Wheeler, but he declined.

9–10–01: Louis Greco's attorney John Cavicchi files a Petition for Pardon to exonerate Greco with the Massachusetts Parole Board by wiping "away 'the stigma of this wrongful conviction' posthumously for the sake of Greco's family.

10–1–01: A few days before he is interviewed by the Committee on Government Reform and three days after a government prosecutor appears to have spoken to him

Robert Daddeico is presented with the following proposal by the FBI: "Robert Daddieco, also known as [Name Redacted by Committee], hereby acknowledges receipt
from the Federal Bureau of Investigation (FBI) of $15,000 for expenses to assist with his relocation, which expenses are being paid in consideration of the assistance he provided to the FBI. Mr. Daddieco acknowledges that the FBI has no further financial obligation
to him. In addition, Mr. Daddieco acknowledges that he is aware of and has been advised by the FBI of potential risks to him as a result of his cooperation with the FBI. In addition, Mr. Daddieco acknowledges that he was offered protection in the Witness
Security Program (hereafter the "program"). Mr. Daddieco acknowledges that he was interviewed by the United States Marshal's Service and was accepted into the "program." However, Mr. Daddieco thereafter indicates that he did not wish to enter the program. Mr. Daddieco acknowledges that he has been advised of and fully understands the risks he is incurring as a result of his decision, and, fully understanding the risks, still wishes to be responsible for his own relocation. The payment of $15,000 to Mr.
Daddieco is intended to allow Mr. Daddieco to relocate on his own in lieu of his participation in the program. Since Mr. Daddieco is not relying on protective assistance from the government and in further consideration of this payment of $15,000 from the FBI, Mr.Daddieco agrees, on his own behalf and on behalf of his heirs and assigns, to hold the United States, its agencies and its employees harmless for any injuries or death to him and/or his family resulting from his cooperation with and assistance to the FBI." Special Agent Mike Buckley handled this matter. Daddieco does not sign this agreement, nor does he accept the $15,000.

10–30–01: Stephen Flemmi's affidavit dated December 13, 1999, is submitted today "by convicted Rhode Island mobster Robert DeLuca, along with a motion to set aside his May 1994 state gambling conviction. DeLuca argues that he is innocent and that St.
Laurent, a co-defendant in his case, set him up for investigators while working as an informant for the FBI and Rhode Island State Police. . . . DeLuca, who gained notoriety as one of four soldiers inducted into the New England Mafia in 1989 during a blood-oath
ceremony that was bugged by the FBI, has about four years left to serve in federal prison on racketeering and extortion charges."

11–6–01: In a letter to Attorney General John Ashcroft, three Massachusetts Congressmen, Representatives Barney Frank, Martin Meehan, and William Delahunt criticize the Justice Department for using "procedural tactics" to try and quash the JohnMcIntyre suit. The Congressmen called the government's motion "embarrassing." They write that "the Justice Department has resorted to the kinds of procedural tactics that give the legal profession a bad name."

11–15–01: In the civil suit *The Estate of John L. McIntyre* v. *U.S.,* Plaintiff McIntyre writes the following in its Opposition to Defendant United States' Motion to Dismiss: "The government's motion to dismiss is all the more striking because in hearings before
Judge Wolf, the government continued in its obstructionist conduct concerning McIntyre's disappearance causing the court to lament that the question concerning McIntyre's disappearance and death could not "be resolved on the present record, in part because of the delayed disclosure of documents by the government and in

part because "it evidently was not in either the interest of Flemmi or of the FBI to have this issue fully developed in this case." *See United States* v. *Salemme,* 91 F.Supp.2d 141, 213 (D. Mass. 1999). The government's shroud of secrecy first began to unravel when
Stephen Flemmi claimed in court pleadings that he was protected from criminal prosecution based upon direct promises made to him by government agents. At first, the government suggested that Flemmi's claim was preposterous, but due to incessant and insistent judicial prodding, Flemmi's 'fiction' became fact—bodies were recovered from the frozen earth of Dorchester and on December 22, 1999 the lead government agent was indicted for a RICO violation, including the allegation of his involvement in two murders. . . . Though plaintiff presented its administrative claim less than *six months* after learning sufficient facts to verify both the government's wrongful conduct and McIntyre's fate, the United States has filed a motion to dismiss pursuant to Fed.R.Civ.P. 12(b)(1) claiming the Estate failed to present its administrative claim within two
years of its accrual as required by 28 U.S.C. § 2401 (b). . . . The government's motion to dismiss is factually insipid, legal deficient, and flirts with Rule 11. How is it that Mrs. McIntyre living alone and caring for her disabled daughter—who was treated as an outcastby law enforcement and did not have the power or authority to investigate criminal wrongdoing, wiretap telephones, conceal electronic eavesdropping devices in private homes and garages, offer immunity to those destined to long prison sentences—could have gained facts sufficient to file a lawsuit when those very facts allegedly escaped or eluded the investigatory power and resources of the federal government, until the government was forced fed them by Judge Wolf."

12–19–01: Roy French is freed from prison. The *Boston Globe* reports, "The only man to admit he helped murder Edward 'Teddy' Deegan in a Chelsea alley 36 years ago saw his convictions wiped out yesterday by Suffolk prosecutors, who decided recently discovered evidence of FBI misconduct denied Wilfred Roy French a fair trial. . . . Assistant District Attorney Mark T. Lee said that while the FBI reports strongly indicated Limone and Salvati were not involved in Deegan's murder, they did not absolve French. 'It has always been our view that he was one of the shooters,' Lee said of French. Deegan was shot by three different weapons. And that hasn't changed, he said. Lee said Martin's office decided to effectively wipe off French's accessory-to-murder convictions from his criminal record because the revelations in the FBI reports seriously undermine their ability to retry French, especially since Barboza is dead. French's attorneys were seeking a new trial based on the FBI reports."

2002

1–10–02: The government files for dismissal in the Brian Halloran lawsuit. The government claims that "plaintiff failed to present its administrative claim within two years of its accrual as required by statute, 28 U.S.C. § 2401(b)." The government argues that the action should have been filed in 1984, which was two years after Halloran's death. In the alternative, it claims that the deadline was April 1998, which was two years after the reporting of Supervisory Special Agent John Morris's testimony.

2–12–02: Jack Zalkind tells reporter J.M. Lawrence that Barboza's testimony was corroborated by others involved in the case.

5–28–02: Former Special Agent John Connolly is convicted of "charges that he shielded the gangsters, accepted a bribe and tipped them to impending indictments. After deliberating two days, a federal jury found Connolly, 61, guilty of one count of racketeering, three counts of obstruction of justice and one count of making a false statement to the FBI. . . . Jurors found

Connolly not guilty of one crime: leaking the identities of three men who had been talking to the FBI. The men were killed by mobsters in retaliation, prosecutors alleged."

7–31–02: Senior U.S. District Judge for the District of Massachusetts Edward Harrington sends a letter to his colleague on the bench, U.S. District Judge Joseph L. Tauro, who is presiding over the John Connolly sentencing matter. The letter outlines the reasons why Connolly's crime-fighting contributions should win him leniency when he is sentenced on September 16, 2002. This conduct is in contravention of the code of conduct governing federal judges, which specifically prohibits judges from initiating contact with a sentencing judge.

8–5–02: Due to public pressure, Senior U.S. District Judge Edward Harrington withdraws his letter urging Judge Joseph Tauro to be lenient on convicted former FBI Special Agent John Connolly when he is sentenced in September. In the letter to Judge Tauro withdrawing his earlier request, Harrington insists that his first letter was proper: "I believed that my letter was entirely proper as it was requested by the defendant, relates to specialized knowledge acquired as a federal prosecutor, and concerns the type of information traditionally considered by courts." He further writes, "Given the present controversy surrounding my letter, I ask that my letter be withdrawn and not be considered in any way." He also apologizes to the court for any inconvenience or distraction his letter caused.

8–14–02: Joseph Salvati files a notice under the Federal Tort Claims Act that he plans to sue the government for $300 million.

8–15–02: The Judicial Council of the First Circuit, a disciplinary committee, brings a complaint against Senior U.S. District Judge Edward Harrington for asking a colleague on the bench to be lenient on former FBI Special Agent John Connolly at his sentencing in September 2002. Harrington responds to the complaint stating: "Upon reflection, I did commit a clear violation of Canon 2(B) of the Code of Conduct for United States Judges in writing a letter to District Judge Tauro relating to the sentencing in a criminal matter." He further states, "For this act, I am exceedingly sorry and sincerely apologize to the Judicial Council and to my fellow judges in the First Circuit."

8–23–02: The Judicial Council of the First Circuit, a disciplinary committee, decides that Judge Edward Harrington has been punished enough after he admitted that he broke ethical rules when he asked Judge Tauro to be lenient on former FBI Special Agent John Connolly at his sentencing next month. The Chief Judge of the U.S. Court of Appeals for the First Circuit writes, "I find that Judge Harrington's withdrawal of his July 31 letter, his admission of a clear violation of the Code of Conduct, his sincere apology, and his agreement to allow all complaint materials to be made public constitute appropriate corrective action to remedy the problem raised by the complaint."

9–16–02: Former Special Agent John Connolly is sentenced to ten years in prison for breaking the law to protect his notorious gangster informants, James "Whitey" Bulger and Stephen "The Rifleman" Flemmi.

NOTE ON TEXT: After sixteen years at large and twelve years on the FBI Ten Most Wanted Fugitives list, Whitey Bulger was arrested in Santa Monica, California, on June 22, 2011

Bulger after his capture

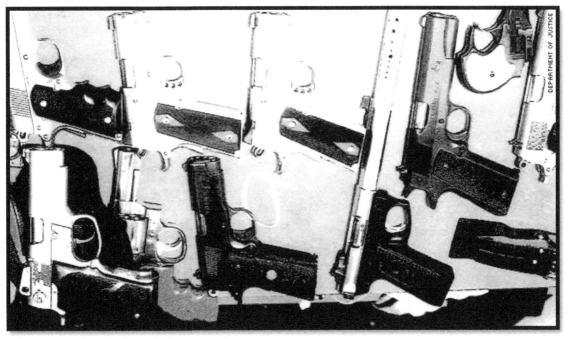

Weapons found in Whitey's apartment

Made in the USA
Middletown, DE
06 July 2021